Building a
Fair Pay
Program
Second Edition

Building a Fair Pay Program
Second Edition

A Step-by-Step Guide

Roger J. Plachy
Sandra J. Plachy

AMACOM
American Management Association

New York · Atlanta · Boston · Chicago · Kansas City · San Francisco · Washington, D.C.
Brussels · Mexico City · Tokyo · Toronto

Library of Congress Cataloging-in-Publication Data

Plachy, Roger.
    Building a fair pay program : a step-by-step guide / Roger J.
Plachy, Sandra J. Plachy. — 2nd ed.
        p.   cm.
    Includes bibliographical references and index.
    ISBN 0-8144-7965-0
    1. Compensation management.   I. Plachy, Sandra J.
HF5549.5.C67P55   1998
658.3'22—dc21

98-20006
CIP

Printing number

10 9 8 7 6 5 4 3 2 1

Forty years, forty wishes.
Who could imagine forty better results?

Contents

List of Tables

List of Figures

Authors' Note

What distinguishes this book from other books on pay management? Here are our main themes:

1. *Pay management is built on an integrated and coherent job results management strategy.* This means that we view jobs, uniquely focused on results to be accomplished, as the focal point for fulfilling the organization's mission.

Job results management aims to accomplish required results starting with recruiting and selecting the right employees, orienting and training them, planning job results, coaching and redirecting job efforts, appraising, rewarding and recognizing job contributions, and developing future employee contributions.

2. *An organization's mission is fulfilled by employees through contributions of job results.* Job contributions are either:

- Job results required
   or
- Extraordinary results—generally innovations or system changes, beyond results required

3. *The critical architecture for managing job contributions is a profile of job results, job duties, and four possible outcomes.* The Job Results Management Profile links job requirements with outcome criteria for appraising and, more important, planning job contributions. Managing is communication first, then measurement. Occasionally the planning and appraisal processes will be a unilateral management action, but they are generally more productive when there is a collaborative dialogue between manager and employee.

4. *Pay is based on job contributions.* The most appropriate pay philosophy (in the United States, given its view of individual rights and capitalistic economy) is to reward job contributions that support and advance the organization's mission.

5. *Results-oriented (nonbehavioral), objective (nonsubjective) thinking is applied in detail to each element of pay management.* Focusing on results establishes and clarifies what we value, guides our actions toward the results we want, and evaluates the impact we have made. Focusing on results is big stuff—a mind-style and lifestyle. Behaviors are *not* results. What you accomplish is a *result*. What you do to accomplish the result is a *behavior*. Objective thinking means focusing on concrete result outcomes (e.g., customers' questions are answered) instead of subjective behavioral measures (e.g., customers are treated pleasantly).

Introduction

Managing Your Pay Project

- Are you faced with the task of designing and implementing a pay program in your organization but don't know where to begin?
- Are you looking for a ready-to-go model you can adapt to the specific needs of your organization?
- Do you want options to consider as you develop your program?
- Would you like advice and guidance on the various approaches open to you?
- Do you want steps to follow that will lead you through the project before you?

If you are nodding your head, don't put this book down.

Pay Management—A Mystery

Pay management is said to be a mystery—at least, that's what many traditionalists who work in pay management would have you believe. Certainly we are entitled to some job protection. The unfortunate effect is that the people who really need to influence a rational pay program—managers who supervise employees in the operations of an organization—are not penetrating the artificial security barrier. Far too many specialists are insulated from the real world and continue to force their organizations to tackle modern issues with age-old tactics.

What about you who do not have specialists available, who are, perhaps, human resources generalists or operations managers in small organizations with little or no pay management experience, but who still have to come up with a pay program? Is there hope?

The whole thing is a lot easier than you might expect. Trust us. You do need to keep your wits about you, you do have to concentrate, and you will have to work hard to cope with a variety of design options of pay management, but nothing in this book is beyond the scope of anyone with a reasonable amount of intelligence and an ample dose of perseverance.

Experienced practitioners will profit from the book too. They will find different perspectives, new twists, and several models to help them review and reevaluate their own procedures and formats, including new ideas on how to involve others fruitfully in a pay program.

A Definition of Pay

The term "pay" refers to the actual dollars received in a paycheck. "Compensation" includes pay, plus short- and long-term benefits and perquisites such as vacations, pension plans, and airline-club memberships, and intangibles such as training and promotion opportunities. Benefits will not be addressed in detail here, as they are a book unto themselves.

Pay implies more than money. It is communication—a statement of human resources values. Pay is not job descriptions, job evaluation, pay range calculations, or any of the other tools we use to establish a program. Pay is a thread in the human relationship between management and employees, a declaration of what is important to the organization and what is not.

Managing Job Contributions

Although only one phase (i.e., a step in the process of building and managing your pay program) in this book discusses how job contributions are managed, it is an incredibly important element in your pay program. It determines how you get to the point of determining how much of a contribution an employee made to the organization, and thus how much he or she ought to share in the rewards of accomplishment. Give this program element a lot of attention.

Nothing Canned

Hang in there! The road ahead requires your attention and diligence. You may be tempted to look for a quick solution, a canned approach. Forget it. First of all, we are going to make the process as painless as we can by offering plenty of options, but you have to stay with it to ensure that your organization's uniqueness receives its just due. Successful organizations customize all their programs, stressing individuality in such areas as marketing, manufacturing, and public relations. The way they pay their employees is just another program to be customized.

Don't be misled. Pay management is not easy. In fact, it requires astute thinking. You need the detailed attention of a technician and the conceptual ability of a professional. Diverse facets of organizational style, group psychology, and individual motivation all must be taken into account to produce a unified and effective program. Yet, as is the case with most other complex issues, understanding is made easy when you take the work a slice at a time.

Adaptable Models

The wheel need not be reinvented again. In the years of pay management history, many of the tasks and steps have been replicated, again and again and again. Let us not start from scratch to design a job analysis or pay survey form. This book will start with models that we already know are workable, if not admirable, and let you fit them to your organization. And since a good part of learning is seeing the bad as well as the good, inadequate examples—properly edited—will also be included.

How You Will Proceed to Build a Pay Program

This book is organized according to the logical, sequential phases of a pay project. Each phase is subdivided into specific considerations or tasks, followed by a series of questions (called "Project Analyzer") to help you analyze your situation. Exercises and examples bring many of the considerations into tangible form. "How to" is what this book is all about. The field of pay management already has plenty of theoretical texts, and you should read them, too, for their useful examination of the issues.

You will address two concerns in this book:

1. *Strategic policy*, which states the philosophical beliefs of your organization and establishes the manner in which the project is conducted.
2. *Tactical procedures*, which determine the manner in which each phase will be executed.

To do this, you will work through the book not once, but *four times*. (Keep calm!)

On your *first* reading, briefly scan the phases of the project to obtain a general sense of the issues. Do not try to deal with any details. At the end of each phase, you will find a section titled "Strategic Planning." Make notes to yourself regarding the strategic policy issues you will have to decide. You may also want to make a few notes about tactical procedures as they begin to occur to you.

On your *second* quick reading, examine your initial thoughts about each phase and decide on an integrated posture for the entire project. Most pay programs are a disarray of piecemeal efforts that treat phases as separate parts. Although each phase deals with a different issue, phases must be harmonized if the total program is to be effective.

Now read through the book a *third* time. This time, think through the practical aspects of implementing each phase of the project. The Project Analyzer questions in most subsections of the phases in the book will help you formulate a detailed, tactical plan of action. *Complete the Master Planner* (in Phase 2) as you read through the phases.

At this point, you should have a firm plan in mind about how to proceed with the project, including a specific information-gathering plan, a work plan, a schedule, a communications plan, and a cost estimate. You should not have started working on specific problems. You should not have presented your ideas to anyone or asked for any commitments. You should know what you need to do, when you need to do it, with whom to do it, and how to obtain the initial project commitment.

Then read the book a *fourth* time. This time, work through project details and take the steps necessary to bring your project to a successful conclusion.

A Warning Before You Begin

You will be consumed shortly with the essentials of a pay program. You will work hard and gain confidence in what you do. You will probably become enamored of your work.

Remember this: your pay program is not what you plan it to be; it is what others say it is. Do not ignore or overlook the perceptions of others.

The tempo and the sequence of the phases derive from our experiences as managers, pay consultants, and course leaders for the American Management Association (AMA). Our work as consultants involves all sorts of organizations, small to large, that need to design and implement, or revamp, a pay and job results management program. Attendees at AMA seminars have the same concern. Lack of experience is common. Thus, this is a book of basics.

"Advanced" pay techniques—translated as "better"—are not allowed here. Either do the job well, or don't do it at all. You can be more or less sophisticated in your approach, depending on the time and the resources you invest in the program, but you can't afford to be inaccurate. If you have only a little time, do what you can, but do it well.

Moving Toward Independence

This book is designed to help you function independently. Ultimately, you are on your own, faced with a need not only for action now, but also for maintaining your program once it has been implemented. You will not be able to rely on someone to bail you out every time you get into a little hot water. Be assured that you are being told everything you need to know about the elements of a pay program; there are no gaps. Think of this book as a friendly resource.

Since the first edition ten years ago, we now know that project managers, just like yourself, have opened the book, followed the steps, and succeeded. Most projects fail because major issues are not anticipated and thought out, the right people are not involved at the right time, details are not organized and scheduled, action is not taken efficiently at the right time, and events are not controlled to produce the desired outcomes. This book is designed not only to point you in the right direction and arm you with the right information, but also to prod you at the right time, especially through the Master Planner you will fill out.

Perhaps this book will serve as an obvious reminder sitting on your desk, almost blinking at you for your response, much as the cursor does on a computer. The information, steps, options, and reminders are here to be studied, restudied, and restudied again. Not all the answers are here, but there is enough guidance to help you make your decisions.

Information is power. Preparation is advantage. The ensuing phases of the book will give you both.

Phase 1

Know Your Organization

> Each organization must design its own pay program.

1.1 Why Start a Pay Project Now?

Understanding why a pay project is being inaugurated tells a lot about its potential for success. Perhaps some employees are complaining that they are being paid less than other employees in a similar job in another department. There could be several causes for this: inaccurate job descriptions, inaccurate job evaluations, incomplete pay surveys, a single incompetent manager who inflates pay increases, or incomplete pay guidelines from which managers make pay decisions. Any one of these problems might be solved individually and easily. It would be a mistake to believe that the entire pay program needs to be revamped.

On the other hand, complaints may be symptomatic of deeper problems. Perhaps managers are thwarting the system because:

- Job descriptions are incomplete.
- Job evaluations are based on a faulty job evaluation plan.
- Pay surveys target regional instead of local data.
- The work appraisal system measures the wrong criteria.
- Many managers inflate pay increases.
- Pay guidelines from which managers make pay decisions are overly rigid, riddled with inconsistencies, or simply not enforced.

The solution here demands an entirely new commitment to pay management.

In this book, we show you each element of a pay program so that you can solve specific problems, but we also emphasize the integration of elements to help you understand the cause and effect of pay problems.

Project Analyzer 1.1

What happened to make you consider building a new pay program?

_____

_____

Why now?

_____

_____

Do you understand the root causes of pay programs?

_____

_____

What do managers think about the current pay program?

_____

_____

What do employees think about the current pay program?

_____

_____

How do you know what managers and employees think?

_____

_____

Is management's opinion based on fact (such as an attitude survey, focus groups, or grievances) or conjecture?

_____

_____

What has to happen in order to make your program right?

_____

_____

1.2 Align Pay Management With Organization Culture

Pay practices are saddled with a badly skewed orientation to "pay what and how other organizations pay." Organizations lose control over their economics and pay practices when they implement programs that emulate competitors or the market. Pay strategies should not contradict the way an organization operates. For example, an organization that encourages teamwork, empowerment, and manager-employee collaboration should promulgate pay policies, practices, and perks that do not contradict these values.

The point for planning pay strategies is to identify the values and practices of your organization realistically and to shape your pay program so that it fits, rather than detracts from, organizational success. Think of pay as communicating and confirming values.

Use Pay to Signal Organizational Change

A change in pay strategies can be used to confirm organizational change or to lead change. For example, an organization may wish to develop a more versatile workforce in which employees can be moved quickly from job to job as needed. This new operating strategy may require rewriting job descriptions, reducing the number of job classifications, rewriting job evaluation degrees within compensable factors, reevaluating jobs, reassigning jobs to fewer job grades, creating special job grades with wider pay ranges, redefining transfer policies, creating competency steps, or changing incentive practices.

Nonpay issues may also have to be addressed. For example, the new operating strategy may require new job skills training, training in decision making (if employees will be expected to make decisions that in the past someone else made), new operating policies and procedures, and attitude adjustment for managers.

Pay policy often serves as an effective outline for debating how proposed operating strategies will actually be implemented and, more important, whether they should be implemented.

Study Your Organization's Structure

Jobs, like bricks, were put together to build an organization and facilitate its function. Some jobs don't change when organizations change. Not that they weren't supposed to change, but no one ever got around to doing anything about them.

Enter you and your proposed pay program. Now you find yourself walking into walls (jobs) that shouldn't be there because the organizational function has changed.

A little skepticism is a good thing. A full-blown pay program starts with a snapshot of the organization in the present. What you see in the "photograph" is one reality; but there are other realities—the reality of what would have been there to be "photographed" if the structure had been updated, plus the reality of what was hidden during the picture-taking session.

You will use a *technical* skill to understand the job content as it is presented, to identify the qualifications for a job, and to write a description of the job in acceptable language. You will use a *professional* skill when you add the question: Is what I am seeing the best way for it to be?

Not only is the introduction of a new pay program an excellent time to question the organization structure, but it would be professionally irresponsible not to do so. You will uncover simple items of duplication of effort among departments, as well as gross cover-ups of incompetence and procrastination. You will offer a new cutting edge of structure as you anticipate future organizational requirements.

Know Your Organization

Start with a clear picture of the purpose and needs of the organization now. These are the main questions to ask:

1. *Why does the organization exist?* What is its purpose? What do we do? Whom do we serve? When, where, and how do we serve them? Who is our competition?
2. *What is our current situation?* Consider quantity of product or service, quality, and costs. Also consider financial, technical, and human resources.
3. *What are our current business objectives?* Weigh sales or service, income and expense, products or services, and prices or charges. And consider innovation, financing, human resources, and social responsibility too.

Don't be surprised if not all the information is available; sometimes organizations work more by instinct than by planning. Your program could be the catalyst for improved managerial performance. What a great opportunity to introduce some good old management development tied to a here-and-now problem.

Where information is available but not circulated to you, go after it. Build rapport with the people who have the information you want. If the information is not given to you, as with sensitive data, be sure to tell the keepers of the inner sanctum why the information is important to your program and what decisions they must make regarding your program.

What Does the Information Tell You?

Study the information you have as you prepare for your project. Understand the implications for future changes. If you identify some concerns or anticipated changes, incorporate them into your planning. As a rule, the organization will *not* remain static, so proceed accordingly.

Pay programs must be designed with the organization in mind. If, for example, your organization anticipates a great deal of growth and change, it cannot afford to be strapped with a rigid and formal program. Your design must include the ability to make rapid changes. If your organization is mature and stable, your planning would differ.

A final warning: when employee relations are not so good in an organization, a revised pay plan is frequently divined as a panacea. Such a beginning portends problems because the program usually becomes a patchwork rather than a unified system that enhances organizational performance. Form follows function. The organization's mission and style dictate the pay program, not the other way around.

Project Analyzer 1.2

What does your organization chart tell you about the way the organization functions?

_____

_____

What is right about the way it functions?

_____

_____

What is wrong about the way it functions?

_____

_____

At which stage is your organization in its development: entrepreneurial, growth, or mature?

_____

_____

How fluid or static does management want the organization to be?

_____

_____

What forces of change are at work?

_____

_____

What do you understand about the purpose of the enterprise?

_____

_____

How does this affect the way it should be organized?

_____

_____

What structure is management thinking about for the future?

_____

_____

What authority do you have to implement the design features you believe are necessary?
_____
_____

Who else has to be, or should be, involved?
_____
_____

If there is a union, what can you expect: support of or opposition to your proposals?
_____
_____

Do you have enough time to introduce a new pay program now?
_____
_____

Does your organization promote employee contribution as an important factor in the success of the organization? If so, how are the two tied to pay?
_____
_____

How are organization results communicated to employees?
_____
_____

Are employees committed to accomplishing organization results?
_____
_____

Does your organization promote employee contribution as an important factor in the team success? If so, how are the two tied to pay?
_____
_____

How are team results communicated to employees?
_____
_____

Are employees committed to accomplishing team results?
_____
_____
_____

1.3 What Do You Want to Accomplish With Your Pay Program?

There are two fundamental reasons that your organization should have an organized pay program: (1) it is an effective way to manage an organization, and (2) it is a reasonable way to manage people.

As an effective way to manage an organization, a pay program does the following:

- Announces management's values.
- Establishes a guide for managers to use when carrying out organizational values.
- Provides a structure for management to use when making business decisions.
- Examines labor expense in a consistent manner so that cost-effective decisions can be made readily.
- Gives management the tool it needs to judge its competitive posture in the labor market.
- Provides a model that management needs to predict the outcomes of specific options in pay, benefits, incentives, and human resources management.
- Serves as a deterrent to, or defense against, legal challenges.
- Discourages union organizing, if that is management's goal, or makes negotiations more objective.

As a reasonable way to manage people, a pay program does the following:

- Pays employees fairly and efficiently for their work.
- Avoids misunderstandings with employees.
- Provides a guide for conversations with employees about their pay.
- Gives managers a guide for improving their rapport with employees.
- Maintains morale.
- Reduces complaints of unfair and arbitrary treatment.
- Rewards outstanding work results.
- Instills a sense of security that individual treatment is not at the whim of individual managers.
- Identifies a hierarchy of value among jobs and clearly identifies what qualifications lead to higher-paying jobs.
- Attracts and retains employees who appreciate a sense of orderliness and opportunity.
- Offers employees an opportunity to participate in shaping the environment in which they work (if management chooses to include employees in the process).

Review the two lists and mark the reasons that are most important to your organization. Identify other goals of a pay program that are unique to your organization. Write a statement of reasons to establish the direction and rationale of your program. Obtain commitment to, and approval of, the purpose of the program from senior management.

Use the purpose of the program to prepare a policy statement describing why the program exists—that is, its goals. Write the statement in your organization's style and language. Do not plagiarize goal statements from other organizations. Be distinctive. Figure 1 contains a sample policy statement.

Figure 1. Example compensation policy statement.

Your compensation includes not only the money you earn as a salary or hourly wage, but also bonuses, incentives, and benefits such as insurance, paid time off, child and elder care, health club, medical services, and retirement investments.

Our pay philosophy is based on the following principles:

1. To pay you fairly for your contribution to our organization in relation to:
   a. The results you accomplish toward organizational objectives.
   b. The results the organization is able to accomplish.
   c. What people earn in other organizations for a similar contribution.
   d. What other people in our organization receive for a similar contribution.
2. To support job learning that will maintain the results the organization needs as well as prepare you for personal and career growth and advancement.
3. To enhance your contribution as an individual, as a member of a work team, and as a member of our organizational team.
4. To adhere strictly to all applicable legal requirements.
5. To ensure equal opportunity to all persons.
6. To explain to you how your pay is determined.
7. To support a collaborative relationship between you, your peers, and your supervisor.

Project Analyzer 1.3

What are the goals of your pay program?

_____

_____

_____

_____

_____

_____

_____

Who needs to be involved in developing these goals?

_____

_____

Whose support and influence are needed for a pay program?

_____

_____

Who approves pay goals?

_____

_____

When are pay goals reviewed for possible change?

_____

_____

What are the pay goals of your organization's employees?

_____

_____

Is this true for all employees?

_____

_____

1.4 Stop! Are People Unhappy With Their Pay?

The national dream among employees in all organizations is to earn more money. Or to put it another way, complaints about low or unfair pay are never-ending.

The caution here is that although management must always be concerned with whether employees are being paid fairly, they must not jump each time employees complain. It may be true that some employees are underpaid and should receive an equity increase, but listen to the basic truths that savvy employees understand about pay and complaints about pay:

> "Who doesn't want to make more money?"
> "No one ever thinks they make enough."
> "If you raised pay, it would be an issue again in a year."
> "Everybody thinks they're overworked and underpaid."
> "If people are unhappy with something else, pay comes to the forefront."

Some managers never seem to learn. For time immemorial, employees have staged holdups: "Give me more money, or I'll quit." Managers give them the money. For the most part, employees quit anyway.

Let's distinguish here between employees who earn near or just above the minimum wage for the job and those who earn at the median or higher pay for their kind of job. For many lower-paid employees, the opportunity for a little increase may well draw them away; at that level, a little more money is very helpful.

For employees who earn a lot more, money is usually not as important. Other influences in the work environment may, and frequently do, take precedence. Just to complicate the issue more, even employees earning the minimum wage will forgo a better wage if the other influences in the new work environment—unsafe working conditions, discrimination, harassment, an overbearing boss, and so forth—are unsatisfactory.

The lesson from seasoned managers is this: Be careful about complaints about pay. Study them. Establish their rationale. Look at history. Look for patterns. Look for other problems in the work environment. Be sure that the issue is really pay, and not something else.

Changing Fashions

Ten years ago, this book stated: "Today's workforce has more knowledge available to apply to situations, and more ways to move knowledge around. Employees are seemingly less committed to institutions than the last generation and more ready to try new options. They are acutely aware of basic human rights and quite vocal about any infringements on those rights. They move around a lot and mix easily. They want to be in on decisions that affect them. They want choices. The whole environment is a lot faster than it used to be."

The same words still apply and probably have been appropriate for a long time. However, the caution we used then still applies: "All of this is true *generally* and only for the workforce as a whole, not for all individuals." We should have added, "*and not for all organizations.*"

Where your organization is now in the development of its business and operating practices determines what human resources policies and practices should be established and implemented. The one thing we know about motivation in relation to pay is that no part of it is obvious or simple. The question, "What can we do to focus our employees on our organization's objectives?" may well be a projection of management's own feelings of inadequacy and impotency.

Project Analyzer 1.4

What has caused employees to applaud pay actions?

_____

_____

What complaints do you hear about pay?

_____

_____

Are managers prone to cave in to pay demands?

_____

_____

What reasons do employees give for demanding more pay?

_____

_____

Do employees' reasons indicate problems with the organization's pay program, or just that employees would like to have more money?

_____

_____

Where is the organization in the development of its pay program?

_____

_____

1.5 Keep Employees Informed

Understand the Difference Between Pay and Benefits

Total dollar compensation is the sum of an employee's paycheck and the monetary value of benefits, such as the dollar value of vacation pay. How much you pay in wages or salaries compared to how much you pay in benefits is an important relationship in your compensation program.

Despite the high ratio of benefits to total compensation, and despite many efforts to communicate the impact of benefits to employees, the lack of acclaim for the less-than-visible benefits persists. They are, after all, more or less expected by employees as a part of the employment process.

Pay is remunerated directly; benefits are given indirectly. More attention and recognition are given to direct payments than to indirect payments. The paycheck is tangible, and frequently it becomes the sole value indicator of work performed. This lack of appreciation among employees adds up to a costly error as your expensive benefits package goes unnoticed. That's too bad because the value of what we used to call fringe benefits is over 40 percent of total pay (pardon the national average), up from around 20 percent forty or so years ago. Obviously, this is no fringe today, and it wasn't one yesterday.

Don't rely on anyone's guess about the future of the pay/benefits ratio. Start with what your organization can afford, not with what other organizations are giving. Certainly find out what other organizations have in their benefits package, so you have a base of comparison, but use the information only as a starting point. Develop a model, cost it out, and decide whether it would be attractive to your employees.

Add the benefits cost to wages and salaries to determine the value of the total package. First, decide whether the program is too costly, given the overall financial program of your organization. Second, try to predict your employees' psychological and social perception of the package and the ratio.

Figure 2 lists common types of employee benefits to consider in calculating the package.

Always Compare Totals

Employees must understand that compensation comparisons with other organizations are based on pay plus benefits. You will particularly need to emphasize this relationship if you choose to give less pay but more benefits than most other organizations. Even though you give them about the same total compensation and are competitive, employees frequently base their initial perception on the obvious payments.

Employees can decide for or against your organization only according to the information they have. Employees easily compare short-term benefits such as vacations,

Figure 2. Benefits to include when calculating the total compensation package (employer's payments only).

- Paid time off (vacations, holidays, sick leave, personal leave)
- Paid time not working (e.g., rest breaks, lunch, wash-up time, clothes changing, travel time)
- Meals
- Discount on goods and services purchased from the company
- Employee education
- Child and elder care
- Short-term disability, sickness, or accident insurance
- State sickness insurance
- Medical, surgical, major medical, and hospital insurance (net), including retirees
- Health care, including dental, vision, physical fitness
- Long-term disability, wage continuation, or long-term care
- Life insurance
- Annuity contracts
- Pension plan (net)
- Defined contribution plan
- Defined benefit pension plan
- Profit sharing
- Employee Stock Option Plan (ESOP)
- Administration expenses for retirement and saving plans
- Stock bonuses
- Social Security and railroad retirement taxes
- Unemployment compensation
- Workers' compensation (estimate self-insured costs)

personal days, and discounts; long-term pension and profit-sharing arrangements take considerably more analysis.

Help Employees Analyze the Pay/Benefits Package

Give your employees plenty of assistance as they make their judgments. The more they know about the care you give to this important aspect of your relationship, the more willing they will be to accept the fairness of the pay program (assuming, of course, that you are being fair). When you are secretive, employees frequently think that you are trying to hide something; they may conclude that you are hiding less-than-fair treatment.

You have a whole separate issue on your hands if you determine that you cannot afford either competitive wages and salaries or benefits, perhaps because you are starting a business or you need to spend much of your money on capital investment. However, the principle remains the same: employees can understand start-up and growth costs—they face the same situation as they invest in their families or themselves. You just need to inform them.

Consider Trends in Pay and Benefits Administration

Trends in the determination of benefits and their mix with pay must be calculated in your planning. Find out what benefits other organizations are offering to their employees in your local area and in your industry. Attend conferences, read current literature, and be aware of legislative deliberations to understand what pay and benefits options are being considered. Come to a decision about the stand your organization wants to take.

Project Analyzer 1.5

What do your employees know about how their total compensation is determined?

_____

_____

How much do your employees want to know?

_____

_____

How do they feel about the pay program?

_____

_____

Do they trust management to develop fair programs?

_____

_____

How do you determine employee attitudes?

_____

_____

What are your total wages and salaries?

_____

_____

What is the total cost of your current benefits? (Refer to Figure 2. State as dollars per year per employee, percentage of payroll, or cents per payroll hour.)

_____

_____

What compensation expenses will your financial structure and strategic plans accommodate?

_____

_____

How do your benefits compare with those offered by other organizations in your industry?

_____

_____

How do they compare with those offered by other organizations in your area?

_____

_____

What do your employees know about their benefits?

_____

_____

How do you keep them informed about the value of their benefits?

_____

_____

Strategic Planning for Phase 1

On your *first* quick walk through the project phases, record your initial thoughts on policy issues that will have to be decided.

_____

_____

_____

_____

_____

_____

Any notes on tactical issues?

_____

_____

_____

_____

On your *second* time through the phases, consider the strategic influences from all phases; decide on an integrated posture for the entire project.

Complete the section for this phase in the Master Planner (in Phase 2.8) during your *third* reading.

Phase 2
Planning and Organizing Your Pay Project

> Don't start your pay project until you know where you're going and how to get there.

2.1 An Integrated Program

Figure 3 demonstrates the integration of organizational elements and the benefits when all elements work well together. The end result of the integrated elements, for our purposes, is pay. We can see that the two primary influences on pay are the pay structure, which determines the worth of the job, and the management of employee job contributions.

The pay structure is determined by job evaluation and pay surveying, both of which rely heavily on the job description. Notice the crucial role of the job description in the overall scheme.

Job analysis is the process by which we gather information about jobs and decide whether they are structured (that is, tasks are organized) according to the needs of the organization, as defined by the purpose of the organization.

The results-oriented job description is the actualizing force of the organization. In the job description, intention meets results.

Organizational objectives—what is to be accomplished over the next year and the next two, five, ten years—emanate directly from the purpose of the organization, as does the structure of the organization. Organizational objectives are translated into specific objectives for individuals in performance plans.

Notice the relationship between organizational objectives and organizational structure (job analysis): what the organization determines as its purpose and its objectives predetermines the way it structures itself. Form follows function. Said another way, an organization must be structured in such as way as to carry out its purpose and its objectives.

Similarly, what is expected of an individual in a results plan this year must match the expectations contracted for in the job description. This avoids the familiar, "It's not in my job description." Individual accomplishments cannot be appraised unless measurable job outcome criteria are established.

Figure 3. How it all fits together: The elements of a well-integrated pay program.

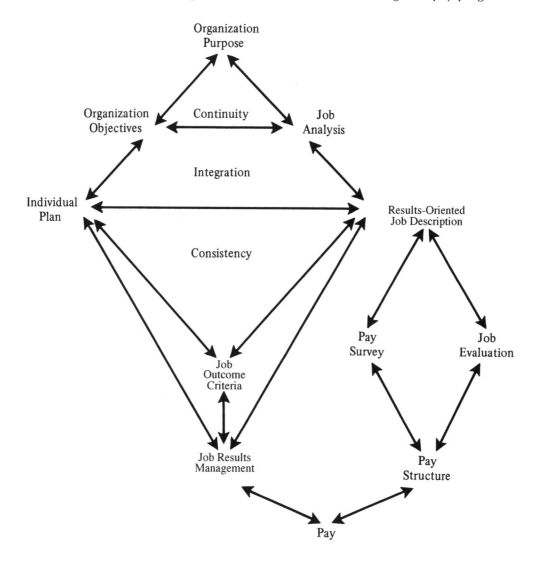

An organization that fulfills all the required processes is described as whole, integrated, and consistent. Opposite conditions spell ineffectiveness, inefficiency, and trouble.

Diagnostic Uses of the Integrated Pay Program Diagram

To jump ahead to pay management concerns, the diagram in Figure 3 helps diagnose problems. For instance, problematic organizational objectives may indeed turn out to be faulty objectives, although defective objectives may be symptomatic of (follow the arrows) an unclear organizational purpose, ineffective organization structuring, wrong job assignment, or vague, unrealistic job outcome criteria.

Complaints about pay may turn out to be a problem with:

- The construction of the pay structure, in either concept or calculation
- The design or execution of the job evaluation system
- How the pay survey was conducted
- Inaccurate job descriptions
- Incomplete job analysis
- Inappropriate job structuring (distribution of job responsibilities)

Then again, maybe the employee just wants to make more money.

Explaining specific aspects of the pay program to employees and managers will take different teaching tactics. If you choose the participatory road to designing and implementing your program, much of the necessary learning will occur by doing. Frankly, a pay project is best understood by doing rather than hearing.

Project Analyzer 2.1

Are all of the elements of a pay program in place now?

_____

_____

If not, which elements need to be developed?

_____

_____

_____

2.2 Formal vs. Informal Programs

Must you have a formal program? No. You can manage without written job descriptions, with unrecorded job evaluations, with telephone pay surveys and unpublished pay guidelines (except under certain federal or state contracts and provisions).

However, you will most likely pay for this informality with time wasted redefining and reexplaining what was forgotten. Worst of all, you will be defenseless if you are ever challenged in a legal proceeding. Human beings, left without the written word, are at a disadvantage; misunderstandings abound.

Formal can mean "in accordance with procedures that ensure validity," and surely that is no problem. Formal can also mean "excessively ceremonious," and that is a problem. What most managers really object to in formality is a restriction of their freedom to act as they desire. But sometimes such restriction is not so bad, when you examine what some managements have done in the name of freedom. But, assuming the best intentions, formal—generally meaning "written"—programs are not necessarily inhibitory. Plenty of flexibility can, and should, be built into a pay program.

Formal should also not be confused with published. We will look at the issue of what to communicate later. For the moment, to dispel anxieties, let's just say that what is formalized need not be published and communicated to employees. Management is entitled to the privacy of its operational plans, so long as it is not doing something illegal.

Project Analyzer 2.2

What kind of flexibility are your managers used to?

_____

_____

How much flexibility do you want to give them?

_____

_____

Are they ready for independence, or do they need to be trained to act independently?

_____

_____

How will what you communicate regarding other programs affect how you will communicate regarding your pay program?

_____

_____

How well does your organization exchange information?

_____

_____

_____

2.3 Obtaining Needed Information

You will need a lot of information to prepare and implement your pay program. Some information will be fact; other information will be opinion. Only your scrutiny will separate the two.

Not everyone has factual information, but everyone has an opinion. Some people will provide information, either fact or opinion, willingly; others will not. Sometimes people are willing to give factual information but not opinion; at other times, their response will be just the opposite.

The phases of this book identify the information, both facts and opinions, necessary to design and implement your program.

Each organization accumulates and disseminates information in its own manner. Knowing the road map is imperative to a successful project. Knowing who the traffic managers are is equally essential. Traffic managers direct information on formal and informal levels. Usually the formal and the informal traffic managers are not the same.

Formal and Informal Information Managers

Formal information managers are those whose names appear on the organization chart and on the official memos; informal information managers are the subculture figures who meet in the hallways and lunchrooms, who talk on the telephone, send e-mail messages, or drop by offices unexpectedly. You must operate on both levels in order to make your program a success. If you ignore or violate either level, your program may suffer, perhaps irreparably.

You usually find out quickly when you miss a formal contact: people become upset, and they, or the person to whom they complained, will inform you. Missing an informal contact is not discernible until you realize that work is not progressing smoothly.

The informal processing occurs whether you want it to or not. What you would like to know, therefore, is how the information flows—that is, who talks to whom. In this way, when you want to get information to certain people without going to them directly, you will know whom to contact.

Information Power and Opinion Power

Having factual information that others want is one form of power; having opinion that others want is another. Having both forms of power is very nice. The trick is getting a person who has either form of power to share it.

A problem occurs when a person has formal authority but no opinion power. Having factual information but no opinion power is not very nice. People have been known to withhold factual information in an attempt to acquire opinion power. Sometimes they even distort information or create information.

Asking for information may be interpreted as asking for power. You will need to clarify your own authority to legitimatize your requests for information and to minimize a perception that you are out to grab power.

A lot of people get more of a kick out of telling others what they think than out of seeing their opinions enacted. After all, if your opinion is enacted, it is your responsibility. The avoidance of responsibility may be so great that no opinions are offered. You can eliminate responsibility concerns and encourage opinions by stating up front that opinions will be gathered from many sources before the final decision is made. Make no commitments that anyone's opinion will be used, only that it will be considered.

Participation

Participation is useful for defusing illusions of self-importance. One on one, people will say nearly anything to convince you of the excellence of their opinion; in a group, they usually hide their preeminence. Some organizations have used focus groups successfully to gather information and opinion and reduce the intensity of interaction.

Focus groups need to be managed carefully, including clarifying the objectives of the groups' discussion. Someone with group management skills should facilitate the discussion for best results, but don't shy away from just sitting down and talking about your situation. Groups can help assess the prospect of change, whether changes or new programs are likely to be successful, which program alternatives are likely to be more effective, what other policies and programs will be affected, how well communication is working, what can be done to improve communication, and what specific communication will now be required.

You need to be concerned not to violate the National Labor Relations Act (NLRA), whether you are unionized or not, by using management-dominated employee teams to deal directly with employees on issues that are legally mandated subjects of bargaining: wages (including benefits), hours, conditions of work, and safety and fitness. However, legislative changes have been proposed to ease the NLRA requirements so that management can involve employees in the development of workplace improvements.

Even now management can create employee teams to share information and ideas on customer service, communications, quality improvement, technical or process re-design, productivity, materials usage, and even operational decisions (except in the restricted areas noted). Where unions exist, team membership and ground rules should be discussed with the union following the provisions of the collective bargaining agreement.

Project Analyzer 2.3

How does your organization accumulate information?

_____

_____

How does your organization disseminate information?

_____

_____

Is your organization open or secretive with information?

_____

_____

How prone is the organization to rumors?

_____

_____

Who are the informal information managers?

_____

_____

What is the best way to obtain information and mobilize resources?

_____

_____

Does your organization use focus groups?

_____

_____

Are employees routinely included in focus groups?

_____

_____

Does your organization conduct attitude surveys?

_____

_____

Would this be a project for breaking new communications ground?

_____

_____

Do you have key contacts in all functional areas?

_____

_____

Are project teams used?

_____

_____

Are they effective?

_____

_____

2.4 Clarifying Your Authority

Pay projects have a way of opening organizational doors that have been closed and avoided for years—a positive result, as the breath of fresh air clears out the staleness, but dangerous for the door opener, who first smells the stench.

Organizational skeletons will be found behind the doors; you can bet on that. Some bones were known to exist, but quietly ignored; others were not suspected. The questions that will be asked during the project—about the definition of job results, about qualifications to fulfill job results, about an equitable rate of pay among jobs, about an appropriate rate of pay for an employee, about measures of job contributions—may provoke consternation among managers and job incumbents.

Given the controversial nature of some expected adjustments and corrections, you will be wise to define your authority at the beginning of the project. Naturally, no one can determine what actions will be required until the problems are defined, but required processes of interaction can be addressed in advance.

Dimensions of Authority

Authority comes in only a few dimensions:

- You can act at your own discretion.
- You can act at your own initiative but must tell someone promptly.
- You can act only after receiving prior approval.

In the Master Planner (see Phase 2.8), which you will fill out on your third reading of the book, identify your authority for each project issue; then verify it with your manager.

Clarifying your communication authority and responsibility for each project issue will be helpful. You may:

- Provide or obtain information.
- Interview or investigate to identify and discover information.
- Interpret or advise to help others understand more clearly.
- Persuade or teach.
- Authorize or arbitrate to initiate action or resolve differences of opinion, where guidelines are available.
- Decide or determine to bring to a conclusion, where autonomous decisions are required.

Do not try to complete the whole project by yourself; get others involved. *Delegate* where you can, and identify all project assignments in the Master Planner.

2.5 Timing and Time

Do not start the project when it is in conflict with other pressing needs of the organization and thus doomed to failure. Admit it: human resources issues typically have lower priority than production, services, marketing, and just about anything else. Seat-of-the-pants methods have worked for years, so what's so urgent about them now?—or so goes the avoidance.

Commitment is the key. The organization must want to do this project now.

Determine How Much Time Is Needed and When

Designing and implementing a pay project is time-consuming. Get the time involved out on the table where managers can look at it and know what they are up against. That way, they can plan their time. Too many projects fail not because they are burdensome but because managers, who have other responsibilities, are not given the courtesy of advance warning so they can plan an efficient schedule. You cannot distribute a memorandum today announcing that next week managers will begin conducting job analysis studies—though, unfortunately, it is done every day in organizations.

As you step through the program phases in your first overview, begin to make some estimate of the time involved and record it in the Master Planner. Later, when you study each element of the project, you can firm up your estimates.

Project Analyzer 2.5

How urgently is a pay program needed?

_____

_____

When can you begin?

_____

_____

When are busy times for the organization?

_____

_____

When are slow times?

_____

_____

What other responsibilities do you have?

_____

_____

What kind of help will be available to you?

_____

_____

When does your fiscal year begin?

_____

_____

When are financial plans due?

_____

_____

_____

2.6 Costs

Eventually, somebody is going to ask, How much is this project going to cost? Each organization considers and computes costs differently, but regardless of the calculation, the investment required to design and implement a pay program must be valued.

The decision to inaugurate a program is a choice among rival opportunities for the use of limited organization resources, not just a matter of actual dollars to be spent. The decision is how we shall spend our time and other resources. Consider noncash opportunity costs, which measure the "profits" that are forgone from other alternatives for which organization resources could have been used.

Actual expenses can be direct external expenditures for the purchase of services, equipment, and materials, or internal expense transfers from your budget for services performed by other departments. One opportunity cost is the salaries or wages per hour for the people involved in the project.

Return on Investment From the Project

Projects are approved on a basis of their return on investment: what the organization will reap from the project. A pay program is measured in reduction of payroll expense and in intangible rewards for management and employees—actually a form of psychic income to the organization.

You will want to develop a program rationale that argues these returns. At this moment, you can argue only psychic income, since you will need the completed pay structure to identify expense reductions.

Project Analyzer 2.6

What actual expenditures do you anticipate?

_____

_____

What have other organizations spent to install new pay programs?

_____

_____

If you plan to hire temporary personnel to help with the project, what costs do you anticipate?

_____

_____

Are there any special resources that you will need? How much will they cost?

_____

_____

How much do pay surveys cost to purchase?

_____

_____

Will you need to add software? How much will it cost?

_____

_____

2.7 Consultants

Having purchased this book, you are probably inclined to design and implement your pay program by yourself—and you will be able to do so. Or perhaps this book will give you the background you need to work intelligently with a consultant. You may intend to accomplish most of the work yourself but want to obtain some expert opinion from time to time about the options presented to you.

Much of consulting occurs in a "comfort" zone; consultants are invited to help out so that the program participants feel as though they are doing the right thing. The organization is purchasing reassurance, so to speak. Sometimes clients purchase disaster avoidance. Consultants point out the implications of various options, especially those hidden deep in the systemic labyrinth.

Using Consultants to Confront Uncooperative Managers

Consultants can say the darndest things and get away with it. Pay project managers almost always find some manager who just does not want to go along with the system:

> "I don't have the time for all the job descriptions or evaluations, and my people don't either."
> "You're going to put people into a box; what are we going to do about all these special situations in my department?"
> "These evaluations are all wrong. What was your task force thinking of when they evaluated my jobs?"

Pay project managers can do battle just so hard and so often before they stretch rapport to the breaking point. Consultants can be a little more direct because they are going to get on their airplane and leave. Do not misunderstand; you should not use a consultant as a hired gun, especially since you will have to handle the dead and wounded after the shootout.

Consultants start their arguments from the premise that they are being paid to tell it like it is, and in the shortest possible time. Vague and waffled discussion does not provide clear options and costs a lot. Moreover, consultants have heard all the objections before. They know what information is necessary to answer the objection and are skilled at presenting the information in a teaching manner.

Using Consultants When Time Is Important

Consultants can help when time is short by doing some of the tedious and time-consuming work—but it will cost you. They can provide quality training for such tasks as writing job descriptions or evaluating jobs when you are going to do most of the work but need someone to present the structure and the guiding principles of the pay program to managers and other employees.

Ensuring Organizational Ownership of the Results

Be aware that work done by the consultant is "owned" by the consultant—psychologically, that is. For example, when you hire a consultant to write job descriptions, managers and employees can avoid accountability ownership by arguing that they did not agree with the description; the consultant wrote it and obviously did not understand the situation. You can avoid this problem by using the consultant's work as a draft to be approved by the manager and the job incumbent.

You can hire a consultant to accomplish specific work for you. You can hire a consultant to teach you. You can hire a consultant to teach you as you accomplish specific work. Generally, learn everything you can, and make an effort to achieve independence.

Project Analyzer 2.7

Does your project deadline suggest that you will need help to meet it?

_____

_____

Is it your inclination to design and install the project yourself or to get some outside help?

_____

_____

On what tasks might a consultant help?

_____

_____

Do you know any consultants who might help?

_____

_____

Who among your peers might know of a consultant, or where would experts in this field demonstrate their expertise?

_____

_____

If you plan to use a consultant, what fees might you anticipate?

_____

_____

2.8 Master Planner

Pay projects will suffer disruptions along the way if they are not thought out completely before project phases are initiated. As you read through this book for the third time, make specific decisions about the way you want to proceed and record them in the Master Planner.

Completing the Master Planner will help you plan, organize, implement, and control your pay project. You will:

- Assess what information and whose opinion you need.
- Schedule activities and develop a project calendar.
- Identify communication targets and techniques.

- Determine your authority to assemble and publish project information.
- Determine your authority to take action on project requirements.
- Identify project costs.

The Master Planner begins on the next page and continues through page 60.

Master Planner: Information/Opinion Access

	Who Has Information	Who Has Opinion	Best Way to Get It

Phase 1. Know Your Organization

	Who Has Information	Who Has Opinion	Best Way to Get It
Establish needs			
Establish program goals			
Identify organization structure			
Determine benefits portion of pay program			

Phase 2. Planning and Organizing Your Pay Project

	Who Has Information	Who Has Opinion	Best Way to Get It
Set time schedule			
Determine costs			

Phase 3. Obtaining Commitment to Pay Strategies

Get support from

	Who Has Information	Who Has Opinion	Best Way to Get It
■ management			
■ employees			
■ the union			
■ others			

Get commitment from

	Who Has Information	Who Has Opinion	Best Way to Get It
■ management			
■ employees			
■ the union			
■ others			

Phase 4. Defining Job Results and Qualifications

Select collection methods					
Edit adaptable questionnaire					
Gather job information from					
■ management					
■ employees					
Get approval					
Identify uses of job descriptions					
Design format of job descriptions					
Write job descriptions					
Get approval					
Determine job qualifications					
Get approval					

Phase 5. Evaluating Job Contributions

Identify job families				
Select compensable factors				
Select benchmark jobs				
Write documentation				
Edit adaptable plan				
Select evaluators				
Train evaluators				

	Who Has Information	Who Has Opinion	Best Way to Get It
Evaluate jobs			
Weight factors			
Review final ranking			
Get agreement			
Get approval			

Phase 6. Evaluating the Price of Jobs in the Marketplace

	Who Has Information	Who Has Opinion	Best Way to Get It
Identify labor markets			
Conduct and obtain surveys			
Edit adaptable questionnaire			
Match jobs and analyze data			

Phase 7. Building the Pay Structure

	Who Has Information	Who Has Opinion	Best Way to Get It
Determine policy line			
Define job grades			
Determine pay range spreads			
Get approval			

Phase 8. Managing Job Contributions

	Who Has Information	Who Has Opinion	Best Way to Get It
Write profiles			
Design job management form			
Train managers			
Develop consensus on outcomes			

Phase 9. Maintaining Your Pay Program

Identify organization reputation					
Identify economic influences					
Identify motivational messages					
Identify perceptions of pay					
Review legal requirements					
Assess implications of new structure and examine options					
Write policies and procedures					
Plan for structural adjustments					
Plan for individual adjustments					
Plan for program maintenance					
Plan for program audit					
Get approval					

Master Planner: Schedule

Project Completion Date: _____

How long will each activity take to complete? When must it be completed? When must it be started? Who will do the work?

	How Long	When Due	Start Date	Who Will Do It

Phase 1. Know Your Organization

	How Long	When Due	Start Date	Who Will Do It
Establish needs				
Establish program goals				
Identify organization structure				
Determine benefits portion of pay program				

Phase 2. Planning and Organizing Your Pay Project

	How Long	When Due	Start Date	Who Will Do It
Determine costs				

Phase 3. Obtaining Commitment to Pay Strategies

Get support from

	How Long	When Due	Start Date	Who Will Do It
■ management				
■ employees				
■ the union				
■ others				

Get commitment from

	How Long	When Due	Start Date	Who Will Do It
■ management				
■ employees				
■ the union				
■ others				

Phase 4. Defining Job Results and Qualifications

Select collection methods				
Edit adaptable questionnaire				
Gather job information from				
■ management				
■ employees				
Get approval				
Identify uses of job descriptions				
Design format of job descriptions				
Write job descriptions				
Get approval				
Determine job qualifications				
Get approval				

Phase 5. Evaluating Job Contributions

Identify job families			
Select compensable factors			
Select benchmark jobs			
Write documentation			
Edit adaptable plan			
Select evaluators			
Train evaluators			

	How Long	When Due	Start Date	Who Will Do It
Evaluate jobs				
Weight factors				
Review final ranking				
Get agreement				
Get approval				

Phase 6. Evaluating the Price of Jobs in the Marketplace

Identify labor markets				
Conduct and obtain surveys				
Edit adaptable questionnaire				
Match jobs and analyze data				

Phase 7. Building the Pay Structure

Determine policy line				
Define job grades				
Determine pay range spreads				
Get approval				

Phase 8. Managing Job Contributions

Write profiles				
Design job management form				
Train managers				
Develop consensus on outcomes				

Phase 9. Maintaining Your Pay Program

Identify organization reputation			
Identify economic influences			
Identify motivational messages			
Identify perceptions of pay			
Review legal requirements			
Assess implications of new structure and examine options			
Write policies and procedures			
Plan for structural adjustments			
Plan for individual adjustments			
Plan for program maintenance			
Plan for program audit			
Get approval			

41

Master Planner: Calendar

Year ——

| Jan. | Feb. | Mar. | Apr. | May | June | July | Aug. | Sept. | Oct. | Nov. | Dec. |

Year ——

| Jan. | Feb. | Mar. | Apr. | May | June | July | Aug. | Sept. | Oct. | Nov. | Dec. |

(Write in project phase number)

Phase 1. Know Your Organization
Phase 2. Planning and Organizing Your Pay Project
Phase 3. Obtaining Commitment to Pay Strategies
Phase 4. Defining Job Results and Qualifications
Phase 5. Evaluating Job Contributions
Phase 6. Evaluating the Price of Jobs in the Marketplace
Phase 7. Building the Pay Structure
Phase 8. Managing Job Contributions
Phase 9. Maintaining Your Pay Program

Master Planner: Communications

Who is the target audience? What communications technique should be employed? Who will communicate?

	Target Audience	What to Do	Who Will Do It

Phase 1. Know Your Organization

Publish

- program goals
- organization structure
- benefits portion of pay program

Phase 2. Planning and Organizing Your Pay Project

Publish

- time schedule

Phase 3. Obtaining Commitment to Pay Strategies

Involve

- management
- employees
- the union
- others

Get support from

- management
- employees
- the union
- others

	Target Audience	What to Do	Who Will Do It
Get commitment from			
■ management			
■ employees			
■ the union			
■ others			

Phase 4. Defining Job Results and Qualifications

	Target Audience	What to Do	Who Will Do It
Announce collection methods			
Distribute questionnaire			
Gather job information from			
■ management			
■ employees			
Get approval of job information			
Get approval of job descriptions			
Publish			
■ uses of job descriptions			
■ format of job descriptions			
Distribute job descriptions			
Get approval of job qualifications			
Publish job qualifications			

Phase 5. Evaluating Job Contributions

Publish

■ job families		
■ compensable factors		
■ benchmark jobs		

Publish

■ documentation		
■ plan		
■ evaluator selection		
Train evaluators		
Get agreement		
Get approval		

Publish

■ evaluations		
■ factor weighting		
■ final ranking		

Phase 6. Evaluating the Price of Jobs in the Marketplace

Contact survey participants	

Publish

■ result of labor market survey	
■ outcome of (participants') survey	

45

	Target Audience	What to Do	Who Will Do It

Phase 7. Building the Pay Structure

Get approval			
Publish			
■ job grades			
■ pay range spreads			

Phase 8. Managing Job Contributions

Write profiles			
Design job management form			
Train managers			
Develop consensus on outcomes			

Phase 9. Maintaining Your Pay Program

Publish			
■ legal requirements			
Present options			
Get approval			
Publish			
■ policies and procedures			
■ structural adjustments			
Convey individual adjustments			

Publish

- policies and procedures
- structural adjustments

Convey individual adjustments

Publish

- program maintenance requirements
- program audit requirements

47

Master Planner: Communication Authority

	Provide or Obtain	Interview or Investigate	Interpret or Advise	Persuade or Teach	Authorize or Arbitrate	Decide or Determine

Phase 1. Know Your Organization

Publish

■ program goals						
■ organization structure						
■ benefits portion of pay program						

Phase 2. Planning and Organizing Your Pay Project

Publish

■ time schedule						

Phase 3. Obtaining Commitment to Pay Strategies

Involve

■ management						
■ employees						
■ the union						
■ others						

Get support from

■ management						
■ employees						
■ the union						
■ others						

Get commitment from

■ management					
■ employees					
■ the union					
■ others					

Phase 4. Defining Job Results and Qualifications

Announce collection methods	
Distribute questionnaire	

Gather job information from

■ management			
■ employees			
Get approval			
Get approval of job descriptions			

Publish

■ uses of job descriptions			
■ format of job descriptions			
Distribute job descriptions			
Get approval of job qualifications			
Publish job qualifications			

49

	Provide or Obtain	Interview or Investigate	Interpret or Advise	Persuade or Teach	Authorize or Arbitrate	Decide or Determine

Phase 5. Evaluating Job Contributions

Publish

- job families
- compensable factors
- benchmark jobs

Publish

- documentation
- plan
- evaluator selection

Train evaluators

Get agreement

Get approval

Publish

- evaluations
- factor weighting
- final ranking

Phase 6. Evaluating the Price of Jobs in the Marketplace

Contact survey participants

50

Publish

■ result of labor market survey				
■ outcome of (participants') survey				

Phase 7. Building the Pay Structure

Get approval	

Publish

■ job grades	
■ pay range spreads	

Phase 8. Managing Job Contributions

Write profiles			
Design job management form			
Train managers			
Develop consensus on outcomes			

Phase 9. Maintaining Your Pay Program

Publish

■ legal requirements	
Present options	
Get approval	

51

	Provide or Obtain	Interview or Investigate	Interpret or Advise	Persuade or Teach	Authorize or Arbitrate	Decide or Determine
Publish						
■ policies and procedures						
■ structural adjustments						
Convey individual adjustments						
Publish						
■ program maintenance requirements						
■ program audit requirements						

Master Planner: Decision Authority

What actions can you take at your own discretion? Which actions do you need to tell someone about? For which do you need prior approval?

	Your Discretion	Tell Someone (Whom)	Prior Approval (From Whom)
Phase 1. Know Your Organization			
Establish program goals			
Identify organization structure			
Determine benefits portion of pay program			
Phase 2. Planning and Organizing Your Pay Project			
Set time schedule			
Determine costs			
Phase 3. Obtaining Commitment to Pay Strategies			
Involve			
■ management			
■ employees			
■ the union			
■ others			
Get support from			
■ management			
■ employees			
■ the union			
■ others			

	Your Discretion	Tell Someone (Whom)	Prior Approval (From Whom)
Get commitment from			
▪ management			
▪ employees			
▪ the union			
▪ others			

Phase 4. Defining Job Results and Qualifications

	Your Discretion	Tell Someone (Whom)	Prior Approval (From Whom)
Select collection methods			
Edit adaptable questionnaire			

	Your Discretion	Tell Someone (Whom)	Prior Approval (From Whom)
Gather job information from			
▪ management			
▪ employees			
Get approval			
Identify uses of job descriptions			
Design format of job descriptions			
Write job descriptions			
Get approval of job descriptions			
Determine job qualifications			
Get approval of job qualifications			

Phase 5. Evaluating Job Contributions

Identify job families					
Select compensable factors					
Select benchmark jobs					
Write documentation					
Edit adaptable plan					
Select evaluators					
Train evaluators					
Evaluate jobs					
Weight factors					
Review final ranking					
Get agreement					
Get approval					

Phase 6. Evaluating the Price of Jobs in the Marketplace

Identify labor markets					
Conduct and obtain surveys					
Edit adaptable questionnaire					
Match jobs and analyze data					

Phase 7. Building the Pay Structure

Determine policy line					
Define job grades					
Determine pay range spreads					
Get approval					

	Your Discretion	Tell Someone (Whom)	Prior Approval (From Whom)

Phase 8. Managing Job Contributions

	Your Discretion	Tell Someone (Whom)	Prior Approval (From Whom)
Write profiles			
Design job management form			
Train managers			
Develop consensus on outcomes			

Phase 9. Maintaining Your Pay Program

	Your Discretion	Tell Someone (Whom)	Prior Approval (From Whom)
Identify organization reputation			
Identify economic influences			
Identify motivational messages			
Identify perceptions of pay			
Determine benefits portion of pay program			
Review legal requirements			
Assess implications of new structure and examine options			
Write policies and procedures			
Plan for structural adjustments			
Plan for individual adjustments			
Plan for program maintenance			
Plan for program audit			
Get approval			

Master Planner: Costs

For what items are expenditures anticipated? Who will incur them? How much?

What Items	Who	How Much

Phase 1. Know Your Organization

Establish program goals		
Identify organization structure		
Determine benefits portion of pay program		

Phase 2. Planning and Organizing Your Pay Project

Set time schedule		

Phase 3. Obtaining Commitment to Pay Strategies

Involve

■ management			
■ employees			
■ the union			
■ others			

Get support from

■ management			
■ employees			
■ the union			
■ others			

	What Items	Who	How Much

Get commitment from

■ management			
■ employees			
■ the union			
■ others			

Phase 4. Defining Job Results and Qualifications

Select collection methods			
Edit adaptable questionnaire			

Gather job information from

■ management			
■ employees			
Get approval			
Identify uses of job descriptions			
Design format of job descriptions			
Write job descriptions			
Get approval of job descriptions			
Determine job qualifications			
Get approval of job qualifications			

58

Phase 5. Evaluating Job Contributions

Identify job families			
Select compensable factors			
Select benchmark jobs			
Write documentation			
Edit adaptable plan			
Select evaluators			
Train evaluators			
Evaluate jobs			
Weight factors			
Review final ranking			
Get agreement			
Get approval			

Phase 6. Evaluating the Price of Jobs in the Marketplace

Identify labor markets			
Conduct and obtain surveys			
Edit adaptable questionnaire			
Match jobs and analyze data			

Phase 7. Building the Pay Structure

Determine policy line			
Define job grades			

What Items	Who	How Much
Determine pay range spreads		
Get approval		

Phase 8. Managing Job Contributions

What Items	Who	How Much
Write profiles		
Design job management form		
Train managers		
Develop consensus on outcomes		

Phase 9. Maintaining Your Pay Program

What Items	Who	How Much
Identify organization reputation		
Identify economic influences		
Identify motivational messages		
Identify perceptions of pay		
Review legal requirements		
Assess implications of new structure and examine options		
Write policies and procedures		
Plan for structural adjustments		
Plan for individual adjustments		
Plan for program maintenance		
Plan for program audit		
Get approval		

Strategic Planning for Phase 2

On your *first* quick walk through the project phases, record your initial thoughts on policy issues that will have to be decided concerning Phase 2.

_____

_____

_____

Any notes on tactical procedures?

_____

_____

On your *second* time through the phases, consider the strategic influences from all the phases; decide on an integrated posture for the entire project.

Complete the section for this phase in the Master Planner (in Phase 2.8) during your *third* reading.

Phase 3

Obtaining Commitment to Pay Strategies

> Commitment is the key to success.

3.1 Getting People Involved

It is foolish and dangerous to begin a pay program without a commitment from management to have it succeed. Commitment comes from an agreement that the program is needed—that it will give new satisfactions, achieve new objectives, and solve old problems.

Employees are resilient beyond imagination, judging by what some managements have pulled on them in the past, but they can have their hopes dashed on the rocks only so many times. One more false start, and you may lose them.

The easiest programs to install are those where the CEO says, and means, "It shall be so." Go for the bell at the top of the pole because when that bell rings, all hear.

Present a Complete Proposal

Start with a complete program proposal, with all phases of this book, to ensure that everybody concerned understands thoroughly what is involved. A total program, which means a big investment of time and expense, demands a thoughtful presentation. The Master Planner will guide you.

Go easy. Lay out the entire pitch, but be ready to take what you can get and run. Only moralists believe that you must swallow the program whole, and in the prescribed manner. Granted, a few program elements are essential, but they are surprisingly few. The psychology here is important: people will make something work if they believe in it. Be ready to give in here and there; many issues are not that big a deal or can be dealt with later.

Top managers want to know that you have thought through the opportunities, options, and obstacles. They want good staff work; they do not want more work than when they started. They usually do not want to examine all your planning details, but they want to know that the details were examined by *someone.*

Some managers will want it all. Assess the managerial style of your top manager and respond accordingly. If you do not interact with the top manager, think beyond any intermediary manager to the ultimate approval authority. Whatever you can do to help others sell your program will come home to help you.

In large organizations, specific support from the top is not essential, though tacit approval is always required. Get formal approval from management one level higher than the highest manager whose employees are affected by the project. Resolve project priorities up front.

Sell Fundamental Benefits

Sell management on the strategic implications of the pay program: productivity and job satisfaction improvements resulting from the pay structure, and clarification of the job relationships between managers and employees. Identify specific benefits as the goals of your pay program.

Get Tangible Support

Push for visible support from top management. Nothing sells harder than unabashed support. On the other hand, keep a low profile if the true support is mere acceptance rather than enthusiasm. Stay on the side of reality, and work with the cards that you are dealt.

Project Analyzer 3.1

Who is the top manager from whom you must obtain support and commitment?

_____

_____

What is the typical posture of the top manager toward human resources programs?

_____

_____

What are the prospects for support for this program?

_____

_____

How will the reasons for inaugurating this project influence potential support?

_____

_____

Has the top manager been involved in a project of this nature before?

_____

_____

What was the outcome of that project?

_____

_____

How will that outcome affect your project?

_____

_____

What is the top manager's style regarding staff work?

_____

_____

Should your presentations be succinct or get down to the nitty-gritty?

_____

_____

Will your presentations be made to one person or to a committee?

_____

_____

Will your presentation include an opportunity to develop ideas, or will you present a finished draft?

_____

_____

What commitment and support do you want?

_____

_____

How will you publish that commitment and support to the organization?

_____

_____

3.2 Building Commitment

People do not inherently resist change. They resist it when they don't understand it or don't agree with it. Resistance is not always permanent. You'll sometimes hear, "I'll support the change, but not at this time."

Focus on acceptance of the pay program from the very start; take every opportunity to help others believe in its merits. Sell, sell, sell. Many good programs have withered for lack of attention and interest, and excellent benefits have been lost to both the organization and its employees.

Solicit support for the program, but also obtain commitment. People can "support" a program by not saying anything negative about it. Commitment arises out of appreciation for the merits of a program and the belief that the benefits will be helpful to the organization. Commitment means advocacy.

The principle of management support we believe in is that a pay program (and the related programs for managing and rewarding work results) ought to provide department managers with the information they need to manage their responsibilities independently. These programs ought not to be HR programs, but rather management programs.

Dealing With "Busy" Managers

Some managers are "always" busy with their "regular" (read, technical) work; human resources projects are secondary issues to them. Mature managers understand that they do not accomplish work as managers except through other people. Sometimes it takes a disaster to capture a manager's attention. If you are starting from a disaster, make the most of this motivational advantage. If you do not have one handy, use the threat of one if you have to.

That managers may object to an incursion into their domain is understandable. A pay project touches the very fiber of the organization: the relationship between manager and employee. But even the most hard-crusted, technically oriented manager realizes, deep down, that departments are collections of people rather than structures and that the most profound and problematic issues involve people, not things.

Dealing With Protective Managers

It should come as no surprise to you that the managers who protest the loudest against programs intended to help them manage are the very managers who need the most help. You undoubtedly suspect that these managers know how much help they need. Of course, they would prefer not to have their weaknesses paraded in front of their peers, subordinates, or bosses, which is what they anticipate will happen once you begin to gather information.

Most of these managers have a problem with their authority—they're afraid of losing it and don't know how to use it. Some managers mistakenly believe that they can accomplish work through others just because authority has been delegated to them. They do not accept that employees may choose to ignore directives or respond less than enthusiastically. These managers want to protect what has been granted to them, and they will resist or attack any program that appears to usurp their authority.

Help, Don't Hurt

Fighting back is not a team tactic. You will lose it all if you counterattack when you are rebuffed. Managers who attack will continue to fight as long as you are willing to scrap, and they will probably win because they have had more practice. Every once in a while you may win a fight, but since you have now shamed your opponent, you must be aware of a new game: "getting even." The whole thing adds up to a lot of wasted energy.

Instead of fighting, follow the ancient martial arts principles and yield to the oncoming force. Step out of the way, but at the same time, gently deflect the force in a way that gives you an advantage. Don't resist in a confrontation. Let an argument go past without a challenge, but as it passes, examine it. Look not only for weaknesses, but for strengths. Acknowledge the strengths, for they are fact; nothing dispels anger better than agreement.

Be patient. You must win your managers' acceptance from the start. Go to them in person, and work for their support. Be willing to explain, and reexplain. Don't catch them out on a limb. Don't give them a final solution. Remember that they are being held accountable for what happens, or fails to happen, in their area of responsibility. How do they know that a program will help them if they do not understand it?

Offering Information

Most managers simply want to know what is going on: how a program will affect them, how they can influence requirements about to be imposed on them, and how they can make adjustments for the demands of their own situation.

Give them information where they lack it or where they misunderstand. Lack of information is easily corrected; uncovering misunderstandings is much more difficult. Be patient. Let them talk; let them ask questions. Be helpful. Accept that people do what seems sensible to them—no matter whether it is right or wrong. Managers fight because it is the only sensible thing for them to do at the moment. With other information and other options, they would choose to do something else.

Managers respond according to their experiences, and you have to know up front that there are far too many inadequate pay programs out there in organizationland. Consequently, you can expect a negative reaction from many managers, because experience tells them that this program is trouble. Although information can eliminate some objections, only positive experience can change some minds.

Acceptance vs. Agreement

If you can obtain agreement with your program, get it, but settle for acceptance that the program should be done if that is all you can get. Pay attention to this subtle but important distinction. If you cannot have positive support, at least stop the fighting.

Why can you afford to wait calmly while recalcitrant managers dissipate their frustrations? Because you know that you are going to win them over in the end. Your program is going to work; it will make their job easier and more satisfying. Yes, you will have your moments of indecision and anxiety, but that's okay. Your confidence will build as you take the steps set out for you in the phases of this book and as you begin to experience the application of your work. Your program will solve problems in your organization and exploit opportunities. What could be more welcome?

Managers might be forced to participate in the program, or they might willingly participate; you will witness many postures, and you will have to use different tactics in encounters with each of your managers. Forcing managers to participate is the least desirable tactic because they will at best give lip service to the project, and their lack of enthusiasm and support will influence employees and other managers.

Engineering Agreement: Get the Opinion Molders Behind You

Opinion molders are useful people to help you win acceptance; they are respected for their thinking, not for their style. They are already vocal, but not loud. Occasionally, of course, mob psychology comes into play and a person stumbles into favor, and that person supposedly speaks for the group.

Opinion molders are informal leaders whose decision to agree or disagree with a program sways other people. If you can get these influential people to support your program, you will achieve your goals; with their commitment, you will alter the course of your organization.

Talk to Employees, Too

Employees, like managers, want to know what is going on and how a program is going to affect them. Employees, we know, have plenty of opinions about their jobs and their pay, and how jobs and pay ought to be managed. Some employees are not particularly interested in discussing these issues and would prefer that you decide; others would like to discuss the issue but figure management will do what it wants anyway.

More and more, however, employees are expressing themselves about issues that affect them, and in some instances, they are expecting an invitation to participate in planning discussions. Occasionally employees want to control the process—unions certainly want a strong voice—but more often than not, employees only want to know that you heard and considered their opinion.

Successful pay projects are built on accurate information, and they blend the organization's needs with the needs of people—both managers and employees. Successful project managers go to the people who have information and opinions. They ask and they listen. They cooperate and coordinate. They personalize an otherwise impersonal program. They build credibility for their project and themselves, not only on the technical merits of the work, but also on the rapport they establish.

Project Analyzer 3.2

Does your organization typically welcome or resist change?

_____

_____

Why has change been resisted in the past?

_____

_____

Why has change been accepted in the past?

_____

_____

Who are your most effective change agents?

_____

_____

How are human resources programs typically received?

_____

_____

Are human resources programs viewed as a help or a hindrance?

_____

_____

What is the reputation of the human resources department?

_____

_____

Are human resources specialists asked for help, tolerated, or avoided?

_____

_____

What tactics have generally helped managers understand and accept human resources programs?

_____

_____

What tactics have managers dismissed?

_____

_____

Are managers generally interested in human concerns?

_____

_____

Should human resources programs be assigned to managers rather than to the human resources department?

_____

_____

Are managers willing to help shape new programs?

_____

_____

What is the reputation of the current pay system?

_____

_____

What strengths can you build on?

_____

_____

What weaknesses must you overcome?

_____

_____

Do managers and employees try to "beat the system"?

_____

_____

Who are the biggest offenders?

_____

_____

What are their strengths?

_____

_____

. . . and weaknesses?

_____

_____

What are their usual tactics?

_____

_____

What are their needs?

_____

_____

Is a planning task force a viable way to build commitment?

_____

_____

Who might be on such a task force?

_____

_____

_____

3.3 A Golden Opportunity to Help Managers Grow

Most managers want to be fair to employees. Unfortunately, their people skills are usually nowhere near as good as their technical skills. A pay program helps managers by narrowing the personal interactive options available to them.

The elements a pay program addresses—job design and descriptions, job relationships and progressions, organized pay improvement, and so forth—are the kind of issues in an employee relationship that technically oriented managers overlook or stumble over. Your pay program can also be a management education program. Properly involved in the development of a pay program, managers will have an opportunity to gain new insights into people and, in the long run, to gain some new skills.

A manager's growth comes as a direct result of participating in successful relationships with employees. As you know, most management development programs are deficient in this regard; classroom beliefs are quickly washed away in the realities of the workaday world. Not so with a pay program that gives managers specific help when they need it.

What is this "good management" we want to teach our managers? We want them to plan, organize, implement, and control. A successful pay program considers the purpose and needs of the organization (planning); the identification and valuing of the tasks that must be performed in order to fulfill the organizational purpose and to meet organizational needs (organizing); the integration of organizational and individual goals (implementing); and the measurement and adjustment of action toward goals, including the distribution of rewards (controlling). A pay program helps managers acquire a managerial perception.

We also want managers to understand that paying employees equitably is good management: organizationally, because the program helps the organization to function better, and humanly, because employees are treated fairly.

Let's state the case bluntly in the negative: the absence of a sound pay program is the absence of management.

Project Analyzer 3.3

How receptive are your managers to management training?

_____

_____

Are they capable managers?

_____

_____

Do they need to learn the essentials of human resources management?

_____

_____

Are your managers used to the idea of talking together and planning program elements?

_____

_____

In what ways might they be involved in this program?

_____

_____

3.4 Collaboration

Is there a managerial nirvana? No, but next door there is a state called *collaboration*. Let us agree that any management style will work so long as the participants agree to it. However, in the long run, some styles probably are not as effective as others.

Autocracy, Democracy, and Collaboration

Autocracy does not build independence, and in our Western culture, at this time, employees highly value the freedom to act without continual direction.

Democracy—giving ultimate governing power to employees—is nearly unworkable at this stage of development of society's interactive skills. Treating management and employees as equals also conflicts with the rights of investors, who have risked economically and are entitled to exert some control over the business through management, which is accountable to them.

Collaboration seems to give us some useful answers. We know that autocracy is more efficient than democracy. We know that democracy gives rights to employees who invest not money but themselves in the enterprise. Collaboration purports to marry these two values.

In short, under a collaborative style, ideas for the management of the enterprise can come from either managers or employees; they should be considered by both, and consensus should be achieved where feasible. Failing consensus, management is accountable for moving forward, and employees must trust in that movement. If we look at such a style from a practical angle, the key to success seems to rest in the opportunity (perhaps even the right) for everyone to speak to the issue and to be considered, but not in the right of refusal.

Authority Retained

Collaboration does not necessarily mean giving up decision-making authority, although this was the impression when the style first hit the textbooks. Collaboration can be as minimal as presenting your decision and asking for comments, or it can include discussions about options available to solve a problem, or free-form discussion to identify the problem.

Collaboration is not a universal style to be applied in all situations. You may choose to collaborate with employees on some issues of your pay program but not on others. The phases of this book offer you some options as you develop your approach.

Undoubtedly, the pay program that you now have in your organization has been there for a while. Change to a new system will take some time; acceptance cannot be decreed. Employees need time to get used to a new idea and to understand it; letting them collaborate along the way does just that.

Do you need to have everyone collaborate? Obviously not. The decision is one of philosophy as well as practicality. You may want to invite every employee to share ideas, fill out forms, and react to opinions, but that would be impractical with thousands of employees. Don't give up on the idea too quickly, however, because there may be some simple ways to reach many people, or some sampling techniques that will give you the breadth of information you need. We will consider all this in subsequent phases as we examine specific aspects of a pay program.

Management's Basic Beliefs

How management chooses to interact with its employees is a matter of style, which stems from the assumptions managers hold about the nature and behavior of employees. No steps can be taken in the design of a pay program until management's style is clearly understood.

If you were, for example, to design a pay program based on so-called modern prescripts of organizational behavior and introduce that program to a group of managers who regard collaboration as an affront to their position authority and think that employees are not able to function effectively and efficiently without direction and control, you would be in for a lot of trouble.

No matter how unclear and informal management's beliefs about employees may be, they do guide its actions. The statement, "We don't have a pay program," is impossible. If you pay employees, you have already decided on a pay policy.

Each organization determines its values in its own manner, be it by decree from the top autocrat or by never-ending debates of laissez-faire committees. The important learning point here is that you must understand and accept where your organization is now before you can consider moving it along in a different direction.

The considerations involved in establishing a pay program profoundly influence an organization and will have to be approached delicately. Do not underestimate the dynamics of the program. You are not dealing with some surface procedures about jobs and paychecks; you are entering an arena that is intertwined with intimate feelings about the value of work and the responsibility of people.

You will not be able to determine management's beliefs about pay until the principals sit down and examine options and outcomes. They don't necessarily have to do this in a group, mind you (some groups would undoubtedly end up in a fistfight if they ever tried to reason together). You don't need more schisms. In such a situation, one person would need to make the rounds of the organization and, in private conversation, elicit ideas about the way management should conduct itself. This person would then distill the divergent opinions into an acceptable draft, which would then be negotiated with the original respondents. The objective is to extract from the members of management a supportable policy without their ever having to discuss it.

Where managers can sit together and debate a policy, they should. Naturally, this process requires someone to manage the discussion in order to achieve fruitful results, but the unification of opinion achieved by this direct approach will be strong.

Collaboration Can Mean Education

We can almost guarantee that announcing and conducting a typical training session in management styles, employee behavior, motivation, and the like will produce yawns. But if you ask managers to gather to express their considered judgment on the important facets of the proposed pay program, they might be willing to do it. And what will they discuss? Management styles, employee behavior, motivation, and the like. But you won't tell.

Gently point out the inevitable success or failure of various suggestions. Bring in new information. Let them talk out the differences. Let them test and try. Let them come to an agreement.

Agreement is easiest at global levels. Get your management group to work on the goals of your pay program first. Why do we want to have this program? Then ease into the discussion of what the program will be and how it should be implemented. Finally, delve into the issue of how much management wants to tell employees about the program, which will most likely be the most heated discussion. We will look at employee communications in detail in Phase 9.

Use the materials in this book to guide your discussions. Generally groups work better when you give them some straw work to tear apart rather than ask them to start with a blank piece of paper. Offer the ideas of this book as sacrificial lambs; it is better that they focus their editorial wrath on those ideas than on you.

Again: take your organization where it's at in management style, even if it does not conform to "modern" theory. It's all you have. Set goals for new ways to act, if change is required. Sometimes you will want to talk out these new directions; in other cases, you will simply start acting that way and let everyone learn from your model.

Project Analyzer 3.4

How does management interact with employees now?

_____

_____

How do managers interact among themselves?

_____

_____

How autocratic and bureaucratic, versus democratic and open, is your organization's management style?

_____

_____

Does management collaborate with employees on goal setting and problem solving?

_____

_____

What is the status of management-employee relations now?

_____

_____

How much confidence do employees have in management's programs?

_____

_____

How much confidence does management have in its employees?

_____

_____

Are employee opinions welcome?

_____

_____

Are employees cooperative?

_____

_____

How honest are employees with management?

_____

_____

How honest is management with employees?

_____

_____

What is the prospect for cooperation between management and employees?

_____

_____

How could cooperation begin?

_____

_____

3.5 Union Relations

Three or four decades ago, it was popular to quote a noted union officer who discerned that the union's responsibility was not to act but only to grieve after management acted. Today, managements and unions generally understand their shared accountability for ensuring the economic security of the organization and its members; they are beginning to accept that unnecessary scrapping in the courtyard is wasteful, and many times destructive.

Pay programs are right at the top of the list of annoyances between management and unions. Certainly pay is near and dear to the hearts of both parties. Pay decisions are never as clean as we would like them, especially when they are made without the benefit of a thoughtful structure. Unions are very concerned about the behind-the-doors, Ouija-board aura that surrounds some pay programs.

Assess Your Situation

Start by assessing your historical and current union relations atmosphere and manner of interacting. Your actions must fit with previous ways of interacting with the union; otherwise, union members might think that something is fishy, especially since money is at issue. Where the union has been involved with job analysis, job descriptions, job evaluation, and so on, keep it involved, unless you want to suffer the consequences of ignoring it. Where the union has not been involved, be careful about giving your rights away.

If you are interested in changing the direction of your relations with labor, especially toward a more cooperative venture, the development of a pay program is a fine opportunity. An effective pay program is based on solid information and builds acceptance from the people affected each step of the way. People who are involved in the considerations that affect the design of the program are more committed to the program than people who either hear about the program through the grapevine or are completely surprised when the program is suddenly announced.

Unions Have Information and Opinions

Unions have information that you need as you design your program, so there is every reason to involve them in the process. Naturally, you will want to be selective in what information and questions you take to a union, but this is true about any group of people. Some issues are not destined to be discussed in a group—if you want to get something accomplished.

Unions are collections of people concerned with the issues of the workplace. Like any other collection of workers, they want to have their opinions heard. What gets union members angry is being ignored. The lesson is the same one we learned about participatory management: employees do not necessarily want to share in making the decisions, but they want to know that their opinion is considered.

Still, unions are political entities; they do things individual members would not. You will want to be careful about when and how to have them participate. As we proceed through the phases of this book, you will be able to consider at what points you want a union's comments.

Remember, today some unions are much more aware of the finesse of pay administration than in the old days. The questions of pay equality in our society have forced them to reexamine traditional solutions. Unions may be just as prepared as, and maybe even more prepared than, you.

Project Analyzer 3.5

What does your labor contract require regarding information and discussions related to the elements of the pay structure: job analysis, job descriptions, job evaluation, market studies, pay progression, and so forth?

_____

_____

What legal precedents have been established?

_____

_____

What information exchange mechanisms between your organization and the union are in place now?

_____

_____

What is the history of labor relations in the organization?

_____

_____

How well do management and the union get along?

_____

_____

What goals have been established for management's relations with unions?

_____

_____

Who are the real decision makers in the union?

_____

_____

Should union officers and members be invited to participate in the development process?

_____

_____

Who would be invited?

_____

_____

What reactions to a proposal for a new or revised program can you expect?

_____

_____

Is there an agreement on the need for a new or revised program?

_____

_____

Do you have the support of your labor attorney for this project?

_____

_____

When are the next contract negotiations scheduled?

_____

_____

Is there enough time before contract negotiations to prepare a pay structure proposal?

_____

_____

Is the timing right to begin your project before negotiations?

_____

_____

When you are able to conclude the project, will the timing be right to implement a new pay structure?

_____

_____

_____

Strategic Planning for Phase 3

On your *first* quick walk through the project phases, record your initial thoughts on policy issues that will have to be decided.

_____

_____

_____

_____

_____

_____

Any notes on tactical procedures?

_____

_____

_____

_____

On your *second* time through the phases, consider the strategic influences from all the phases; decide on an integrated posture for the entire project.

Complete the section for this phase in the Master Planner (in Phase 2.8) during your *third* reading.

Phase 4

Defining Job Results and Qualifications

Jobs—what employees need to accomplish so that the organization fulfills its mission—are the cornerstone of any pay strategy.

4.1 Why Jobs Exist

An organization exists to achieve its purpose. All organization actions must flow from this focus in order to maximize effectiveness and efficiency.

Employees are invited to join an organization to contribute talent and actions that fulfill the organization's mission. The expected contribution is called a job. Employees are paid to accomplish job results that achieve the organization's purpose.

Jobs are the cells of the organization body. Each cell has a function to contribute to the body's success. Cells communicate with each other, especially by adjusting processes in an effort to achieve equilibrium. The key is *communication*.

What keeps cells interacting is the understanding of their common purpose. In the same way, employees who share an understanding of their common purpose can interact to accomplish results. Organizations that fail do not talk to employees about job results that must be produced, or integrated with other jobs, in order for the organization to be successful. Such diseases as job protection occur when employees do not see the relationship of their contribution to other contributions in the organization.

It is important for organizations to be flexible, but it is important as well for job responsibilities to be defined. Chaos will follow when job contributions are not defined. How else would job candidates be evaluated, new employees oriented to their expected contribution, job efforts focused on important requirements, and pay determined fairly?

The key to organizational, job, and employee flexibility is to start with a broad definition of jobs as results to be accomplished *in addition to* the traditional manner of only describing duties to be performed. Employees need to be given as much information as possible—not only about their jobs but about organizational capabilities and demands on the organization—so that they are able to make informed decisions. Managers and employees need to be taught to see organizational possibilities instead of organizational restrictions sometimes ascribed to "narrow" job descriptions.

Focusing on jobs as organization building blocks sets the tone for the next several steps in developing a pay program:

- Gathering information about jobs (job analysis)
- Writing results-oriented job descriptions
- Establishing job qualifications

Project Analyzer 4.1

Is the organization mission clear?

_____

_____

Is the organization mission publicized so that people can rally around it?

_____

_____

How sacred are functional boundaries?

_____

_____

Do employees cross boundaries freely and work with each other collaboratively?

_____

_____

Is the organization stuck in a time warp, adhering to outmoded policies and procedures?

_____

_____

Does the organization need to operate more dynamically?

_____

_____

_____

4.2 Gathering Job Information: Job Analysis

Information used to write job descriptions is gathered in various ways:

- Interviewing people who understand the job
- Asking people who understand the job to complete a questionnaire

- Observing and studying job operations
- Studying outside references of the same job or similar jobs
- Designing the job from scratch

Information may also be gathered at the same time to do the following:

- Establish job qualifications
- Complete job evaluations
- Establish job planning and appraisal outcome criteria
- Reorganize job operations and working relationships
- Change personnel requirements
- Establish hiring and testing requirements
- Develop orientation and training programs
- Develop succession plans

Although information is gathered most often to clarify job results and requirements regarding jobs that already exist, the major question should always be, Is this job designed correctly? That is, Does it fit the way the organization operates or intends to operate?

The method(s) used to gather information depends on:

- Time available
- Costs
- Job circumstances
- Personnel preferences

Who Is a Resource for Information?

Experience demonstrates that the person accomplishing job results usually knows the most about them. Sometimes the supervisor knows best. When the job is a new outgrowth of other jobs in the organization, the incumbents of the jobs that gave rise to the new job are a resource.

Outside resources include other organizations with the same or similar jobs; descriptions published in pay surveys: the Department of Labor's O*NET (Occupational Information Network), which replaces the *Dictionary of Occupational Titles*; books of sample job descriptions; professional associations; and certification requirements.

How Many People Should Be Surveyed?

Theoretically, every job incumbent should be queried to ensure identification of every distinct job duty (important when defending hiring requirements, job outcome criteria, and pay levels). Practically speaking, where 200 people are performing nearly identical jobs, not every incumbent need be invited to respond.

What are your goals? If you intend to maximize employee participation in the project, ask all 200 employees to fill out a questionnaire. Otherwise, identify a random sample of job incumbents, and ask them to participate. Or have all incumbents complete the questionnaire, but read only a random sample of them.

Interviewing is almost always on a sample basis because of the time involved.

Get Management's Approval of Job Content

Regardless of the information-gathering process, all job content must be approved by management—usually the job supervisor and one or two higher levels of management. There are several reasons for this. Management and employees do not always communicate clearly with each other about job expectations. Management may have something else in mind for the job in the future. Employees may exaggerate. Management may exaggerate. The job analyst may misunderstand.

A draft job description can also be verified later with incumbents and management.

Gathering Job Information

Gathering information on job responsibilities can be approached in several ways:

- Ask the job incumbent to identify all job duties, then identify all job results, and then correlate duties and results.
- Ask the job incumbent to identify the major job results, and then list the duties necessary to accomplish each result.
- Ask the job incumbent to identify duties and corresponding results together.

Questionnaire Questionnaires are an efficient technique insofar as they allow the respondent time to answer leisurely and carefully without the constraint of an interviewer waiting for a response. Questionnaires can also be completed in small groups, with time set aside for uninterrupted attention and a knowledgeable person available to answer questions. Questionnaires also save time because answers need only to be read instead of having employees participate in a slower, sometimes rambling, interview.

Effective questionnaires are understood by the respondents and identify the specific information required. Language must be chosen carefully, because the respondent has no one to clarify the intent of a question. Pretesting the questionnaire is a worthwhile precaution.

A questionnaire should reflect the flavor and style of your organization. Casual language, jargon, and colloquialisms are quite permissible if they make questions clearer to the people who need to understand them.

Separate questionnaires may be required for different kinds of jobs. Otherwise, some questions will be extraneous, awkward, or confusing.

Figure 4 shows a job information questionnaire that you can adapt to obtain the data you need to understand the jobs in your organization. It is used to gather two major kinds of job information: (1) what the job is designed to accomplish and (2) the job definition (e.g., number of jobs and people supervised, authority, working conditions).

Almost no one enjoys completing these questionnaires because it takes time, always precious. Similarly, the task of studying the completed questionnaire information and translating it into different formats is very time-consuming. Therefore, shorten the process in any way that you can.

Always provide whatever job information is available to aid the people giving you information. For example, it is frustrating for the person completing the form to know that a job description, no matter how out-of-date, is on file somewhere but the information-gathering process starts all over again as though the job had never existed.

Especially because most people do not have job requirements communicated to them differentiating results from duties, an example job description written in a results-oriented style (see Phase 4.3) should be included with the questionnaire so that anyone who completes the questionnaire will fully understand the new expression of work.

Figure 4. Example of a job information questionnaire.

The information you provide by completing this questionnaire will be used to write a clear and complete job description as well as to define hiring qualifications and special job characteristics. Answer as thoroughly as you can, and don't worry about anyone "grading" your answers; the basic information about the job is what is important.

Your job title _____ Date _____

Name of person to whom you report _____

Department _____ Shift _____

Your name _____ Phone ext. _____

How long have you been in this job? _____

1. Summarize in one sentence your basic job function. (What is the principal reason your job exists? What is your job designed to accomplish?)

   _____

   _____

   _____

   _____

2. Job responsibilities can be described in two ways:

WHAT YOU DO (the duties people can watch you do)	**WHY YOU DO IT** (the effect or result you create)
A waitperson, for example,	
Placing tablecloth, napkins, silverware, plates, glassware (Duties)	Prepares dining table (Result)

List the major responsibilities of your job, including the approximate percentage of time spent on each. (It may be helpful to list duties and then identify the results; or, if you prefer, list the major results expected of your job and then the duties required to accomplish each result.) Remember that sometimes two or three duties combine to produce the same result.

Figure 4. (*continued*)

Duties	Results	Percentage of time spent

(Add additional pages as necessary)

Rank in numerical order the responsibilities in order of importance to the organization:
Mark with a **D** the most difficult part of your job.
Mark with a **C** the responsibilities involving confidential data.

3. What formal course of instruction is required by law to perform this job?

_____

   a. What formal courses of instruction might be helpful?

_____

_____

   b. What licensure or certification is required by law to perform this job?

_____

_____

Figure 4. (*continued*)

4. What specific experiences or skills other than formal education do you feel a person must have in order to start this job today?

_____

_____

_____

_____

   a. Are there any jobs a person must have worked in before this job?

     _____

     _____

5. Given your answers to questions 3 and 4, how long do you feel it should take a qualified new person to perform this job competently?

_____

6. The way you accomplish job results affects other people in terms of quality and quantity of service received, as well as time and money gained or lost.

People you affect	What would be the positive results of your good work on each type of person?	What typically might go wrong for each type of person if job results are not accomplished? (Don't think of the rare catastrophe.)
Customers		
Public		
Employees in your own department		
Employees in other departments		

EXAMPLE:

Customers	Customers receive service as requested on time	Customers complain

Figure 4. *(continued)*

7. What part of your job entails the greatest chance for error?

   _____

   _____

   a. How often does this occur (daily, weekly, monthly)?

   _____

   _____

8. What confidential information do you have access to?

   _____

   _____

   a. What could happen if this information were released?

   _____

   _____

   _____

9. Can you authorize money to be spent? ___ No ___ Yes
   If yes, how much? _____

10. Do you prepare a budget? ___ No ___ Yes
    If yes, how much?
    Planned revenue $ _____
    Planned expenses $ _____

11. Describe the contacts with other persons that you normally make while performing your job.

People contacted	How often (daily, weekly, monthly)	Principal reason for contacting
Customers		
Public		
Employees in your own department		
Employees in other departments		

Figure 4. (*continued*)

12. Which of the following describes the communication you generally use in your job? (Check all that apply.)

   _____ Provide or obtain information   _____ Persuade or teach
   _____ Interview or investigate to identify   _____ Authorize or arbitrate
            and discover information   _____ Decide or determine when
   _____ Interpret or advise to help others   policy guidelines are not
            understand   available

13. Are there any working conditions (e.g., noise, temperature extremes, odors) involved in your job that might be described as uncomfortable or disagreeable?

Condition	*How often encountered (daily, weekly, monthly)?*
_____	_____
_____	_____
_____	_____

14. What physical exertion is required to perform this job?

Exertion (list specific examples)	*How often (hourly, daily, weekly, monthly)?*
_____	_____
_____	_____
_____	_____

15. Describe any unusual time demands on a person in this job, such as travel or being on call. Include the percentage of time each demand requires.

   _____

   _____

   _____

16. Are there any hazardous conditions involved in this job that could result in serious injury?
   __ No __ Yes
   If yes, explain: _____

   _____

   _____

   _____

Figure 4. (*continued*)

17. Describe any other special conditions involved in this job.

_____

_____

_____

18. What equipment must you be able to operate? How often?

_____

_____

_____

19. If you supervise others
    a. List the titles of the jobs supervised:

    _____

    _____

    _____

    _____

    b. Check the activities you do:
       _____ Hire/terminate
       _____ Promote/demote
       _____ Transfer
       _____ Train
       _____ Write a performance appraisal
       _____ Determine or recommend salary increases
       _____ Discipline
       _____ Assign work
       _____ Check work for accuracy and completeness
       _____ Other: _____
    c. How many employees do you supervise?
       Employees reporting directly to you _____
       Employees reporting to people who report to you _____
    d. Percentage of your time spent supervising: _____ %
    e. I do not supervise anyone but I:
       Provide some work direction to other employees _____
       Regularly make recommendations to people's supervisors regarding their job performance _____

20. Where do you get the information you use in your job?

_____

_____

Figure 4. (*continued*)

21. Give examples of the independent decisions you make in your job:

    _____

    _____

    a. What guidance (policy, procedure, supervision) is available to help you with these decisions?

       _____

       _____

    b. Which describes your responsibility?
       _____ Must follow established steps and procedures
       _____ May make some alterations when following established steps and procedures
       _____ Select specific steps from established options
       _____ Develop options by which work can be accomplished
       _____ Set priorities and standards of performance

22. Under what circumstances is your work checked and reviewed by your supervisor?

    _____

    _____

    _____

    _____

23. Is there any other information you want to add in order to help someone understand your job better?

    _____

    _____

24. Attach any documents or examples that may be helpful to explain any of your remarks.

Supervisor's Review and Comments:

_____

_____

_____

_____

_____

_____

_____   _____
Supervisor's signature   Date

Where job responsibilities are fairly well understood except to determine which responsibilities are assigned to which jobs, a standard inclusive list of job results and duties might be provided so that people can simply check off the responsibilities included in their jobs and therefore make the task easier.

You might also consider developing a database so that information can be analyzed or reassembled for different purposes, such as job descriptions, job evaluation, interviewing and hiring, training, career paths, and succession planning.

Interview   Jobs described in writing are not always perfectly clear to the reader; talking to the writer may be necessary to obtain an accurate understanding.

Interviewing a job incumbent without the benefit of a completed questionnaire takes a lot of time: getting together with the person, building rapport, rate of speech versus rate of reading, extraneous discussion, influences of demeanor. Still, personal credibility is essential to a human system, especially one about pay.

Make the most of the interview time. Prepare by gathering whatever information you can and by structuring the questions you want to ask. Follow the questionnaire format. Complete the questionnaire during the interview if it helps guide the dialogue.

Make an appointment and arrange for uninterrupted time, wherever convenient. Many interviewers prefer the incumbent's office or work area, because it is more relaxing for the interviewee and information and examples are at hand.

Develop a conversation, not an inquisition. Let the job incumbent talk approximately 80 percent of the time. Record information for future reference: take notes, draw diagrams, tape-record discussions, videotape actions, and collect written examples.

Do not overlook the possibility of telephone or teleconference interviews when job incumbents travel a lot or are in distant locations.

Observation   Although the job incumbent may work hard to clarify the information exchanged in writing and in person, some things have to be seen to be understood—or touched, heard, or otherwise sensed:

"We climb a tall ladder." (How tall is tall? How dangerous are the conditions?)
"I gather and assemble information." (Where is the information? What's involved?)
"We meet with irate customers all day long." (Irate? What are they complaining about?)
"It's noisy and hot." (How noisy? How hot?)

Being observed can be threatening to some people, but as a rule, people enjoy talking about their work and "showing off." Visiting the job can be a real employee relations boost.

Log   When events need to be recorded over a period of time, job incumbents can be asked to keep a log: number of telephone calls, nature of personal interaction, number of requests for information and reasons for inquiries, pounds lifted and how often, use of equipment, and so forth.

Logs must be designed to minimize inconvenience to the recorder. Provide for checkoff rather than essay responses wherever possible.

Model Approach   In most situations, you will find it appropriate to begin data gathering with an explanation of the process to the respondents, either in writing or in person. Let people know why they are participating. Here are nine steps of a model approach:

1. Give the questionnaire and log to respondents.
2. Study the information returned; identify unclear statements.
3. Gather job content information from other sources.
4. Interview the job incumbent.
5. Observe the job.
6. Clarify perceptions.
7. Prepare a draft job description, qualifications, and job evaluation documentation.
8. Review the draft with job incumbent.
9. Have job description, qualifications, and job evaluation documentation approved by management.

Job Analysis and Job Evaluation

It would be a waste of time to conduct one job analysis to write a job description and another to describe qualifications and gather information for job evaluation. A format can be developed that allows you to accumulate most, if not all, of the required job evaluation information as a part of job analysis.

The job statements gathered for job evaluation purposes have moved from pencil scratchings in the margins of analysis forms of the past to a formal part of the record (see Phase 5). In fact, more of the information gathered during job analysis is used to evaluate jobs than to describe them. Thus, the job evaluation plan is a major guide when designing the data-gathering format for the job analysis.

Project Analyzer 4.2

Who has the job content information needed to understand the jobs?

_____

_____

What outside resources are available?

_____

_____

Is the organizational philosophy to involve all employees in the process, or will management develop job content?

_____

_____

How many people are in the organization?

_____

_____

What is the most efficient method to obtain information from them?

_____

_____

Is a questionnaire appropriate?

_____

_____

_____

Are personal interviews appropriate?

_____

_____

_____

Are logs appropriate?

_____

_____

Is observation appropriate?

_____

_____

Should information be sampled?

_____

_____

Can the same job collection method be used for all jobs?

_____

_____

_____

What adjustments in job collection formats and questions will be required for which jobs or job families?

_____

_____

How will approval be built into the information-gathering method?

_____

_____

_____

Who will approve job content?

_____

_____

_____

4.3 How to Write a Results-Oriented Job Description

It is management's right and responsibility to define jobs, as well as to change them as organizational requirements demand. This right can be exercised at any time (unless it is given away).

A job description is an agreement, much like a contract, between the organization and the employee—except that management always has the right to change the "contract" at its discretion. Treating jobs like contracts makes good interpersonal communications sense, because it creates an understanding between two parties. Some states will hold you to a job description contract; others will not. Problems can arise when management changes the terms of the agreement for inappropriate reasons (e.g., to force someone out of the job, or to prevent someone from getting into the job).

A job description should tell employees what to do. Right?

Wrong! Job descriptions _should_ do that, but the most important aspect is missing in this definition.

What is it that managers get so frustrated about with employees? They get tired of explaining and reexplaining _why_ certain aspects of a job should be performed.

Jobs are traditionally described in terms of the duties, tasks, or activities to be performed by the incumbent. Expressed in such a laundry list fashion, job descriptions are not much fun; actually, they're rather boring and demotivating, if not unmanageable.

Why unmanageable? Because an employee doing duties does not always produce the results management desires.

At hire:	"Your job is keying information."
Later:	"Did you finish the letters?"
	"No."
	"What were you doing?"
	"Keying information."

Yes, you must tell employees what to do—key information—but more important, you must tell them _why_ they do what they do. You have to focus them on results: getting the letters completed.

Obviously employees *can* make the connection, but *will* they? Not after years of "Do what you're told" conditioning. Management has stifled the natural inclination of people to do what is necessary for the good of the enterprise. Traditional job descriptions say, Do these little things. They do not paint the big picture.

When employees are told only what to do, they are unable to integrate that duty with other duties. More important, they are unable to see other possibilities of performing the work in order to accomplish the desired result.

In this era of telecommuting, where managers can no longer always look over the shoulders of employees as they perform their jobs, managing results is the only workable focus. Results planned and appraised are the focal point of the relationship.

Results-Oriented Job Descriptions Educate

Job descriptions have been used for their *contractual purposes:* if you do these things, I will pay you. Job descriptions have not been viewed as a method of education, an opportunity to help employees understand why and how the organization works. Instead of explaining and reexplaining, let's tell employees up front, from day one, why their work is important to the organization and what it is designed to accomplish.

Let us give employees a sense of purpose and participation in the organization; let us tell employees their place in the mission of the organization. We have relied on managers to fill in the gap between the "job duties" we have required of employees and the integration of these activities into an organization. Perhaps we have assumed that employees might not comprehend the total organization—that only management is capable of balancing inputs to achieve the desired outcomes.

Surprise! Managers do not always understand the outcomes either. We have bemoaned the managerial inadequacy of the many technicians who have been promoted to the rank of manager, technicians who do a poor job of integrating the requirements and purposes of managerial action, particularly requirements involving human resources considerations. And we ask these same managers to explain to employees why management does what it does to fulfill the purposes of the organization.

Results-Oriented Job Descriptions Clarify

The development of a results-oriented job description gives a manager an opportunity to clarify why job duties are performed, why they are important. Writing job results forces a manager to think through the essence of the job and then defend that understanding to higher-level or peer managers. Think about the clarity and consistency of management thinking that we can derive from such conversations. Think about the increased clarity of manager-employee relationships when jobs are understood and agreed upon for their intent rather than only for their practice.

Writing job descriptions in terms of results is not just a method of expression; the educational principle is one of defining the purpose first so that the instructions—in this case, job duties—make sense as they are joined into a unified whole. Without this focal point of concentration, an employee must continually search for meaning in the relationship of job duties. "Why am I important?" may sound philosophical, but in practical terms, the answer is a way of guiding employees' efforts to accomplish the organization's goals.

Job descriptions were born in an era when employee involvement was not as prominent an issue as it is today. Employees were simply told what to do; if they did not do what they were told, they could go somewhere else. The old factory term "hired hands" tells much about the mentality of the era. Of course, even then, employees asked themselves about the value of their work, but today we encourage them to do so.

The Results-Oriented Style

Figures 5 through 9 contain job descriptions written in a results-oriented style. Over 450 other models are available in two books to use as they are or to edit to match your own requirements: *Results-Oriented Job Descriptions*, and *More Results-Oriented Job Descriptions* (both from AMACOM), by Roger Plachy and Sandra Plachy.

Notice several things as you read the job descriptions in Figures 5 through 9:

■ The three-line structure focusing on the result expected (highlighted by boldface capital letters) followed by the duty or task to be performed:

Result	**HELPS CUSTOMERS WITH INFORMATION**
	by
[Duty or task]	answering the telephone.

■ The broader contribution of the result beyond the narrower duty.

■ The explanation in the result of *why* the duty is important.

■ The foundation of accountability in the result that will be so important in linking pay to results accomplished or not accomplished (Phase 8).

Where to Begin Writing

The information gathered when jobs are analyzed (see Phase 4.2) determines the content of the job description. The writing process involves ordering the information gathered into job results clusters.

Begin by crystallizing your thoughts to identify the major result areas. There is no rule regarding how many results should be included in a job description; that depends on the job. In our experience, we have found eleven, twelve, or thirteen results to be the mode. Some high-level jobs might have fewer results than lower-level jobs.

Once the results have been identified, arrange them in a logical sequence that helps the reader consider the job, such as steps in the job process, order of importance, or frequency of accomplishment.

We typically approach jobs in a steps-in-the-process manner because it organizes the data-gathering process and the finished product.

(*Text continues on page 103.*)

Figure 5. Results-oriented job description: Assembler.

JOB TITLE:	**ASSEMBLER**

JOB PURPOSE:	**PRODUCES COMPONENTS** by assembling parts and subassemblies.

ESSENTIAL JOB RESULTS:

% of
time

_____ **1. PREPARES WORK TO BE ACCOMPLISHED**
by
studying assembly instructions, blueprint specifications, and parts lists;
gathering parts, subassemblies, tools, and materials.

_____ **2. POSITIONS PARTS AND SUBASSEMBLIES**
by
using templates or reading measurements.

_____ **3. ASSEMBLES COMPONENTS**
by
examining connections for correct fit; fastening parts and subassemblies.

_____ **4. VERIFIES SPECIFICATIONS**
by
measuring completed component.

_____ **5. RESOLVES ASSEMBLY PROBLEMS**
by
altering dimensions to meet specifications; notifying supervisor to obtain
additional resources.

_____ **6. KEEPS EQUIPMENT OPERATIONAL**
by
completing preventive maintenance requirements; following
manufacturer's instructions; troubleshooting malfunctions; calling for
repairs.

_____ **7. MAINTAINS SAFE AND CLEAN WORKING ENVIRONMENT**
by
complying with procedures, rules, and regulations.

_____ **8. MAINTAINS SUPPLIES INVENTORY**
by
checking stock to determine inventory level; anticipating needed supplies;
placing and expediting orders for supplies; verifying receipt of supplies.

Figure 5. (*continued*)

_____   **9. CONSERVES RESOURCES**
by
using equipment and supplies as needed to accomplish job results.

_____   **10. DOCUMENTS ACTIONS**
by
completing production and quality forms.

_____   **11. CONTRIBUTES TO TEAM EFFORT**
by
accomplishing related results as needed.

Figure 6. Results-oriented job description: Compensation manager.

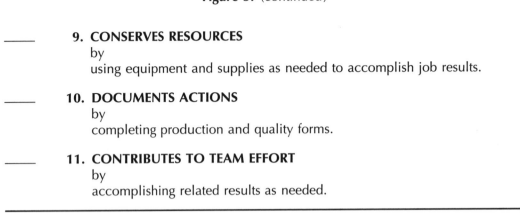

JOB TITLE:	**COMPENSATION MANAGER**

JOB PURPOSE:	**ATTRACTS AND RETAINS EMPLOYEES** by maintaining a pay program.

ESSENTIAL JOB RESULTS:

% of
time

_____   **1. VALIDATES JOB REQUIREMENTS**
by
developing and maintaining a job analysis system; analyzing jobs.

_____   **2. DEFINES JOBS**
by
developing a job description format; writing job descriptions, job
qualifications, and job evaluation documentation.

_____   **3. ESTABLISHES INTERNAL EQUITY**
by
developing and maintaining a job evaluation system; evaluating and
ranking jobs.

_____   **4. ESTABLISHES EXTERNAL EQUITY**
by
defining the labor market; identifying benchmark jobs; selecting
competitor organizations; conducting pay surveys; analyzing pay and
related data.

Figure 6. (*continued*)

_____ 5. **MAINTAINS PAY STRUCTURE**
by
recommending, planning, and implementing structural adjustments;
preparing pay budgets.

_____ 6. **MAINTAINS TOTAL COMPENSATION**
by
studying proportion of pay, benefits, incentives, and intangibles;
recommending program adjustments.

_____ 7. **MAINTAINS PAY DECISION-MAKING GUIDELINES**
by
writing and updating pay policies and procedures.

_____ 8. **COMPLETES COMPENSATION REPORTS AND RECOMMENDATIONS**
by
gathering and analyzing pay data.

_____ 9. **COMPLIES WITH FEDERAL, STATE, AND LOCAL LEGAL
REQUIREMENTS**
by
studying existing and new employment legislation; enforcing adherence to
requirements; advising management on needed actions.

_____ 10. **ENFORCES MERIT RAISE AND INCENTIVE GUIDELINES**
by
comparing recommended pay raises and incentives with budget; notifying
supervisors of variances.

_____ 11. **COMPLETES OPERATIONAL REQUIREMENTS**
by
scheduling and assigning employee; following up on work results.

_____ 12. **MAINTAINS COMPENSATION STAFF**
by
recruiting, selecting, orienting, and training employees.

_____ 13. **MAINTAINS COMPENSATION STAFF JOB RESULTS**
by
counseling and disciplining employees; planning, monitoring, and
appraising job results.

_____ 14. **MAINTAINS PROFESSIONAL AND TECHNICAL KNOWLEDGE**
by
attending educational workshops; reviewing professional publications;
establishing personal networks; participating in professional societies.

_____ 15. **CONTRIBUTES TO TEAM EFFORT**
by
accomplishing related results as needed.

Figure 7. Results-oriented job description: Financial analyst.

JOB TITLE:	**FINANCIAL ANALYST**

JOB PURPOSE:	**ANALYZES FINANCIAL STATUS**
	by
	collecting, monitoring, and studying data; recommending actions.

ESSENTIAL JOB RESULTS:

% of
time

_____ 1. **DETERMINES COST OF OPERATIONS**
by
establishing standard costs; collecting operational data.

_____ 2. **IDENTIFIES FINANCIAL STATUS**
by
comparing and analyzing actual results with plans and forecasts.

_____ 3. **GUIDES COST ANALYSIS PROCESS**
by
establishing and enforcing policies and procedures; providing trends and
forecasts; explaining processes and techniques; recommending actions.

_____ 4. **IMPROVES FINANCIAL STATUS**
by
analyzing results; monitoring variances; identifying trends; recommending
actions to management.

_____ 5. **RECONCILES TRANSACTIONS**
by
comparing and correcting data.

_____ 6. **MAINTAINS DATABASE**
by
entering, verifying, and backing up data.

_____ 7. **RECOMMENDS ACTIONS**
by
analyzing and interpreting data and making comparative analyses;
studying proposed changes in methods and materials.

_____ 8. **INCREASES PRODUCTIVITY**
by
developing automated accounting applications; coordinating information
requirements.

_____ 9. **PROTECTS OPERATIONS**
by
keeping financial information confidential.

_____ 10. **MAINTAINS TECHNICAL KNOWLEDGE**
by
attending educational workshops; reviewing publications.

_____ 11. **CONTRIBUTES TO TEAM EFFORT**
by
accomplishing related results as needed.

Figure 8. Results-oriented job description: Quality assurance analyst—
Information systems.

JOB TITLE: **QUALITY ASSURANCE ANALYST—INFORMATION SYSTEMS**

JOB PURPOSE: **MAINTAINS COMPUTER PRODUCTION QUALITY**
by
analyzing procedures and output; recommending improvements.

ESSENTIAL JOB RESULTS:

% of
time

_____   **1. IMPLEMENTS NEW APPLICATIONS**
by
coordinating quality activities; analyzing impact on current processing
schedules and service levels.

_____   **2. MAINTAINS COST-EFFECTIVE PRODUCTION**
by
reviewing corporate output, mainframe print and fiche, distributed print,
and tape creation.

_____   **3. OPTIMIZES PRODUCTIVITY AND PERFORMANCE**
by
investigating exploitation of infrastructure tools.

_____   **4. ENFORCES QUALITY STANDARDS**
by
recommending resolution of outages; developing new procedures and
standards; implementing automated software version control; implementing
automated distribution software procedures to remote servers and
workstations.

_____   **5. PROTECTS ASSETS**
by
analyzing vaulting procedures; reviewing disaster recovery procedures;
ensuring compliance with Internal Revenue Service regulations.

_____   **6. COMPLETES PROJECTS**
by
planning, organizing, and monitoring assignments.

_____   **7. PREPARES REPORTS**
by
collecting, analyzing, and summarizing information.

_____   **8. MAINTAINS PROFESSIONAL AND TECHNICAL KNOWLEDGE**
by
attending educational workshops; reviewing professional publications;
establishing personal networks; benchmarking state-of-the-art practices;
participating in professional societies.

_____   **9. CONTRIBUTES TO TEAM EFFORT**
by
accomplishing related results as needed.

Figure 9. Results-oriented job description: Vice president—Sales.

JOB TITLE:	**VICE PRESIDENT—SALES**

JOB PURPOSE: **INCREASES REVENUE**
by
directing staff; developing and exploiting markets.

ESSENTIAL JOB RESULTS:

% of
time

_____ **1. MAINTAINS SALES STAFF**
by
recruiting, selecting, orienting, and training employees;
maintaining a safe and secure work environment; developing
personal growth opportunities.

_____ **2. ACCOMPLISHES STAFF RESULTS**
by
communicating job expectations; planning, monitoring, and
appraising job results; coaching, counseling, and disciplining
employees; initiating, coordinating, and enforcing systems,
policies, and procedures.

_____ **3. DEFINES MARKET POTENTIAL**
by
analyzing market surveys and sales statistics; estimating volume
and profit potential; preparing forecasts.

_____ **4. IMPROVES MARKET POSITION**
by
improving current products; researching, testing, and introducing
new products.

_____ **5. DEVELOPS DOMESTIC AND INTERNATIONAL SALES VOLUME**
by
establishing sales policy, objectives, pricing, and discounts;
establishing territories; assigning quotas; maintaining broker
network; negotiating key contracts.

_____ **6. ACHIEVES MARKET SHARE**
by
developing and establishing promotional strategies; implementing
advertising campaigns.

_____ **7. MAINTAINS RAPPORT WITH KEY CUSTOMERS**
by
making periodic visits; exploring specific needs; resolving
problems.

Figure 9. (*continued*)

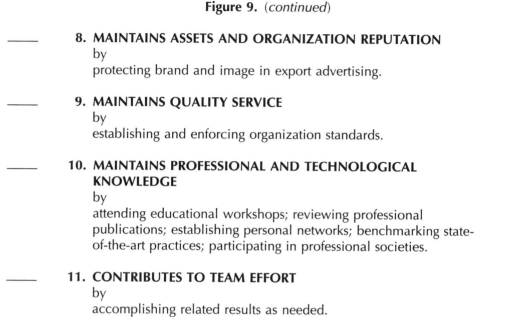

_____ **8. MAINTAINS ASSETS AND ORGANIZATION REPUTATION**
by
protecting brand and image in export advertising.

_____ **9. MAINTAINS QUALITY SERVICE**
by
establishing and enforcing organization standards.

_____ **10. MAINTAINS PROFESSIONAL AND TECHNOLOGICAL KNOWLEDGE**
by
attending educational workshops; reviewing professional publications; establishing personal networks; benchmarking state-of-the-art practices; participating in professional societies.

_____ **11. CONTRIBUTES TO TEAM EFFORT**
by
accomplishing related results as needed.

Basic Structure of the Results-Oriented Job Description

A job results statement has three elements:

1. An action verb
2. What the action produces
3. How the action is produced

Here is a job results statement written correctly:

DETERMINES DRAPERY REPAIR AND REPLACEMENT
[*Action verb, and what the action produces*]
by
completing periodic inspections.
[*How the action is produced*]

Written in a duties-oriented style, the statement would read: *Makes periodic inspections of draperies*. Why the draperies are to be inspected is not clear.

Here are some typical duties that are given meaning when they are expressed in relation to the results desired:

Duty	*Result*
Conducts laboratory tests	Provides diagnostic data to physicians
Polices buildings and grounds	Keeps residents safe
Recruits and screens applicants	Hires qualified employees
Maintains electrical equipment and systems	Supplies power for building and equipment

Try this writing format: identify result to be accomplished by describing how it is to be done. Using this format, the complete statements would be:

PROVIDES DIAGNOSTIC DATA TO PHYSICIANS
by
conducting laboratory tests.

KEEPS RESIDENTS SAFE
by
policing buildings and grounds.

HIRES QUALIFIED EMPLOYEES
by
recruiting and screening applicants.

SUPPLIES POWER FOR BUILDING AND EQUIPMENT
by
maintaining electrical equipment and systems.

Duty vs. Result—A Simple Test

No one learns to write job descriptions by reading about it; you have to practice to get the sense of the flow of words and the relationship of duties to results.

One tip: when you are struggling to say just what you mean, you may wonder whether you are writing a duty or a result. Try placing the expression before the "by" and then after it to gain a sense of proportion and understanding. For example:

COMPLETES INSPECTIONS OF DRAPERIES

by

_____

or

_____

by

completing inspections of draperies.

A result answers the question, Why are we doing this? "Completes inspections of draperies" is not the *why* of anything. If we tried to complete this statement, we would be describing job procedures or protocols—(1) set up a ladder, (2) climb the ladder, (3) remove the drapery from the rods, and so on. That's much too pedantic for a job description.

Such job procedures and protocols are essential instructions and form the basis of job training programs, but they normally are not included in the job description. When might they be? When the job is simple and contains only several results and where the procedures clarify meaning. If you need to list procedures, create a separate section under the results and duties, labeling them "Job Procedures," so that the job results statement is as crisp as it can be.

When you flip the statement around and try "... by completing inspections," you can fit in the missing piece of the puzzle and achieve an understanding of the situation that you did not have before. The result that best states the contribution of the job is:

DETERMINES DRAPERY REPAIR AND REPLACEMENT
by
completing inspections.

One other tip: do not try to write the perfect job description on the first shot. Good writing has much more trial and error than most people understand. Go ahead and get something down on paper, and then try out different possibilities. Work intensely for a while, and then put the writing away. Come back later, when you have regained your objectivity, and do your editing then.

Here is a job description for a senior buyer written in a traditional style:

JOB TITLE: Senior Buyer

REPORTS TO: Materials Manager

JOB PURPOSE: Secure and maintain optimum level of parts and materials for the efficient production of the company's product in accordance with established policies and procedures.

WORK PERFORMED: Remain cognizant of the company's needs for materials and parts to promote efficient production. This is done through monitoring data reflecting inventory needs, stores, warehousing, and change orders. Search out, investigate, select, and negotiate new and tried vendors supplying the company's needs, and maintain the company's competitive position insofar as materials cost is concerned.

Coordinate with engineering and production concerning the changing needs of the company and its products with regard to new products, product innovations, and quality control.

Negotiate in the company's best interest for price and delivery of needed materials and parts consistent with the quality and service required.

Prepare reports and maintain data on the company's transactions.

Coordinate pricing and cost determinations with interested company representatives, (e.g., cost accountants, inventory analysts, etc.).

Lead and direct others in the procurement of goods and services.

Here is the improved, results-oriented job description of the senior buyer:

JOB TITLE: **SENIOR BUYER**

Reports to: Materials Manager

JOB PURPOSE: **SUPPORTS THE PRODUCTION OF PRODUCTS**
                    by
                    purchasing; maintaining an inventory of parts and materials.

ESSENTIAL JOB RESULTS:

% of
time

_____   1. **EVALUATES COMPANY'S NEEDS FOR MATERIALS AND PARTS**
           by
           monitoring production reports and inventory.

_____   2. **KEEPS ABREAST OF NEW PRODUCTS, PRODUCT CHANGES, AND
           QUALITY RESULTS**
           by
           monitoring engineering and production information.

_____   3. **MAINTAINS COMPANY'S COMPETITIVE PRICE POSITION**
           by
           investigating, selecting, and negotiating with vendors.

_____   4. **OBTAINS VENDORS' QUALITY AND SERVICE**
           by
           negotiating service and delivery of parts and materials.

_____   5. **PROVIDES INFORMATION**
           by
           maintaining data on purchasing transactions; preparing reports.

_____   6. **CONTRIBUTES TO PRICING DECISIONS**
           by
           accumulating and providing cost information.

_____   7. **ACCOMPLISHES DEPARTMENT WORK**
           by
           directing others.

Verbs, Verbs, Verbs

Selecting the verb that most accurately describes the action is one of the major concerns when writing a job description. As you might expect, job description writing has somewhat of a jargon of its own. Just how important verbs are will become clearer during the discussion of job evaluation in Phase 5. Figure 10 lists verbs describing job actions, arranged under major categories.

After writing a first draft of a job description (use Figure 12), edit it to make it clear and concise. For example, modifiers such as "good," "effective," "efficiently," "accurately," "properly," which are intended to remind the employee how well something must be done, are unnecessary, since they are commonly implied or will be stated better in outcome criteria. Also, words like "ensure," "make sure," "assure," "provide," or "process" can often be deleted or made more concrete, as in the following examples:

Figure 10. Some verbs describing job actions.

Controls	compiles	clears	codes	*Teaches*
adopts	computes	collates	copies	
anticipates	extends	disassembles	enters	guides
approves	figures	enters	files	instructs
closes	inventories	feeds	indexes	interprets
collects	invoices	handles	itemizes	trains
consolidates	reconciles	opens	lays out	
contracts	totals	processes	lists	*Verifies*
deletes		stacks	places	
disburses	*Directs*	types	posts	affirms
ensures			receives	amends
expedites	administers	*Originates*	registers	checks
finds	assigns		tabulates	compares
follows up	authorizes	arranges	transfers	corrects
locates	delegates	conducts		edits
maintains	determines	creates	*Studies*	proofreads
obtains	manages	defines		revises
orders	oversees	designs	analyzes	
pays	represents	develops	appraises	*Writes*
releases	schedules	establishes	ascertains	
remits	supervises	executes	audits	composes
requires		formulates	estimates	describes
routes		implements	evaluates	drafts
secures	*Distributes*	initiates	examines	outlines
selects		institutes	inspects	summarizes
signs	circulates	organizes	investigates	
traces	disseminates	plans	observes	
	furnishes	prepares	rates	
Counts	issues		reviews	
	renders	*Records*	scans	
adds			screens	
balances	*Operates*	attaches	searches	
bills		catalogs	surveys	
calculates	aligns	charts	tests	
	assembles	classifies		
	carries			

Change This . . .	*. . . to This*
Processes all payrolls and taxes	Pays wages and taxes
Makes sure that shipments are complete	Completes shipments
Ensures payment	Obtains payment
Keeps customer informed	Informs customer
Keeps customer accounts up-to-date	Maintains customer accounts
Generally maintains good relationships with . . .	Maintains relationships with . . .
Prepares all relevant documents and monitors the entire process from beginning to end	Prepares documents and monitors the process
Ensures that automobile fleet is in good condition	Maintains automobile fleet
Ensures that fleet cars are properly registered	Registers fleet cars
Ensures quality and timeliness of administrative services	Provides timely administrative services
Ensures accuracy of data	Verifies data
Makes sure that each manifest is balanced and that product codes agree with customer's order	Balances manifests and correlates product codes with customer order
Provides clerical duties relating to purchase orders, inventory of materials, and vehicle registrations and renewals	Completes, prepares, and files purchase orders, materials inventory, and vehicle registrations/renewals
Provides support to inside and outside salespeople and branches	Manages inventory and provides sales information

The Flow of Job Results to Subordinate Jobs

The jobs in an organization do not stand alone; their results are interconnected. In particular, the results of every job flow down to its subordinate jobs. (See Figure 11.) For example, a higher-level job may be concerned with setting goals. At the next lower level, these goals are translated into objectives. At the level below that, specific methods and procedures for meeting the objectives are developed and enforced. And at a still lower level, employees carry out physical work that follows the methods and procedures.

By being aware of these interconnections, you can anticipate job results expectations in other jobs.

Job Purpose Statement

Every job description should begin with a job purpose. The job purpose follows the same writing structure as a job result. It is a synthesis of the intent of the job in its

Figure 11. Flow of job results from one job to the next.

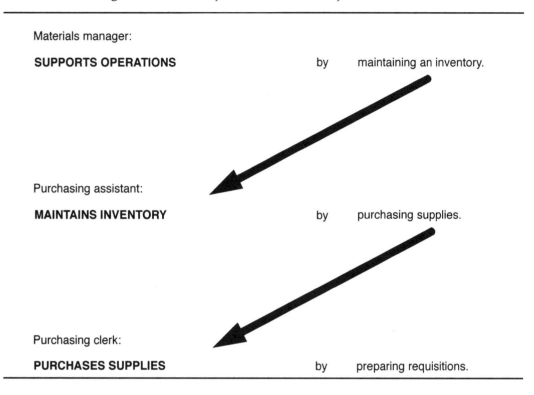

Materials manager:

SUPPORTS OPERATIONS   by   maintaining an inventory.

Purchasing assistant:

MAINTAINS INVENTORY   by   purchasing supplies.

Purchasing clerk:

PURCHASES SUPPLIES   by   preparing requisitions.

entirety. This section might also be named the job mission or job objective since it captures its reason for inclusion in the document. The job purpose, then, is the ultimate overall result expected from the job. Figure 12 is a worksheet you can use to write the job purpose as well as the essential job results.

As an example, here is the job purpose of an inbound marketing operations manager:

JOB PURPOSE: MARKETS PRODUCTS
by
managing staff; maintaining response operations; maintaining quality ratings.

And here is one for a mainframe technical specialist:

JOB PURPOSE: MAINTAINS MAINFRAME OPERATING ENVIRONMENT
by
monitoring and upgrading operations.

Figure 12. Job description worksheet.

RESULT	=	What is accomplished by performing the duty?
		Why is the duty important?
by		
duty	=	What is the activity being performed?

JOB PURPOSE:

RESULT
_____

(Start with an active verb, such as "completes" or "maintains")

by

duty
_____

(Start with an "ing" verb, such as "recording" or "evaluating")   .

_____

_____

ESSENTIAL JOB RESULTS:

RESULT
_____

(Start with an active verb, such as "completes" or "maintains")

by

duty
_____

(Start with an "ing" verb, such as "recording" or "evaluating")

_____

_____

RESULT
_____

(Start with an active verb, such as "completes" or "maintains")

by

duty
_____

(Start with an "ing" verb, such as "recording" or "evaluating")

_____

_____

Figure 12. (*continued*)

RESULT _____

(Start with an active verb, such as "completes" or "maintains")

by

duty _____

(Start with an "ing" verb, such as "recording" or "evaluating")

_____

_____

RESULT _____

(Start with an active verb, such as "completes" or "maintains")

by

duty _____

(Start with an "ing" verb, such as "recording" or "evaluating")

_____

_____

Job Description Format

There is no standard job description format; the formats vary as much as organizations. Use a format that helps your managers and employees identify and retrieve information.

A job description has these basic elements:

- Job title
- Reports to
- Jobs supervised
- Essential job results
- Percentage of time involved in each job result
- Approval authority and date

Job descriptions may include more information that helps to communicate—for example:

- Pay grade
- Pay range
- Exempt/nonexempt status
- Priority (importance) of job results
- Career progression
- Relationship with other jobs

- Budget authority
- Job description author
- Qualifications
- Special demands
- Equipment operated

Uses of Job Descriptions

A description of the actualizing elements of the organization—jobs—is one of the most important documents management needs to accomplish the organization's mission. Unfortunately, job descriptions have been kept in the closet collecting dust. They are frequently viewed as an exercise required by human resources in order to hire somebody, a laborious effort to write out what everybody knows already and will ignore anyway.

Organizations have concocted elaborate appraisal forms to measure how well an employee contributes, but, incredible as it may seem, many forms do not include any reference to the job description.

They use impressive application and interview forms to evaluate job candidates without referring to the job description.

They redesign jobs, bargain with unions, plan human resources needs, post jobs, make all sorts of job-related decisions, including decisions about relative job value and pay—all without the benefit of a job description.

Job descriptions are used for the following reasons:

- Define or revise the organization structure
- Plan human resources requirements
- Advertise jobs and recruit job candidates
- Post jobs
- Interview and select job candidates
- Orient new employees
- Identify training requirements
- Train employees
- Evaluate relative job value
- Determine job pay
- Determine Fair Labor Standards Act exempt/nonexempt status
- Appraise employee performance
- Establish career progressions
- Analyze work flow and work methods
- Conduct pay surveys
- Prepare affirmative action plans
- Comply with equal pay laws
- Establish a base for incentive plans
- Bargain with unions

As you can see, job descriptions are a focal point in the process of managing organizations.

Generic and Specific Job Descriptions

A *generic* job description describes responsibilities in broad terms so that similar jobs can be guided by one description. This avoids having to write a description for each job. For example, where secretaries accomplish nearly identical results in the same or even different departments, the distinctions among jobs might be made more easily in departmental procedure manuals rather than in job descriptions. Similarly, computer programmers need not have different job descriptions just because they work on different types of programs.

Specific job descriptions are needed when the differences among jobs are sufficient to cause miscommunication if the differences are not delineated clearly in separate job descriptions.

Where jobs are different in complexity, and thus would receive different pay levels, either separate job descriptions are required or different qualifications must be documented. Secretaries with vastly different responsibilities should have separate job descriptions. Computer programmers who work with more complex languages may have the same job description but must have supporting differentiation stated under job qualifications. If you keep in mind that a job description must clearly and accurately convey the meaning of the job, you will have no trouble deciding whether to include more than one job under a single description.

Who Should Write and Approve Job Descriptions?

Tradition has it that the job analyst in the human resources department writes job descriptions. But writing implies ownership, so in a sense, the job analyst will "own" the job description. This is not a desirable scenario. A job description is a department management tool, not a human resources record.

The job description is primarily an instrument of communication between a manager and an employee. These are the people who should fashion the document. Certainly, they can obtain advice from the job analyst on technique and expression, but the exercise will be much more meaningful to them when they struggle with the words to say what they mean. They will mean what they say. Besides, for most organizations, writing jobs in a results-oriented manner will be more an exercise in creating results-oriented thinking than in simply writing a job description, and training will facilitate this shift in thinking (actually, the act of identifying and writing job results is a way to produce results-oriented thinking).

The job description writing and approval process usually works in this way:

1. Employees identify job information.
2. Managers approve job content—adding or subtracting results and duties as necessary—and write the first draft of the job description.
3. The job analyst critiques the description style and format.
4. The employee and the manager finalize the first draft together.
5. The manager's manager approves the description for content and integration of job results with the goals, objectives, and policies of the organization.
6. The human resources manager reviews the description for organizational consistency and legal compliance.

Obviously, each organization processes job descriptions according to its own style, resources, and time demands. The message is, however, that human resources departments have typically taken the burden on themselves and have suffered the consequences as department managers have disowned or failed to maintain the product because they have no investment in it.

Sometimes consultants are hired to write job descriptions. You can see that ownership is now even further away from the organization, plus the cost is high. The description will be expertly written, but it may not match the interactive style of the manager and the employee. It's better to have a job description that does not receive an A in style but conveys a clear message to the parties involved.

There is nothing wrong with moving the process along by having writers with more experience contribute their ability. But do not forsake a thoughtful, meaningful product for efficiency.

Where job descriptions are produced by people other than the manager and the employee, it would be prudent to have the employee review the document to create understanding and have the manager approve it to create ownership.

Project Analyzer 4.3

What is management's perception of the value of job descriptions?

_____

_____

What are employees' perceptions?

_____

_____

Do job descriptions exist for all jobs?

_____

_____

Are job descriptions kept current?

_____

_____

In what ways are job descriptions used?

_____

_____

Are job descriptions specific enough to communicate job content accurately?

_____

_____

Are job descriptions too specific, so that jobs are too narrowly defined?

_____

_____

What changes should be made in the way job descriptions are used?

_____

_____

Are job descriptions duties-oriented or results-oriented?

_____

_____

How well are job results understood?

_____

_____

What would it take to get managers to think in terms of job results?

_____

_____

How should the job description format be customized to communicate job information most clearly?

_____

_____

Who writes job descriptions now?

_____

_____

Is this the best way to have them prepared?

_____

_____

Who should be involved in writing them?

_____

_____

What training would be required for managers to be able to write job descriptions in a results-oriented style?

_____

_____

Who will conduct the training?

_____

_____

Who approves job descriptions?

_____

_____

Are the appropriate people included in the approval process?

_____

_____

Who needs to be included in the approval process?

_____

_____

4.4 Establishing Job Qualifications

Job qualifications are the standards that organizations use to determine an employee's capability to accomplish job results. Because some job results are more difficult to accomplish than others, the level of job qualifications required directly affects a pay program.

Any qualification (knowledge, skill, or ability—some people prefer the all-inclusive term, "competency") can be required of an employee if you can demonstrate that the qualification is necessary in order to accomplish a job result. Job qualifications cannot be whatever a particular manager prefers employees to have or even what a manager believes employees must have, if job relatedness cannot be proved.

Suppose that a job requires an employee to complete chemical tests, compare the results to standard ranges, research deviations to understand the problem, and select other tests to analyze results further. The laboratory manager believes that the employee who performs this job needs two years of college chemistry.

We're all for encouraging education and helping people grow in knowledge so that when opportunities present themselves, they can take advantage of them. However, here's what can happen. You have an employee on a production line who begins to take an interest in how the quality of the product varies and is determined, so much so that he or she is promoted to a laboratory assistant. In time, with coaching and experience, this energetic employee learns to complete the chemical tests and analyze the results, just the way the job requires. Now you have an employee accomplishing the job results without the benefit of two years of college chemistry.

If a new candidate were rejected because he or she didn't have the two years of college chemistry, you'd be in trouble. In reality, the moment the production employee was accepted as a laboratory assistant after a probationary period, the qualification was effectively reduced.

Troublesome Qualifications

Never use imprecise distinctions, such as "basic" or "advanced" knowledge. For example, if a manager wants his or her secretary to have "advanced" skills, the question is, What skills qualify as "advanced"? Let's say that the manager means an ability to manage projects. The solution is to make sure that project management is included as a job result in the job description.

Similarly, do not use degree-of-difficulty modifiers such as "simple," "moderately complex," or "extremely complex" in the job description. These kinds of modifiers hardly make the distinction clear. Instead, use a concrete example of job differentiations.

Here is the way to translate generic labels into concrete language—in this case, regarding the kind of equipment problems an employee must solve:

Generic Label	*Concrete Language*
Simple	Verify setup and configuration operations
Moderately complex	Configure features and respond to error messages
Extremely complex	Isolate software faults and design modifications

Avoid identifying general behaviors through words like "self-control," "adaptability," and "spontaneity" when you describe job qualifications. There are two problems here. First, general characteristics are nearly impossible to measure competently. Second, the same job result may be accomplished within acceptable standards using widely varying behaviors. Thus, it would be nearly impossible to defend which behaviors are acceptable and which are not. Here are some other examples of job qualifications that are not stated clearly.

"*Concentration, accuracy, speed, cooperation, and confidentiality.*" Sounds just like the kind of employee you want—actually, the kind of employee that *anybody* would want in just about *any* job. These requirements are global and subject to far too many interpretations—especially the devious kind. Think, too, of the implied rejection of a candidate: your thinking is unfocused; you make mistakes; you are slow, disagreeable, and a security risk. Rather poor public relations.

"*Ability to get along and work well with others.*" By whose standards? What does "getting along" mean?

"*Organized, detail-oriented individual, with excellent interpersonal, communication, and planning skills.*" Organized to accomplish what? What kind of detail? What constitutes excellence? Interpersonal and communication skills aimed at what? Planning what?

"*Must have aptitude for mathematics and accounting.*" Aptitude as in probable success or proven talent? What specific aspects of mathematics and accounting?

"Mechanically inclined." A mental tendency or a demonstrated ability? What kind of machinery?

"Job requires heavy lifting." How heavy?

"Pleasant personality." Pleasant to whom? Why? In what kind of situation?

"Excellent command of the English language." Pulitzer prize stuff?

"Computer experience." Doing what with a computer?

"Self-confidence in handling new responsibilities." The person hasn't even qualified for the first job yet.

"Eagerness to attend seminars." "Willingness" would be more accurate.

"Familiarity with word processing software." Any particular software?

"Knowledge of a second language helpful." Second to which other language? Presumably Welsh, Russian, Arabic, Greek, or Aleut would qualify.

Here are some other job qualification areas that typically cause problems:

■ *Education.* Recently, to support national educational goals, some organizations have begun requiring all employees to have a high school education. Certainly more education for all of our citizens is an improvement for our society. However, this noble effort may not match employment goals or employment law. In a variety of jobs, employees can successfully accomplish job results without a high school diploma.

In addition, a diploma may tell you only that the candidate attended high school, not that he or she learned anything. How many stories have you heard of high school graduates who are unable to read or college graduates who have not developed their skills much beyond basic ones? Furthermore, different schools, offering the same degree, provide vastly different educations.

Some people without a formal education outperform those with a formal education. A degree, then, may be an artificial barrier, as the Supreme Court ruled in *Griggs v. Duke Power* (1954). Stating a degree requirement along with the phrase "or equivalent experience" affords you the protection of not establishing a false barrier yet communicates the difficulty of the job and helps candidates judge whether they think they can handle the responsibility.

Registrations, licenses, and certifications are easy to handle when required by state law, as in the case of a registered nurse, but potentially difficult when they are not. Recognition by a national association may be an excellent credential and may confirm different levels of capability, but the issue is whether a particular job actually requires the credential. Could someone with a lesser credential accomplish the job results? If so, back off and don't be concerned with supporting the goals of some special interest group.

■ *Experience.* Stating that a job requires "two years of experience" is generally standard jargon. Although such a criterion is fairly well understood, "fairly well" is not good enough to communicate or defend. What one person learns from two years' experience is not the same as what another person learns in two years. Experiences required need to be identified specifically.

■ *Physical demands.* Many physical requirements are obvious from the statements on the job description. Add any necessary information in a job qualifications section to clarify the requirement. For example, the job description may specify that an employee in the warehouse is required to load trucks; a statement about qualifications should read: "Able to lift 50-pound items one hour per day." Of course, be ready to make accommodations, especially for people with disabilities.

- *Dress and grooming.* Dress and grooming requirements are typically detailed in organization policy and rules. However, when they are included as qualifications, requirements become a natural part of the hiring process when, for example, the job requirement for serving customers is examined. Be realistic and reasonable. Do not try to impose personal preferences on employees without an objective reason.

- *Religion, age, and gender.* There are few situations where you can defend any requirement in these areas. Defensible situations might be representatives of the faith, counseling where similar age is essential to establish immediate rapport, and situations of privacy and intimacy.

- *Security.* Where you have legitimate concerns about the integrity and trustworthiness of employees, particularly where customers or clients place special trust in your organization, you can demand reputable backgrounds that would reduce concern regarding future conduct. Be aware of potentially conflicting laws regarding reference checking, privacy, libel, and slander.

- *Traits.* Be sure that qualifications are tangible. "Team player" may be a desirable trait, and we all seem to know what that means, but it isn't solid enough to reject someone. How do we make this qualification more certain?

Well, what exactly makes a person a team player? A few characteristics are: freely exchanges information with other members, helps other team members without being asked, warns team members about potential problems. These are the qualifications you should list.

Many managers simply do not understand the guidelines for establishing job qualifications. A few have the attitude that their department is their domain, and they can pretty much do whatever they want. Managers need to be trained to understand legal requirements (and punishments).

By the way, keep track of changing legal requirements and court cases that affect job qualifications.

To get some ideas and standard language for qualifications statements, use the Department of Labor's O*NET. At the same time, follow our cautions for exacting standards since some of the department's statements are still activity-based. The statements for math, language, and physical demands are very helpful.

Results Statements as Job Qualifications

For the most part, the job description results statements can be used effectively as a statement of job qualifications. Traditionally, job qualifications are shown in a separate section of the job description after the essential results:

```
┌─────────────────────────────────┐
│ Essential job results:          ├──┐
│                                 │  │
└──────┬──────────────────────────┘  │
       │ Job qualifications:         │
       │                             │
       └─────────────────────────────┘
```

But separate documentation is usually redundant and may lead to vagueness.

Use the job results statements as the documentation of job qualifications to provide a consistent reference for all decisions regarding the job (very helpful legally); to explain requirements more fully, clearly, and concretely; and certainly to save the time of double recording.

Some qualifications are not obvious from the job results statement and must be noted. For example, although the job result for a secretary requires the use of word processing software, a job description usually does not specify which software. Furthermore, some qualifications are absolutely essential before someone can begin in the job; this would also need to be noted. Figure 13 shows a job description, including a section on qualifications where reference is made to the applicant's capability to accomplish essential job results, but the section also states qualifications that are not perfectly clear or are not negotiable.

Figure 13. Job description with job qualifications section.

JOB RESULTS MANAGEMENT PROFILE

JOB TITLE:	DATA PROCESSING MANAGER

JOB PURPOSE:	PROVIDES INFORMATION SYSTEMS AND SERVICES by defining and solving user requirements; developing computer applications.

ESSENTIAL JOB RESULTS:

% of
time

_____   **1. MAINTAINS STAFF**
            by
            recruiting, selecting, orienting, and training employees; maintaining a safe and secure work environment; developing personal growth opportunities.

_____   **2. ACCOMPLISHES STAFF RESULTS**
            by
            communicating job expectations; planning, monitoring, and appraising job results; coaching, counseling, and disciplining employees; initiating, coordinating, and enforcing systems, policies, and procedures.

_____   **3. DEFINES MANAGEMENT AND EMPLOYEE INFORMATION REQUIREMENTS**
            by
            conferring with users; studying user functions.

Figure 13. (*continued*)

_____ 4. **SOLVES USER INFORMATION REQUIREMENTS**
by
developing information procedures; recommending computer system hardware and applications.

_____ 5. **PREPARES PROGRAMS**
by
writing, testing, modifying, and documenting programming language.

_____ 6. **PREPARES USERS TO USE MAINFRAME AND PERSONAL COMPUTER SYSTEMS**
by
conducting training sessions; providing individual coaching.

_____ 7. **PROVIDES SYSTEM RESOURCES**
by
documenting procedures; maintaining a library of user manuals; answering
questions.

_____ 8. **SECURES INFORMATION AND PROGRAMS**
by
establishing backup policies, procedures, and programs.

_____ 9. **IMPROVES PROGRAM AND SERVICE QUALITY**
by
devising new applications; updating procedures; evaluating system results
with users.

_____ 10. **PRODUCES ROUTINE AND SPECIAL REPORTS**
by
scheduling operations; assigning employees.

_____ 11. **ACHIEVES FINANCIAL OBJECTIVES**
by
anticipating requirements; submitting information for budget preparation;
scheduling expenditures; monitoring costs; analyzing variances.

_____ 12. **MAINTAINS PROFESSIONAL AND TECHNICAL KNOWLEDGE**
by
attending educational workshops; benchmarking professional standards;
reviewing professional publications; establishing personal networks.

_____ 13. **KEEPS MANAGEMENT INFORMED OF TECHNOLOGICAL TRENDS**
by
collecting, analyzing, and summarizing state-of-the-art information.

_____ 14. **MAINTAINS CONTINUITY AMONG CORPORATE, AREA, AND COMMUNITY WORK TEAMS**
by
documenting and communicating actions, irregularities, and continuing
needs.

Figure 13. (*continued*)

_____ **15. CONTRIBUTES TO TEAM EFFORT**
by
welcoming new and different work requirements; exploring new opportunities to add value to the organization; helping others accomplish related job results as and where needed.

Job Qualifications

Job qualifications are already stated as Essential Job Results in the Job Description. The Essential Job Results are what the employee must be able to accomplish in order to be competent in the job.

Some candidates will apply for the job with all, or nearly all, of the knowledge (education, skills, or equivalent job or life experiences) to accomplish the Essential Job Results. Other candidates will learn job requirements based on a learning plan after they enter the job.

All employees will need to demonstrate their ability to accomplish Essential Job Results by the end of their probationary period.

In some cases, basic learning cannot occur on the job. Job candidates must know certain principles, processes, or skills before entering the job.

Job knowledge absolutely required before entering the job:

B.S. in data processing, or equivalent experience in data processing systems, programming, and operations. AS/400 and PC operations experience. Managing people and projects.

Project Analyzer 4.4

Are job qualifications established for all jobs?

_____

_____

Are they job-specific?

_____

_____

Are they realistic and necessary to accomplish job results?

_____

_____

Do managers understand the dangers of introducing indefensible job qualifications?

_____

_____

Have you had any legal challenges to hiring qualifications?

_____

_____

_____

Strategic Planning for Phase 4

On your *first* quick walk through the project phases, record your initial thoughts on policy issues that will have to be decided.

_____

_____

Any notes on tactical procedures?

_____

_____

On your *second* time through the phases, consider the strategic influences from all the phases; decide on an integrated posture for the entire project.

Complete the section for this phase in the Master Planner (in Phase 2.8) during your *third* reading.

Phase 5

Evaluating Job Contributions

> Employees want to be paid fairly in relation to what other employees in their organization are being paid to accomplish comparable basic job results.

5.1 Redefining Job Evaluation

The basic truth that has never changed in pay management is that an organization should pay employees fairly for their contribution to the success of the organization.

Employee contribution comes in two forms:

1. The job contribution required to accomplish organization objectives
2. The employee's personal contribution above and beyond the basic job contribution

Two separate systems are required to pay for these different contributions:

1. *Job evaluation*, which values the worth of the basic job contribution
2. *Job results management*, which values the worth of the employee's personal contribution beyond the basic job contribution (see Phase 8)

Job evaluation is a decision-making process used to determine job worth. The process begins with a clear definition of job responsibilities and the qualifications necessary to fulfill the responsibilities (developed in Phase 4). The core mechanism of job evaluation is a set of criteria against which jobs can be valued. There are two options for implementing job evaluation: let human resources experts do it, or use a task force of job incumbents with experts guiding the process. We favor the task force.

Job evaluation looks and acts like a measurement process and is frequently described as such. Using the most popular job evaluation approach, which we will discuss in a moment, jobs are assigned points based on weighted criteria and on calculated degrees of worth within each criterion. One job might be counted as 437 points and another as 444 points. This all looks very exacting. However, this mathematical orientation misses the point completely.

You will succeed much better with job evaluation if you recognize it first as a communication process for building consensus among people throughout the organization regarding the different value of different job contributions, and second as a mathematical process for calculating points to place jobs into a pay structure. The core goal of job evaluation is to establish agreement within the organization regarding the worth of jobs in order to eliminate the constant pressure from managers and employees to increase job worth and therefore to obtain a higher pay rate.

Given a propensity for disagreement among managers and employees regarding the worth of jobs, getting interested parties together to discuss and debate accurate application of the job evaluation criteria is essential. For this reason alone, be skeptical of computer-aided job evaluation schemes that purport to eliminate the need for an evaluation task force. Not only may this form of job evaluation be viewed as secretive when it is accomplished behind the closed doors of the human resources department, but it may also be viewed as mysterious because of the unknown value system residing in the black box of a computer.

The criteria used to determine job worth are words. As you know, different people may give the same word a different meaning, especially when emotions run high—and emotions certainly can run high when job worth and eventually pay are being determined. Settling on an agreed-on definition of job evaluation criteria is another reason that people should come together in a task force to talk out the application of the criteria to various jobs. The history of job evaluation in an organization, and therefore the effectiveness of the organization's job evaluation process, is the special meaning that people in that organization give to the criteria.

While most managers accept job evaluation as a system developed and managed by human resources professionals, managers appreciate understanding the construction of the system as well as participating in the actual process of evaluating jobs. They want to know what's happening and how it happens when a major element of the pay structure is being determined.

Internal Equity

Get this straight: job evaluation does not mean determining a job's pay rate. Forget money and markets. Concentrate on the relative worth of jobs *within* your organization. In the next phase of your pay project, you will identify market pay rates that, with job evaluation, are the major building blocks of the pay structure that finally determines job pay rates.

Job evaluation criteria can be mathematically linked to market pay rates, but doing so upsets the concept of internal equity—that is, the fairness with which different jobs are viewed within the organization. In other words, the clerical job in Department A really is more demanding than a similar-looking clerical job in Department B.

When you tie job evaluation directly to market pay rates, you accept the market as a given. Organizations often decide to be out of line with the market; perhaps they want to pay a premium to attract higher-quality job candidates, or they can't afford to pay market rates, or they choose to spend their money on training or benefits instead of on direct pay.

Job evaluation gives an organization an opportunity to examine its own organizational structure carefully, independent of market influences. In this way, it can isolate and correct internal idiosyncrasies that affect pay. Market data may mask a multitude of sins.

You will undoubtedly find that your organization has unique jobs that will not be matched in the marketplace, which means that if you rely exclusively on market pay rates to drive your pay program, you still need some method for assessing the worth of jobs for which you cannot obtain data.

Arguments Against Job Evaluation

Some people don't think much of job evaluation. They argue that internal equity becomes too important; that most compensable factors are out of line with contemporary organizational issues; that the job evaluation process is time-consuming, cumbersome, prone to exaggeration; that job evaluation reinforces hierarchy and bureaucracy; and that job evaluation narrows employees' attention to specific skills rather than integrating with other functions in the organization.

These arguments, however, are not really the mistakes of the job evaluation system but rather of the people who manage or work within the system. One of the tenets of job evaluation is that the job evaluation process must be tailored to the unique requirements of each organization. Thus, job evaluation will be as contemporary and meaningful as you make it.

Pay the Market?

Some organizations decide to align more with market pay rates (external equity) than with internal equity, so they skip over job evaluation. This is not an unreasonable position, but it does risk the wrath of employees who do make internal comparisons and find them wanting and of investigators who find Equal Pay Act deficiencies.

Job evaluation puts reasonableness into a pay program. It discourages individual employees and managers from seeking excessive rewards. When organizations align themselves on the side of orderliness, they are responding to a basic need that each of us feels. Employees respect organizations for reducing aberrations in the pay system.

Most pay structures are determined by the dynamic interplay of job evaluation and market pay rates. If you were to pay solely according to either, you would make an incomplete decision. In short, properly designed pay structures are important precisely because they attempt to resolve the often differing demands of the two forces of internal and external equity. Job evaluation never prevents an organization from paying what the market demands, but it does make the organization completely aware of the magnitude and significance of any variation it chooses.

Project Analyzer 5.1

On what basis is job worth now determined in your organization?

How well has the organization communicated this process to managers and employees?

_____

_____

Are basic job contributions and employees' personal contributions above and beyond the basic job contribution differentiated now?

_____

_____

What do people in your organization know about job evaluation?

_____

_____

What experiences have they had with job evaluation?

_____

_____

What misconceptions need to be corrected?

_____

_____

How measurement-prone is the organization?

_____

_____

Could this interfere with the job evaluation process?

_____

_____

Is internal equity viewed as more important, equal to, or less important than equity with the market?

_____

_____

Is a job evaluation plan tied to market data desirable for your organization?

_____

_____

Are a substantial number of the organization's jobs readily found in the marketplace so that pay comparisons can be made, or are many of your jobs unique so that no comparisons are available?

_____

_____

Have you had any grievances regarding inequitable pay?

_____

_____

What was the outcome?

_____

_____

Are there any agreements or programs in place as a result of the equity settlements?

_____

_____

_____

5.2 Don't Do It If You Don't Mean It

The announcement of a job evaluation project creates expectations that pay or status inequities will be resolved. Misjudge these expectations, and you will be in deep trouble.

Some inequities exist only in the minds of the participants; nevertheless, the inequities are very real to these people. It is not impossible to demonstrate with logic that the "inequity" felt is not an inequity of fact, but the discussion can be difficult. However, a total job evaluation program, thoughtfully conceived and executed, can convey a reasonable argument about job equity as it is defined by the organization.

Job Relationships Defined

Job evaluation declares which relationships are equitable as far as your organization is concerned; individuals will have to adjust their personal preferences about what is equitable and what is not. It's a bit "stonewallish" but not unfair.

A way to run into all kinds of trouble is to decide that you don't like the results after the jobs have been evaluated. That's very unsporting.

Management must be willing to face the issues when they arise. As a practical matter, however, some inequities may not be addressable (e.g., they are the result of long-standing seniority systems) or may not need to be addressed the moment they are discovered (e.g., they are not significant or there are compensatory compensations). Experience demonstrates that this is almost always the case.

Distinguish Between Job Equity and Pay Equity

As a basic distinction, inequities of job evaluation are not the same as inequities of pay. Job evaluation looks at jobs only; until the pay structure is calculated, nobody can know that an actual pay inequity exists. Job evaluation inequities may precipitate pay inequities, but more often, job inequities stem from incomplete or inaccurate job definitions. Some inequities are not connected to job or pay but are the result of not giving the employee's personal job contribution proper recognition.

Use job evaluation to promise a thorough consideration of job relationships within the organization. Promise a thoughtful review by management. Do not promise pay adjustments, since pay involves consideration of market pay rates and personal job contribution, neither of which is addressed during the evaluation of jobs. Hammer away at the distinction between job equity and pay equity.

The Quiet Option

Where the organization's situation is recognizably desperate and the mere mention of job or pay equity is likely to evoke emotional outbursts, management can closet itself to evaluate the jobs and ascertain the dimensions of the problem without exciting expectations. Identified problems can be corrected or minimized quietly. Management can still bring the program out in the open later to validate its own work.

Employees are not unreasonable if their interests are not ignored, though they are not always happy with judgments that are in the best interests of the organization. Happy or unhappy, employees need to understand that management did what it could to establish a reasonable relationship among jobs within the organization.

Project Analyzer 5.2

What is the situation regarding job relationships now?

_____

_____

Will you be clearing up just a few problems, or do you need to correct years of inequities?

_____

_____

Does management realize what is involved in the project?

_____

_____

Is management able to distinguish between evaluating jobs and dealing with pay adjustments?

_____

_____

How open has management been about pay problems?

_____

_____

Is problem solving a way of life? Do people accept that problems can exist and can be solved? Or do people look for the culprit and try to extract their measure of blood?

_____

_____

Has management expressed its commitment?

_____

_____

_____

_____

5.3 Choosing a Job Evaluation System

The four traditional approaches to job evaluation are ranking, classification, factor comparison, and point factor comparison. The first three are a waste of time if you want to minimize arguable challenges to the results. Point factor comparison (referred to simply as a "point" plan) is the most systematic approach and will produce the most thoughtful and most accurate rankings of jobs according to their relative value to the organization. However, we will briefly summarize the four methods.

Ranking

The ranking method considers the whole job without reference to any objective criteria that attempt to break it down into components. Each rater uses personal, unspecified criteria to compare jobs. The method is based on what your gut tells you is the difference among jobs—not very convincing or defensible. Hybrid approaches state the criteria so that all raters are at least using the same reference.

The product of ranking looks like this:

1. Accountant
2. Buyer
3. Human resources assistant
4. Mail clerk

The ranking method does not yield the real distance between jobs. The four jobs just ranked appear to be equally separated from each other. In reality, the jobs might be truly evaluated in this way:

1. Accountant
2.
3. Buyer
4. Human resources assistant
5.
6.
7. Mail clerk

This true ranking has substantial implications for determining pay accurately.

Actually, the ranking method is not completely useless because people who really know the jobs being ranked "know" with some degree of accuracy which jobs are worth more to the organization than others. The ranking thought process can be used to uncover evaluation mistakes made when using the point system.

Ranking is unworkable when evaluating a large number of jobs. Evaluators cannot comprehend, in an orderly hierarchical fashion, more than just a few jobs. To rank a large number of jobs, benchmark jobs are ranked first to establish references. Then the remaining jobs are ranked in relation to the benchmark jobs.

A hybrid method, the *paired comparison*, can also be used to accommodate a large number of jobs. Each job is compared to every other job (valued as more or as less than the other job), one pair at a time. The job that is valued most often (when compared in pairs) is the most valued job. Of course, the ranking still shows jobs as equally separated and does not yield the real value distance among jobs.

Classification

The classification method uses one criterion with degrees of value, much as a thermometer or ruler does. Each job is assigned the level that best describes the job's value. The point system, in contrast, uses several criteria and thus produces a more balanced and equitable outcome. In reality, such as in the General Schedule of the U.S. Civil Service, the one criterion is jam-packed with subcriteria that complicate the process; a rater may find some wording in one degree applicable and yet some other wording in a different degree also applicable.

More important, whereas other job evaluation systems produce a ranking of jobs without reference to pay levels, the classification method equates each job level directly with a different pay level. Thus, there is enormous pressure for managers and employees to "try for" the next highest level.

Factor Comparison

The factor comparison method uses several criteria but no degrees within each criterion. Jobs are simply ranked separately according to each criterion. For each job, some pay rate, usually the average market pay rate, is apportioned among the criteria according to how much of the rate is attributable to each criterion—for example:

Job Title	Average Market Rate	Criterion A	Criterion B	Criterion C
Technician	$10.00	$4.35	$3.75	$1.90
Clerk	$7.00	$2.00	$2.95	$2.05

The ranking of jobs and the ranking within each criterion must be in accord—and it never is after the first attempt. The tediousness of the process of reranking and reapportioning makes the system unpopular; more important, the introduction of the market pay rate into the evaluative process contaminates the internal ranking of relative job worth.

Point Factor Comparison

Point methods evaluate each job according to several criteria, weighted to place emphasis as desired by the organization. Each criterion contains degrees of value, much as a thermometer or ruler does. Each degree is assigned a point value; the higher the degree, the more points awarded. The points for each criterion are added to a total, and the totals are arranged from most points to least points to produce a hierarchy of job worth. Here's a general overview of the approach:

Job Title	Criterion A	Criterion B	Criterion C	Total Points
Criteria Weighting	40	25	35	
Technician	40	62	34	136
Clerk	35	55	30	120

The pay management guidelines offered in this book are keyed to the use of this method, which will be explained in detail in the rest of this phase, along with a complete and adaptable job evaluation plan that you can use.

Project Analyzer 5.3

Is your organization ready to commit to a thorough evaluation of jobs?

_____

_____

Is there any reason to argue for an abbreviated approach, such as job ranking?

_____

_____

5.4 A Job Evaluation Plan for Each Job Family vs. One Plan for All Jobs

Adopting one job evaluation plan to value all of the jobs in an organization establishes internal equity throughout the entire organization. This prevents pay discrimination against women and minorities, whose pay is typically lower than the market average. Most organizations prefer this approach.

Jobs may be grouped for pay management when they:

- Are in the same department.
- Involve similar job processes.
- Make similar demands on job incumbents (see Figure 14).
- Are scheduled together.
- Interact closely.
- Are located together geographically.
- Have a common supervisor.

Figure 14. Equal Employment Opportunity affirmative action categories.

Officials and managers. Personnel who set broad policies, exercise overall responsibility for execution of these policies, and direct individual departments or special phases of a firm's operations. (Senior executives, who might be owners or subject to the board of directors' compensation committee, whose pay is determined on an individual basis, and who are eligible for special incentive benefits, are usually separated from the routine pay families and are subject to executive compensation policies and procedures.)

Professionals. Occupations requiring college graduation or experience of such kind and amount as to provide a comparable background.

Technicians. Occupations requiring a combination of basic scientific knowledge and manual skill that can be obtained through about two years of post–high school education, such as is offered in many technical institutes and community colleges or through equivalent on-the-job training.

Sales workers. Employees engaging wholly or primarily in direct selling.

Office and clerical personnel. All clerical workers whose activities are predominantly nonmanual (though some manual work may be included) and not directly involved with altering or transporting products.

Craft workers. Manual workers of relatively high skill level having a thorough and comprehensive knowledge of the processes involved in their work. They exercise considerable independent judgment and usually receive an extensive period of training.

Operators. Workers who operate machines or processing equipment or perform other factory-type duties of intermediate skill level that can be mastered in a few weeks and that require limited training.

Laborers and service workers. Occupations that require no special training.

- Are guided by common policy and procedure.
- Are grouped in training.
- Lead to similar jobs.
- Follow parallel career paths.
- Are represented by the same union.

If job families are established, they should parallel and support the management of the organization, as well as facilitate pay management.

Some organizations group jobs for pay management according to their exempt or nonexempt status under the Fair Labor Standards Act or according to the method of pay calculation (hourly or salaried). Both groupings are structurally dangerous. Whether a job must be paid overtime and how pay is calculated have nothing to do with the relative worth of a job to the organization. Under these distinctions, jobs might inadvertently be placed in an inappropriate category and compared with dissimilar jobs, using unfair criteria.

One advantage of job families is that they allow more precise market comparisons. For example, clerical jobs can be compared with the clerical job pay market, and technical jobs can be compared with the technical job pay market. If the clerical pay market increases 2 percent but the technical pay market increases 6 percent, then where the two markets are combined into one organization pay structure, the average increase of 4 percent is overly generous to the clerical jobs and unfair to the technical jobs.

Still, most organizations prefer to pursue the goal of internal job equity, placing all jobs in the same structure and using one job evaluation plan, where fairness is based on the worth of the job contribution to the organization, not on the whim or potential discriminations of the market. Organizations prefer to control their pay structure to the degree possible.

Figure 15 shows a bank's initial plan for switching from two plans based on an exempt/nonexempt division to four job families. Figure 16 shows additional analysis of job movement in the bank to help determine which families and how many would

Figure 15. One bank's initial proposal for a transition to the job family concept.

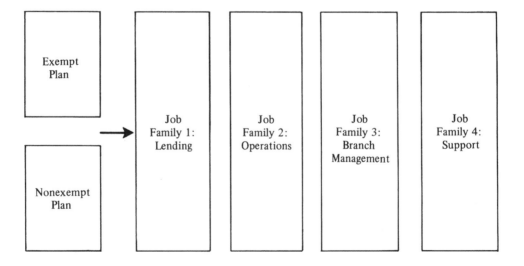

Figure 16. Analysis of job changes and career development for the four proposed job families in the bank.

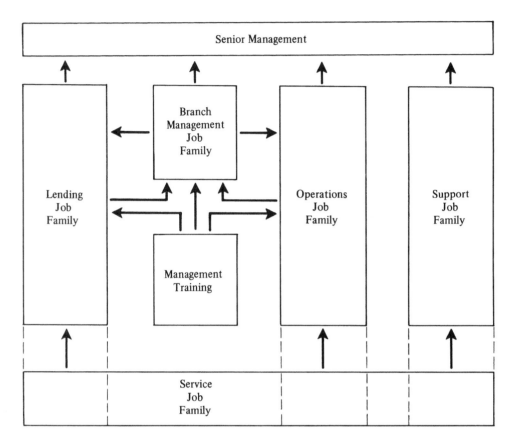

make the most sense. Entry-level service jobs differ for each job family, yet they are similar in job demands.

Management trainees move into defined jobs according to a training schedule and the quality of their performance; the relative value of the job is not a consideration. There is substantial movement among the lending, operations, and branch management families—especially between branch management and lending.

One solution is to recognize three job families: sales and service (the combination of branch management and lending), production (operations), and support. Service jobs are included in their respective job families.

You are not stuck with your decision, however. You can use one job evaluation plan or several, examine the outcome, and switch your approach. True, this will mean more work, but not as much as you might anticipate. Regardless of the work, you must have a program that is helpful to your organization; you must invest what it takes to get the results you desire.

During actual evaluations, you will have the flexibility to redefine families, rewrite plans, and evaluate some jobs according to different plans to assess which yields the most equitable results. If you establish one plan for technical jobs and another for service and support jobs, you may discover that a particular job in a technical area, evaluated according to the technical plan, is truly a service job and is more fairly evaluated according to the service-and-support plan.

One Job Evaluation Plan Is Usually Best

Separate job evaluation plans may complicate matters more than they are worth. Most organizations feel that simpler is better, not only to reduce administrative burdens but, more important, to send a message that all jobs in the organization are on the same wavelength.

You must understand what you wish to accomplish, the goals of your compensation program. What are your managerial principles? What is the message you wish to convey to your employees? What can you afford? Certain advantages and disadvantages will derive when you separate jobs into families and when you do not. Consider these implications and make the best decision you can.

Project Analyzer 5.4

What is your reaction to the various job evaluation approaches?

_____

_____

What does your organization want to accomplish by evaluating jobs?

_____

_____

Will management commit itself to a thorough effort?

_____

_____

What do you need to do to convince top managers if they are not ready now?

_____

_____

Would one job evaluation plan for all jobs be simpler to manage, be fairer to all jobs, and demonstrate job integration and relatedness across functional lines?

_____

_____

Would more than one plan support operating distinctions when there is no need to combine jobs under the same plan?

_____

_____

What job families exist?

_____

_____

What different pay markets are involved?

_____

_____

5.5 A Job Evaluation Plan You Can Use

The adaptable point factor comparison plan in Figure 17 provides a technically efficient base that can be tailored to the unique jobs and requirements of your organization. Study the plan. Modify the compensable factor definitions and degree wording to reflect the jobs you will evaluate. Move the degree definitions around to match the structure of your organization. Combine the language of degrees. Use language in harmony with your organization. Substitute the name of your organization for the generic reference to "the organization." From our experience, except to modify specific areas that inherently demand unique definition for your organization, not much usually needs to be changed.

Start out with your best word forward, but as you learn more about the meaning of the words during the actual evaluating process, be prepared to reword. Make further adjustments in the plan as you discover words that need to be changed, added, or deleted. You or someone else will notice that the meaning of a word is usually explained in conversation by use of a synonym; put that synonym into the plan. Remember, the application (changing) of the degrees to the unique jobs of your organization is the conversion that gives the job evaluation plan its usability and credibility.

The first day of your evaluation sessions will be the toughest, and the most important, because words and the meaning of words will be new. Later, you will finesse the meaning of the words again—not often, of course, but in response to subtle, nagging problems of interpretation or application. When you are delayed at one place or another in the plan, don't be discouraged. Instead, look for ways to clarify interpretation.

The essential communication lesson for job evaluation is this: the words of the plan mean what your task force interprets them to mean. The only requirement is that the task force applies the interpretation consistently.

Feeling the pressure of responsibility to do a credible job, some task force members occasionally fall prey to the disease of wordsmithing and fail to remember the goal to achieve consensus. Refocus them when they get a little crazy.

(Text continues on page 149.)

Figure 17. A job evaluation plan you can use in your organization.

KNOWLEDGE

What kind and level of information must be recalled and applied to accomplish job results competently? Information can be acquired through formal education, apprenticeship, experience, self-learning, or on-the-job operation and training.

Quick Key	Description	Degree
	Comprehension of the basic requirements of daily living (*Example: laborer*)	1
Elementary	Reading, writing, arithmetic (*Examples: janitor, landscape helper, kitchen helper, mailroom support clerk*)	2
	(*Examples: courier, purchasing assistant*)	3
	(*Examples: receptionist, construction worker, mailroom equipment operator*)	4
Vocational	Mechanical, technical, dexterity, or interpersonal skills that can be applied immediately and directly to job requirements without specific experience (*Examples: word processor, data entry operator, switchboard operator, inventory clerk, truck driver, teacher aide, child care worker, home closing coordinator, home quality assurance coordinator, marketing research specialist, PC specialist, building materials buyer*)	5
	(*Examples: records management clerk, general maintenance technician, cash clerk, accounts payable clerk, social work assistant, lifeguard, CAD operator, computer operator, telephone customer service representative, cash administrator, office administrative services manager*)	6
	Proficiency or occupational seasoning in mechanical, technical, dexterity, or interpersonal skills, such as through experience in unique organization requirements, or specialized training (*Examples: payroll supervisor, credit analyst, cost accounting clerk, outside salesperson, dispatcher, programmer, clerical supervisor, camp counselor, telephone cable locator*)	7

Figure 17. (*continued*)

	(*Example: instructor*)	8
	(*Examples: payroll accountant, business manager, safety manager*)	9
Professional	Knowledge of professional practices including sources of information and commonly accepted standards that can be applied immediately and directly to job requirements without explicit instruction—including the ability to discern when important information is missing; master tradesman (*Examples: staff accountant, inventory manager, product manager, inside sales manager, counselor, teacher, public relations assistant, executive secretary, programmer/analyst, operations analyst, nurse, social worker I, contract administration specialist, telephone field engineer, telephone installation and repair technician, home building manager, financial analyst, general accounting supervisor, home salesperson*)	10
	(*Examples: telephone cable technician, home building estimator*)	11
	Knowledge of professional practices including sources of information and commonly accepted standards that must be interpreted before being applied to the unique requirements of the organization (*Examples: senior business analyst, human resources manager, branch controller, certified family therapist, fund-raiser, social worker II, resident house parent, regional home construction manager, home sales manager*)	12
	(*Example: controller*)	13
	Understanding of a profession in order to influence its principles and practices (*Examples: social worker III, nurse practitioner, data processing manager*)	14
Interdisciplinary	Understanding of professional practices of more than one knowledge area in order to develop organization strategies typically involving a planning horizon of three to five years (*Examples: information services director, director of marketing, social worker IV, telephone switching and transmission engineer*)	15
	(*Examples: program director–day care, telephone engineering manager*)	16
	(*Example: deputy director–social service agency*)	17

Figure 17. (*continued*)

Understanding, integration, and creation of organization strategies involving diverse knowledge areas (*Example: executive director–social service agency*)	18

INFORMATION PROCESSING
What mental processes are involved in using job knowledge?

Quick Key	Description	Degree
	Uses or transfers information as is, without changing its basic format (*Examples: mail clerk, cafeteria helper, data entry operator, housekeeper, file clerk, receptionist*)	1
Rearranges information	Enters information into a prescribed format, without changing its basic content, rearranges or calculates information (*Examples: inventory clerk, computer operator, word processor, payroll clerk, department secretary, bookkeeper, cook, courier, purchasing agent*)	2
	Organizes information; sets priorities (*Example: telephone construction worker*)	3
	(*To be filled in as needed by the organization*)	4
	Studies information to identify what it is (*Example: home quality assurance coordinator*)	5
Analyzes information	Determines what information means; interprets data (*Examples: inventory specialist, credit analyst, assistant controller, counselor, nutritionist, administrative assistant, programmer, child care worker, mailroom equipment operator, PC specialist*)	6
	Resolves discrepancies after interpreting data (*Examples: general maintenance technician, lifeguard, camp counselor, CAD operator, cash administrator, home closing coordinator, computer operator, junior accountant*)	7

Figure 17. (*continued*)

	Determines how information fits together; identifies relationships within information (*Examples: senior programmer, financial analyst, market research associate*)	8
	Determines cause of a problem in a subsystem (*Examples: social worker I, telephone cable locator, general accounting supervisor, office administrative services manager, building materials buyer*)	9
	Draws a conclusion based on inference (*Examples: resident house parent, telephone customer service representative, home building manager, safety manager, home salesperson*)	10
Builds information	Combines and synthesizes information from various sources into a unified system (*Examples: human resources manager, controller, public relations manager, purchasing supervisor, programmer/analyst, social worker II, telephone cable technician, telephone field engineer, telephone install and repair technician, home building estimator*)	11
	Develops new information (*Examples: fund-raiser, social worker III*)	12
	Creates organizational concepts (*Example: social worker IV*)	13
Evaluates systems	Determines the relevance of information to total organization strategies—"reads between the lines" (*Examples: telephone switching and transmission engineer, regional home construction manager, regional home sales manager, data processing manager*)	14
	Anticipates the relevance and impact of several information systems to total organization strategies—"sees around corners, and beyond where we are" (*Examples: program director–day care, controller*)	15
	Integrates diverse information systems into new organization possibilities (*Examples: deputy director–social service agency, executive director–social service agency*)	16

Figure 17. (*continued*)

DECISION MAKING
How much autonomy does the job incumbent have to decide job issues? What kind of decisions are made?

Quick Key	Description	Degree
Follows procedures	Follows prescribed steps/methods/procedures on how work is to be performed, without alteration (*Examples: file clerk, housekeeper, data entry operator, switchboard operator, order puller, mail clerk, purchasing assistant, receptionist*)	1
	Alters prescribed steps/methods/procedures on how work is to be performed to meet specific requirements (*Examples: word processor, purchasing clerk, department secretary, incoming mail supervisor, driver, telephone construction worker*)	2
	(*Examples: accounts payable clerk, home quality assurance coordinator*)	3
Selects option	Selects suitable steps from several prescribed and obvious options in order to accomplish job results (*Examples: administrative secretary, credit analyst, personnel supervisor, word processing supervisor, programmer, public relations assistant, mailroom equipment operator, junior accountant, market research associate*)	4
	Alters selected option to meet specific requirements (*Examples: general maintenance technician, accounts payable clerk, cash administrator, home closing coordinator*)	5
	Determines which method (several steps) from several prescribed but not obvious options will accomplish job results; sets priorities (*Examples: executive secretary, nutritionist, production scheduler, social worker I, telephone cable locator, CAD operator, senior programmer, financial analyst, PC specialist*)	6

Figure 17. (*continued*)

	Modifies selected method to meet specific requirements (*Examples: instructor, telephone customer service representative, home building estimator, general accounting supervisor, home materials buyer, home salesperson*)	7
Develops systems	Recommends or develops a subsystem of steps/methods/procedures to solve a problem (*Examples: certified family therapist, microcomputer specialist, programmer/analyst, accounting manager, nurse, home building manager, office administrative services manager, safety manager*)	8
	Integrates subsystems to solve a problem (*Examples: social worker II, telephone cable technician, telephone field engineer, telephone installation and repair technician*)	9
	Recommends or develops a unified system to accomplish given objective (*Examples: social worker III, resident house parent, telephone switching and transmission engineer, regional home construction manager, regional home sales manager, data processing manager*)	10
Sets objectives	Defines unit objectives (*Examples: controller, human resources manager*)	11
	Recommends or develops total organizational strategies (*Examples: program director–day care, controller*)	12
	(*Example: deputy director–social service agency*)	13
	Establishes organizational strategies and policies—time horizon of three to five years (*Example: executive director–social service agency*)	14
	Creates organization culture (*Example: division president*)	15

Figure 17. (*continued*)

INTERPERSONAL COMMUNICATION

What are the purpose and complexity of communication with others?

Quick Key	Description	Degree
	Provides or obtains information (*Examples: data entry operator, file clerk, housekeeper, mailroom clerk*)	1
	Inquires to identify specific information (*Examples: kitchen helper, courier*)	2
Interviewing	Interviews to understand information (*Examples: receptionist, switchboard operator, order confirmation clerk, driver, records management clerk, construction worker, programmer, computer operator*)	3
	Investigates to discover unanticipated information; explains data (*Examples: bookkeeper, accounts payable clerk, purchasing clerk, general maintenance technician, mailroom equipment operator, cash clerk, home closing coordinator, junior accountant*)	4
Training	Trains/coaches others to understand steps and methods (*Examples: benefits specialist, credit analyst, counselor, representative, microcomputer specialist, vehicle maintenance technician, PC specialist, building materials buyer*)	5
	Coordinates among differing expectations (*Examples: home building estimator, marketing research associate*)	6
	Interprets information to help others understand concepts (*Examples: accountant, telephone cable locator, CAD operator, quality assurance coordinator, programmer/ analyst, financial analyst*)	7

Figure 17. (*continued*)

	Establishes an emphatic rapport with another person (*Examples: nurse, child care worker, telephone cable technician*)	8
Persuading	Persuades others to accept a course of action: hires, terminates, transfers, demotes, disciplines employees; plans, monitors, and appraises job results; administers pay; supervises two or more people* (*Examples: business analyst, public relations manager, executive secretary, outside salesperson, office administrative services manager, general accounting supervisor*)	9
	Establishes rapport with emotionally disturbed individuals; difficult customer contact (*Examples: certified family therapist, instructor, social worker I, telephone customer service representative, telephone installation and repair technician*)	10
Getting people to act	Develops a unified effort among people who have different expectations by convincing, compromising, or developing suitable alternatives (*Examples: fund-raiser, social worker II, nurse practitioner, telephone field engineer, safety officer*)	11
	Settles matters where guidelines are available (*Examples: social worker III, resident house parent, telephone switching and transmission engineer*)	12
	Resolves differences of opinion in conjunction with others (*Examples: social worker IV, home building manager, controller, data processing manager, home salesperson*)	13
Maintaining policy and organization direction	Resolves differences of opinion autonomously to accomplish total organization strategies (*Examples: store manager, branch manager, personnel manager, director of public relations, program director–day care, regional home construction manager, regional home sales manager*)	14
	(*To be filled in as needed by the organization*)	15
	(*To be filled in as needed by the organization*)	16

Figure 17. (*continued*)

Negotiates resolution among diverse points of view in order to achieve organization goals (*Examples: deputy director–social service agency, executive director–social service agency*)	17

*Supervisory responsibilities are included here because of their nature as a communication process. There is no separate factor for supervision, although you may choose to add a factor to the plan to give credit for the number of people supervised if that makes sense for your organization. See Additional Compensable Factors.

IMPACT ON ORGANIZATION RESULTS

What is the impact on, or risk to, the organization by acting or failing to act?

Quick Key	Description	Degree
Accomplishing individual results	Results are immediately obvious and can be adjusted with minimal rework and negligible cost; poor results would cause an inconvenience (*Examples: janitor, receptionist*)	1
	(*Examples: purchasing assistant, receptionist*)	2
Integrating organization subsystem results	A portion of the work must be redone to adjust results; poor results would cause an interruption of effort (*Examples: kitchen helper, accounts payable clerk, courier, quality assurance coordinator, financial analyst, PC specialist*)	3
	Analyzing an organization subsystem (*Examples: construction worker, bookkeeper, cash clerk, programmer, junior accountant*)	4
	(*To be filled in as needed by the organization*)	5
Planning organization subsystem results	Designing an organization subsystem; poor results would cause a waste of resources (*Examples: child care worker, camp counselor, office administrative services manager, programmer/analyst, general accounting supervisor, marketing research associate, home materials buyer*)	6

Figure 17. (*continued*)

	Nearly all results must be redone; missed production schedule (*Examples: instructor, social worker I, accounts payable specialist, CAD operator, mailroom equipment operator, home building estimator*)	7
	Analyzing a system for the entire organization (*Example: safety officer*)	8
	(*Examples: nurse practitioner, resident house parent, staff accountant, telephone customer service representative*)	9
Integrating organization results	Designing a system for the entire organization; poor results would cause a loss of organization momentum (*Examples: fund-raiser, telephone cable locator, telephone cable technician, telephone installation and repair technician, home closing coordinator, controller, home salesperson*)	10
	(*Examples: social worker II, telephone field engineer, data processing manager*)	11
	(*Examples: social worker III, social worker IV*)	12
Planning organization results	Integrating results for the entire organization; poor results would cause an organizational failure—time horizon from three to five years (*Examples: program director–day care, telephone switching and transmission engineer, regional home construction manager, regional home sales manager*)	13
	(*Example: deputy director–social service agency*)	14
	(*Example: executive director–social service agency*)	15

*An analogy for the terms in this section is building a better mouse trap:
  a. Gathers mouse trap parts for assembly. It is an *inconvenience* (degree 1) when the mouse trap doesn't work and the correct parts need to be retrieved.
  b. Assembles the mouse trap. It is an *interruption of effort* (degree 3) when problems with parts are discovered during assembly and some of the assembled parts need to be reassembled.
  c. Assembles and tests the mouse trap. It is a *waste of resources* (degree 6) when the mouse trap doesn't work properly because some of the parts do not meet specifications and the trap has to be taken apart and rebuilt with new parts.
  d. Designs the mouse trap. It is a *loss of organization momentum* (degree 10) when the mouse trap doesn't catch more mice and a new trap must be designed.
  e. Manages mouse trap manufacturing. It is a *failure* when the concept of mouse traps needs to be abandoned and the use of cats needs to be considered.

Figure 17. (*continued*)

+---+
| **ENVIRONMENT** |
| |
| What physical demands or exposures are involved in the job? |
+---+

Quick Key	Description	Degree
Comfortable	No special physical demands or exposures—everyday risks or discomforts	0
	Lifting 10 to 20 pounds; standing; pushing; pulling; visual strain; working in an awkward position for less than 50 percent of the time (*Examples: supply clerk, home building manager, mailroom clerk*)	1
	Lifting 10 to 20 pounds; standing; pushing; pulling; climbing; visual strain; working in an awkward position for more than 50 percent of the time (*Example: warehouse person*)	2
	Whining noise; airborne particles; fumes (*Examples: van driver, child care worker*)	3
Disagreeable	Temperature variations; hot materials; coolants; working at heights (*Examples: kitchen helper, general maintenance technician, mailroom equipment technician*)	4
	Flying debris; odor; rare exposure to dangerous circumstances (*Example: lifeguard*)	5
Strenuous	Lifting 20 pounds or more continually; exposure to emotionally upset clients for more than 50 percent of the time (*Examples: telephone field engineer, counselor*)	6
	Noise greater than 85 dba; welding flash (*Examples: punch press operator, welder*)	7
	Rotating machinery, such as blades and spindles (*Examples: lathe operator, vehicle maintenance repair technician*)	8

Figure 17. (*continued*)

	Caustics (*Examples: janitor, laboratory technician*)	9
	Toxicants; infectious diseases (*Examples: nurse, telephone installation and repair technician*)	10
Dangerous	High voltage; supervise children 24 hours per day (*Examples: electrical repair technician, resident house parent*)	11
	Supervise children in a wilderness camp 24 hours per day where close support found in a city is not readily available (*Example: camp counselor*)	12
	Physical attack (*Examples: police officer, telephone cable technician*)	13

Compensable Factors

Because job evaluation is a decision-making process, the decision-making criteria (known as *compensable factors*) constitute a point plan's essential nature. What gets measured is a statement of organization values.

People have a pretty clear idea of why one job might be valued more than another job in an organization:

- What does the job holder need to know?
- How difficult is the information to work with?
- What decisions does the job holder have to make?
- How difficult and risky are the decisions?
- With whom does the job holder interact, and why?
- Is the job physically demanding?

You want to be certain that the people in your organization understand that these questions will be answered by the job evaluation plan and that the plan measures what it is supposed to. You may want to conduct some focus groups to identify and discuss the issues, and to hear some observations that will affect the way that you adapt the model job evaluation plan in this book to your organization. Focus groups are an excellent way to begin the buy-in process for the results produced by job evaluation.

The compensable factors of the adaptable job evaluation plan in this book are:

- Knowledge
- Information Processing

- Decision Making
- Interpersonal Communications
- Impact on Organization Results
- Environment (physical)

These same factors can be used if you choose one job evaluation plan for your organization, or they can be weighted differently (see Phase 5.6) and the degrees within the factors edited differently if you choose to establish different job evaluation plans for different job families.

Education and Experience Related to the Knowledge Factor

In Phase 4, we warned about generalizations involving education and experience. We hesitate to offer the following education and experience references because they might distract from the more accurate job-specific descriptions, but because they are so commonly used, we thought it would be helpful to show how education and experience *generally* relate to the Knowledge factor.

KNOWLEDGE

Description	Approximate Equivalent Reference		Degree
	Education	Work Knowledge	
Comprehension of the basic requirements of daily living			1
Reading, writing, arithmetic	High school		2
		1 year	3
		2 years	4
Mechanical, technical, dexterity, or interpersonal skills that can be applied immediately and directly to job requirements without specific experience	Technical training	3 years	5
		4 years	6
Proficiency or occupational seasoning in mechanical, technical, dexterity, or interpersonal skills, such as through experience in unique organization requirements, or specialized training	Associate of arts (A.A.) degree	5 years	7

		A.A. plus 1–2 years or 6 years	8
		A.A. plus 3–4 years or 7 years	9
Knowledge of professional practices including sources of information and commonly accepted standards that can be applied immediately and directly to job requirements without explicit instruction, including the ability to discern when important information is missing	Bachelor's degree	A.A. plus 5–6 years or master's trade license or 8 years	10
		B.A. or B.S. plus internship	11
Knowledge of professional practices including sources of information and commonly accepted standards that must be interpreted before being applied to the unique requirements of the organization		B.A. or B.S. plus 3–4 years	12
	Master's degree	B.A. or B.S. plus 5–6 years	13
Understanding of a profession in order to influence its principles and practices		B.A. or B.S. plus 7–8 years	14
Understanding of professional practices of more than one knowledge area in order to develop organization strategies typically involving a planning horizon of three to four years	Multiple disciplines		15
Planning horizon five to six years			16
			17
Understanding, integration, and creation of organization strategies involving diverse knowledge areas			18

Additional Compensable Factors

The factors in the job evaluation plan have adequately measured the basic job requirements in a variety of organizations. Your organization's jobs may present a unique situation for which an additional factor may be helpful, or your task force may simply feel more comfortable with an additional factor. One bank, for example, added a factor it called Branch Bank Measurement to measure loan and deposit volume, type of customer, and number of accounts and transactions.

The factors in Figure 18 will give you some ideas. However, make sure that anything else the task force thinks it needs to measure is not already covered in the basic factors. In job evaluation, more measurements do not necessarily produce a more accurate ranking of jobs. More criteria may mean nothing more than more work. The task force will do well to keep the job evaluation plan as simple as possible. As an alternative, instead of adding another factor, some of the language in the suggestions in Figure 18 may be added to the basic plan factors for additional clarification. The factors in Figure 18 are numbered according to the real and equitable value between degrees, which will be explained later.

Figure 18. Additional job evaluation factors.

TIME TO DISCOVER AN ERROR

Measure the time elapsed and the absolute investment/commitment of organization resources from action until an error is discovered and all implications are understood.

1. Errors are discovered immediately.
2. Errors are discovered on routine follow-up, generally within several days.
4. Errors are discovered on random inspection, generally within a month or two.
8. Errors are discovered on audit and commit the organization for approximately one year.
12. Errors are discovered on audit and have long-term implications—several years—for the organization.

Example: Although an erroneous report may be filed away for one year, if the error can be discovered immediately upon retrieving the report and there are no implications other than the correction, Time to Discover an Error should be measured as degree 1.

SEVERITY OF ERROR

Measure whether a unique/extraordinary possibility exists that errors will cause a major expense/injury/embarrassment to the organization.

0. No
1. Yes

CONFIDENTIAL AND SENSITIVE INFORMATION

Measure the access to confidential and sensitive information, the effect on the organization if the information were divulged, and the realistic opportunity to divulge information.

0. No access
1. Embarrassment; wasted time to correct misunderstandings or ameliorate feelings
3. An invasion of personal or organizational privacy
6. Subjects organization to potential or actual lawsuit
10. Loss of competitive advantage

Figure 18. (*continued*)

AUTHORITY

Measure the authority to conduct work.

1. May act only after receiving approval
3. May act but must inform supervisor promptly
6. May act at own discretion, subject to short-term review
10. May act at own discretion, subject to long-term audit

TIME SPAN TO COMPLETE WORK

Measure the amount of time typically required to bring work to a conclusion so that results can be accurately judged.

1. One day
2. One week
3. One month
4. Three months
5. Six months
6. One year
8. Two years
12. Five years
18. Ten years

SCOPE OF FINANCIAL RESPONSIBILITY

Measure the responsibility for expenditures and funding.

1. Requests expenditures
2. Recommends expenditures
4. Monitors expenditures
8. Authorizes expenditures
15. Develops funding sources

FINANCIAL IMPACT OR ACCOUNTABILITY

Measure the amount of money the job incumbent can commit and is required and able to control.

*Real
Value**

_____	Up to $_____
_____	Up to $_____
_____	Up to $_____
_____	Up to $_____
_____	Up to $_____
_____	Up to $_____

*To be filled in as needed by each organization.

Figure 18. (*continued*)

NUMBER OF EMPLOYEES SUPERVISED

Measure the number of employees supervised, including both those supervised directly by the incumbent and those supervised indirectly (employees supervised by subordinate supervisors).

Real Value
Factors
to Be
Determined

_____	Two to _____
_____	_____ to _____
_____	_____ to _____
_____	_____ to _____
_____	_____ to _____

SUPERVISORY COMPLEXITY

Measure the complexity of the jobs supervised, as defined by the highest degree of Knowledge assigned to a subordinate job.

  1. Supervises jobs requiring Knowledge degree 1
  2. Supervises jobs requiring Knowledge degree 2
  4. Supervises jobs requiring Knowledge degree 3
  6. Supervises jobs requiring Knowledge degree 4
  9. Supervises jobs requiring Knowledge degree 5
11. Supervises jobs requiring Knowledge degree 6
15. Supervises jobs requiring Knowledge degree 7

PROJECT MANAGEMENT

Measure the planning, organizing, leading, and controlling skills used to manage projects.

  1. Determines which steps/methods/procedures among several prescribed options are required to fulfill an identified project objective
(*Examples*: specialist, technician)
  4. Develops steps/methods/procedures for fulfilling an identified project objective
(*Example*: analyst)
  7. Defines project objectives
(*Example*: team supervisor)
11. Establishes project goals

Project Analyzer 5.5

Which compensable factors are appropriate for the organization?

_____

_____

Are the factors defined accurately?

_____

_____

Is the wording in each degree suitable?

_____

_____

Who will decide which factors are appropriate and whether or not the factors are defined accurately?

_____

_____

_____

5.6 Adapting the Job Evaluation Plan to Your Organization

Here are some guidelines to follow when editing compensable factors and degrees:

- Limit the definition of a compensable factor to one criterion. Multiple possible combinations of criteria only confuse the mind.
- Describe criteria only once in one compensable factor. Do not measure nearly the same thing in another factor.
- Describe what the criterion intends to measure. Measure observable conditions instead of subjective opinions.
- State ideas concisely. Too many words cause more questions than they answer.
- Use specific, precise words. Vague words cause debate and waste time.
- Avoid trendy words, such as "leadership," "teamwork," "collaboration," and "innovation" until they are accurately defined for your organization. Then use the definition.
- Make the distinctions between degrees obvious. Unclear distinctions result in confusion and measurement errors.
- Define the number of degrees needed. Too many will cause debate over which degree applies; too few will not be able to account for the relative distance between jobs.
- Use gender-free language.

Here are examples of language changes that may help your task force with changes it wants to make:

- Adjust quantitative definitions, such as percentages of time.
- Add quantitative indicators, such as dollars—but if you use dollars, remember to keep them current.
- Change words—for example, "one sales season" for "approximately one year"; "questions" for "interviews"; "loss of image and integrity" for "loss of competitive advantage"; "revenue sources" for "funding sources."
- Add words, such as "explain" in addition to "interpret."
- Delete words that do not fit your organization.
- Add examples for organization jobs, such as, "files quarterly tax return," "prepares policy recommendations," "computes benefit allocations," "explains pension plan," "obtains information for new accounts."

Job References in Plan

Some job titles are cited in the job evaluation plan to help you understand how the generic words of the plan apply to common jobs, but *use them with caution*. Obviously, the same job title will have different job requirements in different organizations. Examples to clarify the meaning of the degrees can provide at least some basis for your task force to understand the level of the degree or levels adjacent to the indicated level. Even when the task force says, "Well, our programmer/analyst job is higher than this degree," you've learned something about the interpretation of the degrees. Be sure to delete the job title references that do not apply to your organization, and add those that do.

A purist might say that the language of the degrees can be interpreted in only so many ways. Language should be defined within a plausible range of interpretation so that communication among people is easier. However, each task force will have a mind of its own and define words as the members see fit. Some tend to underrate all jobs in one factor, and others tend to overrate all jobs in another factor. Almost always in our experience, regardless of which way the words are applied, each task force puts its mark on the job evaluation plan and interprets the words consistently.

Defining Degrees

Not all of the degrees in each factor of the job evaluation plan are defined because there aren't enough generic words to describe each of the levels. The blank degrees may be filled in when the task force identifies a specific job that is more demanding than the next-lower-level defined degree and less demanding than the next-higher-level defined degree. In some cases, the task force will not use a degree, and that's fine. Just leave it there, or else the calculation of the degree points will be wrong.

Avoiding Traditional Problems With Job Evaluation Plans

In order to understand what's effective about the job evaluation plan, you need to understand some of the problems that can arise.

Number of Degrees   Most job evaluation plans have only several degrees in each factor, not enough to determine the relative worth of jobs. For example, in the Knowledge factor, only seven or eight degrees might be shown. In the plan in Figure 17, there are eighteen degrees because the highest level of knowledge required is eighteen times greater than the lowest level.

Over twenty years ago, we discovered this inequity in most plans. Geometric mathematical progressions between degrees were used occasionally to calculate degree points, but math alone couldn't solve the problem of an incorrect number of degrees. After years of correlating job pay to job evaluation plans and surveying human resources professionals regarding the actual value of degrees instead of the value by routine calculation, we arrived at the real number of degrees that are required to produce an equitable relationship among jobs within an organization. Do not reduce the number of degrees in any factor without careful consideration.

Subjective Language   As you edit the job evaluation plan to meet your organization requirements, don't fall into traps that have plagued job evaluation for decades. Most plans use subjective instead of objective degrees. Here is some traditional language that you'll want to recognize and avoid because it is imprecise:

Initiative
1. Minimum of mental concentration
2. Light mental concentration
3. Normal mental concentration
4. Considerable mental concentration
5. Close mental concentration

There are a number of problems here. "Initiative" is a poor choice as a compensable factor because the word, regardless of specific definition, is subject to a variety of personal interpretations. Worse, the grading of initiative necessarily implies that some jobs require less personal initiative than others, which is demeaning. All jobs require people to begin the effort and follow through energetically.

Similarly, the factor of complexity would imply that some jobs are less complex than others. This may be true, or a lower-level job may be just as complex to its incumbent as a higher-level job may be to its incumbent, which means that the explanation, "Your job is not as complex as this other job," is useless.

Mental concentration is difficult to explain, and the difference between minimum, light, normal, considerable, and close is open to widely varying interpretation. What should be measured instead is the effect when initiative is taken.

When an organization used initiative as a compensable factor, it created additional definitions in what turned out to be a failed attempt to clarify the meaning:

1. Minimum of mental concentration on *largely repetitive operations where routine is closely defined.*
2. Light mental concentration *on largely repetitive operations.*
3. Normal mental concentration *on largely variable operations for short periods of time.*
4. Considerable mental concentration *on variable operations for long periods of time.*
5. Close mental concentration *on highly variable operations for long periods of time.*

So now we have additional confusion over largely repetitive operations versus largely variable operations as opposed to highly variable operations, further complicated by short and long periods of time.

Here are some additional examples to demonstrate the danger areas:

Diversity
1. Limitedly diverse
2. Slightly diverse
3. Moderately diverse
4. Considerably diverse
5. Extensively diverse

Notice the various possible definitions attributable to "limitedly," "slightly," "moderately," "considerably," and "extensively," and the confusion that would result among evaluators.

Contacts
1. With employees within the same department.
2. With employees of different agencies or with the general public.
3. With individuals who have some impact on the programs or policies involved in the work.
4. With persons, officials, or representatives of organizations who could have a significant impact on the programs and policies involved in the work.

The point in valuing contacts is not with whom you talk, it is what you talk about. Service organizations typically give more credit for talking to customers than for talking to employees, without recognizing that very important and difficult interactions occur between employees, whereas very undemanding interactions may occur with customers. A similar mistake gives more credit for "contacts with senior managers," presumably on the basis that you would be dealing only with high-level and tough stuff when you talk to senior managers.

Another erroneous twist is to attempt to define contacts as

1. Simple
2. Routine
3. Responsible
4. Important
5. Complex

These words are open to personal definitions and can be degrading for people in jobs that are important but not complex.

Accuracy
1. Requires normal accuracy
2. Requires careful attention
3. Requires a high degree of accuracy

Should we really attempt gradations in accuracy? Don't we want all employees to be accurate all the time? What should be measured instead is the *consequence of inaccuracy.*

Here the focus is better, but the subjective modifiers still leave a problem:

1. Errors would result in a minor reduction in the quality of service.
2. Errors definitely would reduce the quality of service.
3. Errors would result in a marked reduction in the quality of service.

Physical Exertion
1. Light
2. Moderate
3. Partially heavy

Obviously, what is "partially heavy" exertion to one person may be "moderate" to someone else.

Judgment
1. In the frame of professional knowledge
2. In the frame of great professional knowledge

Great professional judgment? Judgment should be measured as the amount and kind of guidance given to the job incumbent.

Thinking
1. Strictly routine
2. Routine
3. Semiroutine

If "semiroutine" is not clear enough for you, try this as someone's idea of clarification:

> Thinking is guided by somewhat diversified procedures and precedents. The thinking environment has the somewhat less limiting aspects of procedures rather than instructions or the past practice of doing something the company way. Thinking is guided by examples in carrying out proceduralized assignments. Typical examples include various fundamental secretarial functions, applied fundamental accounting, laboratory procedures of moderate complexity, or operating specialized equipment of moderate complexity or difficulty.

A lot of words that only obfuscate the meaning.

Working Conditions
1. Very favorable
2. Generally good—rarely unavoidable exposure to outside conditions
3. Fair—occasionally unavoidable exposure to variable environment
4. Poor—frequent exposure to unpleasant conditions
5. Disagreeable—predominant exposure to disagreeable surroundings

Rarely? Outside? Occasionally? Variable? Frequent? Unpleasant? Predominant? Disagreeable? Nothing is made clear.

Weighting (Valuing) the Factors

Each organization values jobs differently. Mathematical weighting of compensable factors puts organizational values where you want them.

Weighting ensures equitable results when the relative importance of jobs is compared. Not weighting factors means that each factor will have the same relative importance as every other factor, which is never the case. Factors that are not weighted properly will produce a distorted pay structure.

To produce the weighting, each factor is assigned a proportional value—a percentage of the total—of the job evaluation plan. The proportional value is the influence that the factor should have in determining the relative value of the job. For example, if the organization tends to value jobs that are physically very demanding more than jobs that require great interpersonal communication skills, then the factor Environment should be given more weight than the factor Interpersonal Communication.

Do not weight the factors at the beginning of the project or at the beginning of the evaluation sessions. Introduce the *concept* of weighting to the task force because you will receive questions about the relative influence of the factors, but it would be premature to assign values early. You may, for example, change your mind about which factors to use as you proceed through the evaluations. Nothing is final until you reach the end of the project.

More important, you and your task force will develop a better understanding of the meaning of each factor as you work with it during the evaluation sessions, and your valuing will become more accurate. Then, too, attaching points to job concepts in the beginning may distort the job evaluation deliberations. Knowing how many points each degree is worth is not necessary to evaluate jobs. Maintaining objectivity will be tough enough when evaluating jobs without the temptations and distractions of "points." Relying on the degree words alone will provide the best results from your efforts to compare and contrast jobs. Assigning points comes later.

When you weight the factors, start by dividing 100 percent among the factors according to your understanding of the general character of the jobs being evaluated. One way to achieve this is to let each task force member offer his or her opinion of a percentage distribution. You can then calculate the mode and the average of the opinions to find the consensus value for each factor.

Table 1 shows a completed example of the weighting process for a task force of six. As illustrated in Table 2, you can use the *mean* (the arithmetic average of the values) to determine the final weightings, with the *mode* (the most frequent value) as an additional decision aid. (See Phase 6.5 for more information about mean and mode.)

An explanation of the final consensus follows to demonstrate how the final weighting is determined:

K: Although the mode is at 15, the mean is pulling toward 20. If you take away 5 points from the 25 and redistribute them to a 15, you will have four indications that the weight should be 20.

IP: Here the mean and the mode are rather close.

DM: Mean and mode are close.

IC: Mean and mode are close.

IOR: This factor shows the same problem as K.

E: A clear picture.

Table 3 gives random weighting opinions to let you practice resolving different opinions. An answer is given in Table 4. (Practice before looking at Table 4.)

Table 1. Example of weightings of compensable factors by task force members.

Factor	Weighting					
	Jenson	Sara	Randy	Rod	Erik	Robin
Knowledge (K)	20	15	15	25	15	20
Information Processing (IP)	15	15	15	20	20	15
Decison Making (DM)	25	30	25	25	25	30
Interpersonal Communication (IC)	25	25	20	15	20	10
Impact on Organization Results (IOR)	10	10	15	10	15	20
Environment (E)	5	5	10	5	5	5
Total	100	100	100	100	100	100

Table 2. Using the mean and the mode of factor weightings to arrive at final weightings.

Factor	Jenson	Sara	Randy	Rod	Erik	Robin	Mean	Mode	Final
K	20	15	15	25	15	20	18.3	15	20
IP	15	15	15	20	20	15	16.6	15	15
DM	25	30	25	25	25	30	26.6	25	25
IC	25	25	20	15	20	10	19.2	20	20
IOR	10	10	15	10	15	20	13.3	10	15
E	5	5	10	5	5	5	5.8	5	5
								Total	100

Table 3. Random weighting opinions for five factors. Determine mean, mode, and final weighting.

Factor	Weighting Opinions						Mean	Mode	Final
	1	2	3	4	5	6			
A	45	20	30	35	25	25	_____	_____	_____
F	20	45	35	35	45	35	_____	_____	_____
M	15	15	25	20	25	25	_____	_____	_____
Q	5	10	10	5	5	10	_____	_____	_____
W	25	20	15	10	5	20	_____	_____	_____

Table 4. A solution for the hypothetical weightings in Table 3.
(*Note:* These random samples will not add up to 100 percent.)

Factor	Weighting Opinions						Mean	Mode	Final
	1	2	3	4	5	6			
A	45	20	30	35	25	25	30.0	25	30
F	20	45	35	35	45	35	35.8	35	35
M	15	15	25	20	25	25	20.8	25	25
Q	5	10	10	5	5	10	7.5	5/10	?
W	25	20	15	10	5	20	15.8	20	20

Explanation of the final consensus:

A: The mode is not mathematically significant; give credence to the very high vote of 45 and the high vote of 35.
F: Plenty of agreement here.
M: Go with the majority at 25.
Q: Go back to the group for more discussion to determine the final weighting.
W: Given the countervailing split among the opinions, the two votes at 20 point the direction because more opinions are in the 15–25 range than in the 5–10 range.

Gathering Opinions on Factor Weighting

Opinions on weighting for compensable factors can be gathered in a variety of ways and from a variety of people, depending on your circumstances. The job evaluation task force is the most likely group to wrestle with this information. Again, it will do a better job on factor weighting once it has worked with the factors during the evaluation process.

Other people in the organization, however, will also have opinions and may need to be invited into the process. For people outside the job evaluation task force to participate in this decision, you usually need to explain how the information will be used, why it is important, and why opinions are being solicited.

If you intend to use more than one job family plan, plenty of opinions will be required to substantiate the variation of weightings for the same factors among different job groups.

The weight of a compensable factor is the base for calculating points, which in turn are used to assign the final ranking of jobs (see Phase 5.12). Each different opinion about factor weights will produce a different job ranking. Only one ranking is the best expression of the organization's ranks. Later in the project, you can test different weighting options to produce and evaluate different job rankings.

Critics will ask: "How can you be certain that the weighting is correct?" They will challenge you: "That's just your opinion of how much each factor is worth; other people could decide differently." Critics may protest: "Did you allocate the weighting accurately, properly reflecting the relative importance of the job measurements?" They may demand validation of the allocation process.

Yes, it is your opinion, and the opinion of people who have information about the jobs being measured, who may have accountability for the way jobs are designed and performed. Ultimately, the board of directors and the chief executive officer decide what kind of an organization it shall be, what it is designed to accomplish, how it distinguishes itself from other organizations, how it operates, and what it values.

Weighting is an expression of these intentions. Valuing is in the minds and hearts of the participants of the organization, and asking people what they believe to be the values of the organization is the only way to obtain a core understanding of what drives an organization.

Some professionals in the field would argue that the values can be determined statistically (that is, more precisely). They would say that the factor values can be determined by starting with the pay that employees already receive, or with the market value of the job, and calculating backward to measure how much impact each compensable factor had in determining that pay or market value. That is okay if you are willing to accept the pay or market value as the real, accurate, uncontaminated value of the job. But such a judgment is questionable when we reflect on the many varied, unpredictable, uncontrollable, and biased influences that affect pay and market rates.

Validation derives from the logical, systematic, reasonable, and thorough procedures, applied consistently, that you use to obtain and analyze the information to design your pay program. Validation (that is, credibility) comes from the aura of the program, from the quality and conduct of the people who work to build the program.

Calculating Job Evaluation Plan Points

After each compensable factor is weighted, the point value of each degree within each factor must be calculated, according to the following steps:

Step 1. To determine points for the first (lowest) degree, use the same as the weighted value of the compensable factor.

Degree	Points
1	20

Step 2. The points for the highest degree at the opposite end of the scale are determined by multiplying the first-degree points by any multiplier. (A multiplier of 10 is simple to use, and it yields a reasonable range of numbers for future calculations of the pay structure. Be sure to use the same multiplier for each factor. In this example, degree 11 is the highest degree. In the job evaluation plan compensable factors—for example, Knowledge—the highest degree is 18.)

Degree	Points	Calculation
1	20	20 × 10
2		
3		
4		
5		
6		
7		
8		
9		
10		
11	200	

Step 3. To determine the points of the degrees in between the lowest degree and the highest degree, start by subtracting the lowest-degree value from the highest-degree value:

$$200 - 20 = 180$$

Step 4. Calculate the increment between degrees by dividing the difference determined in Step 3 (in this example, 180) by 1 less than the number of degrees in the factor (in this example, $11 - 1 = 10$):

$$180 \div (11 - 1) = 18$$

Step 5. Determine the points of the second degree by adding the increment (in this example, 18) to the first degree. The points of the third degree are determined by adding the increment to the second-degree points, and so forth throughout the remaining degrees. Round off any fraction after all additions have been made. The math will be proved when the last calculation (in this example, from the tenth degree to the eleventh degree) matches the predetermined highest-degree value (in this example, $182 + 18 = 200$). Don't worry when you miss by an insignificant fraction, but recalculate when a gap occurs.

Degree	Points	Calculation
1	20	20 + 18
2	38	38 + 18
3	56	56 + 18
4	74	74 + 18
5	92	92 + 18
6	110	110 + 18
7	128	128 + 18
8	146	146 + 18
9	164	164 + 18
10	182	182 + 18
11	200	

To demonstrate the calculation of degree points, here are the points for the Knowledge factor in the adaptable plan presented earlier. Assume a factor weighting of 25 percent.

KNOWLEDGE

Quick Key	Description	Degree	Points
	Comprehension of the basic requirements of daily living	1	25
Elementary	Reading, writing, arithmetic	2	38
		3	51
		4	65
Vocational	Mechanical, technical, dexterity, or interpersonal skills that can be applied immediately and directly to job requirements without specific experience	5	78
		6	91
	Proficiency or occupational seasoning in mechanical, technical, dexterity, or interpersonal skills, such as through experience in unique organization requirements or specialized training	7	104
		8	118
		9	131
Professional	Knowledge of professional practices including sources of information and commonly accepted standards that can be applied immediately and directly to job requirements without explicit instruction—including the ability to discern when important information is missing	10	144
		11	157
	Knowledge of professional practices including sources of information and commonly accepted standards that must be interpreted before being applied to the unique requirements of the organization	12	171
		13	184
	Understanding of a profession in order to influence its principles and practices	14	197

Interdisciplinary	Understanding of professional practices of more than one knowledge area in order to develop organization strategies typically involving a planning horizon of three to five years	15	210
		16	224
		17	237
	Understanding, integration, and creation of organization strategies involving diverse knowledge areas	18	250

Avoid Mathematical Problems

We have mentioned the problem of too few degrees in a compensable factor. We can now use the point calculation to demonstrate that problem. Education is not an effective factor for reasons discussed in Phase 4, but it provides a simple example to which we can all easily relate to demonstrate the issue of an inequitable number of degrees. If the factor has only five degrees—one for each diploma—then a doctorate would seemingly be worth only five times a high school diploma, as follows:

Degree	Degrees Valued Equally
1	High school
2	Associate of arts
3	Bachelor's
4	Master's
5	Doctorate

Most people, however, would say that the difference looks more like this:

Degree	Degrees Valued Equitably
1	High school
2	Associate of arts
3	
4	Bachelor's
5	
6	
7	Master's
8	
9	
10	
11	Doctorate

The mistake becomes clearer when points are calculated based on the two different numbers of degrees, as follows:

Degree	Degrees Valued Equally	Incorrect Point Calculation	Degrees Valued Equitably	Correct Point Calculation
1	High school	20	High school	20
2	Associate of arts	40	Associate of arts	38
3	Bachelor's	60		56
4	Master's	80	Bachelor's	74
5	Doctorate	100		92
6				110
7			Master's	128
8				146
9				164
10				182
11			Doctorate	200

Here you can see the importance of keeping all of the degrees in the factor even though they may not be used.

Notice the mistaken mathematical approach used to produce the incorrect point calculation. The second-degree points are determined by adding the points of the first degree to itself; the third-degree points are determined by adding the same number of points of the second degree; and so forth. The reason for multiplying the weighted value of the compensable factor (the points of the first degree) by some constant multiplier in the correct calculation is to ensure that the weighting (value) assigned to the compensable factor is carried throughout the calculation. Otherwise, a factor with more degrees than another factor will receive unintended and unfair credit.

Project Analyzer 5.6

Who has opinions about the values/weightings that should be assigned to compensable factors?

_____

_____

_____

Who should be invited to contribute opinions?

_____

_____

_____

What is the best way to capture these opinions?

_____

_____

_____

Can people be brought together to talk out the value of each compensable factor?

_____

_____

_____

_____

Could data be gathered efficiently through paperwork exercises?

_____

_____

_____

_____

5.7 Job Evaluation Information and Documentation

Use the job results statements in the job description as the basis for evaluating the job. Some organizations develop separate documentation records for recording job evaluation information, but we find this is mostly redundant to the information already contained in the job description. Using the job description saves time when collecting information, eliminates double recording, and provides a consistent reference for all decisions regarding the job.

As with job qualifications, occasionally the job results statements do not provide complete information, and other information will need to be added as additional job evaluation documentation to clarify job demands.

The best time to obtain job evaluation information is during the job information-gathering process described in Phase 4. The compensable factors of the job evaluation plan from the outline for collecting the required information. Figure 19 shows the questions used to obtain necessary information for each compensable factor if the information is not already contained in the job description.

More information, not uncovered at this time, may be noted during the task force's actual deliberations as the members clarify job demands and assign degrees. Documentation should be adjusted as a result of job evaluation deliberations. Figure 20 shows a form you can use during task force deliberations to record specific reasons that one degree was selected instead of another.

In Figure 13, we showed three key sections of a job description for a data processing manager—job title, job purpose, and essential job results—plus a section for job qualifications. Now we add a section on job evaluation information. Only information that is not included in the job description needs to be added.

Getting Concrete Job Evaluation Information

Evaluators need solid information in order to make sound judgments. Vague job assessments only confuse the issue.

(Text continues on page 172.)

Figure 19. Questionnaire based on compensable factors to collect job evaluation information.

Job evaluation plan factors:

Knowledge: What does the job incumbent need to know in order to perform the job competently? (Consider formal education, experience, and self-learning.)

_____

_____

_____

Information processing: What mental processes are involved in using job knowledge?

_____

_____

_____

Decision making: How much autonomy does the job incumbent have to decide job issues? What kinds of decisions are made by the incumbent?

_____

_____

_____

Interpersonal communication: What are the purpose and complexity of communication with others?

_____

_____

Impact on organization results: What is the impact on, or risk to, the organization by acting or failing to act? (Think about normal work occurrences rather than the rare exception.)

_____

_____

_____

Environment: What physical demands or exposures are involved in the job?

_____

_____

_____

Figure 19. (*continued*)

Additional factors or issues that might be added:
Time to discover an error: How long does it usually take to determine that an error has been made by the incumbent?

_____

_____

_____

Severity of error: Describe any constant high risks involved in this job.

_____

_____

_____

Confidential and sensitive information: What confidential and sensitive information will the job incumbent have access to?

_____

_____

_____

Authority: Describe the authority invested in the incumbent.

_____

_____

_____

Time span to complete work: How much time is usually required to finish a work project?

_____

_____

_____

Scope of financial responsibility: What responsibilities does the job incumbent have for expenditures, funding, and revenues?

_____

_____

_____

Financial impact or accountability: How much is the incumbent authorized to spend?

_____

_____

_____

Figure 19. (*continued*)

Supervision—number of employees to be supervised: How many employees are supervised (including those supervised indirectly, that is, by subordinate supervisors)?

_____

_____

_____

Supervisory complexity: What is the highest degree of *knowledge* assigned to a subordinate job? (To be completed after job evaluation.)

_____

_____

_____

Project management: Describe the planning, organizing, and control skills used to manage projects.

_____

_____

_____

_____

Figure 20. Job evaluation documentation (completed by the task force recorder).

Job title _____ Date _____

Department _____

Compensable Factor	Degree Assigned	Rationale
Knowledge		
Information Processing		
Decision Making		
Interpersonal Communication		
Impact on Organization Results		
Environment		

Use the evaluation deliberations as an opportunity to clarify job understandings. There should be no competition between the evaluators and the manager who describes and documents the job; there should be collaboration so that everyone understands the job. Send job descriptions back, telephone, or invite the manager to the evaluation meeting when clarification is required.

As a reminder, look back over the differences between clear and unclear job descriptions and qualifications, between duties-oriented and results-oriented styles. "Must be pleasant, courteous, innovative, well organized, and willing to make commonsense decisions" describes an employee who would make a welcome addition to any organization—any employee, in any job. Such general comments do not clarify the value of a particular job. For example, how would you evaluate this executive secretary's job?

1. Coordinates staff itineraries
2. Maintains a filing system
3. Assists in developing and administering the budget
4. Assists in coordinating meetings
5. Coordinates information with other departments

Depending on your interpretation of the vague terms in this duties-oriented description, you could attach almost any value to the job.

Now suppose you had this results-oriented job description plus additional clarifying information:

JOB TITLE: Executive Secretary

1. MAINTAINS PROJECT SCHEDULES
by
coordinating staff itineraries.

2. RETRIEVES INFORMATION
by
maintaining a filing system.

3. MAINTAINS THE BUDGET
by
preparing statistical analyses; verifying and forwarding expense reports; monitoring and reporting variances.

4. CONSERVES STAFF'S TIME
by
identifying optimal meeting times; organizing and publishing meeting agenda; arranging facilities, equipment, and requirements.

5. MAINTAINING DEPARTMENT CALENDAR
by
coordinating project and staff itinerary information with other departments.

ADDITIONAL JOB EVALUATION INFORMATION

Knowledge: Must know the detailed operational procedures of the department in order to be effective.

Information Processing: Covered adequately in the job description.

Decision Making: Makes independent judgments regarding administrative schedule based on department policy.

Interpersonal Communication: Interpersonal contacts require the utmost diplomacy.

Impact on Organization Results: An executive will rely on the secretary's organizational ability for the administrative management of the department and budget and should not need to establish priorities. Reports and information will be relied on as thorough and accurate. Access to organizationally sensitive department information.

Environment: No significant impact.

Valuing jobs is easier and more accurate when you have all the information, clearly described, on which to base your judgments. Figure 21 shows one more example of the job description and additional job evaluation information.

Figure 21. Job description and additional job evaluation information.

JOB RESULTS MANAGEMENT PROFILE

JOB TITLE: **DATA PROCESSING MANAGER**

JOB PURPOSE: **PROVIDES INFORMATION SYSTEMS AND SERVICES**
by
defining and solving user requirements; developing computer
applications.

ESSENTIAL JOB RESULTS:

% of
time

_____   **1. MAINTAINS STAFF**
by
recruiting, selecting, orienting, and training employees; maintaining a safe
and secure work environment; developing personal growth opportunities.

_____   **2. ACCOMPLISHES STAFF RESULTS**
by
communicating job expectations; planning, monitoring, and appraising
job results; coaching, counseling, and disciplining employees; initiating,
coordinating, and enforcing systems, policies, and procedures.

_____   **3. DEFINES MANAGEMENT AND EMPLOYEE INFORMATION
REQUIREMENTS**
by
conferring with users; studying user functions.

_____   **4. SOLVES USER INFORMATION REQUIREMENTS**
by
developing information procedures; recommending computer system
hardware and applications.

_____   **5. PREPARES PROGRAMS**
by
writing, testing, modifying, and documenting programming language.

_____   **6. PREPARES USERS TO USE MAINFRAME AND PERSONAL COMPUTER
SYSTEMS**
by
conducting training sessions; providing individual coaching.

_____   **7. PROVIDES SYSTEM RESOURCES**
by
documenting procedures; maintaining a library of user manuals;
answering questions.

Figure 21. (*continued*)

_____ 8. **SECURES INFORMATION AND PROGRAMS**
by
establishing backup policies, procedures, and programs.

_____ 9. **IMPROVES PROGRAM AND SERVICE QUALITY**
by
devising new applications; updating procedures; evaluating system results with users.

_____ 10. **PRODUCES ROUTINE AND SPECIAL REPORTS**
by
scheduling operations; assigning employees.

_____ 11. **ACHIEVES FINANCIAL OBJECTIVES**
by
anticipating requirements; submitting information for budget preparation; scheduling expenditures; monitoring costs; analyzing variances.

_____ 12. **MAINTAINS PROFESSIONAL AND TECHNICAL KNOWLEDGE**
by
attending educational workshops; benchmarking professional standards; reviewing professional publications; establishing personal networks.

_____ 13. **KEEPS MANAGEMENT INFORMED OF TECHNOLOGICAL TRENDS**
by
collecting, analyzing, and summarizing state-of-the-art information.

_____ 14. **MAINTAINS CONTINUITY AMONG CORPORATE, AREA, AND COMMUNITY WORK TEAMS**
by
documenting and communicating actions, irregularities, and continuing needs.

_____ 15. **CONTRIBUTES TO TEAM EFFORT**
by
welcoming new and different work requirements; exploring new opportunities to add value to the organization; helping others accomplish related job results as and where needed.

Job Qualifications

Job knowledge absolutely required before entering the job:

B.S. in data processing. Data processing systems, programming, and operations. AS/400 and PC experience. Managing people and projects.

Figure 21. (*continued*)

Additional Job Evaluation Information

Knowledge: Already stated in job description and job qualifications.

Information Processing: Analyzes software applicability, but information services committee evaluates enterprise system integration.

Decision Making: Already stated on job description.

Interpersonal Communication: Information services committee establishes information objectives.

Impact on Organization Results: Computer service company on standby at all times.

Environment: Occasional travel to all locations within region.

Project Analyzer 5.7

What job evaluation documentation is recorded now?

_____

_____

Do managers understand the need to substantiate job evaluation decisions?

_____

_____

Have job evaluators complained that they do not have enough information to make informed decisions?

_____

_____

5.8 Who Will Do the Evaluating?

The integrity and saleability of your pay program rests substantially in the hands of the person(s) evaluating the jobs.

It is management's responsibility to define the values of jobs; management can share this responsibility with other employees if it chooses. If management retains its authority, it manages by decree, which is certainly appropriate.

In this era, however, it is in vogue to invite employees in the ranks to participate in the deliberations that assign values to jobs. This, too, is appropriate on the theory that the people who perform the jobs know more about them than the people who supervise them. Experience tends to support this notion.

Leave It to the Professionals?

The starting point in this decision is whether the organization's professionals in job analysis and pay management should do the evaluating. Evidence clearly points away from the professionals to collective wisdom. The word of the human resources professional regarding the management of people is not accepted without question. Everybody is an "expert" in the affairs of other people.

Whoever decides which jobs are more valued by the organization owns the decision, and anything that goes wrong with the decision will be blamed on the person who made the decision. The process of evaluating jobs can be viewed as a social decision-making procedure. The extent to which those affected by the decision are allowed to participate in the process through the exercise of control and voice is a measure of procedural justice. Since human resources professionals are frequently the "lawyers" and "police," pointing out what can and cannot be done or taking violators to task, there is a general feeling that whatever HR people decree should be challenged (sometimes just for the sake of the challenge). Some managers and employees believe that the HR department does not really know what is going on in the jobs of the organization. On the other hand, where the HR staff has been integrated into the organization and has earned the respect of managers and employees, it is not impossible for the HR staff to evaluate the jobs. Any HR department that has earned such respect will naturally involve managers and employees from other functions in the process.

The important issue at stake is acceptance of the project. The organizing tactic ought to minimize the opportunity for people to poke holes in the results. If HR professionals are susceptible to accusation because they do not live with the job, why give the opposition an opportunity to blow a hole in the structure? In a positive vein, why not let the people who will be most affected by the decision participate in the decision?

Sometimes the place of the professional is to advise, not to do. There is plenty of work for the professional: to understand the intricacies of the job evaluation plan, to know how to train others to do the work, even to manage the process. For example, if a task force is formed, the HR professional might be the chairperson rather than a voting member of it, remaining objective and above the subjective deliberation, using an understanding of group dynamics to manage the process, keeping the group focused on the proper goal, resolving conflicts, maintaining efficiency, and pointing the group one way or the other.

Should one person or many people value the jobs? The essence of job evaluation is to resolve legitimate but varied views of the same job. Clearly, no one person is capable of such unbiased and unprejudiced opinion. You need only to sit through a few hours of job evaluation discussion and deliberation, and sometimes argument, to realize that letting one person evaluate jobs is foolhardy.

A Task Force of Knowledgeable People

A task force of knowledgeable people, mostly management but including others, seems like a workable model.

Let senior management reserve final judgment.

Let the HR professional provide expert knowledge, thoughtful and efficient staff work, and guidance.

But, anything goes. The theme so often overlooked is that the situation dictates the strategy. While some strategies are weak and even prone to error, almost any will work if the people involved agree that it will. The style in your organization suggests the most appropriate method. At the same time, maybe this is the moment to change the style and produce a more fruitful return.

Top management may decide that it knows best or that this is not the time to begin a participatory style of management. Top management may assign the task to department managers who may meet as a task force. Or they may evaluate their jobs individually and send the ranking to you to incorporate them in an organization-wide scheme. Maybe first-line supervisors will get the nod. "We are too busy with other projects" may mean that the HR department will do the work and bring it to a select management task force for approval. In an egalitarian atmosphere, employees might choose some people from their own ranks to be the council that recommends a ranking to management. Anything goes if you are willing to trust and work at it.

Still, the most popular process is a task force of knowledgeable people. Add respectable and reasonable, and start looking for those qualities first.

At the opening of this section, we stated that the integrity and saleability of your pay program rests substantially in the hands of the people who evaluate the jobs. We can now expand on this by emphasizing that the people chosen must be *respectable*. The names of these people must evoke confidence among the populace if you want to start on the right foot as you walk into the meeting room to begin your work.

Pick Your Favorites

Stack the task force with the people who are already your best organization contributors, your loyal and willing participants, folks who know themselves and others and can put personal prejudices aside to focus on the purpose, reasonable people who are able to look at both sides of an issue and talk about differences. Try to get one person who nitpicks a little, to keep the group from skimming over important and sometimes hidden facts, and one slightly brash type, to prevent bogging down in minutiae.

Remember that someone, perhaps you, will be the nonvoting chairperson to help task force members focus on their mission, to encourage quiet members to comment, to move the conversation politely away from a monopolizer. The chair is an important responsibility because the decorum will dictate whether the project will be taken seriously.

As much as you want congenial characters, nice people who do not know what they are talking about will be a disaster. To rely only on personal affability in your selection would put you in a precarious position to explain to someone why he or she was not selected to participate.

You need a task force that collectively knows most of the jobs very well. You should therefore invite members who represent the major areas of your organization. Look for people who have moved around and can speak about a variety of jobs. Invite people from different levels of the organization—officers, managers, supervisors, professionals, technicians, clerical personnel, operators—to get a thoughtful balance of perspectives.

Members should have some tenure in the organization rather than be brand-new so that they have a real sense of the way things are. Don't forget retirees, who can bring invaluable knowledge to the process (and have the time).

Once you have identified your people, invite them as soon as you can. Let them plan for the time they will need to devote to the cause. Tell them up front what is involved, that the meetings will mean hard work and possibly long hours. Tell them approximately how much time must be invested and what kind of arrangements you will make. (See Figure 22 for a sample invitation.)

Figure 22. Sample invitation to join task force.

To:

From:

Date:

Subject: Job Evaluation Task Force

Congratulations!

I am pleased to invite you to participate in a program designed to understand better and compensate all of (organization's) jobs. Specifically, I am inviting you to join a task force to study each job and to help management examine the demands of each job in the overall organization.

To be clear about what will be expected from the task force, you are not being asked to evaluate the job contributions of anyone, and you are not being asked to determine pay rates for either jobs or people. You are being asked to develop information about the value of the contributions of jobs that will be used to structure our pay program.

You will receive training to participate on this task force so that you feel comfortable with the process. You will use our results-oriented job descriptions and supporting information to examine the jobs. You will work with fellow task force members as a group to arrive at a consensus. Time will be scheduled for the task force to work together.

In order for you to schedule your time, an introductory meeting will be held on (date), from (time) to (time). Training for the job evaluation process will be on (date), from (time) to (time). The actual task force discussions will begin on (date), from (time) to (time).

If you have any questions about the process or time requirements, please contact me at (telephone extension) or (e-mail address).

I hope that you will agree to participate in this very worthwhile project. You will have a rare opportunity to make important recommendations toward the development of our compensation program and to work with others in a productive process that you will find rewarding.

Do give us the benefit of your contribution.

You will never have all the knowledge you want on the task force, or else you would fill an auditorium. There are two questions here: How many members do you need, and, What do you do when you run out of knowledge?

How Many People?

Group dynamics experience suggests that seven to nine people, not counting the chairperson, make a workable group. Too few is too cozy and not enough of a database, whereas too many can fragment the conversation or even make it unruly. Again, the situation will dictate. Keep in mind that these people will be your prophets to spread the word that the project is serious business.

Even a group twice as big will find itself lacking information about some jobs. Do not hesitate to call the supervisor of the job or the job incumbent on the telephone or into the meeting to provide the information. For one reason, you'll obtain the correct information; for another reason, the message will get out that the task force really wants to do a good job.

As an option, you could invite the supervisor of the jobs being evaluated, or the job incumbent, to sit in on the deliberations in order to provide immediate commentary when it is needed. People called upon for information may (or may not) sit in for the actual voting, but they should not vote, since they do not know how the job evaluation plan was applied to jobs already evaluated. The more open you are, the less you can be accused of trying to hide something.

Project Analyzer 5.8

If jobs have been formally evaluated in the past, how was the work received by the organization?

_____

_____

Was it successful?

_____

_____

Why?

_____

_____

Who was involved?

_____

_____

Was the project a failure laden with suspicion?

_____

_____

What went wrong?

_____

_____

How should you proceed now?

_____

_____

Which functional areas in your organization should be represented on a job evaluation task force?

_____

_____

Who knows most about the jobs in each functional area?

_____

_____

How many people will you choose to invite?

_____

_____

Who can meet the "congeniality" requirements?

_____

_____

Who cannot?

_____

_____

What can be done to minimize interference within the selection process?

_____

_____

Who might resent not being chosen?

_____

_____

What can be done to ameliorate feelings?

_____

_____

Who else should be involved in selecting the task force?

_____

_____

What is the authority of the task force: to recommend or to decide?

_____

_____

Will there be a review group of senior management who will approve the task force's work?

_____

_____

If so, who will be the reviewers?

_____

_____

What is the role of the human resources staff?

_____

_____

When will the task force meet?

_____

_____

When should task force members be notified of their involvement?

_____

_____

5.9 Arranging and Managing Meetings

So you have decided to make the design and development of your pay program a collaborative experience with your employees. Practical (pessimistic?) people will remind you of the old saw that a camel is what someone got when he asked a group to design a horse. A lot of truth there.

A task force is a group of persons elected or appointed to perform some service or function, such as to investigate, report on, or act upon a particular matter. So says the lexicographer who never had to deal with one.

Take Charge

A task force can be a real pain, or more precisely, the chairperson can be when he or she fails to manage the experience efficiently. The first trick is to take control and establish your authority. You are in charge; you are not one of the voting members. Your job is to plan, organize, lead, and control—that is, manage. You have a mission, and people through whom you will work to accomplish your mission.

Plan the entire pay project before the first task force meeting; read through this book, and chart a rough course of what you want to accomplish. You will make specific navigational changes once you are underway, but your destination port and the major stops along the way will probably not change. Knowing where *you* want to be at the end of the project gives you a substantial advantage and leverage when working with your task force. You will also want to gain some commitments from the powers that be in advance of your first meeting.

Organize your materials and time so that work is accomplished efficiently. You must be a little compulsive in order to make this project succeed. Chart the course of events to the conclusion of the project so that you know what will occur when, and how much time is involved. Integrate your plan into the timetable of other events in the organization. Avoid conflicts before they occur. Show your chart to everyone who will be involved in the project. Gain commitment now.

Schedule meetings well in advance so that everybody has enough time to make arrangements. Stick to the schedule unless there are disasters. Do everything right the first time you meet so that task force members know that you mean business. Agendas might be helpful, though many of your meetings will have only one item.

Look good. Be ready before the meeting. Have the room set up neatly, with materials assembled and distributed to each place. Start on time if everyone is present; in any case, for the benefit of busy people who are on time, start no more than two minutes late. Late people should not be ignored but should not be catered to.

You are skeptical, we're sure. You have worked with groups before, and no matter how much you prepare, it seems, the discussions are a disaster because everybody wants to make his or her point, perhaps even look good. What is the difference between a successful and unsuccessful task force? The answer is: task force members.

You may get stuck with certain people who are there because of their position and not because of their team membership abilities. All is not lost. Good management techniques regarding materials and process will make an important difference.

Ask task force members for their commitment to the project. Tell them what is expected, give them an opportunity to understand the time and energy demands, and ask them to commit themselves, or not. Send them a "commitment agreement" giving the goals and objectives of the program, the dates of evaluation meetings, procedures, a timetable, a deadline, a list of resources, and the dates of follow-up meetings.

Lead your people to success. Important as it is for you to plan, organize, and control the paperwork of your project carefully, success is won in the encounter with people. Most commonly, pay programs fail because of the arrogant tactic of managing the system as if the people involved were pawns. Because pay is a personal issue, personal opinions will be expressed—sometimes loudly, sometimes quietly—in all their diversity.

Leadership is not the art of giving everybody what he or she wants, but the ability to coalesce differing needs. Management and leadership work in tandem: careful planning, organizing, and controlling coupled with thoughtful personal attention. As you interact with others on the project, do your homework so that you have confidence in your position, but don't get locked into it. Use your knowledge as a benchmark and to help others reach a conclusion. Do not set out to "beat" the others.

Mostly, you will listen to other opinions and guide your task force to a consensus. The important skills here are to manage the conversation, keep the discussion on course, keep track of the relevant points, ensure thorough consideration of each issue, prevent people from monopolizing the argument, and elicit opinions from quiet members.

You also need to decide how to present the various issues to the task force. You have a variety of tactics available, and chances are that you will use all of them throughout the course of deliberations. You can:

- Decide what will be done and announce your decision.
- Decide what will be done and give an explanation in order to persuade.
- Develop what will be done, and ask for task force members' reactions, but be ready to use authority to install the decision.
- Develop a course of action, ask for members' reactions, and be ready to accept other options.
- Identify a problem and ask members to identify options, but you select the best option.
- Identify a problem and invite members to join in finding a solution.
- Identify and solve problems with your members.
- Identify a problem, specify limits for possible solutions, and trust members to solve the problem by themselves.

Control the progress of the project. You determined what you intend to accomplish and set your timetable when you planned and organized the project. If all goes well (which it never does), you will complete your project just as you planned. In the real world, however, you will have to adjust your schedule according to new demands. You can do that intelligently only from an existing plan. Otherwise, your reaction will be helter-skelter. Your task force will respect your desire and action to keep the project on course and will be motivated to participate in a worthwhile effort.

You have the opportunity to provide one of the most productive pieces of work that your organization has witnessed in a long time. With concentrated effort, your task force will set the structure of jobs for your organization.

Ensure Physical Comfort

Make the experience physically comfortable but work-oriented. A conference table, plenty of space to spread out materials, room to walk around, comfortable chairs, writing materials, refreshments, casual attire: all can contribute to the effectiveness of the task force work.

Meeting at Home or Away?

When groups meet "in the conference room," they are more readily subject to distraction than if they meet away. Even with ground rules that interruptions should be made only for emergencies—and such a ground rule should be made in any event—the proximity invites the "It will only take a second" interruption. Committee members themselves are tempted to "Check in just to see what's going on." Even brief breaks may subject task force members to hallway conferences. All of this means time wasted or attention diverted.

When groups move to the local hotel—or, with luck, to a mind-freeing retreat lodge—the message is clear that you mean business. Let them call the office once a day if they really have to, but the focus is work, work, work on the project at hand.

Work, work, work can also be accomplished back at the office, and fun and games can occur away; your good management will make the most out of the meeting wherever it is held. Management starts with planning, following the guides found in the first phase.

When groups go away to a hotel or resort, they get a bit of a "vacation" and can take advantage of the physical amenities to relax and enjoy themselves. Do not overlook the advantage that the group will spend more time together and will be able to foster an even stronger camaraderie.

How Much Time Is Required?

Once your task force members have been selected, notify them well in advance of the first meeting to allow them to arrange their calendar. How much time will they have to devote? Obviously, a number of factors will influence this decision, the first being your timetable to complete the entire project.

The best bet is to go away and do all the jobs at once. That way, the task force can internalize the job evaluation scheme with maximum concentration. If the task force were to meet once a week, the members would have to "relearn" again and again the meaning given to the factors and degrees. Can't go away and do all the jobs at once? It's not a prohibition to your success; it just means a little extra time will be required to get it right.

Some groups work at the effort for two days a week; others work about six hours a day, at the office, allowing members to check into their departments at the beginning of the day; others go to the mountaintop for a long weekend; others rent a room nearby, start a little later to give everyone a chance to stop by the office, but then work until 7 P.M. or 8 P.M. and end each day with a nice dinner.

Rules of thumb are always misleading, and so the question of how many jobs can be done in a day detracts from the concern that the jobs be evaluated properly and carefully. Some groups work fast, some with more deliberation; the nature and complexity of the jobs being evaluated, as well as the clarity of the job descriptions, dictate the speed of the process.

The number of minutes per job is misleading, as tougher and easier jobs will balance the time used. The first day is the slowest, because committee members must orient themselves to everything—process, plan, people, and place. Fifteen jobs on the first day is just fine, but you might do thirty. Production on the second day should double and might even triple. On the third day, production will not be too much higher than on the second day, and it won't increase after that.

One group did only seven jobs the first day, from 8:30 A.M. to 4 P.M., with one hour off for lunch as scheduled (quitting time was announced as 3:30 P.M., but the group decided to continue, because the members wanted to finish one group of jobs). On the second day, they did twenty-three jobs, reducing their lunch time, by consensus, to one-half hour and again quitting close to 4 P.M. Although this group was a little more deliberate than others, its members were certainly sincere and were able to feel very confident about their work. This comfort with the decisions will pay off when the program needs to be interpreted to other managers and employees.

Other groups might do eighteen or twenty jobs the first day and not degrade the process, though this number approaches an upper limit and warns that the jobs might not be studied thoroughly and thoughtfully. On the other extreme, to do only four or five jobs the first day may suggest examination to the point of exhaustion. Take your cues from task force members; if some people are trying to get a word into the discussions but the majority is being induced to move along, intercede and get other opinions on the table. Where conversation continues endlessly into minutiae, call for a vote as to which degree applies.

Be Organized

Have a workable portion of the job descriptions distributed around the table at the start to minimize paper shuffling. A copy of the job evaluation plan, including the rules for evaluating jobs, should be at each person's place. An informal scoring sheet for each committee member (see Figure 23) allows each person to remember earlier and related degree assignments and reduce the "What degree did we give so-and-so?" questions.

Get extra clerical help if you can: a job analyst, personnel assistant, or secretary to move papers, document reasoning, record decisions, get refreshments, check on other arrangements, and so on—anything to facilitate the concentration of the task force members.

Rewards

Good job evaluation is exhausting intellectually, psychologically, emotionally, and physically. Having accomplished an important task for the organization has its intrinsic rewards, which may be completely satisfactory. But you may want to consider something more tangible, such as a dinner at the conclusion of the task or a thoughtful letter from the CEO.

Figure 23. Task force member scoring sheet.

Job Title	Factors					
	K	IP	DM	IC	IOR	E
Notes:						

K = Knowledge
IP = Information Processing
DM = Decision Making

IC = Interpersonal Communication
IOR = Impact on Organization Results
E = Environment

Note: See Phase 5.7 for details on compensable factors.

Project Analyzer 5.9

Is a task force the best project method for your organization?

_____

_____

What successes has your organization had with task forces?

_____

_____

How can you build on these strengths?

_____

_____

What failures has your organization had with task forces?

_____

_____

How can you avoid these weaknesses?

_____

_____

Are you prepared to be in charge?

_____

_____

If not, who can give you some advice?

_____

_____

Or is there someone else who should be in charge?

_____

_____

Is there agreement that the task force should be formed?

_____

_____

Is the authority of the task force clear?

_____

_____

Whom would you like to have on your task force?

_____

_____

Are they the best you can find?

_____

_____

Is there a good balance of personalities—one driver, one thinker, one humorist?

_____

_____

Are these people available to work with you?

_____

_____

Do they want to?

_____

_____

Do they represent the organization fairly in terms of the different functions of the organization, different levels of jobs, and different EEO categories?

_____

_____

_____

Is this a good time to form a task force and begin working on the project?

_____

_____

What do you want the task force to accomplish?

_____

_____

What tasks in the project will it be working on?

_____

_____

What tasks won't it work on?

_____

_____

When do you want the task force to meet?

_____

_____

What day is best?

_____

_____

What time is best?

_____

_____

How long are the members willing to let the meetings last?

_____

_____

_____

Should you meet on premises or off?

_____

_____

What facilities are available?

_____

_____

Where will concentration be easiest?

_____

_____

How many jobs will be evaluated?

_____

_____

How much time needs to be set aside?

_____

_____

Who will help with the meeting arrangements?

_____

_____

_____

What do you need in terms of materials, supplies, rooms, and refreshments?

_____

_____

Should you be answering all these questions, or should you be discussing them with your task force?

_____

_____

Are all the job descriptions completed?

_____

_____

. . . and assembled?

_____

_____

Are the job evaluation plans printed?

_____

_____

In what sequence will the jobs be evaluated?

_____

_____

Which jobs should be chosen as benchmarks? (Remember to select jobs with anticipated high, medium, and low relative value, and to include jobs from nearly all departments.)

_____

_____

_____

_____

_____

_____

_____

_____

_____

_____

_____

5.10 Training Evaluators

Evaluating jobs is the best way to learn job evaluation. Talking about the process is confusing, and role playing fails to convey the proper sense of responsibility. Give evaluators some orientation, but don't be long-winded.

Start by explaining the important role each task force member is going to fulfill in the overall scheme of the pay project (see Figure 24). Be honest. Let them know that

Figure 24. Job evaluation task force objectives.

- The purpose of job evaluation task force deliberations is to produce a ranking of all organization jobs. It is built on a group consensus, using a job evaluation plan that you will adapt for our organization.
- Job evaluation identifies the internal worth of each job to the operation of our organization.
- The job ranking forms one of the major building blocks of a pay structure. The other building blocks are market value and organization policy.
- Job evaluation is not the same as pay rates.
- You were chosen for your knowledge of jobs and, more important, for your ability to deliberate the issues fairly and consistently for all jobs within the organization. Don't "fight" for your department.
- After you consider all jobs individually, you will assess the ranking of all jobs together.

the process will be tedious, but that it will also be rewarding. You can make a safe bet that few other task force members will have produced as much in as short a time or made as substantial a contribution. You can tell the task force members with confidence that they will know a great deal more about their organization at the conclusion of their effort than they know at the start. They will walk away from their task feeling tired but good.

Explain why the job evaluation is necessary and how the results fit into the total program. The goal is pay. Pay is the product of the value of the job and how well the job is performed. How well the job is performed is not the province of the job evaluation; it's the domain of the manager. The value of the job is what the work of the task force is all about.

Help the task force understand that the product of job evaluation is a ranking of jobs, from the job that makes the greatest contribution to the organization to the job that demands the least of an incumbent. The product is typically expressed in points to facilitate the comparison of value.

Explain that jobs are examined in terms of compensable factors—values that the organization considers important when measuring the demands placed on individuals. (We will study compensable factors in more detail later.) Factors are considered one at a time, and a decision is made regarding the relative value of the job within each factor; in job evaluation jargon, a *degree of the factor* is assigned (degree 1 is always low). After all factors have been considered, the decisions for all factors are totaled. Each degree in each factor is assigned a certain number of points; thus, the total is derived by adding all the points (assuming that you use a point plan).

Tell the task force that its job is to determine the value of each job in the structure of the organization. Each task force member is selected for his or her knowledge of jobs, since no one person can know all jobs intimately. When the task force needs more information about a particular job, someone will be summoned to provide clarification.

Which Job to Evaluate First

It is helpful to use a model, or sampling, of the organization to test a job evaluation plan before building the pay structure, especially where a substantial number of jobs —say, 400 or more—are involved. A good guide is to choose 20 percent of the jobs as benchmarks, or as many as you can find.

Benchmark jobs are references against which other jobs can be compared. They are usually well known, clearly describable, and easily understood, thus making their evaluation easier and more reliable. As references, benchmark jobs facilitate evaluating less known and less understood jobs.

Some of the jobs selected as benchmarks must be unique to your type of organization so that appropriate pay surveys can be conducted with similar organizations. An example would be the job of nurse in a hospital. Other jobs, such as secretary or bookkeeper, will be selected because they can be compared with those in other organizations in your local labor market. More on this in Phase 6.

Benchmark jobs must represent the different levels and kinds of jobs in the organization. Anticipating the relative value of the jobs selected (use your gut computer) ensures that a few will be on the high end of the hierarchy, a few on the low end, and a few in the middle. Be sure to include jobs from nearly all departments.

Usually, the task force starts by evaluating some benchmark jobs in order to get a feel for the entire plan and how all the factors and degrees are applied. When job family plans, that is, job evaluation plans specifically designed for a job family and different from other plans for other job families, are used, starting with benchmark jobs will not be as useful because of the homogeneity of jobs and the relatively small range of degrees. Still, the first jobs selected should include one you expect to come out low and another you expect to come out high, so the task force can start working with the low and high degrees in order to appreciate their relative impact on the others.

After the introductory jobs have been evaluated, select a department and work through all the jobs in that area; task force members can immerse themselves in similar tasks, jargon, and relationships without having to disrupt their concentration by major changes in job content.

Make Adjustments Along the Way

Make adjustments in the language of the job evaluation plan as you discover words that need to be changed, added, or deleted. Make changes directly on the written plan, and if convenient, have the changes processed at the end of the day and corrected versions printed for use the next day.

Because the plan must be fine-tuned throughout the evaluating process, you and the task force must remind yourselves that the evaluations are tentative until you complete the process and say that the evaluations are final. You will probably change the plan here and there to accommodate your unique situation. You will need to review earlier decisions. All that is acceptable.

You may want to examine the consistency of degree application (jobs listed by factor and ordered by degree within each factor in order to assess that similar jobs are receiving the same degree in a factor) at the beginning of each day rather than at the conclusion of the exercise. In this way, misassignments can be mended as you proceed. See the section entitled "The Final Ranking" later in this phase for more details.

Project Analyzer 5.10

When should job evaluation orientation occur?

_____

_____

Is the orientation scheduled far enough in advance so that everyone has an opportunity to schedule it?

_____

_____

Who will conduct the orientation?

_____

_____

Are the objectives for the job evaluation task force written, clear, and understood by task force members?

_____

_____

Are the rules for evaluating jobs prepared?

_____

_____

How will the job evaluation plan be tested?

_____

_____

Which jobs will be tested?

_____

_____

_____

5.11 Rules for Evaluating Jobs

Although each organization has unique requirements, a few rules are universal when evaluating jobs. They are summarized in Figure 25.

1. *Base your judgments on actual job requirements.* Each task force member knows some jobs very well and others only in passing or hardly at all. People may "think" they know job requirements. Stick to the job requirements as stated in the job description. When a question arises, obtain clarification. Perhaps another task force member has the answer. If not, telephone supervisors or job incumbents or invite them to the meeting. The message will go out that the task force wants to rely on accurate information.

Occasionally someone will say, "This job is going to change." Unless the task force has clear documentation of anticipated changes, evaluate only what is known for sure.

Sometimes a task force will be given more responsibility to make changes—for example, where reengineering might be included. The task force will be studying jobs closely and will be able to make recommendations for changes in job design or organization structure. For example, when the group evaluates a certain job result and then finds the same responsibility in another job, it may be appropriate to take advantage of that observation and bring the redundancy to someone's attention. Or the task force might recommend changes in working conditions, such as moving a loud paper cutter

Figure 25. Rules for evaluating jobs.

1. Base your judgments on actual job requirements.
2. Evaluate the job, not the person.
3. Consider the job contribution of a competent employee.
4. Consider what happens in the job 95 percent of the time; do not consider what might occur rarely (5 percent of the time).
5. In each factor, select the degree that most closely describes the job; each degree includes the values of all lower degrees.
6. Consider the worth of the job within the organization; do not consider the current or anticipated market rates of the job.
7. Measure the worth of the job according to each separate factor; do not try to make the job "come out" where you think it ought to.
8. Achieve a consistent consensus.
9. Communicate effectively.

that makes talking to customers difficult instead of giving the job a higher degree for environmental conditions.

2. *Evaluate the job, not the person.* Task force members will know some job incumbents. In small organizations, everybody knows everybody. It is only human that a judgment about the job will be influenced by the results the incumbent produces, be they superior or poor. To assign a higher or lower value to the job based on the personal contribution of the incumbent would distort the normal and fair relationships among jobs.

3. *Consider the job contribution of a competent employee.* Job contributions may be thought of as entry level—that is, what a new employee is able to accomplish—or superior contributions—what a seasoned employee is able to accomplish. To establish parity, jobs must be evaluated according to relatively equal demands. The goal of a base pay program is to pay employees to accomplish basic job results in a way that accomplishes organization objectives according to basic requirements.

Think about what it takes to accomplish job results, without being deflected by the way some jobs have developed over time as people with different talents and aspirations have accomplished them.

4. *Consider what happens in the job 95 percent of the time; do not consider what might occur rarely (5 percent of the time).* If the task force evaluates the extraordinary occurrences or conceives of the worst thing that could go wrong in a job, all jobs will be inflated or valued at the top of the scale. "But what if the boiler blows up?" and "Do you know what would happen if the whole system were purged accidentally?" are valid concerns but unrealistic expectations where safety devices and backups are employed. The job will get its fair due if it is viewed in the light of normal conditions.

5. *In each factor, select the degree that most closely describes the job; each degree includes the values of all lower degrees.* The meaning of each degree of a compensable factor will not be fully understood until the task force settles the subtle differences in interpretation of each word. Then, the words in the degree that most accurately identify the job are chosen. Words can be changed as required; the plan should be adapted to the language of the organization to convey as clear a meaning as possible. In one organization, the

word "explain" will be most meaningful and accurate; in another, "interpret" will be preferable; in a third, "counsel" will work better; and in a fourth, "advise" will convey the right meaning. Still another organization might use any of these words interchangeably. Be flexible, and be accurate.

The degrees should be designed to be as distinct as possible so there is plenty of "space" between them. If they are too close in definition, a decision could go toward either one degree or another. The greater and clearer the gap is between degrees, the easier the judgment is as to which degree is appropriate.

Even though the degrees may be distinct, jobs do not break neatly into the same slices as degrees on the value continuum, which may tempt the committee to assign a value between degrees. This spells disaster.

Given that one degree may be worth 20 points and the next higher degree worth 30 points, why not give a job 25 points when it seems not to be described exactly by either of the degrees but seems to fall somewhere in between? The reason is that if you can give one job 25 points when it falls halfway between the degrees, then you should be able to assign another job 27.5 points when it seems to be closer to the one degree than to the other, and you should be able to assign 29 points because the job almost, but not quite, matches the higher degree. The options are as many as we can count with numbers.

However, jobs cannot be described so precisely that human beings can agree with a narrow assignment. Since there are no words between the degrees, and since each task force member has a personal interpretation of the meaning of differences, some imprecision is inherent in the ratings.

What if there are no degrees to describe the situation? Write them or make an exception. Edit the degrees to fit the unique situation of the organization, or make an exception to the plan to give credit when credit is entirely deserved.

For example, in one retail organization that sells diamonds along with other merchandise, only three people have the combination to the safe containing millions of dollars' worth of inventory: the diamond buyer, the assistant diamond buyer, and an inventory clerk in the diamond department. The job evaluation plan for the clerical position in no place gives credit for the trust placed in this job. When evaluating the job, the task force could adjust the plan permanently, which would be awkward, or it could make an exception: the job is simply given more points by the task force. (With this action, the task force also makes the point that the plan and the system are not inflexible.)

Do not let the task force get carried away with bonus points, however. The preceding example was the only exception in the company, and in many organizations, there are no exceptions at all.

6. *Consider the worth of the job within the organization; do not consider the current or anticipated market rate of the job.* Job evaluation is the measure of internal equity, the value of a job relative to other jobs in one organization, with the job uniquely defined by that organization. The value of a job in the marketplace is a product of other influences, influences not in control of the organization. "How are we ever going to attract people into this job if it is rated too low?" is a realistic concern, but it's a pay management problem, which will be addressed once the pay structure is constructed.

7. *Measure the worth of the job according to each separate factor; do not try to make the job "come out" where you think it ought to.* Compensable factors state the reasons some jobs should be valued more than others in the organization. It is mentally simpler to break this value analysis into its components than to compare one whole job to another.

"If we give this job a higher degree in this factor, we can give it a lower degree in another factor" may sound equitable, but it is unnecessary. The factors must stand alone.

At times, the task force will raise the question of whether a job should take into account a particular demand under this factor or that. The task force will change previous decisions in order to give credit where credit is due, or take away credit where it had been placed erroneously. Such deliberations are the essence of evaluating jobs. So long as they do not turn into trading this degree in a job in my area for that degree in a job in your area, they are perfectly in order.

Explain that the factors are not equally important to the final outcome; each factor may be weighted differently to recognize the true job values of the organization. You may invite the task force to help assign the weightings after it has worked with the plan.

8. *Achieve a consistent consensus.* If all the job description and job evaluation words were perfectly clear, there would be no disagreement on the assignment of degrees; in fact, there would be no need for a task force. Because value perceptions vary, it is the task force's task to exchange information and opinions in order to get a clear understanding of every job. Where unanimous agreement is not possible, a clear majority of opinion is required. Sixty or seventy percent of the group's thinking one way suggests an unclear definition, translation, or interpretation of the job requirements. More information and discussion are needed.

Occasionally, a task force member may want to reconsider a previous decision. "If we give this job a degree 3, we really should go back and change the degree we gave this other job" is not necessarily vacillation, especially during the first day or so when the plan is still new to everyone. The task force is just working out its own interpretation of the words.

At the conclusion of the evaluation process, consistency in the application of degrees to all jobs should be checked. More about this later, when we discuss the final ranking (see Phase 5.12).

Notice the danger mentioned in rule 7: the temptation of making the job come out where people think it should. Although errors can be made, trust the system. Investigate concerns, but live with the decisions made by the task force in its thoughtful deliberations. Remember that many of the problems that you or the task force anticipates will be issues of pay management, not job evaluation.

9. *Communicate effectively.* Follow these simple rules:

- Only one person talks at a time.
- Talk only about the decision being made.
- Be nice.

Project Analyzer 5.11

Do task force members understand and accept the rules for evaluating jobs?

Are they prepared to evaluate jobs openly and objectively?

_____

_____

Would communication training be useful to help them exchange information and reach a consensus?

_____

_____

5.12 The Final Ranking

The product of a point plan evaluation is a ranking of jobs from most points to fewest—the more points, the more valuable the job is to the organization.

Theoretically, the individual factor/degree decisions made by the task force will add up to equitable relationships among jobs.

Theoretically. If job evaluation were a scientific system, the points would add up accurately. But job evaluation is not a scientific system; it is a human system. Human beings make mistakes. They lose their objectivity and consistency, no matter how hard they try, no matter how great their integrity.

Picture a task force discussion with the person whose job is being evaluated sitting at the table. The other members, who have worked with this reasonable and cooperative person, may be tempted to grade the job on the high side.

Face it, we all are prone to inflate our work just a tiny bit. You turn to the person and ask, "How do you do that?" The answer will sound a lot better from the person sitting right next to you than the answer you would get from a piece of paper.

Validate the Work

From the beginning, tell the task force that it will have an opportunity to review its work and assess the fairness of its decisions. After all detailed factor/degree decisions have been made, give the task force members time to relax and regain their objectivity. After all, they will be tired from their demanding work.

Now they need to look at the big picture. The best bet is to conclude the deliberations and meet again in a few days. Have the total ranking ready for the task force's perusal.

Present the ranking in three ways:

1. All jobs by total points.
2. Jobs by factor/degree (all jobs that received a degree 1 in the Knowledge factor, all jobs that received a degree 2 in Knowledge, and so on; then all jobs that received a degree 1 in Information Processing, all jobs that received a degree 2 in Information Processing; and so on through all factors).

3. All jobs within each department by factor/degree and by total points.

Where different job families are used, the analysis is made for each family.

Let the task force examine the product of its labor and assess whether the ranking makes sense according to a hierarchy of value to the organization. Are jobs that intuitively make approximately the same contribution to the organization ranked roughly equal?

Actually, the process of viewing the relative value of jobs within an organization without reference to specific criteria was described earlier (Phase 5.6), when we discussed job evaluation systems; it is called *weighting*. So, the task force is using another job evaluation system to validate its work.

The task force may not be able to prove that its work is specifically verifiable, but by taking this precautionary step, it should be able to convince detractors that its approach was reasonable.

Oddities will stick out. Strange things can happen when people deliberate. Let each member of the task force make a personal examination of the ranking. Compare observations. Identify concerns. Refer to your documentation, and try to reconstruct the discussion. Was this the job where you argued and argued and finally took a vote, which was close? Perhaps you should have argued some more and voted the other way.

Did the discussion occur at the end of the day, when everyone was tired and wanted to go home? Was the job one of the first you evaluated, before you had settled on your interpretation of some of the words?

Is this the job where you invited the job incumbent into the discussion room and heard an impassioned plea about the mental stress involved in the job? Nice employee; he or she deserves better. Maybe this was the job where some silver-tongued supervisor slipped one past the deliberators.

Let the task force talk out this global perspective of jobs to understand why they now believe, in contrast to their inductive reasoning, that the job seems out of place. Be careful. Do not cave in at this crucial moment. The task force worked diligently during its deliberations. If it discovers that it made a mistake, make an adjustment. Determine which factor was erroneously applied, and change the degree points and the total.

Do not, however, allow one task force member to use this opportunity to make a point he or she was unable to make during the discussions. Be stingy, but be fair.

If validation of results is paramount, consider having two task forces work separately, and then meld the results.

Getting Agreement From Department Managers

After the task force is satisfied with the result of its work, show the department rankings to department managers privately. Ask their opinion on the consistency of the ranking within their department. Listen to their concerns and their reasoning. You may find that their definitions of some jobs differ from the descriptions given to the committee. Things change. Communications are not always clear.

Again, be careful. The manager's reaction is based on a unique set of criteria. The manager does not have the benefit of separate views of the job according to the individual compensable factors. The manager has only a global, holistic view. But that global view is important and real.

Remember the discussions about agreement and commitment in Phase 3. Each manager will have to live with the results of the task force decisions. Put yourself in the manager's place: you're accountable for the management of your department, and along comes some group that wants to dictate how the jobs within the department are to be arranged and paid. That's important stuff—important enough to make the manager fight for satisfaction.

This is why it is important to select people who are respected for your task force. How much easier it is to convince department managers that the task force work is valid when you can point to individual members whose opinions are respected!

Examine the department managers' concerns with the results, and make adjustments where they are defensible. Typically, you will find that where changes are indicated, they are based on a new definition or required by a misperception of the job; it hardly ever is a matter of one opinion against another. Take your time, and make changes only if they are reasonable.

Let managers know that you made changes according to their comments. Keep building their commitment, for you still have to convince top management and employees of the results, and having the managers on your side will be a big advantage. You also have to convince each manager that the results are equitable not only within each department but also across departments.

It is one thing to get a manager to agree that his or her departmental ranking is in order; it is another to get agreement that the jobs are equitably aligned alongside other departments. Face it, managers will be biased toward their jobs. "My jobs are very complex; you really have to be there to understand them."

Emphasize the individual agreements with department managers regarding intradepartmental rankings. The organizationwide ranking is an integration of the departmental, agreed-upon rankings. You may want to bring your managers together for a group discussion to compare perceptions of jobs across departmental lines and to resolve differences.

Getting Executive Approval

Executives have a global perspective of the organization and know how they want jobs to fit together. They are more used to this view than anyone else who has reviewed the rankings. Their opinion is an excellent validation. Listen to them.

Once you have agreement from your managers, present the final recommendations for executive approval, however the structure and authority of your organization dictate. Authorization and commitment from the top are essential.

The process is the same as with other groups: have the ranking reviewed; listen to concerns; be aware of the macroanalysis of the individual versus the microanalysis of the task force; identify whether differing opinions are based on feelings or on a different understanding of job requirements, or possibly on a decision that "The job may be this way today, but I want it to be different tomorrow." As before, *be careful:* only a few changes should be made.

At the same time, prevent the executives from acting on a misunderstanding. Executives normally interact only with a few other jobs. They have a concept of what the organization needs, but usually not an intimate knowledge of what actually goes on or why some jobs are more demanding than others from a worker's point of view.

Also, executives are usually very concerned with market rates: "How much does it cost us to hire a person for that job?" Managers are concerned with costs too. It is not inappropriate to think about market rates when you review job rankings, but they should be viewed only as another, separate index of value.

Knowing, for example, that job A is ranked near jobs P, R, and V but commands a significantly higher pay in the marketplace than P, R, and V may help you understand that job A is underranked. Seeing the misalignment of pay rates may remind you of problems with the job when the job was being evaluated. Do not change rankings only because the market rates are different. External pay rates at variance with internal worth are pay policy considerations (Phase 7).

Project Analyzer 5.12

Who needs to review job rankings?

_____

_____

When should they be reviewed?

_____

_____

Who needs to approve job rankings?

_____

_____

When should the approval be done?

_____

_____

_____

5.13 Software Spreadsheet Example

In this case study of Quality Condominium Builders (a fictitious company), we show examples of software spreadsheets as applied to job evaluation.

Table 5 shows the job evaluation plan presented in this book with an example of factor weightings. The degrees are the same as the model plan since they rarely change, even though you have the option to change them.

Table 6 shows the recording of job titles of Quality Condominium Builders and the degree for each factor that was assigned to each job by the task force during job evaluation deliberations.

Table 7 shows the total points for each job as a result of summing the points assigned for each factor. The degree entered in Table 6 performs a lookup function for the value assigned in Table 5 for the corresponding degree.

Table 8 shows the sorting of total points for all jobs into a ranking from high to low points. Thus, the task force produced the information it needed to identify natural job clusters in the organization, which turn out to be the job grades of the organization's pay structure (in Phase 7).

Table 5. Adapting job evaluation plan compensable factors.

1. *Change the number of degrees in each compensable factor, if necessary.*
2. *Enter the weight of each compensable factor. Value must equal 100.*
   Weights equal 100.
3. *The point value of each degree in each factor will calculate automatically.*

	Knowl-edge	Informa-tion Processing	Deci-sion Making	Interpersonal Commu-nication	Impact on Organization Results	Environ-ment
Degrees	18	15	16	17	15	14
Weight	20	17	20	18	20	5
1	20	17	20	18	20	5
2	31	28	32	28	33	8
3	41	39	44	38	46	12
4	52	50	56	48	59	15
5	62	61	68	59	71	19
6	73	72	80	69	84	22
7	84	83	92	79	97	26
8	94	94	104	89	110	29
9	105	104	116	99	123	33
10	115	115	128	109	136	36
11	126	126	140	119	149	40
12	136	137	152	129	161	43
13	147	148	164	140	174	47
14	158	159	176	150	187	50
15	168	170	188	160	200	0
16	179	0	200	170	0	0
17	189	0	0	180	0	0
18	200	0	0	0	0	0
19	0	0	0	0	0	0
20	0	0	0	0	0	0

Table 6. Recording job titles and degrees.

1. Enter job titles for the organization.
2. Enter degree assigned for each job title for each compensable factor.

Maximum Degrees	18	15	16	17	15	14
Job Titles	Knowledge	Information Processing	Decision Making	Interpersonal Communication	Impact on Organization Results	Environment
Accounts Payable Clerk	5	5	3	4	3	
Administrative Manager	6	9	8	9	6	
Bookkeeper	7	6	5	5	3	1
Building Maintenance Technician	5	3	4	3	2	1
Building Manager	10	10	8	13	10	
Cash Manager	6	7	5	4	5	
Closing Coordinator	5	7	5	4	4	
Computer Operator	6	7	6	5	6	
Construction Accountant	10	9	7	7	6	
Construction Accounting Coordinator	4	6	4	5	3	
Construction Secretary	5	5	5	4	5	
Construction Site Assistant	4	3	1	3	3	1
Controller	13	15	12	13	10	
Cost Analyst	6	7	6	5	4	
Decorator	7	8	4	6	4	
Designer	7	6	3	3	5	
Director of Quality	10	14	10	13	6	
Estimator	7	11	7	6	7	
Executive Secretary	8	8	7	8	6	
Financial Analyst	10	8	6	7	3	
General Accounting Supervisor	10	9	7	9	6	
Information Systems Manager	10	14	10	13	11	
Information Systems Programmer/Analyst	7	8	6	7	6	
Junior Accountant	10	7	4	4	4	
Land Development Manager	10	10	9	13	13	1

Mail Clerk	2	1	1	2	3	1
Marketing Research Assistant	5	8	4	6	6	
PC Specialist	5	6	6	5	3	
Purchasing Assistant	3	2	1	3	3	
Quality Assurance Coordinator	5	4	4	5	3	
Quality Assurance Manager	7	10	8	13	10	1
Quality Assurance Technician	5	3	4	5	3	1
Quality Services Manager	5	5	3	7	3	
Receptionist	4	1	1	3	2	
Regional Construction Manager	12	14	10	14	13	1
Regional Coordinator	5	5	5	4	5	
Regional Sales Manager	12	14	10	14	13	
Safety Officer	9	10	8	11	8	1
Sales Administrator	5	7	5	4	4	
Sales Associate	10	10	7	13	10	
Secretary, Administration	6	8	6	5	5	
Senior Accounts Payable Clerk	5	6	4	5	4	
Senior Buyer	6	9	7	5	6	
Senior Designer	8	8	8	9	6	

Table 7. Calculating total points for each job.

1. *Format and job titles are copied from Table 6.*
2. *The points for each job in each factor perform a lookup from Table 5 based on the degrees entered in Table 6.*

Job Titles	Knowledge	Information Processing	Decision Making	Interpersonal Communication	Impact on Organization Results	Environment	Total Points
Accounts Payable Clerk	62	61	44	48	46	0	261
Administrative Manager	73	104	104	99	84	0	465
Bookkeeper	84	72	68	59	46	0	327
Building Maintenance Technician	62	39	56	38	33	5	233
Building Manager	115	115	104	140	136	5	615
Cash Manager	73	83	68	48	71	0	343
Closing Coordinator	62	83	68	48	59	0	320
Computer Operator	73	83	80	59	84	0	378
Construction Accountant	115	104	92	79	84	0	475
Construction Accounting Coordinator	52	72	56	59	46	0	284
Construction Secretary	62	61	68	48	71	0	311
Construction Site Assistant	52	39	20	38	46	5	200
Controller	147	170	152	140	136	0	744
Cost Analyst	73	83	80	59	59	0	353
Decorator	84	94	56	69	59	0	360
Designer	84	72	44	38	71	0	309
Director of Quality	115	159	128	140	84	0	626
Estimator	84	126	92	69	97	0	468
Executive Secretary	94	94	92	89	84	0	453
Financial Analyst	115	94	80	79	46	0	413
General Accounting Supervisor	115	104	92	99	84	0	495
Information Systems Manager	115	159	128	140	149	0	690
Information Systems Programmer/Analyst	84	94	80	79	84	0	420
Junior Accountant	115	83	56	48	59	0	361
Land Development Manager	115	115	116	140	174	5	665
Mail Clerk	31	17	20	28	46	5	146

206

Marketing Research Assistant	62	94	56	69	84	0	365
PC Specialist	62	72	80	59	46	0	318
Purchasing Assistant	41	28	20	38	46	0	173
Quality Assurance Coordinator	62	50	56	59	46	0	272
Quality Assurance Manager	84	115	104	140	136	5	583
Quality Assurance Technician	62	39	56	59	46	5	266
Quality Services Manager	62	61	44	79	46	0	292
Receptionist	52	17	20	38	33	0	160
Regional Construction Manager	136	159	128	150	174	5	752
Regional Coordinator	62	61	68	48	71	0	311
Regional Sales Manager	136	159	128	150	174	0	747
Safety Officer	105	115	104	119	110	5	558
Sales Administrator	62	83	68	48	59	0	320
Sales Associate	115	115	92	140	136	0	598
Secretary, Administration	73	94	80	59	71	0	376
Senior Accounts Payable Clerk	62	72	56	59	59	0	307
Senior Buyer	73	104	92	59	84	0	412
Senior Designer	94	94	104	99	84	0	475

Table 8. Sorting total points, high to low.

1. Format and data are copied from Table 7.
2. Press Ctrl+s to copy data range from Table 7 and to sort all jobs in descending order based on total points.

Job Titles	Knowledge	Information Processing	Decision Making	Interpersonal Communication	Impact on Organization Results	Environment	Total Points
Regional Construction Manager	136	159	128	150	174	5	752
Regional Sales Manager	136	159	128	150	174	0	747
Controller	147	170	152	140	136	0	744
Information Systems Manager	115	159	128	140	149	0	690
Land Development Manager	115	115	116	140	174	5	665
Director of Quality	115	159	128	140	84	0	626
Building Manager	115	115	104	140	136	5	615
Sales Associate	115	115	92	140	136	0	598
Quality Assurance Manager	84	115	104	140	136	5	583
Safety Officer	105	115	104	119	110	5	558
General Accounting Supervisor	115	104	92	99	84	0	495
Senior Designer	94	94	104	99	84	0	475
Construction Accountant	115	104	92	79	84	0	475
Estimator	84	126	92	69	97	0	468
Administrative Manager	73	104	104	99	84	0	465
Executive Secretary	94	94	92	89	84	0	453
Information Systems Programmer/Analyst	84	94	80	79	84	0	420
Financial Analyst	115	94	80	79	46	0	413
Senior Buyer	73	104	92	59	84	0	412
Computer Operator	73	83	80	59	84	0	378
Secretary, Administration	73	94	80	59	71	0	376
Marketing Research Assistant	62	94	56	69	84	0	365
Junior Accountant	115	83	56	48	59	0	361
Decorator	84	94	56	69	59	0	360
Cost Analyst	73	83	80	59	59	0	353
Cash Manager	73	83	68	48	71	0	343

208

Bookkeeper	84	72	68	59	46	0	327
Closing Coordinator	62	83	68	48	59	0	320
Sales Administrator	62	83	68	48	59	0	320
PC Specialist	62	72	80	59	46	0	318
Construction Secretary	62	61	68	48	71	0	311
Regional Coordinator	62	61	68	48	71	0	311
Designer	84	72	44	38	71	0	309
Senior Accounts Payable Clerk	62	72	56	59	59	0	307
Quality Services Manager	62	61	44	79	46	0	292
Construction Accounting Coordinator	52	72	56	59	46	0	284
Quality Assurance Coordinator	62	50	56	59	46	0	272
Quality Assurance Technician	62	39	56	59	46	5	266
Accounts Payable Clerk	62	61	44	48	46	0	261
Building Maintenance Technician	62	39	56	38	33	5	233
Construction Site Assistant	52	39	20	38	46	5	200
Purchasing Assistant	41	28	20	38	46	0	173
Receptionist	52	17	20	38	33	0	160
Mail Clerk	31	17	20	28	46	5	146

Project Analyzer 5.13

What software capability do you have now?

_____

_____

Do you have independent computer support, or will you need support?

_____

_____

If needed, when will you orient information services support specialists to your project requirements?

_____

_____

_____

Strategic Planning for Phase 5

On your *first* quick walk through the project phases, record your initial thoughts on policy issues that will have to be decided.

_____

_____

_____

Any notes on tactical procedures?

_____

_____

On your *second* time through the phases, consider the strategic influences from all the phases; decide on an integrated posture for the entire project.

Complete the section for this phase in the Master Planner (in Phase 2.8) during your *third* reading.

Phase 6

Evaluating the Price of Jobs in the Marketplace

> Jobs are worth what other organizations are willing to pay, what the job candidate is willing to accept, and what your organization is willing to pay. Fair pay is complicated.

6.1 Job Value

Up to this point in the development of a pay program, the focus has been internal: what the organization values, what the organization wants to accomplish with its pay program, what results jobs are designed to accomplish, and what the relative value of each job's contribution is to the organization's mission. These questions must be answered to provide an operating structure for the organization and to define its management policy and practices with regard to pay.

To complete the pay picture, one other factor must be evaluated: how much other organizations are willing to pay to attract job candidates. This place where pay offers are accepted or rejected is called the *job marketplace*. It closely parallels the marketplace of goods and services where the equilibrium of supply and demand dictates price, except that in the labor market, the "goods and services" (that is, job candidates) have a mind of their own.

In a sense, the pay marketplace has three components: the value of the organization's offer, the value of offers of other organizations, and the value the job candidate places on himself or herself.

An organization may place a logical value on a job based on an internal analysis of the organization's jobs and an external analysis of how much other organizations value the same job, and its job offers may be rejected. Personal decisions about pay may well defy logical statistical analysis.

Still, each organization needs a structure to guide its pay management decisions, or it will sail like a rudderless boat. Surveying the competition, just as organizations do regarding their products and services, makes good sense. What doesn't make sense is following the market blindly.

Some organizations ignore the concept of an internal job value, as defined by job evaluation. They argue that job evaluation isn't reliable, as we discussed in Phase 5. And they figure that when the value determined by job evaluation differs from the value in the marketplace, the marketplace value will be more highly regarded—in other words, if you don't pay the price, you won't get the employee. As we also mentioned, some organizations use the job evaluation process but weight compensable factors and calculate degrees using market rates directly in the job evaluation plan.

It is wisest not to rely solely on either job evaluation or the market but instead to blend the internal and external values in a pay structure in order to do the best job possible of reconciling sometimes conflicting influences. Actually, the ranking produced by job evaluation typically parallels the marketplace hierarchy of jobs.

As uncontrollable as the marketplace is, the one thing that an organization can control is its own pay structure. The bottom line is that an organization may force itself into pay freezes or layoffs by trying to keep pace with a market that it cannot afford.

Following the market alone ignores the significance of an organization's benefits, which may be substantial, and also ignores the goodwill intangible of the organization's reputation for thoughtful human relations, which will do a lot more in the long run than pay alone to build a stable, dedicated workforce. Paying the market may well produce a workforce that responds mainly to monetary motivations—and to offers for more money elsewhere.

6.2 Surveying Market Pay Rates

Pay surveys are conducted to determine how much other organizations currently pay employees for specific jobs. Knowing what the competition is willing to pay is a crucial piece of information when determining how much your organization is willing to pay to attract and retain employees.

Uses of Surveys

Pay surveying is based on an exchange of information: if you tell me what you are paying for certain jobs in your organization, I will tell you what I pay for those jobs in my organization.

Surveying the price of jobs in the market means comparing the economic status of one organization to that of other organizations that can attract similar job candidates or hire employees away.

At the installation of a pay program, surveys, along with job evaluation information, are used to establish the pay structure. The market price is another barometer of value; it can be compared with the job evaluation measurements taken within the organization. In this way, a pay survey is a substantiating technique for the internal valuation.

Once a pay structure has been established, surveys are conducted to track shifts in market pricing so that adjustments, if necessary, can be made to the structure.

Surveys can also be conducted to prepare for labor negotiations, forecast markets and prepare budgets, make specific job pay recommendations, determine the hiring range for new jobs, study turnover, assess recruitment problems, give special pay adjustments, demonstrate relevance of economic decisions, signal dangerous situations, or maintain pay leadership.

What to Survey

The number used in pay structure calculations (which will be discussed in Phase 7) is the price of a job, expressed in dollars of actual pay: "Job A is paid, on the average, X dollars per hour [week, month, year]." The number represents the most common pay rate for that job in the labor market—the number around which other rates tend to cluster, the number that is typical of what people are being paid in the job.

Besides asking about the pay rate of the job, you also need to ask questions that will help you understand the organizations with which you are making job comparisons. An adaptable survey form (Figure 26) is included in this phase. You can ask just about anything that you want; however, the more cumbersome and time-consuming the survey, the less inclined people will be to complete it.

The market mixes all kinds of people together: those who are new in their jobs, those who are contributing just as organizations want them to contribute, those who are contributing more than required, those who have been in their jobs a long time, those who are not contributing well, those who are favored by their supervisor, and any and all other people.

You can assume that all sorts of rates, and reasons for them, exist in the market; hence, measures of central tendency—where the most representative number exists— wash out the many variations and produce a pay rate that represents what satisfactory performers tend to earn.

Where to Survey and Obtain Survey Information

Your labor market is wherever employees and job candidates come from in order to work for you, and where they might go if they leave. In other words, it's the area in which organizations compete for employees. (We are excluding here job candidates who decide for a variety of reasons, typically not work related, that they wish to live in an area, move there, and begin to look for a job.)

Start with present personnel records to ascertain where employees live now and where they moved from in order to work with your organization. Discussions with employees will point out some of the natural barriers: "We prefer not to drive all the way downtown." Thus, "downtown" pay rates are not in the competitive area and should not be used. Records of past employees can be analyzed in the same way.

Exit interviews with employees who leave may provide some clues on changing labor markets and new competition.

Some jobs draw candidates from anywhere in the city, county, state, region, nation, or world. Surveying must consider all geographic areas in which a candidate may choose to apply. Obviously, large geographic areas require different elements of analysis; just because an organization could draw employees from New York City, San Francisco, or Houston, it doesn't have to pay rates competitive with these cities if it is located in Winston-Salem. But knowing that candidates could opt for these other locations, you may want to gear recruiting to other attractions.

Other organizations, especially their human resources departments that work with this information all the time, are a good source on what surveys are available, and dependable, in the area. For example, other organizations in your industry will know about surveys that aim particularly at your unique jobs.

The federal government's Bureau of Labor Statistics publishes a wealth of information. State and local governments—especially those eager to attract industry to their area—also have surveys, as do civic and business associations. All government and many quasi-government pay schedules are public information.

Employment agencies and recruiters have current information. Consulting firms that specialize in compensation services sell surveys. Professional associations interested in specific jobs have pay data. Human resources management associations publish information.

Employment ads are another valuable source of information on pay rates and other components of compensation.

Finally, managers and employees in your own organization have ideas on where to look for information; they know comparable jobs, their industry and related industries, their counterparts and others with whom they relate, and their opportunities.

If nothing suitable is available, you may have to conduct your own survey by contacting appropriate sources.

Size of the Survey

The most perplexing question of all is, How much information do I need? There is no absolute guide. A few lonely numbers on a piece of paper are not enough to price a job. A stack of pages loaded with data is too much. In medium-size organizations where jobs are not diverse, participating in approximately six major surveys, each of which includes information gathered from twenty to thirty organizations, should gather just about all the pricing information needed.

The Real Issue: Quality of the Survey

The most important thing in pay surveying is to collect, analyze, and disseminate the information with care and understanding. Mistakes can be made in which organizations are invited to participate, in what questions are asked, in how the information is assembled and analyzed, and in how it is reported. Sloppy surveys are useless.

Talk with the people who conduct the survey, in person if you can. Judge from their discussion whether they know what they are talking about and care about what they are doing. If you run into nonsense anywhere along the line, try to salvage what you can from the data, or dump the survey.

Know the database: what kinds of organizations participated; where they are located; how big they are, by meaningful standards; how many employees they have; how old they are; whether they are unionized; whether they are family-owned; and anything else you find out.

Where possible, and especially when you have confidence in the numbers, use the same surveys year after year to spot trends more easily.

Another aspect of quality refers to the currency of the data. Surveys are published throughout the year, while the value of the dollar changes. By the time the data are published, the value of the dollar may have changed. Consequently, the pay data must be made current by an adjustment for the rate of change in the value of the dollar. For example, if the rate of inflation is 3 percent annually and the data are six months old, increase the pay rates by 1.5 percent. Use your own organization's economic estimates to get the adjustment rate.

Adjust data from different geographic areas using the government cost-of-living index or another generally accepted index. The most important influences are cost of housing and state and local taxes, but costs of utilities and transportation, as well as medical, clothing, and recreation costs, also play a role.

Project Analyzer 6.2

What pay information is routinely collected now?

_____

_____

If jobs are divided into families, which markets (sublocal, local, area, state, region, national, international) apply to which families?

_____

_____

Where do current employees live?

_____

_____

Where did they live?

_____

_____

Where did they work?

_____

_____

_____

Why do they work for your organization now?

_____

_____

_____

Where do employees go to work when they quit?

_____

_____

Why?

_____

_____

Who uses which surveys?

_____

_____

What information do managers and employees have about sources of information?

_____

_____

What sources of information will you use?

_____

_____

_____

6.3 A Pay Survey Questionnaire You Can Use

Figure 26 is an adaptable pay survey form that can be edited to meet your needs. *A legal warning:* ask nearly anything you want in order to understand the job and other organizations as they are now or as they were in the past, but *be careful not to ask for information regarding the future.* Specifically, never ask by how much they intend to adjust their pay structure, individual salaries, or hiring rates. Such information might be construed as a concerted attempt by a group of employers to hold pay down or fix pay rates. On the other hand, don't dump surveying because your lawyer gets anxious. Just make sure you are not colluding with any other organization.

6.4 Matching Jobs

The key to surveying is to obtain prices for jobs that are identical, or nearly identical, to the jobs in your organization. Given the various factors at work in the market, a true match is impossible, but many matches will be close enough.

The benchmark jobs selected earlier in the project and used during the job evaluation process come back into the picture now. The "obvious" jobs in your organization will match up more readily with "obvious" jobs in other organizations.

Figure 26. Sample pay survey form.

	In Our Organization	*In Your Organization*

Job title _____ | _____

Reports to _____ | _____

Supervises

      (titles) _____ | _____

                  _____ | _____

   (number) _____ | _____

In career ladder

Next higher job: _____ | _____

Next lower job: _____ | _____

How does our job description differ from the one in your organization?

_____

_____

_____

_____

Estimate on the scale how much "bigger" or "smaller" your job is than our job:

15% _____ 10% _____ 5% _____ 0% _____ 5% _____ 10% _____ 15%
     your job is bigger   equal   your job is smaller

Number of employees in this job title _____

Average salary paid to these employees $ _____ (annual)

   Median salary paid $ _____   Highest salary paid $ _____

   Normal hours of work per week _____

   Average seniority of employees in this job _____

Pay range for this job:

   Minimum $_____ Midpoint $ _____ Maximum $ _____

   Hire up to $ _____

   Date of last structure adjustment _____

Can employees in this job earn a bonus? Yes _____ No _____

Are they paid a shift differential? Yes _____ No _____

   How much? $ _____

Are they paid overtime? Yes _____ No _____

   How is overtime computed? _____

_____

Be careful. In the interests of space conservation, some surveys publish only scant descriptions of jobs, not enough to confirm that similar jobs are being compared. In some very obvious jobs, the mismatch might be minor, but poor comparisons are, nonetheless, poor comparisons.

Consider these job descriptions:

ACCOUNTING CLERK II: Uses principles of accounting and statistical analysis for maintaining general accounts and financial operating reports. Organizes and directs posting of general accounts payable or receivable. Examines posted entries in ledgers and journals for accuracy. Verifies source data. Has skill and experience with bookkeeping machines, calculators, and EDP equipment. Usually has two or more years of college training and two or more years of experience.

CLERK TYPIST: Performs, according to standard procedures, routine to moderately difficult clerical work, which requires a limited degree of decision and in which typing is an essential duty. Answers phone and may in other ways assist the public. Entry position, with prior experience not required.

PAINTER: Performs skilled work in painting and redecorating furniture, equipment, and buildings.

PAYROLL CLERK: Computes employee earnings, compiles department payrolls, handles and records payroll deductions, makes labor distributions, compiles payroll statistics, and performs other related payroll functions, under medium supervision.

These descriptions are tempting because they "seem to be just like ours." The problem is that they are too general. Such data can be used only when you are convinced that your job fits right in the middle of the definition. Even then, did the other people in the survey read the description the same way and submit appropriate data?

Here are two job descriptions for executive secretaries for you to match. Are they comparable jobs? Can you use the pay information directly?

JOB TITLE: **EXECUTIVE SECRETARY** (your organization)

JOB PURPOSE: **FACILITATES THE WORK OF AN EXECUTIVE**
by
completing secretarial and administrative responsibilities.

ESSENTIAL JOB RESULTS:

% of
time

_____   **1. SUPPORTS AN OFFICER OF THE COMPANY**
by
keying and transcribing information; maintaining files.

_____   **2. PROVIDES ADMINISTRATIVE SUPPORT**
by
managing projects.

_____   **3. ACTS FOR OFFICER**
by
initiating and answering correspondence.

_____ **4. FACILITATES MEETINGS**
by
making arrangements; preparing agenda; recording discussions.

_____ **5. PREPARES REPORTS AND PRESENTATIONS**
by
collecting, assembling, and analyzing data, including preparing information for graphics.

_____ **6. ADMINISTERS PERSONNEL RECORDS AND PROGRAMS**
by
completing all administrative and clerical requirements, such as for pension plan, profit-sharing plan, insurance plan.

_____ **7. ACCOMPLISHES DEPARTMENTAL WORK**
by
directing other secretaries and clerks.

JOB TITLE: Executive Secretary (nearby organization)
JOB PURPOSE: Performs secretarial duties for a manager of the company.

WORK PERFORMED:

1. Keys information, takes machine dictation, and maintains files for an executive.
2. Assists company manager in administrative duties.
3. Answers telephone inquiries and routes calls to proper department; drafts responses to written inquiries.
4. Makes arrangements for meetings; takes notes during meetings; keys and distributes minutes.
5. Operates switchboard communications equipment and delivers incoming messages.
6. Receives and opens mail daily, and routes to the proper department.
7. Gathers data for reports.
8. Performs special projects as may be necessary from time to time.
9. May schedule work for clerical personnel.

Sound similar, don't they? But they are not a match. The job in the nearby organization is that of a departmental secretary, not an executive secretary. These are the crucial differences:

1. "Managing projects" is more responsible than "assisting in administrative duties."
2. "Answering correspondence" indicates greater authority and independence than "drafts responses to written inquiries."
3. "Prepares reports by . . . analyzing data" is a higher-level responsibility than "gathers data for reports."
4. In view of the first two mismatches, "operates switchboard communications equipment and delivers incoming messages" seems not to be an omission to be taken for granted in the first description as much as a lower-level duty the executive secretary probably does not perform.

5. "Administers personnel records" conveys more responsibility than the very general "performs special projects as may be necessary from time to time."
6. "Directing other secretaries and clerks" suggests a higher-level responsibility than "may schedule work for clerical personnel."

How much a new automobile is worth cannot be answered until the specific model and options are known; the same is true in job comparisons.

Adjusting for Imperfect Matches

Job matches are rarely perfect. Occasionally, some aspects of a job indicate that it is more responsible than the job compared to, while other aspects of the job suggest that it is less responsible; this indicates a wash and is an acceptable match.

When jobs do not match and miss by a mile, do not count the data and keep looking for a match. When the match is close but not perfect, adjustments are appropriate. Adjustments of up to 10 percent are reasonable, but beyond 10 percent seems to indicate a mismatch. Thus, if you believe that your job is almost but not quite like the job in the survey—say, you estimate your job to be approximately 5 percent less responsible—reduce the pay rate of the other job by 5 percent before entering it into the database.

Project Analyzer 6.4

Of the pay surveys currently available to your organization, what is your estimate of the quality of information in them?

_____

_____

What needs to be done to improve the information (if it needs to be improved)?

_____

_____

Can you meet with the survey administrators to clarify information?

_____

_____

6.5 Analyzing Pay Survey Numbers

There are several measures you will use when analyzing pay data. Here is a list of them, with brief explanations:

■ *Range*—the difference between the low and the high pay rate. For example, in 2, 4, 6, 8, and 10, the range is 8.

■ *Mean*—the arithmetic average. Add all the rates and divide the sum by the number of pay rates in the list. In the preceding example (rates of 2, 4, 6, 8, and 10), the mean is 6 (the sum, 30, divided by the number of pay rates, 5). Generally, the mean of the pay market is the measure you're looking for.

In computing the mean, be sure to count all the actual rates. Take this example:

1 employee earning	2 (1 × 2) = 2
2 employees earning	4 (2 × 4) = 8
1 employee earning	6 (1 × 6) = 6
3 employees earning	8 (3 × 8) = 24
1 employee earning	10 (1 × 10) = 10

There are 8 pay rates here because the example includes data for 8 employees, not 5. Thus, the mean is 50 (the sum) divided by 8, or 6.25.

■ *Mode*—the most frequently observed pay rate. For example, if you have pay rates of 2, 4, 6, 6, 6, 6, 8, and 10, the mode is 6.

■ *Median*—the pay rate in the middle of a list of pay rates arranged from lowest to highest. For example, in 2, 4, 6, 8, and 10, the median is 6. Use the median instead of the mean when the range is very large and when you can't recalculate because you don't have the raw data.

■ *Standard deviation*—the extent of dispersion of pay rates from the mean (a routine calculation in spreadsheet software). The dispersion indicates the scattering of raw data, such as a narrow scattering (a small standard deviation) or a wide scattering (a large standard deviation). For pay surveying purposes, the smaller the deviation, the better.

In the second example in this section, the mean is 6.25. The standard deviation is 2.71. The calculated standard deviation is added to and subtracted from the mean to identify the most meaningful data:

$$
\begin{array}{ccc}
6.25 & & 6.25 \\
-2.71 & & +2.71 \\
\hline
3.54 & \text{to} & 8.96 \qquad \text{dispersion}
\end{array}
$$

While the range of the pay rates is from 2 to 10, the most representative data are found between 3.54 and 8.96. Data beyond these limits are suspect; they indicate pay rates of jobs that are not a good match. Typically, these rates are discarded from the analysis.

Another list of pay rates might produce the same average but have a different dispersion. A smaller standard deviation means that more of the representative numbers cluster closer to the mean:

$$
\begin{array}{ccc}
6.25 & & 6.25 \\
-2.00 & & +2.00 \\
\hline
4.25 & \text{to} & 8.25 \qquad \text{dispersion}
\end{array}
$$

In other words, the pay rates are less varied and more similar. A larger standard deviation means that the numbers scatter further away from the mean, that they are more varied and less similar:

$$
\begin{array}{cc}
6.25 & 6.25 \\
-3.00 & +3.00 \\
\hline
3.25 \quad \text{to} & 9.25 \quad \text{dispersion}
\end{array}
$$

Central ranges can be calculated for one, two, or three standard deviations from the mean; one is normally used. When the frequency distribution of all pay rates collected is a normal distribution—and we assume that it is—approximately two-thirds of all pay rates that might be collected would fall within this one deviation.

Applying this to the example, approximately two-thirds of the pay rates that we might expect to collect will be between 3.54 and 8.96.

By using the standard deviation, we are able to focus on the data that most accurately represent the pay market. After reducing the data to the best, we then calculate the mean.

■ *Percentile*—the percentage of pay rates equal to or below a stated percentage of all the pay rates in the list. Take the following example:

2	6
2	6
4	7
5	8
6	8
6	10

In this case, the 10th percentile is 1.2 pay rates (10 percent of 12 pay rates) from the lowest, which in this list is the pay rate 2. The 25th percentile is 4 pay rates (25 percent of 12 pay rates) from the lowest, which in this list is the pay rate 4. The 50th percentile is 6 pay rates (50 percent of 12 pay rates) from the lowest, which in this list is the pay rate 6. And the 75th percentile is 9 pay rates (75 percent of 12 pay rates) from the lowest, which in this list is the pay rate 7.

Groups of 25 percent are called *quartiles*. The second quartile, or 50th percentile, is the same as the median.

■ *Pay range spread*—the percentage difference from the minimum of the pay range to the maximum. If the minimum of the pay range is $20,000 and the maximum is $28,000, the spread is 40 percent ($28,000 divided by $20,000 = 1 plus 40 percent). Some people alternatively calculate the spread as a percentage below and above the midpoint. Be careful to know which calculation is being used when you make comparisons.

■ *Compa-ratio*—the relationship between a pay rate and the midpoint of the range. If the midpoint of a pay range is $30,000, the compa-ratio of $26,000 is .87 ($26,000 divided by $30,000). Compa-ratios can be expressed for a pay rate in relation to the mean or the median.

■ *Common sense*—the appreciation for what the numbers mean, regardless of the statistical measures involved.

Manipulating numbers is tedious work, prone to error. Spreadsheet software makes the work nearly effortless and allows you to concentrate on the important decisions about pay data rather than on the statistical exercises; the software frees you to do more number crunching when you otherwise might give up from boredom or fatigue.

Here are some examples to help you understand how to select a representative pay rate for a pay market. First, consider the following series of pay rates:

$602	$524	$488	$460	$448	$420
600	521	480	459	444	410
591	510	471	459	443	409
588	505	470	458	438	409
574	494	469	458	437	409
537	494	469	450	427	408
531	492	461	450	425	390
525	489	461	450	420	385

The *range* between the low and the high value is $217, or 56 percent. Such a range is large and suggests that the jobs being compared are not matched properly.

An inspection of the list reveals a large gap between $574 and $537. Another large gap exists at the bottom of the list between $390 and $408. Common sense tells us to discard the rates above $537 and below $408 and use the remaining data as most representative of the common pay rate for the job. Let us see what the numbers say.

The *mean* for the reduced data is $463. (The mean for the entire original list is $472.) There is no usable *mode*; there are just three rates at $450 and another three at $409. The *median*—the rate in position 20 or 21 out of 41 rates in the list—is $459. (The median for the original list is $460.)

The *standard deviation* is $37, which, when added to and subtracted from the mean, gives a central range of $426 to $500. (The standard deviation for the original list is $55—the range from $417 to $527, close to the range identified.) The quartiles are: third, $489; second, $459; and first, $437.

Notice that the mean is lower when using the reduced list than when using the entire original list; the standard deviation also demonstrates a much tighter grouping around the mean—$37 rather than $55. By discarding poorly matched rates and studying the remaining data using the statistical methods presented here, you can be confident that the rates you use in your subsequent pay structure calculations represent the market rate accurately and will produce a reliable pay guide.

Table 9 shows another example. The following discussion will clarify the situation depicted, including the organization code number (e.g., R31), the pay range spread from minimum to maximum in each organization, the actual low and high rates of incumbents, and the mean.

First, since all the low and high rates, except one (R41), are identical, it is obvious that only one person is in each job. Second, the fact that the low and the high pay of the exception are identical to the minimum and the maximum of the range, respectively, suggests that the respondent misunderstood the reporting requirements and simply copied the range numbers into the actual columns; it would be most unlikely that the incumbents just happen to be at the minimum and the maximum of the range.

What does common sense tell you about these numbers? Do they all give the same message about a common rate, or should some of them be dropped from the list?

Table 9. Sample data from a pay survey.

Code	Minimum	Midpoint	Maximum	Low	High	Mean
R31	$25,000	$32,500	$40,000	$33,500	$33,500	$33,500
R18	26,350	33,600	40,850	33,000	33,000	33,000
R41	25,971	30,721	35,471	25,971	35,471	30,420
R40	25,507	29,359	33,793	30,769	30,769	30,769
R39	18,183	21,732	24,837	—	—	—
R34	22,178	27,716	33,254	28,561	28,561	28,561
R48	33,840	43,992	54,144	35,832	35,832	35,832
R46	30,249	37,811	45,373	38,040	38,040	38,040
R43	32,959	40,604	48,249	41,400	41,400	41,400
R13	41,800	54,300	66,800	—	—	—
R10	—	—	—	32,500	32,500	32,500
R91	31,356	39,192	47,040	37,999	37,999	37,999
S60	23,015	28,770	34,525	25,760	25,760	25,760

The range is $15,640. The mean is $33,434. There is no mode. The median is $33,000. The standard deviation is $4,595 ($28,839 to $38,029).

The high and low rates in this situation ($41,400 and $25,760) are uncommon, suggesting a mismatch of jobs. They should be dropped from the list, and a new mean should be calculated for the reduced data and used in further calculations.

Table 10 shows another example. In this example, some new and important information has been added: the number of employees involved in each organization and the calculation of a weighted mean. The weighted mean is the number of employees times the mean. Without the number of employees being reported, all data are suspect, though you may have to use them if no other data are available.

The weighted mean calculates each job incumbent's rate rather than allowing only a comparison of means for each organization (there is no such statistical expression as the mean of the means). The best data, of course, are the actual numbers on each incumbent from each organization.

Common sense suggests that the two high rates ($27,950 and $23,324), and possibly also the low rate ($12,650), are out of line. Let's check the numbers.

The range is $15,300. The mean is $18,325. There is no mode. And the standard deviation is $4,327 ($13,998 to $22,652).

Common sense was on target with the calculated standard deviation. So drop the two highest and the lowest rate from the list, and calculate new indices.

For the reduced list, we get a range of $5,600, which is much better. The mean now is $17,182; it is calculated by adding the remaining weighted means (other than those indicated by the asterisks in Table 10), which yields $257,738, and dividing that sum by the number of employees involved, 15.

Remember the Other Elements of Compensation

It is just about now that some pay management specialists lose their perspective. Buried in a sea of numbers, they can easily lose sight of the relationship of pay to the

Table 10. Sample data from a pay survey incorporating the weighted means of pay rates.

Code	Low	High	Mean	Number of Employees	Weighted Mean Calculation
R18	$18,120	$18,120	$18,120	1	$18,120
R31	11,200	14,000	12,650	3	37,950*
R41	14,556	17,390	15,675	2	31,350
R15	18,800	18,800	18,800	1	18,800
R39	—	—	—	—	—
R34	16,653	21,164	18,403	4	73,612
R35	—	—	—	—	—
R47	16,500	19,380	17,818	2	35,636
R46	19,600	19,600	19,600	1	19,600
R43	27,950	27,950	27,950	1	27,950*
R13	—	—	15,220	1	15,220
R12	14,000	—	14,000	1	14,000
R91	18,499	31,500	23,324	2	46,648*
S60	15,609	15,791	15,700	2	31,400

*Data dropped after the first analysis.

overall concern of how employees of the organization should be compensated. Pay is one element; benefits, incentives, and intangibles are the other elements. Actual dollars in the paycheck are important, and pay survey work must be thoughtful and accurate—but it has to be kept in perspective.

Project Analyzer 6.5

How thoroughly have you analyzed pay survey data in the past?

_____

_____

What specific analysis do you need to add?

_____

_____

Strategic Planning for Phase 6

On your *first* quick walk through the project phases, record your initial thoughts on policy issues that will have to be decided.

_____

_____

_____

Any notes on tactical procedures?

_____

_____

    On your *second* time through the phases, consider the strategic influences from all the phases; decide on an integrated posture for the entire project.

    Complete the section for this phase in the Master Planner (in Phase 2.8) during your *third* reading.

Phase 7

Building the Pay Structure

> The pay structure is a guide for management's actions.

7.1 Pay Structure as a Management Guide

Typically some department in the organization is assigned to be the keeper of the pay structure. In most organizations, this is the human resources department or perhaps the finance or administration department. In the long run, we believe this is *not* the best way to manage pay.

Certainly someone has to assemble the information needed to design and maintain the pay structure and its components: job descriptions, job evaluation, pay surveys. Senior management must review the information and establish pay policy and procedures. But a keeper usually looks like and acts like a controller who doles out pay. The responsibility for pay management is thereby shifted from the department manager to the keeper. A department manager's "decision" looks more like a recommendation that gets reviewed and approved, denied, or argued with.

If the human resources department is the keeper, then the program is an "HR" program. Managers not worthy of their title may cry to employees that they wanted to do the right thing, but HR wouldn't allow it. Good managers, on the other hand, spend too much time explaining themselves during procedural debates with HR.

Department managers are the key decision makers. It is at their discretion that employees are hired, promoted, and terminated and do or do not receive pay increases and rewards. Authority and responsibility need to be placed squarely in the hands of department managers. They need to have both the flexibility and the accountability to manage the pay resources of their department. They are in the best position to understand the nuances of job satisfaction and dissatisfaction of individual employees and groups of employees.

What managers need, of course, is information and support. They need to understand pay relationships in other parts of their organization and in other organizations. They need someone to turn to who can help them sort options.

The pay structure is a strong but not immutable economic guide for managers and employees. Managers need to know how to respond to specific situations in order to maintain organizational consistency and to get the best results; they cannot respond solely as they choose. Employees need to know that pay management is equitable and predictable.

How firmly the guide is managed is a matter of organizational style—strict or flexible. The mathematical precision of the structure suggests rigidity. But pay management is anything but rigid; consistent, yes, but not rigid.

Having reached this point in the construction of a pay structure, you are certainly aware of the many judgments on which it is based. No one claims that the judgments are perfect, only that they are thoughtful. No human system can accommodate all the nuances of employee relations.

Exceptions to the pay guide will be necessary. How many? Very, very few. The value of the guide is that a pay judgment can be considered in relation to all other pay decisions, using established and agreed-on reference points. The pay guide helps managers answer pay policy and related issues:

- Is the pay program a problem for holding on to or hiring people?
- If we have difficulty hiring people, is the job evaluated correctly?
- Was the market analyzed correctly?
- Is the market out of whack temporarily?
- If the situation involves a request for an increase, is this employee a star contributor?
- Is an increase warranted because of an increase in job responsibilities (a movement higher on the job evaluation scale) or because the employee is contributing more than the basic job requirements (a movement higher in the pay range, or a bonus)?
- If the pay policy seems to be in line, are our management practices out of line?

Managing without a pay structure is like a sandlot game where offside is never certain. It's better to put the references on the ground. Then managers can decide for themselves whether to step over the boundary when necessary.

Project Analyzer 7.1

Who is the keeper of the pay structure?

_____

_____

Are department managers capable of making their own pay decisions?

_____

_____

Do managers have enough information to manage their pay program?

_____

_____

Would holding department managers accountable for managing their own pay program fit with your organization culture?

_____

_____

What training and information support would be necessary in order to hold department managers accountable for managing their own pay program?

_____

_____

7.2 Designing and Calculating the Pay Structure

In a moment you will be reading about job grades and pay grades, pay minimums and pay maximums. Pay structures are often attacked as inflexible boundaries, clubs over the heads of well-meaning managers, the core of bureaucracy.

The pay structure can be used in a negative way, but it can just as easily be used as a positive resource for making decisions regarding pay. After all, the pay structure is a thoughtful response to the question, What is fair pay for job contributions? Certainly this is a question that every organization needs to answer. Be prepared to adjust vocabulary and applications to suit your organization's culture. This flexibility will increase the effectiveness and acceptance of the program.

Let us start with a picture of where you are heading. (See Figure 27.) The pay structure answers the question: How much should an organization pay for what kind of work?

The width of the box is the job evaluation measure—how valuable the work is to the organization. The farther to the right on the horizontal scale, the more valuable the job.

The height of the box is the pay value: the value of the job in dollars. The higher on the vertical scale, the more dollars.

Each box is a pay grade, starting with the lower grades at the bottom left.

The nomenclature of the box, measured in dollars, is as follows:

- *Maximum*—the top of the box, which states the greatest amount of money that a job in the pay grade is worth. This is the most an employee should earn for accomplishing the job.

- *Midpoint*—the middle of the box, which is the distance halfway between the maximum and the minimum. This is the amount of money an employee should earn for accomplishing job results competently.

- *Minimum*—the bottom of the box, which states the smallest amount of money that a job in the pay grade is worth. This is the least an employee should earn for that job.

Figure 27. General view of a pay structure.

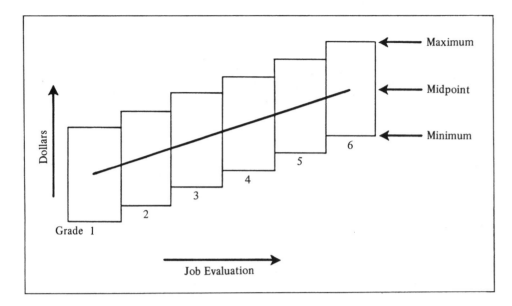

Table 11 shows some job evaluation and pay survey data. We will use these sample data to demonstrate the five basic steps of calculating a pay structure. Then we'll show you a complete software spreadsheet example in Phase 7.6 for a fictitious organization.

Step 1: Determine Job Grades

A good place to start is by determining the number of job grades that will make up the pay structure. A job grade should include jobs that have similar demands made on them so that they will be paid similarly. Job evaluation is the key here, since it produces a hierarchy of job worth. The range of job evaluation points is inspected to identify job clusters where job evaluation points cluster together. Obversely, the range is also inspected for gaps between job points.

For practice, study the job evaluation points in Table 11 (the second column). Identify clusters and gaps. In your own organization, you would also consider normal job and career progressions and routine operating relationships to identify which jobs should be grouped together and which jobs should be separated. For example, Machine Operator A, B, and C might be separated into three different grades (although recognition for learning new job skills might also be accomplished with a specified increase within the same pay grade). Then compare the clusters you identify with our solution, where the gaps are indicated by asterisks:

Table 11. Sample data for a pay structure.

Job Title	Job Evaluation Points	Mean Rate of Pay in the Marketplace	Mean Rate of Pay in the Organization
A	100	$1,220	$1,285
B	105	1,230	1,280
C	125	1,260	1,295
D	130	1,240	1,265
E	150	1,320	1,330
F	160	1,380	1,385
G	165	1,360	1,370
H	170	1,335	1,325
I	180	1,380	1,320
J	210	1,390	1,340
K	215	1,460	1,400
L	220	1,420	1,380
M	225	1,440	1,370
N	240	1,680	1,525
O	290	1,560	1,480
P	295	1,540	1,560
Q	305	1,580	1,500
R	315	1,560	1,510
S	320	1,340	1,480
T	340	1,620	1,540
U	350	1,660	1,480
V	355	1,640	1,570
W	360	1,650	1,590
X	390	1,780	1,705
Z	395	1,820	1,715

Job Evaluation Points

100	165	*	355
105	170	290	360
*	180	295	*
125	*	305	390
130	210	315	395
*	215	*	
150	220	340	
160	225	350	

If the job grades are published based solely on natural clusters, the pay structure would look haphazard, but some grades narrow and some grades widen with no symmetrical relationship. A symmetrical grade progression where the percentage increase from one grade to the next is the same (or gradually increasing) presents a greater degree of orderliness.

Typically, the first grade starts with the lowest job evaluation points that can be assigned, and pay grades increase at a set percentage. First efforts will be trial and error as you experiment with different percentages. Try increasing at 10 percent intervals from 100 job evaluation points, and observe where breaks occur in the list of points.

(The calculation is 100 × 1.10; that product × 1.10; that new product × 1.10; and so on. In this example, 100 × 1.10 = 110, × 1.10 = 121, × 1.10 = 133, and so forth.)

Try other percentage increases until you find one that comes closest to the natural job clusters you identified. Compare your opinion with the symmetrical clusters below.

Here are the job grade points resulting from 16 percent intervals that keep the significant clusters together:

    100
    116
    135
    156
    181
    210
    244
    282
    328
    380
    441

This interval produces ten job grades, which seems manageable. Figure 28 shows the graphic presentation. Other intervals (tried and discarded) divided natural clusters and, in the case of smaller intervals, produced too many grades.

Percentage interval increases need not remain static. The first grades might be narrow—say, 8 or 9 percent—to offer rapid movement and pay increases through entry jobs; then the intervals may increase to 10 percent or 12 percent, and end with 15 percent or 17 percent at the higher-level jobs. While percentages may increase, they should not decrease or bounce around.

Some people use a constant real-number increase rather than a percentage, but most do not.

Using a percentage increase, such as 16 percent, gradually increases the job evaluation points in higher-level job grades. In the preceding list, the first grade was 16 points from the beginning to the end, whereas the final grade was 61 points. The small spread of the first grade recognizes the limited demands on lower-level jobs, where the addition of just a few responsibilities should elevate the job to the next higher grade. The wide spread of the highest grade accommodates the addition or subtraction of major chunks of responsibility in higher-level jobs without requiring a job reevaluation.

Job grades can be numbered according to organizational preference, starting at 1, or 3, or 20, or something else. The number of job grades parallels the number of natural job clusters. There is no rule of thumb for deciding how many grades are appropriate for an organization. For a target, the appropriate number for many organizations is around sixteen to twenty-two. However, the correct number of grades depends on the diversity and kind of jobs and the need to establish equitable pay relationships among jobs.

Sometimes job grades are referred to as *job bands*. Broad bands may refer to wider job grades (meaning more jobs in the same grade) or larger pay ranges (meaning more distance from minimum pay rate to maximum pay rate), or a combination of both. Broadbanding generally involves converting several existing grades into one band, with the use of reference dollar points instead of minimums, midpoints, and maximums to guide pay management—for example:

Old Pay Grade		New Broad Band
13	Maximum	
	Midpoint	Reference point
	Minimum	
12	Maximum	
	Midpoint	Reference point
	Minimum	
11	Maximum	
	Midpoint	Reference point
	Minimum	
10	Maximum	
	Midpoint	Reference point
	Minimum	

Figure 28. Job grade points produced by 16 percent intervals between job grades.

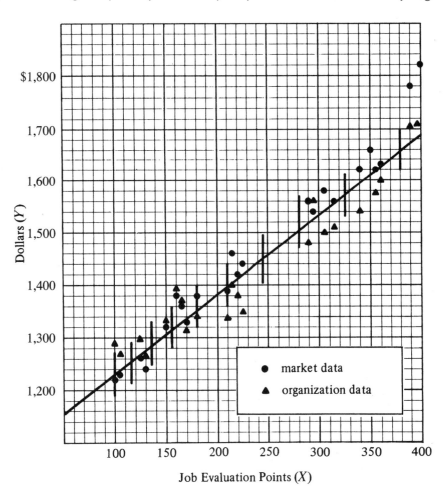

Broadbanding can be carried too far. Within a few years after its introduction into pay management literature, mistakes are being admitted. For example, thirty-three pay grades for nonexempt employees were reduced to six in one organization, which later proved to be too few to distinguish jobs with widely varying degrees of responsibility. Additionally, large pay ranges allowed managers too much freedom to grant pay increases, and payroll costs increased as a result.

Broadbanding can be thought of as an approach to pay management that provides flexibility to meet individual pay requirements. On the other hand, it is also a tactic for reducing unnecessary job grades. In the example, thirty-three grades were too many. Six, on the other hand, are too few. Someone forgot to identify the natural job clusters that fit the operating environment of the organization.

Step 2: Calculate the Market Line

Begin with a picture of the job evaluation and pay data so you can evaluate the data visually instead of having to read numbers in columns. (See Figure 29.) This type of picture is called a *scatter plot*. You can create your own plot using a spreadsheet program. As you can see, the dots are indeed scattered. "Plotting" refers to the process of determining where the dots should be placed.

How is each point marked in the scatter plot? Let's take the first line of data, for job title A in Table 11. For this job, the job evaluation points are 100. On the horizontal scale, read across until you find 100. The mean rate or pay in the marketplace for job A is $1,220. So, on the vertical scale, read up until you come to $1,220.

Now follow the $1,220 line across until you come to the 100 line of the horizontal scale. Then mark the intersection of these two imaginary lines with a dot (see Figure 32).

To understand the process better, use Figure 30 to plot some of the other data in Table 11. When you have finished, verify your work against Figure 29.

Eliminate Widely Varying Data   Notice that two plottings on Figure 29 are quite apart from the others: JE240 (job N), $1,680; and JE320 (job S), $1,340 (where JE stands for *job evaluation points*). In other words, these plottings do not fit logically with the other data points. The variance from the norm is large, and one has to ask why these plots do not fit the pattern.

How would you know that these plots do not fit "logically"? What is the "norm"?

Bear in mind that you are building a model that will ultimately represent all jobs. Models can never represent every single job; if your model does a good job of representing 80 percent or 90 percent of the jobs, that's fine. Stated in the obverse, you can expect 10 percent or 20 percent of the jobs not to fit logically. After following the steps through this phase, you will understand what fits "logically" and what does not. Figure 31 shows the plot map without the two plots that do not fit.

What is the "norm"? In pay management, it usually is a line that you can visualize running through the middle of the plots, upward and to the right.

Data points that do not fit the model, that are not representative of the situation, are eliminated from the calculation. If these strange data were not eliminated, the calculation of the line would be distorted; it would not be representative of the bulk of the jobs. The accuracy of the line is crucial, because it is the basis of important comparisons and additional calculations.

Figure 29. Scatter plot of job evaluation points and market mean. (The data are from Table 11.)

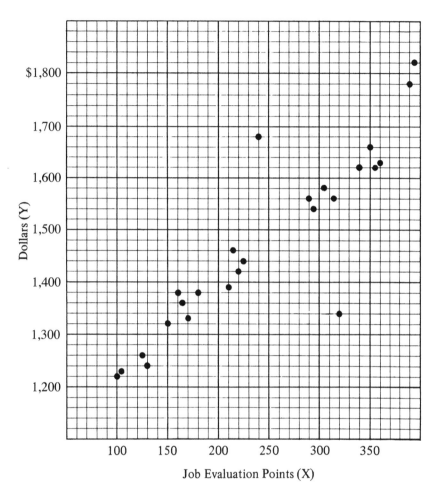

Why would the plottings be so out of line? One innocent possibility is that the points were marked incorrectly. Or the problem may lie in job evaluation: if you check back, you may discover that the job was one that the task force argued about—the wrong argument prevailed, and the wrong degree was selected. Or you may remember some confusion about just what was meant in the job description. Perhaps the job analysis was conducted incompletely. Maybe the weighting of a compensable factor favors this kind of job and gives credit that is not due.

The problem may also originate in the market rate data. You may discover a mathematical error in the survey calculations. Or you may conclude that, as you had suspected, the data submitted by some other organization were poor. Maybe the job was not matched accurately with a comparable job. Perhaps insufficient data prevent a proper assessment of the market, or data from the wrong market area were included.

If you discover such errors, you should usually be able to revise the numbers and replot the data. In some cases, however, the error is nearly unsolvable because a combination of errors in both job evaluation and pay surveying created the problem.

Figure 30. Practice scatter plot for step 2. Draw a scatter plot for the data in Table 11.

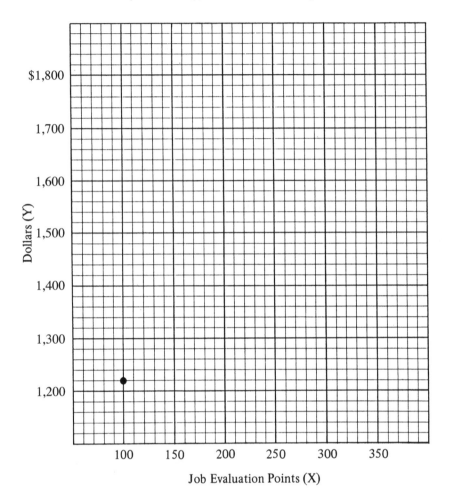

Notice that there are two issues here. First, we need to be sure that all the prior work in the project is accurate. Assessing the validity of the data is one of the major reasons for assembling them into a structure. Second, we must make sure that the model is representative. Some pay managers ignore the opportunity of trying out what-if questions with the model.

Here are some useful what-if questions to ask. What if we:

- Use different jobs in our model?
- Weight the compensable factors differently?
- Add a factor?
- Eliminate a factor?
- Add a degree?
- Change a degree?

Figure 31. Scatter plot of job evaluation points and market mean in Table 11 without widely varying jobs N and S.

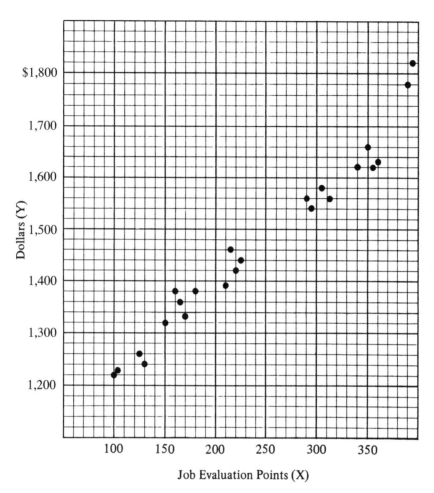

- Use different pay markets?
- Compare with different organizations?
- Select different rates?

You may have to try some or all of these scenarios to build a model that best organizes your jobs into an equitable relationship of job evaluation points and pay market rates.

The Line of Best Fit The process of calculating the *line of best fit* is called *regression analysis*. When the calculation produces a straight line, the process is *linear*. Lines that bend one way or the other are called *curvilinear*. We'll use a straight line for this beginning example (see Figure 32), and then we'll show you a fictitious organization

Figure 32. Market line for the data in Table 11.

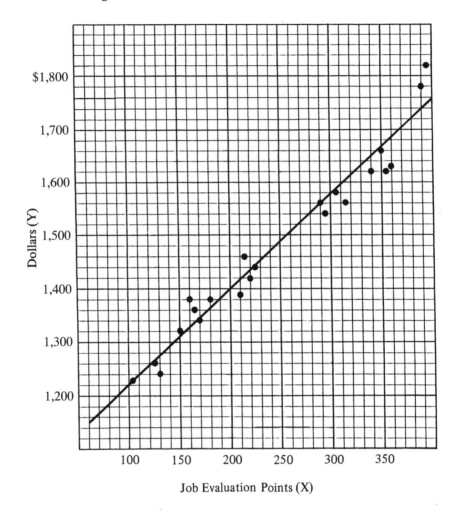

Job Evaluation Points (X)

involving a curved line. You always need to test for a curved line situation so that the line is the best fit for the data. It would be incorrect to use a straight line when a curved line is called for.

Some background information will be helpful to understand regression analysis. Each relationship of job evaluation points to mean market rate is recorded, and the average relationship of all relationships is determined. The line showing the average relationship is drawn down the "middle of the road" of plots. Two points to connect are needed to draw a straight line. The two points are determined with the algebraic formula

$$Y = a + bX$$
(stated as Y equals a plus b times X)

In other words, with a value of X (job evaluation points), the corresponding value

Figure 33. Using the line of best fit to determine the pay rate for a new job with a given number of job evaluation points.

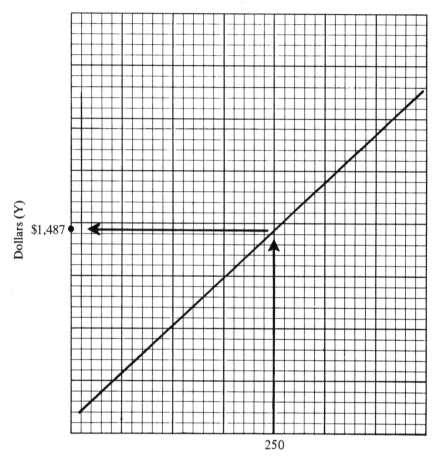

Job Evaluation Points (X)

of Y (pay rate) can be determined for that line. Having entered the job evaluation and pay data as shown in Table 11, spreadsheet software will complete the calculation and display the line.

The line of best fit forms the basis of the entire pay structure. (Actually, several lines will be drawn.)

Predicting pay rates is another value of regression analysis. Each plot represents a relationship between a job and equivalent pay, on the average, in the market. These are known relationships of existing situations. Suppose that a new job is created for which there are few or no market data. The line tells you what to pay, on the average, for this job, as follows: find the job evaluation value of the job on the horizontal scale (say, 250 points), read up to the regression line, then turn left 90 degrees to the pay scale and read the related pay rate. See Figure 33.

Notice that the job evaluation points are labeled X (always the horizontal scale) and dollars as Y (always the vertical scale); these are just shorthand symbols.

Figure 34. Comparing the organization line to the market line.

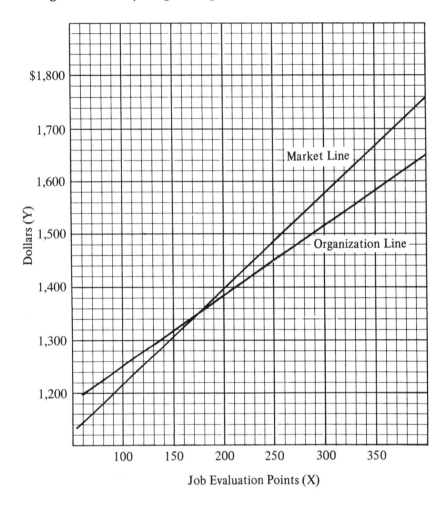

Now enter pairs of data into your program to calculate a straight line for jobs A through Z, except jobs N and S, which we will take to be at too great a variance from the anticipated line to be useful as representative jobs in building the model.

Step 3: Calculate the Organization Line

In order to make a comparison of the organization to the market, you must determine the mean rate of pay of employees in the jobs in your organization (that is, for the jobs for which you obtained market information). In short, you have to calculate a second line for your data just as you did to calculate the market line.

Do that, using the mean rate of pay in the organizational data in Table 11 (do not use jobs N and S since they were eliminated in the market rate analysis). You should arrive at Figure 34, with two lines to compare: the market line and the organization line.

Figure 35. Choose a policy line on the basis of your organization's wants and needs for its pay program.

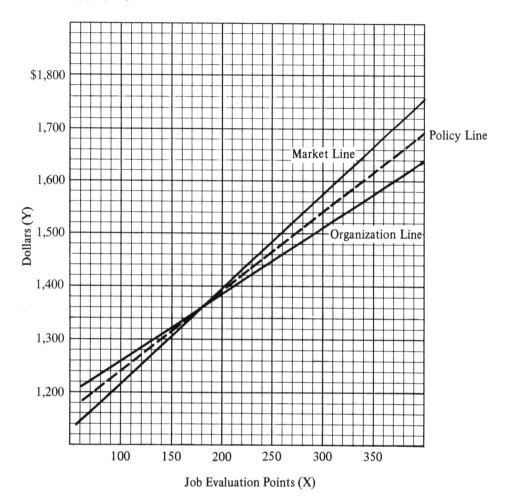

What does the hypothetical picture in Figure 34 tell you? It tells you that this particular organization is overpaying people on lower-level jobs and underpaying people on upper-level jobs, according to the market. Of course, in your organization, the picture may be quite different.

Step 4: Determine a Policy Line

The next decision is far-reaching, for it establishes the organization's posture with employees and determines what the organization considers fair pay for job contributions according to management's expectations. You may not be in a position to make this decision; your role may be to examine the options and make a recommendation. Return to the organization's pay goals in Phase 1.3. What does the organization want to do? What does the organization need to do? Figure 35 shows an example policy line.

Figure 36. Degrees of correlation: (*a*) perfect correlation, (*b*) moderate to strong correlation, (*c*) weak or nonexistent correlation.

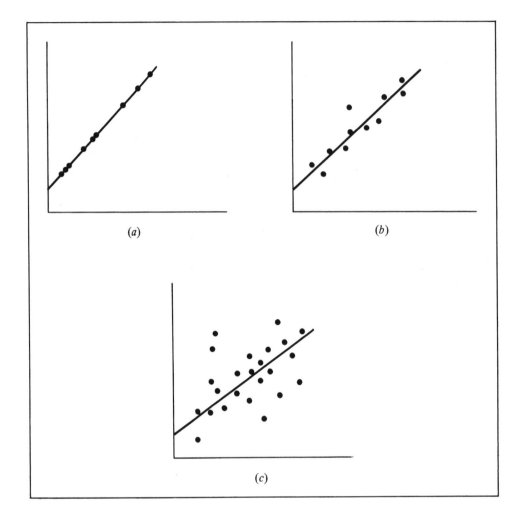

In this case, the organization is moving toward the market but is not willing to meet all market rates.

Coefficient of Correlation How good is the structure? Are the job evaluation data accurate and consistent? Are the pay survey data reasonable? Although these questions cannot be answered precisely, there is a measure of reliability: the coefficient of correlation.

Notice Figure 36. In the drawing *a*, all the plots are on the line—a condition called *perfect correlation*. All the relationships of points to dollars are identical. In drawing *b*, the plots are scattered slightly away from the line, meaning that the correlation is moderate to strong. In drawing *c*, the plots are scattered around, meaning that the relationship between points and dollars is weak, if existent.

The closer the plots are to the line, the stronger is the correlation. A higher correlation suggests that the data are more reliable. The coefficient for the market line in the example is .98, and for the organization line, .94; both are very reliable. You'll do fine to be above .80.

The coefficient is calculated as a product of the regression analysis and is reported in the following way:

> 0 to .19 = no relationship
> .2 to .49 = weak correlation
> .5 to .69 = moderate
> .7 to .89 = strong
> .9 to 1.0 = very strong

Step 5: Determine the Pay Range Spread

With the job grades and the policy line connecting the midpoints of the pay ranges established, the pay ranges can be determined. The midpoint of the job grade in points and the midpoint of the pay range in dollars (see Figure 37) represent the X plus Y values of a single point.

The middle of the grade in job evaluation points is found by adding the low points to the high points of the job grade and dividing the result by two. For example: 100 + 116 = 216 ÷ 2 = 108.

Job evaluation midpoints are converted to the midpoints in dollars by using the regression values from the policy line to find the corresponding dollar value. Table 12 shows the results for our example.

Range spreads are typically defined as the percentage distance from minimum to maximum. For the purpose of demonstrating the calculation, let's use a range spread of 50 percent.

The minimum is found by dividing the midpoint, $1,250 in grade 1, by 1 plus one-half of the selected range spread (one-half of 50 percent is 25 percent). Thus, divide $1,250 by 1.25. (Since the midpoint is half the distance between the minimum and the maximum, 1.25 answers the question: The midpoint of $1,250 is 125 percent of what dollar minimum?) The minimum therefore is $1,000. The maximum is found by multiplying the minimum by 1 plus 50 percent ($1,000 × 1.50). The maximum therefore is $1,500. See Figure 38.

In an actual situation, experiment with different pay range spreads to determine the most appropriate impact. Obviously if the percentages you use produce a large number of pay rates falling below the minimum and/or above the maximum, the range spreads are too small. If almost all of the pay rates are within the pay range, and, furthermore, almost no pay rates are near the minimum or maximum, the pay range spread is too large.

As a general rule, pay range spreads for lower-level jobs are generally calculated at 25 to 30 percent. These jobs don't require much opportunity for pay increases because the jobs are rather static, and individual accomplishments do not influence results as much as they do in higher-level jobs. Pay range spreads for technical and administrative jobs might be from 30 or 35 percent to 40 or 45 percent. Professional jobs require more potential pay movement within the range so that spreads of 45 to 60 percent are more appropriate. Senior professional and middle management jobs are more suited to 60 to

Figure 37. Midpoint of the job grade in points and midpoint of the pay range in dollars. The points meet at the same point on the line of best fit.

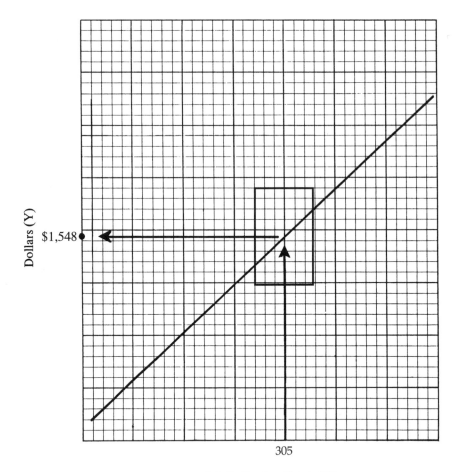

Job Evaluation Points (X)

80 percent spreads. You need to try a number of options in order to determine the pay range spreads that best meet your organization's goals and situation. The pay range spreads as reported in some pay surveys offer another guide as to what spreads are used by other organizations.

For practice, complete the calculations for the pay ranges according to the percentages listed in Table 13, and then compare your results to the minimums and maximums listed there.

Some people use another method of calculating minimums and maximums: they select a pay range spread (let's say 20 percent) and multiply the midpoint by 120 percent to find the maximum, and by 80 percent to find the minimum.

The completed pay structure for the example is in Figure 39.

In the End, Does the Structure Make Sense? Be careful. About now, you may have lost sight of the big picture. Perhaps there were just too many calculations.

Table 12. Pay grade midpoints, expressed as job evaluation points and as dollars.

Grade	Job Evaluation Points	Job Evaluation Midpoint	Dollar Midpoint
1	100–115	108	$1,250
2	116–134	125	1,276
3	135–155	145	1,306
4	156–180	169	1,342
5	181–209	196	1,382
6	210–243	227	1,430
7	244–281	263	1,484
8	282–327	305	1,548
9	328–379	354	1,622
10	380–440	411	1,707

Figure 38. Minimum-maximum calculations, given a 50 percent range spread.

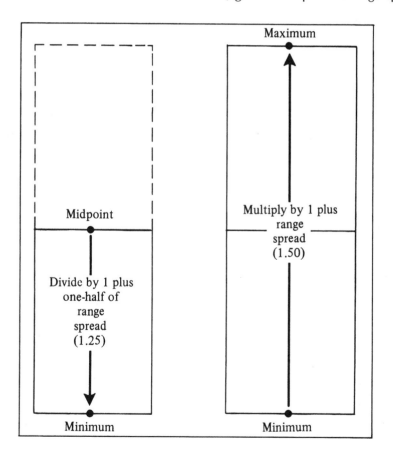

Table 13. Calculated dollar minimums and maximums for job grades, using a pay range spread of 50 percent.

Grade	Job Evaluation Points	Pay Range Spread	Minimum	Midpoint	Maximum
1	100–115	25%	$1,111	$1,250	$1,389
2	116–134	25	1,134	1,276	1,418
3	135–155	30	1,136	1,306	1,476
4	156–180	30	1,167	1,342	1,517
5	181–209	35	1,176	1,382	1,588
6	210–243	35	1,217	1,430	1,643
7	244–281	40	1,237	1,484	1,731
8	282–327	40	1,290	1,548	1,806
9	328–379	45	1,324	1,622	1,920
10	380–440	45	1,393	1,707	2,021

Figure 39. Final pay structure.

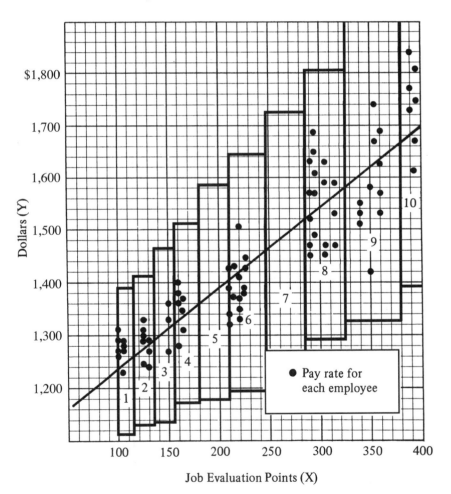

The big picture is this: you are trying to develop an organizational guide to recognize and reward employees who contribute their effort to the enterprise. It's an important goal, so make sure it doesn't get lost in the maze of numbers.

Project Analyzer 7.2

Was your current pay structure calculated according to the protocol for determining job grades and pay ranges?

_____

_____

If grades and ranges are not calculated properly, does this explain some of the equity problems your organization has been experiencing?

_____

_____

7.3 Evaluating the New Structure

Once the calculations of the new pay structure have been completed, the time is at hand to assess its implications for the organization and the people who are being paid.

This is a delicate time. While management will probably be surprised to learn that it has not done too badly in managing pay with informal guides (maybe it will use the "I told you so" routine), it will also learn about the mistakes made along the way.

Do not shy away from the lessons to be learned. If you have done your work thoroughly and diligently, pay attention to the results, for they are accurate and they have a message for your organization.

You may realize that employees are paid, on the average, slightly below the market, or slightly above the market, or perhaps at the market.

You may realize that the low average rates are a result of high turnover; no one gets a chance to move up into the range. Or the high average rates may support the observation that people who have seniority do not leave and are sitting near the maximum of their grade.

You may discover that a few or a lot of people are being paid below the minimum for their pay grade, or that a few or a lot of people are being paid above the maximum for their pay grade.

All such findings require an explanation. Things do not just happen. Conscious managerial decisions have produced the results—all right, maybe some unconscious ones, too. What happened? Why? Having these answers helps fashion an appropriate response. The answers are there; you need only ferret them out.

Examine the Options

Return to the compensation goals and objectives. What does the organization want to achieve? Identify and evaluate options that will achieve goals and objectives. Now that a structure exists, examine a variety of what-if scenarios.

Some options will deal with problems (such as pay rates below the minimum), for they need to be corrected. Other options will consider opportunities (such as new career paths), for you need to take advantage of them.

Have several options, with implications, ready to present to the decision makers of your organization. Have a recommendation too.

What to Do About Jobs Below the Minimum or Above the Maximum

There can be any number of pay rate situations that require attention even though the rates are within the pay range. The most treacherous are pay rates that fall below the minimum or above the maximum. Recognize what these conditions say to the people involved: below the minimum says, "We have been underpaying you"; above the maximum, "We have been overpaying you."

In many cases, the employees paid above the maximum are the long-service, loyal employees of the organization. Be very careful about the way these folks are treated. Find out who is involved and why. This is not the time to set a general policy without understanding the implications for each human being.

Okay, some of the employees are not pulling a fair share, and, yes, something should have been done about the situation before. Be careful. The construction of a pay structure is not the excuse someone has been waiting for to do the dirty deed.

Remember, the success of this program rests on its acceptance. If other employees view the program as a lame excuse to "get" some people, the whole thing will be rejected.

Employees whose pay rates are below the minimum generally are brought up to the minimum at the installation of the program. Occasionally, where the adjustment is quite large, two increases are made, perhaps three, four, or six months apart. You can sense the difficulty in this approach: an employee can argue, "The minimum is the minimum; bring me up now." On the other hand, you *are* making the adjustment.

Pay rates above the maximum are another story (see Figure 40 on page 272, especially noting grades 1 and 8). The rates could theoretically be dropped into the range, but this is rarely done. Here are your choices:

- Leave the rates high and accept that the person warrants the extraordinary pay.
- Stop all pay increases until the rate comes within the range.
- Allow the employee to continue to receive increases, but in smaller amounts and/or over longer review periods.
- Develop a plan to increase job skills so that the employee can qualify for a job in a pay grade commensurate with the pay rate.
- Add bona fide responsibilities to the job so that it will be reevaluated at a higher pay grade.

Look at the options and evaluate them carefully.

The choice of the pay range spread depends on the number of rates outside the range. Obviously if the range spread is large enough, there will be no rates outside the range, but then the long-run costs are prohibitive. Try different range spreads; consider the impact of each new calculation.

Costs of the Program

There are two categories of costs you must consider: immediate costs and long-term costs. The immediate costs of installation are the immediate payroll adjustments to bring people up to their new minimums (again, see Figure 40; note grades 6 and 9) plus the costs of this change over the remainder of the financial planning cycle. The long-term costs are the costs of allowing all employees to reach new maximums.

Timing of Implementation

Some managements will want to implement the program immediately. Others may prefer to have the pay project identify the problems but not force them to act immediately; they want the time to consider options carefully and to begin to make changes quietly without the scrutiny of the entire organization. This is perfectly acceptable, even prudent, reasoning. The other side of the coin is that if an organization has decided on a collaborative style to develop the program, the word is out and everyone will be anxious for the results. Still, deliberate action is laudable.

Addressing Personal Concerns

People want to know how the new pay structure will affect them. Why are we doing this? Who worked on the project? What pay grade am I in? How was it decided? Who decided? What is a pay grade? How is it calculated? Where am I in the grade? What happens when I get to the top? How long will it take? How can I earn a bonus? Will my pay be cut? What happens now? Does this change my review date? What about merit increases? When will changes be effective? How do I move to a higher grade? What if my job description has changed? Or what if it changes later? Does this program affect everybody? What about opportunities for the future?

The questions will be endless, but most can be anticipated. What are your answers? Be prepared. Train managers to respond cogently and consistently to employees throughout the organization. Be ready for "special" questions and "special" situations. Management's demeanor at this moment will make or break the program.

Project Analyzer 7.3

What does the new structure say about the organization's human resources and management practices?

_____

_____

What do you know about the reasons for pay conditions as they now exist?

_____

_____

In what ways do these reasons influence the actions that need to be taken to implement the new structure?

_____

_____

What will be done about pay rates below the minimum?

_____

_____

What will be done about pay rates above the maximum?

_____

_____

What are the costs of implementing the program?

_____

_____

What optional range spreads should you consider?

_____

_____

_____

Should changes be implemented now or later?

_____

_____

7.4 Managing Pay

Now that the pay structure has been calculated, the next consideration is how pay will be managed within the structure. In fact, having calculated a sound basic model, you are now in a position to adapt your pay management guide to support the pay strategies that your organization wishes to embrace. Remember that the pay structure is not immutable. If it becomes sacrosanct, the organization runs the risk of losing its flexibility to stay abreast of a dynamic environment. Heed warnings of rigidity.

Pay and Motivation

You will read and hear much about aligning pay strategies to support organization strategies on the theory that correctly defined and managed pay programs will motivate employees to work for rewards based on organization success. Don't get sucked into a false premise.

Is pay a motivator? It is when an employee decides to accept the inducement. It is *not* a motivator when the employee rejects the inducement.

Decades ago, Frederick Herzberg, an organizational psychologist, offered his hygiene/motivation theory in which he identified work satisfiers (motivators) and dissatisfiers (demotivators). His analysis is still correct. Pay, he concluded, is largely a dissatisfier. (Other dissatisfiers are company policy and administration, supervision—both technical and human relations—and working conditions.) Work satisfiers are recognition, achievement, advancement, responsibility, and the work itself.

The beauty of Herzberg's work is the understanding that correcting dissatisfaction, such as correcting poor pay, will not convert pay from a demotivator to a motivator. What is achieved by correcting the problem with pay is to eliminate the dissatisfaction.

Ask a group of managers how long the good effect of a pay increase will last. Most will say, "Until the next paycheck." Perhaps that reply is a bit cynical, but it is more true than not. The moment a pay increase is granted, the value of the increase begins to diminish, and dissatisfaction begins to set in.

The reality is that most all employees either are dissatisfied with their pay or accept it as a given. Complaining about pay is a badge of acceptance among employees. Almost no one stands up and announces, "My pay is great!" More pay is better because it affords a better standard of living. Wanting more pay is part of our national fabric. Even executives who earn millions of dollars a year want to earn more money.

Pay Range Minimum, Midpoint, and Maximum

The minimum of the pay range is the target pay rate for employees newly hired or promoted into a job. The minimum signifies the least amount of money an employee should earn to accomplish the job. When their qualifications warrant, employees may be placed in a job at a pay rate above the minimum, but typically not above the midpoint.

Learned job responsibilities is the most obvious criterion for awarding pay increases to move employees through the bottom half of the pay range until they are fully qualified, at which point they will be paid at the midpoint (competent rate or performance rate). The midpoint is maintained equitably with rates paid in the marketplace for similar jobs.

Rather than pay employees as each new qualification is learned, most organizations prefer the administratively easier procedure of reviewing employees' pay at set times, such as on the employee's anniversary date of entry into the job or when all employees' pay rates are reviewed annually.

Because the midpoint signifies the pay of a fully qualified employee, the top half of the pay range, from midpoint to maximum, is designed to reward employees who accomplish extraordinary results. Unfortunately, this turns out not to be the case when pay increases are based on seniority or so-called merit.

Seniority and Merit Pay Increases

Seniority pay increases are awarded, typically once a year, as long as an employee remains in a job. Seniority increases assume that the job results produced by the employee meet organizational expectations and that more experience in the job equates to better job results. Both assumptions may be false. Especially as desired by unions, seniority increases eliminate management's opportunity to grant pay increases to favorite employees. Seniority pay systems are not common.

Merit pay increases are the most prevalent pay strategy in organizations. Pay increases are awarded for meritorious job performance, usually judged in a performance review and tied to a performance rating (such as superior, outstanding, competent, marginal, or poor). Pay budgets are calculated on expected revenues and expenses, anticipated staffing, inflation of market pay rates, and estimated pay increases. Disastrously, employees may conclude that their increases were budgeted "last year" so that there is nothing they can do to obtain a bigger increase.

There are problems with merit increases. First, increases are almost always distributed even if an employee does not deserve an increase, much the same problem as with seniority increases. If an employee is still employed at review time, some increase is awarded. Second, although the merit increase is based on the final performance rating, most managers collapse and figure out some way to pay everyone the same in order to avoid both grumbling among the troops and becoming the target of outright verbal abuse. Using the performance rating scale above as an example, most managers would shun the competent rate as merely average and attempt to rate most employees as outstanding (above average). Some managers, on the other hand, hold down increases in order to give a little extra to superior performers, but this amount turns out to be not enough of an increase to signal an exceptional contribution, and it certainly upsets the employees who receive a minimal increase.

Merit increases are viewed as an expected addition to pay by most employees. In most employees' view, the pay increase is never enough to cover the change in cost of living—and, in many cases, aggregate economic indicators prove this is true. Merit increases, besides being tied to a performance rating, are typically determined in a pay matrix of pay range divisions and time intervals (sometimes the time interval is a standard twelve months). The following matrix numbers are merely examples and are simplified in order to demonstrate the concept. Instead of relating pay increases to every employee's pay rate, the pay range is divided into four groups (quartiles) to simplify identifying position in the range, which guides the timing and amount of pay increases. The first quartile is identified for employees new in their jobs, and the fourth quartile is identified for employees who have been in their jobs the longest.

Performance Rating	First Quartile 3 months[a]	Second Quartile 6 months[a]	Third Quartile 12 months[a]	Fourth Quartile 18 months[a]
Superior	8%	7%	6%	5%
Outstanding	6	5	4	3
Competent	4	3	2	1
Marginal	1	1	0	0
Poor	0	0	0	0

[a]Refers to interval between pay reviews.

Pay increases are more rapid and larger in the first two quartiles to relate to the typically greater learning acquired when first in the job and to move employees up to the midpoint, or competent rate, as soon as possible. The timing and amount of the increases are slowed and lowered in the third and fourth quartiles to relate to less learning, but also to slow reaching the range maximum, which means no more increases until the maximum is adjusted upward.

Obviously the precise, calculated, and rigid nature of a matrix stifles most thoughts of flexible rewards based on better contributions. All kinds of questions can be raised about how the matrix was constructed. Certainly employees will want to know why their increases are less as they move toward the top of the pay range and will need to be reminded that a smaller percentage of a larger base may produce a nearly equal or even greater increase than a larger percentage of a smaller base. Unfortunately, employees may walk away in utter dismay at receiving a performance rating better than last year yet a smaller pay increase percentage.

Employees progress rather automatically to the maximum. Remember, however, that the range above the midpoint to the maximum signifies extraordinary employee accomplishments. But for most employees, this is not the case. Stated the other way around, employees who are more competent may be earning less than their counterparts. Obviously, this inequity is a major frustration of so-called merit pay. Additionally, with most employees eventually working their way into the top portion of the pay range and with the midpoint being tied to the average market pay rate, the merit increase approach becomes very expensive as pay increases mount on top of previous pay increases.

Pay for Job Contribution

Problems with merit pay increases have led many organizations to emphasize a pay philosophy of rewarding employees according to their job contribution (sometimes referred to as *pay for performance, pay for results,* or *variable pay*). Organizations are demanding more production and productivity, more new ideas, improved operations, reduced expenses, greater acceptance of responsibility, and independent decision making, and they say they are willing to pay for this greater job contribution.

Paying for performance (the most popular term) has been a new theme in pay management—for a number of years. That's because most organizations can't quite break away from the administrative simplicity and security of a merit increase system, yet they continue to be drawn to the allure of the noble American tradition: we only pay for what we get.

There are several drags on the implementation of this pay strategy. First, although organizations welcome the opportunity to pay out rewards in return for the results, they are reluctant to upset or penalize employees who do not accomplish objectives.

Second, the inherent assumption of paying for performance is that all results must be positive in order to be rewarded. However, organizations also know that people learn from mistakes, and withholding pay increases when mistakes are made may derail enthusiasm. Worse, employees may waste energy trying to cover up mistakes, or to avert risk, in order to obtain or protect rewards.

Third, the great organizational hope is that results will always get better, and therefore employees will always be able to earn more. However, recessions occur, business plans don't always pan out, and then there is no pot of money to share.

These realities are crucial in the assessment of whether a job contribution approach is right for your organization. That pay ought to vary in relation to the contribution an employee makes to the organization, whether the contribution is measured as an individual job contribution, a portion of team accomplishment, or a portion of organization accomplishment, is widely accepted, especially since it fits with the American economic fabric that success reaps rewards. This pay philosophy rests not only on the courage of managers to live up to the standard, but also on the fairness of pay and work management systems. Otherwise, organizations will remain mired in giveaway merit pay programs.

Let's look at an illustration of the pay-for-job contribution approach. The noticeable difference from most other approaches doesn't occur until the employee reaches the midpoint (competent rate), although according to the philosophy, employees must be held accountable for contributing expected job results from the first day of their employment.

An employee is hired in year 1 at the minimum of the pay range. The employee learns the job following an orientation program, training, and on-the-job experience. The focus is on rewarding the employee for learning the job essentials. Bonuses may be awarded based on extraordinary individual, team, or organizational accomplishments. Let's say that by year 3, the employee has progressed to the midpoint (competent rate) of the pay range—$20,000.

Pay will continue at the competent rate as long as job results meet job expectations. The competent rate may change as the pay range and pay structure are adjusted to maintain equity with the market.

Once the employee is fulfilling all job expectations competently, the manager and the employee can begin to set objectives that exceed basic job expectations so that the employee can earn a bonus. Let's assume the employee chooses to contribute more than basic job expectations in order to earn a bonus, accomplishes the objectives, and is awarded a bonus of $3,000. The employee now earns $23,000, except that the $23,000 is composed of the $20,000 competency base pay plus the $3,000 bonus. The base, unlike merit pay programs, does not become $23,000.

The employee may take the $3,000 bonus as a lump sum payment or may have it spread out evenly in the paychecks during the following year. Tax issues must be investigated to assess the implications of each way of taking the bonus payment. Similarly, changes in benefit programs based on pay may be required.

At the beginning of year 4, the manager and the employee again set job objectives to exceed basic job expectations. Let's suppose that the employee accomplishes extraordinary results and again earns a bonus, even better than the previous year—$5,000. Now the employee is earning $25,000 (the base pay of $20,000 plus the bonus of $5,000).

The employee is not earning $28,000—that is, $20,000 plus last year's $3,000 plus the new $5,000 bonus. This bonus system is designed to prevent employees from stacking pay increases and coasting on previous accomplishments. The organization benefits from reduced fixed payroll expense. Follow the illustration one more step, and you will see another impact of the system.

In year 5, the employee does well again and earns a bonus, but not as much as in previous years; this time the bonus is $1,000. In a system where pay increases accumulate, this employee would earn $29,000 ($20,000 plus previous pay increases of $3,000, $5,000, and $1,000) instead of $21,000. Other employees might have accomplished more than this employee in this year but would not have earned as much unless they too had been in the system long enough to accumulate previous increases.

Converting to a job contribution pay strategy requires managers who can plan, monitor, and appraise job contributions and who are willing to hold employees accountable for success, as well as for failure. Furthermore, organizations must accept that employees may choose to come to work, accomplish basic job expectations, collect their paychecks, and go home. Unfortunately, many organizations can't leave well enough alone and believe that employees can and should be "motivated" to accomplish extraordinary results.

Some organizations even put a portion of base pay at risk (meaning that it may be lost) in exchange for an opportunity to earn a reward of perhaps two, three, or four times greater than the amount risked, depending on results accomplished. Organizations use pay at risk as a way to induce employees to think and act like owners.

For most people, risk is okay so long as the risk pays off. When bad times come along, and they always do, all the rationale of having known the risks up front will not ameliorate bad feelings. Most employees have a strong need for security, principally based on the predictability of what will or will not happen to them. Despite the possibility of huge rewards, the demand of paying bills motivates most people to prefer security over risk when faced with the choice, especially because most people do not earn sufficient income to provide a cushion from which to risk. Nevertheless, when an organization dangles the opportunity for more money in front of the average worker, sensibilities are lost, the offer is not rejected, and disappointment is risked. The job contribution approach provides a secure base but adds the spice, if accepted by the employee, of extra rewards for extra results.

In sum, paying employees for their contribution is a time-honored concept. It fits with an American sense of individual responsibility. It is straightforward. More enticing and intricate schemes are not necessary. Solid pay structures built on a realistic understanding of human motivation and behavior, coupled with competent and fair management practices aimed at delivering effective job contributions, win out every time.

Competency-Based Pay

Some organizations choose to match pay to personal competencies mastered by the employee instead of to job contributions (sometimes referred to as "paying for the person" instead of "paying for the job"). Competencies have been defined as the specific knowledge, skill, or ability required to accomplish a job, such as writing sales contracts, but also defined as abstract knowledge areas or behaviors, such as customer service or teamwork.

The purpose of tying pay to competencies is to encourage employees to acquire more competencies. Focusing on personal competencies aims to encourage employees to think more broadly about how they can contribute their talents anywhere in the organization, not just in their jobs. Some organizations believe that the concept of a job that the employee is supposed to accomplish, and a pay range within which pay is matched to job accomplishments, is a narrow and confining point of view. Furthermore, it is argued, the organization can save time by not having to manage complex job grade systems and is able to adapt more quickly to changing work environments by not having to work through tedious job evaluation schemes.

Managing competencies may not turn out to be so simple. Even if jobs don't have to be valued, competencies do. Somehow time will be required to identify, value, and test employee competencies. Pay market information will be uncertain because market information is organized around job information, not competencies. Organizational costs might even increase as employees acquire competencies that employees have to pay for but are not able to be used by the organization.

A major theme of this book is to focus on jobs as an organizational unit supporting the organization's mission. Competencies should be directly linked to the qualifications required to accomplish jobs. If you desire to reward employees for competencies as they grow in job capability, use special bonuses, or increase job responsibilities based on the new competencies and increase base pay. As for organizational flexibility to use employee talents wherever they may be helpful, no major pay system needs to be constructed to accomplish this; just let them do it.

Team-Based Pay

When employees work together on a team, it is appropriate to divide rewards among team members for accomplishing team results in production, quality, efficiency, service, costs, waste, and safety, for example. Team rewards can also be used to emphasize a unified, cooperative effort with other employees versus individual achievement or functional isolation.

Teams need to flow naturally from the organization's operating structure and practices before rewards can be associated with team results. Teams established to provide a mechanism to distribute teams are unrealistic. Teams anointed for the sake of "teamwork" will fail because teamwork does not necessarily come from teams.

Remember that a team is a group of individuals who depend on one another to accomplish a common objective. If the demand on individual team members is absolutely equal (which doesn't happen very often), then develop a reward program that shares rewards equally and reinforces the concept of equal participation. When participation is not equal—some members influence team results more than others—recognize individual results in addition to team results.

Employees may say that equal shares are acceptable, but deep down, the old individual contribution bug will infect the system. If employees who contribute substandard results received the same distribution as employees who contribute exceptional results, you can be sure there will be an outcry.

Beware also of triggering counterproductive competition among teams. If you are trying to build commitment to the enterprise based on cooperation and participation, teams in competition with one another for rewards may be the very thing that you do not want to do.

Organization Reward Sharing

Sharing the rewards of organizational accomplishments with each employee, or with groups, recognizes that all employees, or all groups, contribute to the organization's success.

Rewards can be based on production, quality, efficiency, service, costs, waste, safety, and so forth, but mainly they are based on operating profit. The concept of operating profit takes into account revenues generated minus how well the organization used the revenue. Operating profit does not calculate increases or decreases over which employees have no control, such as changes in material costs. Profit is not a complicated concept to understand, but its calculation based on operating influences is. Provide plenty of information to help employees understand profit results.

The downside of organization rewards is that each employee's contribution, or each group's contribution, is typically small relative to the total organization effort, and some employees, or some groups, by the nature of job or group responsibilities, or by personal effort, contribute more than others. It is difficult for individuals or groups to relate their contribution to total organization results.

Organization rewards therefore symbolize the collaborative nature of enterprise achievement. Because of the many influences between individual or group effort and organization payout, not much stock should be placed in using organization rewards to encourage esprit de corps and maximum contribution.

Reward Criteria   Regardless of how rewards are based—on individual, team, or organization accomplishments—the criteria used to determine them require a great deal of attention. Rewards are generally conceived of as an incentive to produce desired results ("If you accomplish this, you will get that"). Thus, reward criteria are established before work begins toward results.

Most organizations make the mistake of focusing rewards too narrowly—for example, on increased production. The result may be that production increases but costs may also increase or quality may decrease. In an attempt to take these possibilities into account, organizations have tried to develop complicated formulas and measurements to the point that the reward mechanism becomes difficult to understand or is fraught with countervailing value judgments susceptible to argument.

An after-the-fact judgment runs contrary to the design concept of most reward programs as a motivator. The theory is that people need to know up front what rewards they will receive in order for them to agree to work for the desired result. Built on simplistic incentive systems popular in the early part of the twentieth century, current incentive systems have continued to be designed on questionable psychological tenets. The lesson to be learned, after many, many incentive program failures, is that employees understand that results are unpredictable: rewards can't be fairly distributed unless all of the results are considered, organizational success is dependent on a number of influences, it doesn't make sense to give rewards for one improvement while other problems detract from the improvement, and employees can commit to broader and more complicated objectives.

The best way to understand reward criteria is in relation to the total and final result produced when all of the influences on results can be examined and explained. For example, successful delivery of a product is the sum of the correct production, meeting quality standards, at the least possible cost, on time, without hurting anyone. All of these factors must be taken into account.

The best time to understand reward criteria is when actual results have been delivered, when all of the facts are known, when all of the pluses and minuses can be assessed.

Reward System Considerations   Here are some issues you should consider when installing individual or group reward systems:

■ *Design system objectives to meet specific needs in your organization.* Do not pick a system off the shelf just because everyone else is using it. Gain a commitment among managers, before the program is implemented, to reward objectives. Study the implications and what-ifs of the program to preclude disasters and disgruntlements with reward payments. Many rewards look good until they are analyzed for their faults.

■ *Clarify who can receive what rewards.* Principally, be sure that employees can influence the factors that will earn them rewards. Make sure that the rewards are tied to all aspects of an employee's job, the profitable and the unprofitable, and all responsibilities of the job, the favorable and the unfavorable, so that employees share in all dimensions of performance.

■ *Make sure reward criteria fit with the organization's objectives, so you avoid contradictory motivations.* If long-term growth of the organization is needed, short-term rewards will impair the long-term objective. New organizations cannot be hampered by high salaries as a fixed expense; these organizations should offer greater incentive rewards to employees for meeting growth objectives. Growth in mature organizations is usually more stable, so that there is less opportunity for substantial rewards for few employees and more opportunity for rewards among many employees.

■ *Match rewards criteria with operational cycles and time them to coincide with revenues.* For example, if revenues are high in only one quarter of the year, rewards should be tied to a yearly cycle instead of a quarterly cycle so that employees not only receive the benefit of the good quarter but also share equally in the difficult times of the other three quarters.

■ *Discuss expectations before effort is expended in the pursuit and management of reward objectives.* Many times, "subjective" criteria can be made measurable with only a little effort when managers and employees discuss their perceptions of success. Not all important organizational values are quantifiable in the measurable sense of how many dollars were saved or how many more tickets were processed. Particularly in the area of human rapport and service, measurements are elusive. The components of *courtesy and tact*, for example, and how to teach our ideals to someone else, are not certain. Yet we cannot drop these values from our organizations just because they are difficult to measure. In fact, customers *know* when they have been treated *discourteously and tactlessly.* At least in discussion, criteria can be clarified sufficiently so that employees can accomplish the organization's expectations.

■ *Focus rewards on those gains that are most desirable for the organization, the individual, or the group.* Reward payments may be immediate or deferred, cash or something else of value, mandatory or voluntary, and various combinations of these. Tax considerations are essential when the organization is planning requirements and options in the system.

■ *Match reward payments to the difficulty of attaining the objective.* Three different conditions of difficulty and reward may exist: (1) The next objective is just as difficult to achieve as the previous one, and therefore the reward payment is the same for each new objective attained; (2) the next objective is *more* difficult to achieve than the previous one, and therefore the reward payment is larger for each new objective attained; or (3) the next objective is *less* difficult to achieve than the previous one, and therefore the reward payment is smaller for each new objective attained.

■ *Consider the scheduling of reward payments.* Reward payments can be scheduled to begin only after certain conditions are met—for example, no reward, or a limited reward paid, until a certain amount of revenue is received. Reward payments might be paid only if the employee were still employed when the reward was earned.

Project Analyzer 7.4

What experience has your organization had with various pay strategies?

_____

_____

Does the organization favor rigid operating policies and procedures?

_____

_____

Is the organization willing to give department managers the authority to manage their own pay budgets?

_____

_____

Does the organization hold department managers accountable for pay decisions, or is some other department (human resources, administration) the controller?

_____

_____

What is current policy for awarding pay increases?

_____

_____

When are pay reviews conducted?

_____

_____

What do managers and employees think of the pay review policy?

_____

_____

Do employees seem to get pay increases automatically, without much regard to the results they accomplish?

_____

_____

Are managers honest when they recommend pay increases, or are they forced to play games because of a restrictive system?

_____

_____

Are managers consistent among themselves when they make pay recommendations?

_____

_____

Do employees have an entitlement mentality toward pay?

_____

_____

What would happen if employees were told that in the future their pay will depend on the contribution they make to organization objectives (if they haven't been told that already)?

_____

_____

Would managers be willing to confront employees who are not contributing required results?

_____

_____

Are employees willing to risk some of their pay in order to win bigger rewards?

_____

_____

Are criteria adequate to measure job contributions?

_____

_____

Does the organization use incentive programs?

_____

_____

Have the incentives increased the organization's accomplishments?

_____

_____

Have incentives increased employee satisfaction?

_____

_____

Do employees play games to beat the incentive schemes?

_____

_____

Are incentives worth the investment?

_____

_____

Has the organization thought about or experimented with paying for competencies?

_____

_____

What was the organization's experience with paying for competencies?

_____

_____

What have you learned about the practice from other organizations?

_____

_____

Would managers be willing to evaluate competencies and develop learning programs to develop them?

_____

_____

Has your organization defined its core competencies?

_____

_____

Do the organization's operating practices naturally center on organization results, team results, individual results, or a combination?

_____

_____

Do teams flow naturally from operating practices?

_____

_____

How well can team results be documented?

_____

_____

What experience does the organization have with rewarding team members for team results?

_____

_____

What do employees think about participating on teams?

_____

_____

What do managers think about managing teams?

_____

_____

How complicated is it to communicate understandable organization results to employees?

_____

_____

Do employees seem to be interested in organization results?

_____

_____

What communication programs are in place to explain organization results?

_____

_____

What new communication programs would be needed?

_____

_____

_____

7.5 Alternatives to Pay

There is no universal guide for determining when employees should be rewarded with pay for their job contribution and when they should be recognized personally with symbols, gestures, and payments in kind. The most effective mix of pay rewards and personal recognition for an individual depends on the needs and desires of that individual.

Recognition may be anything that the employee considers meaningful—for example:

Professional Recognition

- A trip to a trade show
- Membership on a task force
- A new job title
- Attendance at a seminar
- Exclusive training
- A conference with a consultant
- The performer-of-the-year (day, week, month, quarter) award
- A suggestion award

- A certificate
- Publication of research findings
- A professional announcement
- A plaque inscribed for outstanding achievement
- A picture in the organization newsletter or local newspaper
- An introduction before assembled peers

Esteem Recognition

- A stripe on uniform
- A patch
- A hat
- An embroidered shirt or blouse
- A pin
- A name tag with descriptive title
- Selection privileges for office furniture or equipment

- Distinctive accessories
- A larger office
- An office with a window
- A more convenient or comfortable work location
- A private parking space
- Use of a special automobile for the month

Esteem Recognition (continued)

- An extended break
- Flexible work schedule
- Extra time off
- A credit card

- Carpeting
- Privacy
- A uniform
- Limousine service

Social Recognition

- A letter of congratulations
- A personal visit from the chief executive officer
- A photograph of the winning team
- A visit by famous personalities
- A celebrity autograph
- A birthday or anniversary card

- A flower
- A gift for the spouse
- A thank-you note
- A visit by the manager to off-shifts
- Lunch with an executive
- A party

In-Kind-Value Recognition

- A fishing trip to the company lodge
- A ticket for children's events
- A purchase discount
- A loan
- A food basket

- A ticket to a sporting event
- A prize
- A lottery
- A vacation
- A lunch

Some forms of recognition are more subtle. For example:

- *Communication* recognizes employees as capable participants in organizational efforts.
- *Managing participatively* recognizes employees' creativity and dignity.
- *Promotion from within* recognizes the value of diligence and loyalty.
- *Allowing professionals to develop new programs or products* recognizes their knowledge as a direct contribution to the organization.

Organizations are searching desperately for ways to tap the value of the "different" employee—the person who wants more than the status quo, the person who questions the system in order to make it better. Ironically, this potential contribution has always been within organizations. People with unlimited energy come to work every day. Unfortunately, by the end of the day, their energy has been effectively sapped and squelched by systems, conformity, or the psychological inadequacy of their managers.

When people are treated as machines—remunerated for each output, or restricted because someone is emotionally unable or unwilling to recognize the value of their contribution to the organization—they give up and respond according to the dictates of the system. They perceive no value in results and thus perform perfunctorily to maintain compliance. The promise of results is lost.

Recognition is an important force that must be integrated into the total compensation program along with pay, benefits, and results options. Without personal recognition, compensation programs bring out the worst mercenary motivations of people: to extract the most coins out of the organization. The organization becomes nothing more than a cash drawer, which sooner or later becomes empty.

Pay reward and personal recognition reinforce outcomes most powerfully when they are given, or communicated (as in the case of long-term, deferred benefits), shortly after they are earned. When a manager waits too long to reward or recognize an employee's results, the value of the reward or recognition is diminished, or it may even turn into an insult if the employee believes that the manager forgot or, worse, had to be reminded to express the appreciation.

On the other hand, when rewards and recognition are "administered" immediately after every special outcome, the appreciation becomes a conditioned reflex of the organization, fully anticipated by the employee, with no benefit derived by the employee or the organization.

Project Analyzer 7.5

How important is pay to employees in your organization?

_____

_____

How important are other forms of recognition?

_____

_____

What is the basis of your opinion?

_____

_____

_____

What is your organization's experience with using other forms of recognition? (List the forms your organization has used and the results of using each.)

_____

_____

_____

Have you used special awards?

_____

_____

_____

Have you used the subtle "goodwill" forms of recognition, such as better communication programs?

_____

_____

_____

_____

7.6 Software Spreadsheet Example

In this case study of Quality Condominium Builders (a fictitious company), we show examples of software spreadsheets applied to building the pay structure.

Step 1: Determine Job Grades

Table 14 shows the testing of different multiplier percentages, such as 11.6 percent or 11.8 percent, until a constant multiplier is found that matches job grades with natural job clusters.

The lowest number of points that can be assigned in the job evaluation plan is 100. In some organizations, such jobs do not exist. Therefore, the lowest points of the first grade can be higher—perhaps the lowest number of total points actually assigned.

Table 15 shows the effect of the various percentages tested in Table 14. The testing of various multiplier percentages in Table 14 provides a gross assessment. Table 15 specifically confirms the placement of jobs in grades. The multiplier percentage that seems to do the best job of creating job grades in Table 14 is entered into Table 15.

Step 2: Calculate Market Line

Table 16 shows the calculation of the market mean, median, and standard deviation for each benchmark job (discussed in Phase 6). Pay rates were collected in surveys and entered as market survey 1, market survey 2, and so on.

Figure 40 shows a scatter plot of job evaluation points and the selected market pay rate from Table 16.

Step 3: Calculate Organization Line

Table 17 shows the calculation of the organization mean for each benchmark job. Pay rates are the actual pay of employees and are entered as employee 1, if there is only one employee in the job, and employee 2, employee 3, and so on, if there is more than one employee in the job.

Figure 41 shows the comparison of the selected market pay rate from Table 16 and the organization mean from Table 17 regressed against job points for the benchmark jobs.

(*Text continues on page 276.*)

Table 14. Determining job grades.

1. Enter the lowest number of points assigned, or a lower number, where job grades will begin to calculate. Starting point of job grade

   1. → **146**

2. Establish natural clusters of jobs in grades by changing the multiplier percentage to test various job clusters. See Table 15 for the effect of different multipliers. Changing the starting point of job grade 1 will also affect the job groups.

Multiplier Percentage	11.0%		11.2%		11.4%		11.6%		11.8%		12.0%		12.2%		12.4%	
Job Grade	Minimum Grade Points	Maximum Grade Points	Minimum Grade Points	Maximum Grade Points	Minimum Grade Points	Maximum Grade Points	Minimum Grade Points	Maximum Grade Points	Minimum Grade Points	Maximum Grade Points	Minimum Grade Points	Maximum Grade Points	Minimum Grade Points	Maximum Grade Points	Minimum Grade Points	Maximum Grade Points
1	146	162	146	162	146	163	146	163	146	163	146	164	146	164	146	164
2	163	181	163	182	164	182	164	183	164	184	165	184	165	185	165	186
3	182	202	183	203	183	204	184	205	185	206	185	207	186	209	187	210
4	203	225	204	227	205	229	206	230	207	232	208	234	210	235	211	237
5	226	251	228	253	230	256	231	258	233	260	235	263	236	265	238	267
6	252	280	254	283	257	286	259	289	261	292	264	295	266	298	268	302
7	281	312	284	316	287	320	290	324	293	328	296	332	299	336	303	340
8	313	347	317	352	321	357	325	362	329	368	333	373	337	378	341	383
9	348	387	353	393	358	399	363	406	369	412	374	419	379	425	384	432
10	388	430	394	438	400	446	407	454	413	462	420	470	426	478	433	487
11	431	479	439	488	447	498	455	507	463	517	471	528	479	538	488	548
12	480	532	489	544	499	556	508	567	518	580	529	592	539	605	549	617
13	533	592	545	606	557	620	568	634	581	649	593	664	606	679	618	695
14	593	658	607	675	621	692	635	709	650	727	665	745	680	763	696	782
15	659	732	676	752	693	772	710	792	728	814	746	835	764	858	783	881
16	733	814	753	837	773	861	793	886	815	911	836	937	859	963	882	991
17	815	904	838	932	862	960	887	989	912	1,000	938	1,000	964	1,000	992	1,000
18	905	1,000	933	1,000	961	1,000	990	1,000								

267

Table 15. Evaluating job grades.

1. Enter the percentages of points growth from Table 14 that establish natural clusters of jobs in grades. ⟶	11.8%
2. Enter the starting point of first job grade. ⟶	146
3. Enter the lowest number of the job grade where you want to start numbering. ⟶	1

Job Titles	Totals	Job Grade	Job Titles	Totals	Job Grade
Regional Construction Manager	752	15	Closing Coordinator	320	7
Regional Sales Manager	747	15	Sales Administrator	320	7
Controller	744	15	PC Specialist	318	7
Information Systems Manager	690	14	Construction Secretary	311	7
Land Development Manager	665	14	Regional Coordinator	311	7
Director of Quality	626	13	Designer	309	7
Building Manager	615	13	Senior Accounts Payable Clerk	307	7
Sales Associate	598	13	Quality Services Manager	292	6
Quality Assurance Manager	583	13	Construction Accounting Coordinator	284	6
Safety Officer	558	12	Quality Assurance Coordinator	272	6
General Accounting Supervisor	495	11	Quality Assurance Technician	266	6
Senior Designer	475	11	Accounts Payable Clerk	261	6
Construction Accountant	475	11	Building Maintenance Technician	233	5
Estimator	468	11	Construction Site Assistant	200	3
Administrative Manager	465	11	Purchasing Assistant	173	2
Executive Secretary	453	10	Receptionist	160	1
Information Systems Programmer/Analyst	420	10	Mail Clerk	146	1
Financial Analyst	413	10			
Senior Buyer	412	9			
Computer Operator	378	9			
Secretary, Administration	376	9			
Marketing Research Assistant	365	8			
Junior Accountant	361	8			
Decorator	360	8			
Cost Analyst	353	8			
Cash Manager	343	8			
Bookkeeper	327	7			

Table 16. Calculating mean of market pay rates (dollars per year).

1. Job titles and points are copied from the results of Table 8.
2. Enter raw market data as market survey 1, market survey 2, etc.
3. The market mean, market median, and standard deviation are calculated based on market data entered.
4. The selected market pay rate is a value that must be entered by you. Enter either the market mean, market median, or a number you desire.
5. A value for selected market pay rate must be entered to establish market trend lines in Figures 42 and 44.

Job Titles	Points	Selected Market Pay Rate	Market Mean	Market Median	Standard Deviation	Market Survey 1	Market Survey 2	Market Survey 3	Market Survey 4	Market Survey 5	Market Survey 6
Regional Construction Manager	752	$72,233.33	$72,233.33	$66,750.00	$11,724.62	$64,900.00	$81,000.00	$62,000.00	$67,500.00	$92,000.00	$66,000.00
Regional Sales Manager	747	70,000.00									
Controller	744	77,683.33	77,683.33	71,800.00	21,244.33	71,600.00	120,000.00	60,000.00	72,000.00	70,500.00	72,000.00
Information Systems Manager	690	41,750.00	41,300.00	41,750.00	3,200.00	42,000.00	42,000.00	46,500.00	41,500.00	38,000.00	37,800.00
Land Development Manager	665	42,220.00	42,220.00	41,800.00	2,008.38	42,220.00	46,000.00	40,000.00	42,000.00	41,500.00	41,600.00
Director of Quality	626	42,000.00									
Building Manager	615	39,500.00	39,416.67	39,500.00	1,158.30	40,000.00	41,000.00	39,000.00	39,500.00	39,500.00	37,500.00
Sales Associate	598	37,500.00									
Quality Assurance Manager	583	37,500.00									
Safety Officer	558	35,230.00	34,960.00	35,230.00	2,479.19	34,960.00	38,000.00	33,500.00	31,000.00	35,500.00	36,800.00
General Accounting Supervisor	495	32,470.00	32,470.00	32,250.00	2,140.23	30,220.00	32,500.00	33,600.00	30,500.00	36,000.00	32,000.00
Senior Designer	475	44,786.67	44,786.67	44,750.00	3,484.40	42,220.00	46,000.00	43,500.00	48,000.00	40,000.00	49,000.00
Construction Accountant	475	31,661.67	31,661.67	30,610.00	2,570.76	30,220.00	33,500.00	36,000.00	29,500.00	29,750.00	31,000.00
Estimator	468	35,790.00	34,513.33	35,790.00	3,087.57	35,580.00	37,500.00	32,000.00	36,500.00	29,500.00	36,000.00
Administrative Manager	465	30,520.00	30,290.00	30,520.00	2,547.43	29,540.00	31,500.00	33,200.00	26,000.00	29,500.00	32,000.00
Executive Secretary	453	39,730.00	38,743.33	39,730.00	5,837.74	38,460.00	42,000.00	30,000.00	46,500.00	41,000.00	34,500.00

Table 16. (*continued*)

Job Titles	Points	Selected Market Pay Rate	Market Mean	Market Median	Standard Deviation	Market Survey 1	Market Survey 2	Market Survey 3	Market Survey 4	Market Survey 5	Market Survey 6
Information Systems Programmer/Analyst	420	36,450.00	35,700.00	36,450.00	3,372.24	35,400.00	39,500.00	31,000.00	38,300.00	37,500.00	32,500.00
Financial Analyst	413	32,911.67	32,911.67	32,375.00	2,915.27	30,220.00	36,000.00	33,750.00	31,000.00	36,500.00	30,000.00
Senior Buyer	412	33,600.00	33,600.00	32,650.00	3,547.39	32,300.00	38,300.00	31,000.00	29,500.00	33,000.00	37,500.00
Computer Operator	378	28,520.00	28,520.00	28,060.00	1,703.64	28,620.00	31,000.00	27,500.00	26,500.00	27,500.00	30,000.00
Secretary, Administration	376	30,000.00									
Marketing Research Assistant	365	29,100.00	29,100.00	28,600.00	2,194.54	29,400.00	32,300.00	27,800.00	26,900.00	27,200.00	31,000.00
Junior Accountant	361	25,563.33	25,563.33	25,440.00	2,643.00	24,080.00	26,800.00	23,150.00	22,600.00	27,750.00	29,000.00
Decorator	360	28,795.00	28,465.00	28,795.00	2,018.45	28,840.00	31,000.00	26,400.00	25,800.00	28,750.00	30,000.00
Cost Analyst	353	30,678.33	30,678.33	30,610.00	3,021.26	30,220.00	33,600.00	27,800.00	26,950.00	31,000.00	34,500.00
Cash Manager	343	34,710.00	34,053.33	34,710.00	4,655.09	36,420.00	39,000.00	28,500.00	28,900.00	33,000.00	38,500.00
Bookkeeper	327	28,488.33	28,488.33	28,240.00	2,984.03	27,480.00	31,000.00	26,800.00	24,200.00	29,000.00	32,450.00
Closing Coordinator	320	27,500.00									
Sales Administrator	320	27,500.00									
PC Specialist	318	26,750.00	26,716.67	26,750.00	2,387.82	26,000.00	28,500.00	24,500.00	23,800.00	27,500.00	30,000.00
Construction Secretary	311	21,456.67	21,456.67	21,220.00	1,813.96	20,440.00	22,500.00	20,000.00	19,500.00	22,000.00	24,300.00
Regional Coordinator	311	22,500.00									
Designer	309	21,401.67	21,401.67	21,305.00	1,717.79	20,860.00	21,750.00	20,000.00	19,500.00	22,000.00	24,300.00
Senior Accounts Payable Clerk	307	26,965.00	26,355.00	26,965.00	2,859.26	27,480.00	26,450.00	24,200.00	22,000.00	28,000.00	30,000.00
Quality Services Manager	292	18,690.00	18,646.67	18,690.00	1,923.82	17,880.00	19,500.00	17,500.00	16,000.00	19,500.00	21,500.00
Construction Accounting Coordinator	284	21,230.00	20,835.00	21,230.00	2,264.10	20,460.00	22,300.00	18,500.00	18,000.00	22,000.00	23,750.00

Position	Code										
Quality Assurance Coordinator	272	20,000.00									
Quality Assurance Technician	266	20,620.00	20,581.67	20,620.00	20,240.00	2,041.57	21,750.00	19,500.00	17,500.00	21,000.00	23,500.00
Accounts Payable Clerk	261	19,358.33	19,358.33	19,125.00	18,100.00	1,310.88	20,800.00	18,750.00	18,000.00	19,500.00	21,000.00
Building Maintenance Technician	233	20,970.00	20,490.00	20,970.00	20,440.00	2,846.16	21,500.00	17,500.00	17,000.00	22,000.00	24,500.00
Construction Site Assistant	200	24,000.00	23,823.33	24,000.00	22,440.00	2,469.67	26,000.00	23,000.00	20,000.00	26,500.00	25,000.00
Purchasing Assistant	173	18,800.00	18,391.67	18,800.00	18,100.00	1,476.62	19,500.00	17,500.00	16,000.00	19,500.00	19,750.00
Receptionist	160	23,470.00	23,073.33	23,470.00	22,640.00	1,899.33	24,300.00	22,000.00	20,000.00	24,500.00	25,000.00
Mail Clerk	146	18,863.33	18,863.33	18,500.00	17,880.00	1,210.98	19,500.00	17,800.00	18,500.00	18,500.00	21,000.00

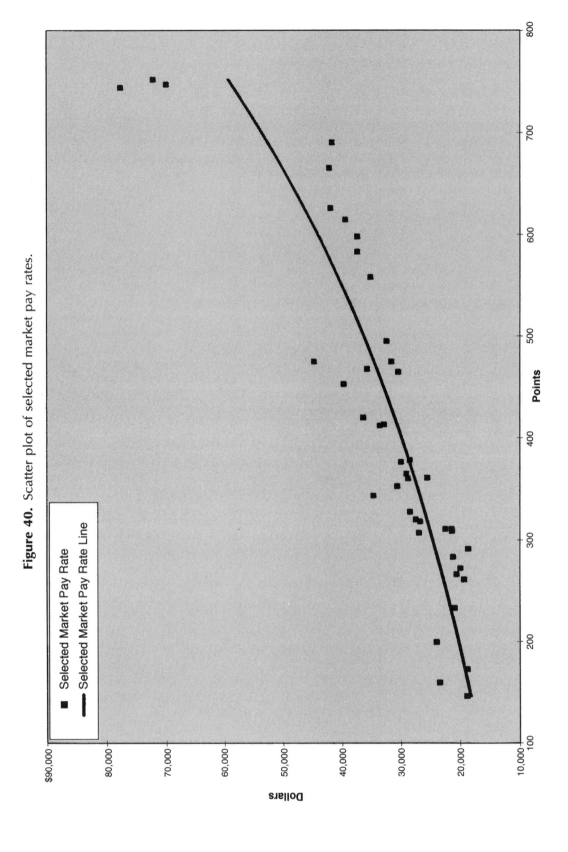

Figure 40. Scatter plot of selected market pay rates.

272

Table 17. Calculating mean of organization pay rates (dollars per year).

1. Job titles and points are copied from the result of Table 8.
2. Enter raw data as employee 1, employee 2, etc.
3. The organization mean is calculated based on market data entered.

Job Titles	Points	Organization Mean	Grade	Employee 1	Social Security Number	Grade	Employee 2	Social Security Number	Grade	Employee 3	Social Security Number	Grade	Employee 4	Social Security Number
Regional Construction Manager	752	$61,996.25	15	$48,000.00	011-22-3333	15	$55,391.00	022-33-4444	15	$85,594.00	033-44-5555	15	$59,000.00	044-55-6666
Regional Sales Manager	747	65,000.00	15	65,000.00	011-22-3334	15			15			15		
Controller	744	73,464.00	15	73,464.00	011-22-3335	15			15			15		
Information Systems Manager	690	38,750.00	14	38,750.00	011-22-3336	14			14			14		
Land Development Manager	665	44,961.00	14	44,647.00	011-22-3337	14	45,275.00	022-33-4445	14			14		
Director of Quality	626	45,621.00	13	45,621.00	011-22-3338	13			13			13		
Building Manager	615	37,000.00	13	41,000.00	011-22-3339	13	33,000.00	022-33-4446	13	36,000.00	033-44-5556	13	38,000.00	044-55-6667
Sales Associate	598	42,950.00	13	42,950.00	011-22-3340	13			13			13		
Quality Assurance Manager	583	38,442.00	13	39,602.00	011-22-3341	13	37,282.00	022-33-4447	13			13		
Safety Officer	558	32,702.00	12	32,702.00	011-22-3342	12			12			12		
General Accounting Supervisor	495	26,826.00	11	26,826.00	011-22-3343	11			11			11		
Senior Designer	475	44,410.00	11	44,410.00	011-22-3344	11			11			11		
Construction Accountant	475	26,098.00	11	26,098.00	011-22-3345	11			11			11		
Estimator	468	32,673.75	11	26,002.00	011-22-3346	11	20,792.00	022-33-4448	11	35,901.00	033-44-5557	11	48,000.00	044-55-6668
Administrative Manager	465	29,361.00	11	29,361.00	011-22-3347	11			11			11		
Executive Secretary	453	38,000.00	10	38,000.00	011-22-3348	10			10			10		
Information Systems Programmer/Analyst	420	33,946.00	10	33,946.00	011-22-3349	10			10			10		
Financial Analyst	413	25,002.00	10	25,002.00	011-22-3350	10			10			10		
Senior Buyer	412	31,629.50	9	33,322.00	011-22-3351	9	29,937.00	022-33-4449	9			9		
Computer Operator	378	31,857.00	9	31,857.00	011-22-3352	9			9			9		
Secretary, Administration	376	27,550.00	9	27,550.00	011-22-3353	9			9			9		
Marketing Research Assistant	365	28,513.00	8	28,513.00	011-22-3354	8			8			8		
Junior Accountant	361	22,402.00	8	22,402.00	011-22-3355	8			8			8		
Decorator	360	23,180.50	8	24,045.00	011-22-3356	8			8			8		

273

Table 17. (*continued*)

Job Titles	Points	Organization Mean	Grade	Employee 1	Social Security Number	Grade	Employee 2	Social Security Number	Grade	Employee 3	Social Security Number	Grade	Employee 4	Social Security Number
Cost Analyst	353	28,677.00	8	28,677.00	011-22-3357	8			8			8		
Cash Manager	343	35,216.00	8	35,216.00	011-22-3358	8			8			8		
Bookkeeper	327	27,496.00	7	27,496.00	011-22-3359	7			7			7		
Closing Coordinator	320	25,327.00	7	25,327.00	011-22-3360	7			7			7		
Sales Administrator	320	22,421.00	7	22,421.00	011-22-3361	7			7			7		
PC Specialist	318	19,600.00	7	19,600.00	011-22-3362	7			7			7		
Construction Secretary	311	19,049.00	7	20,500.00	011-22-3363	7	23,194.00	022-33-4451	7	18,502.00	033-44-5558	7	14,000.00	044-55-6669
Regional Coordinator	311	31,000.00	7	31,000.00	011-22-3364	7			7			7		
Designer	309	21,734.00	7	21,734.00	011-22-3365	7			7			7		
Senior Accounts Payable Clerk	307	22,922.00	7	22,922.00	011-22-3366	7			7			7		
Quality Services Manager	292	16,160.00	6	16,160.00	011-22-3367	6			6			6		
Construction Accounting Coordinator	284	20,136.75	6	21,609.00	011-22-3368	6	20,696.00	022-33-4452	6	18,242.00	033-44-5559	6	20,000.00	044-55-6670
Quality Assurance Coordinator	272	16,590.00	6	16,590.00	011-22-3369	6			6			6		
Quality Assurance Technician	266	22,152.00	6	22,152.00	011-22-3370	6			6			6		
Accounts Payable Clerk	261	17,137.00	5	11,137.00	011-22-3371	5			5			5		
Building Maintenance Technician	233	17,754.50	5	18,000.00	011-22-3372	5	15,016.00	022-33-4453	5	17,002.00	033-44-5560	5	21,000.00	044-55-6671
Construction Site Assistant	200	22,587.00	3	25,000.00	011-22-3373	3	24,001.00	022-33-4454	3	18,760.00	033-44-5561	3		
Purchasing Assistant	173	18,135.67	2	16,305.00	011-22-3374	2	18,302.00	022-33-4455	2	19,800.00	033-44-5562	2		
Receptionist	160	22,400.00	1	22,400.00	011-22-3375	1			1			1		
Mail Clerk	148	16,738.75	1	14,080.00	011-22-3376	1	16,680.00	022-33-4456	1	15,224.00	033-44-5563	1	20,971.00	044-55-6672

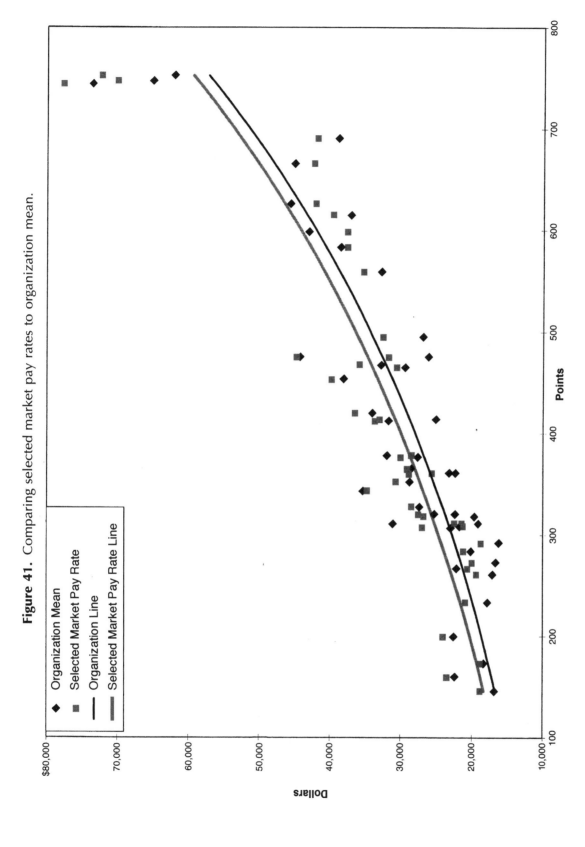

Figure 41. Comparing selected market pay rates to organization mean.

275

Step 4: Determine Policy Line and Step 5: Determine Pay Range Spread

Table 18 shows the development of a pay range spread based on the market in Figure 41. Figure 42 shows the pay ranges graphically, including individual pay rates below the minimum of the pay range, within the pay range, and above the maximum of the pay range, based on the market mean line that is based on the data entered in Table 17.

Table 19 shows current employee pay rates in relation to potential pay range minimums and maximums based on the market pay rate line. Table 20 shows the determination of a new policy line as above, equal to, or below the market line and the resultant new pay range minimum, midpoint, and maximum.

Figure 43 shows a comparison of three lines: the selected market pay rate, the organization mean, and the proposed new policy line. Figure 44 shows the pay ranges graphically, including rates below the minimum of the pay range and above the maximum of the pay range, based on the new policy line.

Table 21 shows current employee pay rates in relation to potential pay range minimums and maximums based on the new policy line.

Table 18. Comparing potential pay ranges to selected market pay rate trend line.

| 1. Enter the exponential curve constant from Figure 42. $\longrightarrow$ | | | | | | **13,742** |
| 2. Enter the exponent multiplying constant from Figure 42. $\longrightarrow$ | | | | | | **0.0019** |

Job Grade Range	Job Grade	Job Grade Midpoint	Market Midpoint	Pay Range Spread	Pay Range Minimum	Pay Range Maximum
146–163	1	154.6	$18,434.49	30.0%	$15,669.32	$21,199.66
164–184	2	173.9	19,123.16	32.5	16,015.64	22,230.67
185–206	3	195.5	19,923.59	32.0	16,436.96	23,410.22
207–232	4	219.6	20,858.20	37.5	16,947.29	24,769.12
233–260	5	246.6	21,955.10	40.0	17,564.08	26,346.13
261–292	6	276.8	23,249.88	42.5	18,309.28	28,190.48
293–328	7	310.5	24,788.04	45.0	19,210.73	30,365.35
329–368	8	348.2	26,628.50	47.5	20,304.23	32,952.77
369–412	9	390.3	28,848.39	50.0	21,636.30	36,060.49
413–462	10	437.4	31,550.04	52.5	23,268.16	39,831.93
463–517	11	490.1	34,871.12	55.0	25,281.56	44,460.68
518–580	12	549.0	38,999.66	57.5	27,787.26	50,212.06
581–649	13	614.8	44,196.71	60.0	30,937.70	57,455.72
650–727	14	688.4	50,831.15	62.5	34,946.41	66,715.88
728–814	15	770.7	59,434.31	65.0	40,118.16	78,750.46
815–911	16	862.8	70,787.66	67.5	46,896.82	94,678.49
912–1,000	17	955.9	84,494.28	70.0	54,921.28	114,067.28

Figure 42. Pay ranges based on market mean line.

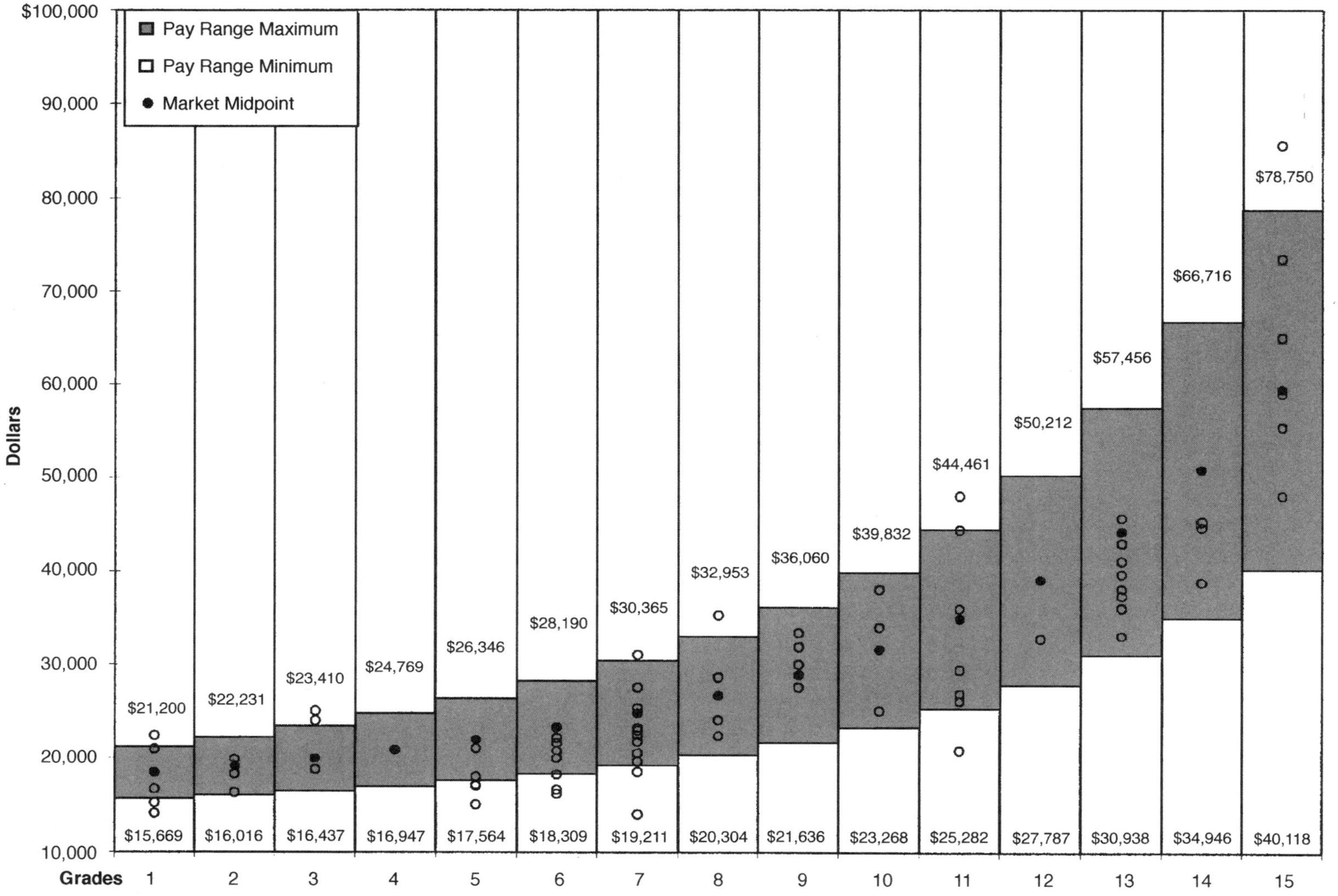

Table 19. Comparing organization employees' pay rates to selected market minimum

1. Job titles and points have been copied from Table 8.
2. Organization mean, grades, employee pay, and Social Security numbers are from
3. The analysis tool for Under/Over/OK is dynamic based on parameters within
4. See which employees are underpaid/overpaid based on the market minimum

Job Titles	Points	Organization Mean	Grade	Employee 1	Social Security Number	Under/ Over/OK	Grade	Employee 2
Regional Construction Manager	752	$61,996.25	15	$48,000.00	011-22-3333	OK	15	$55,391.00
Regional Sales Manager	747	65,000.00	15	65,000.00	011-22-3334	OK	15	
Controller	744	73,464.00	15	73,464.00	011-22-3335	OK	15	
Information Systems Manager	690	38,750.00	14	38,750.00	011-22-3336	OK	14	
Land Development Manager	665	44,961.00	14	44,647.00	011-22-3337	OK	14	45,275.00
Director of Quality	626	45,621.00	13	45,621.00	011-22-3338	OK	13	
Building Manager	615	37,000.00	13	41,000.00	011-22-3339	OK	13	33,000.00
Sales Associate	598	42,950.00	13	42,950.00	011-22-3340	OK	13	
Quality Assurance Manager	583	38,442.00	13	39,602.00	011-22-3341	OK	13	37,282.00
Safety Officer	558	32,702.00	12	32,702.00	011-22-3342	OK	12	
General Accounting Supervisor	495	26,826.00	11	26,826.00	011-22-3343	OK	11	
Senior Designer	475	44,410.00	11	44,410.00	011-22-3344	OK	11	
Construction Accountant	475	26,098.00	11	26,098.00	011-22-3345	OK	11	
Estimator	468	32,673.75	11	26,002.00	011-22-3346	OK	11	20,792.00
Administrative Manager	465	29,361.00	11	29,361.00	011-22-3347	OK	11	
Executive Secretary	453	38,000.00	10	38,000.00	011-22-3348	OK	10	
Information Systems Programmer/Analyst	420	33,946.00	10	33,946.00	011-22-3349	OK	10	
Financial Analyst	413	25,002.00	10	25,002.00	011-22-3350	OK	10	
Senior Buyer	412	31,629.50	9	33,322.00	011-22-3351	OK	9	29,937.00
Computer Operator	378	31,857.00	9	31,857.00	011-22-3352	OK	9	
Secretary, Administration	376	27,550.00	9	27,550.00	011-22-3353	OK	9	
Marketing Research Assistant	365	28,513.00	8	28,513.00	011-22-3354	OK	8	
Junior Accountant	361	22,402.00	8	22,402.00	011-22-3355	OK	8	
Decorator	360	23,180.50	8	24,045.00	011-22-3356	OK	8	22,316.00
Cost Analyst	353	28,677.00	8	28,677.00	011-22-3357	OK	8	
Cash Manager	343	35,216.00	8	35,216.00	011-22-3358	Overpaid	8	
Bookkeeper	327	27,496.00	7	27,496.00	011-22-3359	OK	7	
Closing Coordinator	320	25,327.00	7	25,327.00	011-22-3360	OK	7	
Sales Administrator	320	22,421.00	7	22,421.00	011-22-3361	OK	7	
PC Specialist	318	19,600.00	7	19,600.00	011-22-3362	OK	7	
Construction Secretary	311	19,049.00	7	20,500.00	011-22-3363	OK	7	23,194.00
Regional Coordinator	311	31,000.00	7	31,000.00	011-22-3364	Overpaid	7	
Designer	309	21,734.00	7	21,734.00	011-22-3365	OK	7	
Senior Accounts Payable Clerk	307	22,922.00	7	22,922.00	011-22-3366	OK	7	
Quality Services Manager	292	16,160.00	6	16,160.00	011-22-3367	Underpaid	6	
Construction Accounting Coordinator	284	20,136.75	6	21,609.00	011-22-3368	OK	6	20,696.00
Quality Assurance Coordinator	272	16,590.00	6	16,590.00	011-22-3369	Underpaid	6	
Quality Assurance Technician	266	22,152.00	6	22,152.00	011-22-3370	OK	6	
Accounts Payable Clerk	261	17,137.00	5	17,137.00	011-22-3371	Underpaid	5	
Building Maintenance Technician	233	17,754.50	5	18,000.00	011-22-3372	OK	5	15,016.00
Construction Site Assistant	200	22,587.00	3	25,000.00	011-22-3373	Overpaid	3	24,001.00
Purchasing Assistant	173	18,135.67	2	16,305.00	011-22-3374	OK	2	18,302.00
Receptionist	160	22,400.00	1	22,400.00	011-22-3375	Overpaid	1	
Mail Clerk	146	16,738.75	1	14,080.00	011-22-3376	Underpaid	1	16,680.00

and maximum pay ranges.

Table 17.
Tables 16 and 18 and Figure 43.
and maximum; search for the row(s) corresponding to the grade within Figure 43.

Social Security Number	Under/Over/OK	Grade	Employee 3	Social Security Number	Under/Over/OK	Grade	Employee 4	Social Security Number	Under/Over/OK
022-33-4444	OK	15	$85,594.00	033-44-5555	Overpaid	15	$59,000.00	044-55-6666	OK
		15				15			
		15				15			
		14				14			
022-33-4445	OK	14				14			
		13				13			
022-33-4446	OK	13	36,000.00	033-44-5556	OK	13	38,000.00	044-55-6667	OK
		13				13			
022-33-4447	OK	13				13			
		12				12			
		11				11			
		11				11			
		11				11			
022-33-4448	Underpaid	11	35,901.00	033-44-5557	OK	11	48,000.00	044-55-6668	Overpaid
		11				11			
		10				10			
		10				10			
		10				10			
022-33-4449	OK	9				9			
		9				9			
		9				9			
		8				8			
		8				8			
022-33-4450	OK	8				8			
		8				8			
		8				8			
		7				7			
		7				7			
		7				7			
		7				7			
022-33-4451	OK	7	18,502.00	033-44-5558	Underpaid	7	14,000.00	044-55-6669	Underpaid
		7				7			
		7				7			
		7				7			
		6				6			
022-33-4452	OK	6	18,242.00	033-44-5559	Underpaid	6	20,000.00	044-55-6670	OK
		6				6			
		6				6			
		5				5			
022-33-4453	Underpaid	5	17,002.00	033-44-5560	Underpaid	5	21,000.00	044-55-6671	OK
022-33-4454	Overpaid	3	18,760.00	033-44-5561	OK	3			
022-33-4455	OK	2	19,800.00	033-44-5562	OK	2			
		1				1			
022-33-4456	OK	1	15,224.00	033-44-5563	Underpaid	1	20,971.00	044-55-6672	OK

Table 20. Determining new pay policy line for your organization.

1. Job grade, job grade range, job grade midpoint, and market midpoint have been copied from Table 18.
2. Determine new pay policy line by creating the new pay range midpoint by choosing whether to "increase" or "equal" or "decrease" the market midpoint.
3. Enter the desired variance percentage from the market midpoint.
4. By choosing "equal," the corresponding variance percentage must equal 0.
5. See Figure 44 for the impact on new pay trend line.

Job Grade	Job Grade Range	Job Grade Midpoint	Market Midpoint	Increase Equal to Decrease	Variance	Job Grade Midpoint	New Pay Midpoint	Pay Range Spread	Job Grade	New Pay Range Minimum	New Pay Range Maximum
1	146–163	154.6	$18,434.49	Decrease	2.00%	154.6	$18,065.80	30.0%	1	$15,355.93	$20,775.67
2	164–184	173.9	19,123.16	Decrease	2.00	173.9	19,505.62	32.5	2	16,335.96	22,675.28
3	185–206	195.5	19,923.59	Decrease	2.00	195.5	20,322.06	35.0	3	16,765.70	23,878.42
4	207–232	219.6	20,858.20	Decrease	2.00	219.6	21,275.37	37.5	4	17,286.24	25,264.50
5	233–260	246.6	21,955.10	Equal to	0.00	246.6	21,955.10	40.0	5	17,564.08	26,346.13
6	261–292	276.8	23,249.88	Equal to	0.00	276.8	23,249.88	42.5	6	18,309.28	28,190.48

7	293–328	310.5	24,788.04	Equal to	0.00	310.5	24,788.04	45.0	7	19,210.73	30,365.35
8	329–368	348.2	26,628.50	Equal to	0.00	348.2	26,628.50	47.5	8	20,304.23	32,952.77
9	369–412	390.3	28,848.39	Increase	4.00	390.3	30,002.33	50.0	9	22,501.75	37,502.91
10	413–462	437.4	31,550.04	Increase	4.00	437.4	32,812.04	52.5	10	24,198.88	41,425.21
11	463–517	490.1	34,871.12	Increase	4.00	490.1	36,265.96	55.0	11	26,292.82	46,239.11
12	518–580	549.0	38,999.66	Increase	6.00	549.0	41,339.64	57.5	12	29,454.49	53,224.79
13	581–649	614.8	44,196.71	Increase	6.00	614.8	46,848.51	60.0	13	32,793.96	60,903.07
14	650–727	688.4	50,831.15	Increase	6.00	688.4	53,881.02	62.5	14	37,043.20	70,718.83
15	728–814	770.7	59,434.31	Increase	6.00	770.7	63,000.36	65.0	15	42,525.25	83,475.48
16	815–911	862.8	70,787.66	Increase	6.00	862.8	75,034.92	67.5	16	49,710.63	100,359.20
17	912–1,000	955.9	84,494.28	Increase	6.00	955.9	89,563.94	70.0	17	58,216.56	120,911.31

Figure 43. New pay trend line compared to market and organization means.

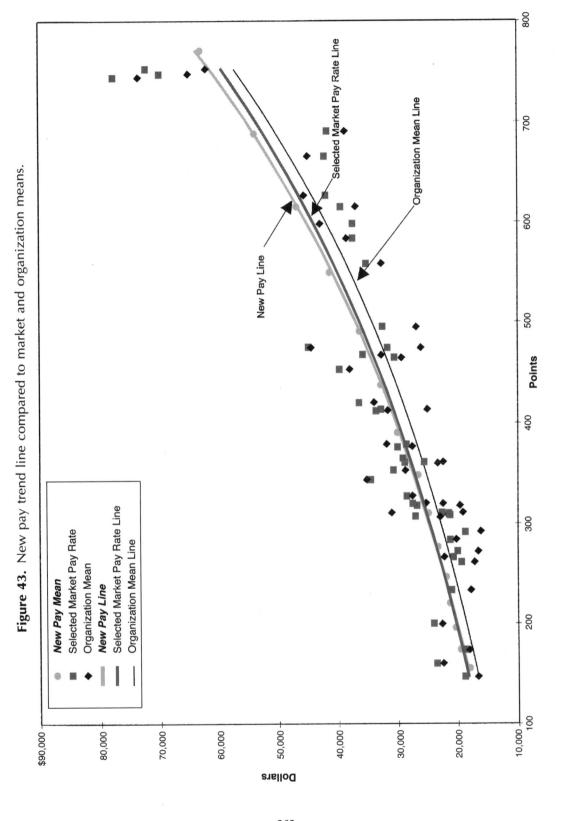

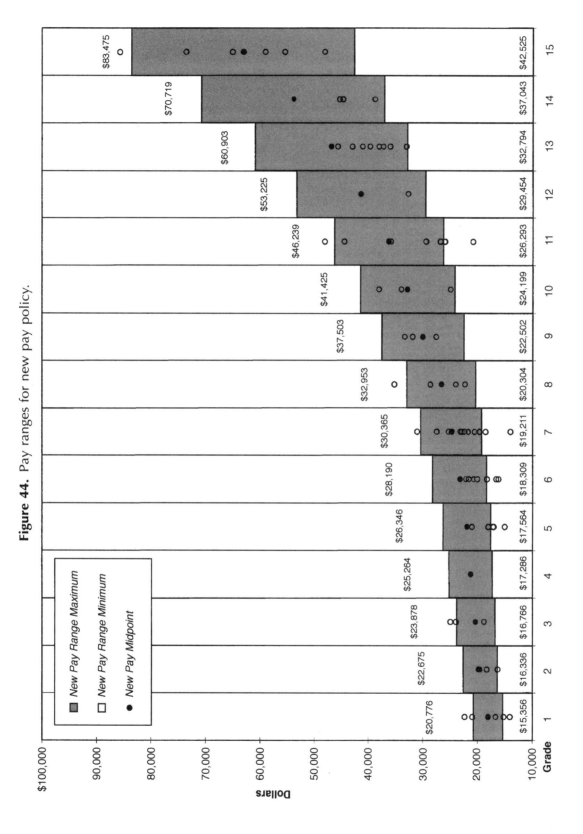

Figure 44. Pay ranges for new pay policy.

283

Table 21. Comparing organization employees to the new pay minimum and maximum

1. *Job titles and points have been copied from Table 8.*
2. *Organization mean, grades, employee pay, and Social Security number have been*
3. *The analysis tool for Under/Over/OK is dynamic based on parameters within Tables 19*
4. *See which employees are Underpaid/Overpaid based on the new pay minimum and*

Job Titles	Points	Organization Mean	Grade	Employee 1	Social Security Number	Under/ Over/OK	Grade	Employee 2
Regional Construction Manager	752	$61,996.25	15	$48,000.00	011-22-3333	OK	15	$55,391.00
Regional Sales Manager	747	65,000.00	15	65,000.00	011-22-3334	OK	15	
Controller	744	73,464.00	15	73,464.00	011-22-3335	OK	15	
Information Systems Manager	690	38,750.00	14	38,750.00	011-22-3336	OK	14	
Land Development Manager	665	44,961.00	14	44,647.00	011-22-3337	OK	14	45,275.00
Director of Quality	626	45,621.00	13	45,621.00	011-22-3338	OK	13	
Building Manager	615	37,000.00	13	41,000.00	011-22-3339	OK	13	33,000.00
Sales Associate	598	42,950.00	13	42,950.00	011-22-3340	OK	13	
Quality Assurance Manager	583	38,442.00	13	39,602.00	011-22-3341	OK	13	37,282.00
Safety Officer	558	32,702.00	12	32,702.00	011-22-3342	OK	12	
General Accounting Supervisor	495	26,826.00	11	26,826.00	011-22-3343	OK	11	
Senior Designer	475	44,410.00	11	44,410.00	011-22-3344	OK	11	
Construction Accountant	475	26,098.00	11	26,098.00	011-22-3345	Underpaid	11	
Estimator	468	32,673.75	11	26,002.00	011-22-3346	Underpaid	11	20,792.00
Administrative Manager	465	29,361.00	11	29,361.00	011-22-3347	OK	11	
Executive Secretary	453	38,000.00	10	38,000.00	011-22-3348	OK	10	
Information Systems Programmer/Analyst	420	33,946.00	10	33,946.00	011-22-3349	OK	10	
Financial Analyst	413	25,002.00	10	25,002.00	011-22-3350	OK	10	
Senior Buyer	412	31,629.50	9	33,322.00	011-22-3351	OK	9	29,937.00
Computer Operator	378	31,857.00	9	31,857.00	011-22-3352	OK	9	
Secretary, Administration	376	27,550.00	9	27,550.00	011-22-3353	OK	9	
Marketing Research Assistant	365	28,513.00	8	28,513.00	011-22-3354	OK	8	
Junior Accountant	361	22,402.00	8	22,402.00	011-22-3355	OK	8	
Decorator	360	23,180.50	8	24,045.00	011-22-3356	OK	8	22,316.00
Cost Analyst	353	28,677.00	8	28,677.00	011-22-3357	OK	8	
Cash Manager	343	35,216.00	8	35,216.00	011-22-3358	Overpaid	8	
Bookkeeper	327	27,496.00	7	27,496.00	011-22-3359	OK	7	
Closing Coordinator	320	25,327.00	7	25,327.00	011-22-3360	OK	7	
Sales Administrator	320	22,421.00	7	22,421.00	011-22-3361	OK	7	
PC Specialist	318	19,600.00	7	19,600.00	011-22-3362	OK	7	
Construction Secretary	311	19,049.00	7	20,500.00	011-22-3363	OK	7	23,194.00
Regional Coordinator	311	31,000.00	7	31,000.00	011-22-3364	Overpaid	7	
Designer	309	21,734.00	7	21,734.00	011-22-3365	OK	7	
Senior Accounts Payable Clerk	307	22,922.00	7	22,922.00	011-22-3366	OK	7	
Quality Services Manager	292	16,160.00	6	16,160.00	011-22-3367	Underpaid	6	
Construction Accounting Coordinator	284	20,136.75	6	21,609.00	011-22-3368	OK	6	20,696.00
Quality Assurance Coordinator	272	16,590.00	6	16,590.00	011-22-3369	Underpaid	6	
Quality Assurance Technician	266	22,152.00	6	22,152.00	011-22-3370	OK	6	
Accounts Payable Clerk	261	17,137.00	5	17,137.00	011-22-3371	Underpaid	5	
Building Maintenance Technician	233	17,754.50	5	18,000.00	011-22-3372	OK	5	15,016.00
Construction Site Assistant	200	22,587.00	3	25,000.00	011-22-3373	Overpaid	3	24,001.00
Purchasing Assistant	173	18,135.67	2	16,305.00	011-22-3374	Underpaid	2	18,302.00
Receptionist	160	22,400.00	1	22,400.00	011-22-3375	Overpaid	1	
Mail Clerk	146	16,738.75	1	14,080.00	011-22-3376	Underpaid	1	16,680.00

ranges.

copied from Table 17.
and 20 and Figure 44.
maximum; search for the row(s) corresponding to the grade within Figure 44.

Social Security Number	Under/ Over/OK	Grade	Employee 3	Social Security Number	Under/ Over/OK	Grade	Employee 4	Social Security Number	Under/ Over/OK
022-33-4444	OK	15	$85,594.00	033-44-5555	Overpaid	15	$59,000.00	044-55-6666	OK
		15				15			
		15				15			
		14				14			
022-33-4445	OK	14				14			
		13				13			
022-33-4446	OK	13	36,000.00	033-44-5556	OK	13	38,000.00	044-55-6667	OK
		13				13			
022-33-4447	OK	13				13			
		12				12			
		11				11			
		11				11			
		11				11			
022-33-4448	Underpaid	11	35,901.00	033-44-5557	OK	11	48,000.00	044-55-6668	Overpaid
		11				11			
		10				10			
		10				10			
		10				10			
022-33-4449	OK	9				9			
		9				9			
		9				9			
		8				8			
		8				8			
022-33-4450	OK	8				8			
		8				8			
		8				8			
		7				7			
		7				7			
		7				7			
		7				7			
022-33-4451	OK	7	18,502.00	033-44-5558	Underpaid	7	14,000.00	044-55-6669	Underpaid
		7				7			
		7				7			
		7				7			
		6				6			
022-33-4452	OK	6	18,242.00	033-44-5559	Underpaid	6	20,000.00	044-55-6670	OK
		6				6			
		6				6			
		5				5			
022-33-4453	Underpaid	5	17,002.00	033-44-5560	Underpaid	5	21,000.00	044-55-6671	OK
022-33-4454	Overpaid	3	18,760.00	033-44-5561	OK	3			
022-33-4455	OK	2	19,800.00	033-44-5562	OK	2			
		1				1			
022-33-4456	OK	1	15,224.00	033-44-5563	Underpaid	1	20,971.00	044-55-6672	Overpaid

---

Strategic Planning for Phase 7

On your *first* quick walk through the project phases, record your initial thoughts on policy issues that will have to be decided.

_____

_____

_____

Any notes on tactical procedures?

_____

_____

On your *second* time through the phases, consider the strategic influences from all the phases; decide on an integrated posture for the entire project.

Complete the section for this phase in the Master Planner (in Phase 2.8) during your *third* reading.

Phase 8

Managing Job Contributions

> Manage organization and job results; then pay for the results contributed.

8.1 Job Results Management Strategy

Employees are paid for accomplishing job results that fulfill the organization's mission. This suggests that managing job contributions well will produce a more direct benefit toward fulfilling the organization's mission than hyping pay rewards to "motivate" employees to accomplish job results. Pay, insofar as it is a part of the employer-employee relationship, is the result of valuable job contributions.

In the 1980s, to offset the shortsightedness of performance appraisal, the concept of performance management was introduced to bring planning, monitoring, and *appraising* work into a unified process.

Managing job contributions expands the performance management concept to the level of an organization management strategy. The architecture is job results management, which includes:

- Recruiting job candidates
- Selecting employees
- Orienting and training employees
- Planning job results
- Coaching job efforts
- Redirecting job efforts
- Appraising job contributions
- Rewarding and recognizing job contributions
- Developing future employee contributions

Missing in most organizations is an integrated and coherent management strategy. Organizations are quick to introduce new initiatives such as total quality management, teamwork, collaboration, customer service, open-book management, strategic business planning, Japanese-style management, MBO (management by objectives), competency-based pay, reengineering, core organization competencies, social contracts, learning as an organization principle.

These initiatives, inaugurated at the enterprise level, are seldom developed at the level of organizational implementation: jobs. Organizations are formed to accomplish a mission. Resources are assembled. Work is organized and assigned. Work is accomplished. Right here, where work is accomplished—where prospective customers are enticed, products are manufactured, service is rendered, bills are paid—organization philosophy, strategy, and tactics must be pinpointed to fulfill the organization mission in the manner that the organization wants it fulfilled. This is where successful organizations make it happen. This is where unsuccessful organizations fail. Figure 45 sets out an integrated and coherent job results management strategy.

Figure 45. Job results management: An integrated and coherent management strategy.

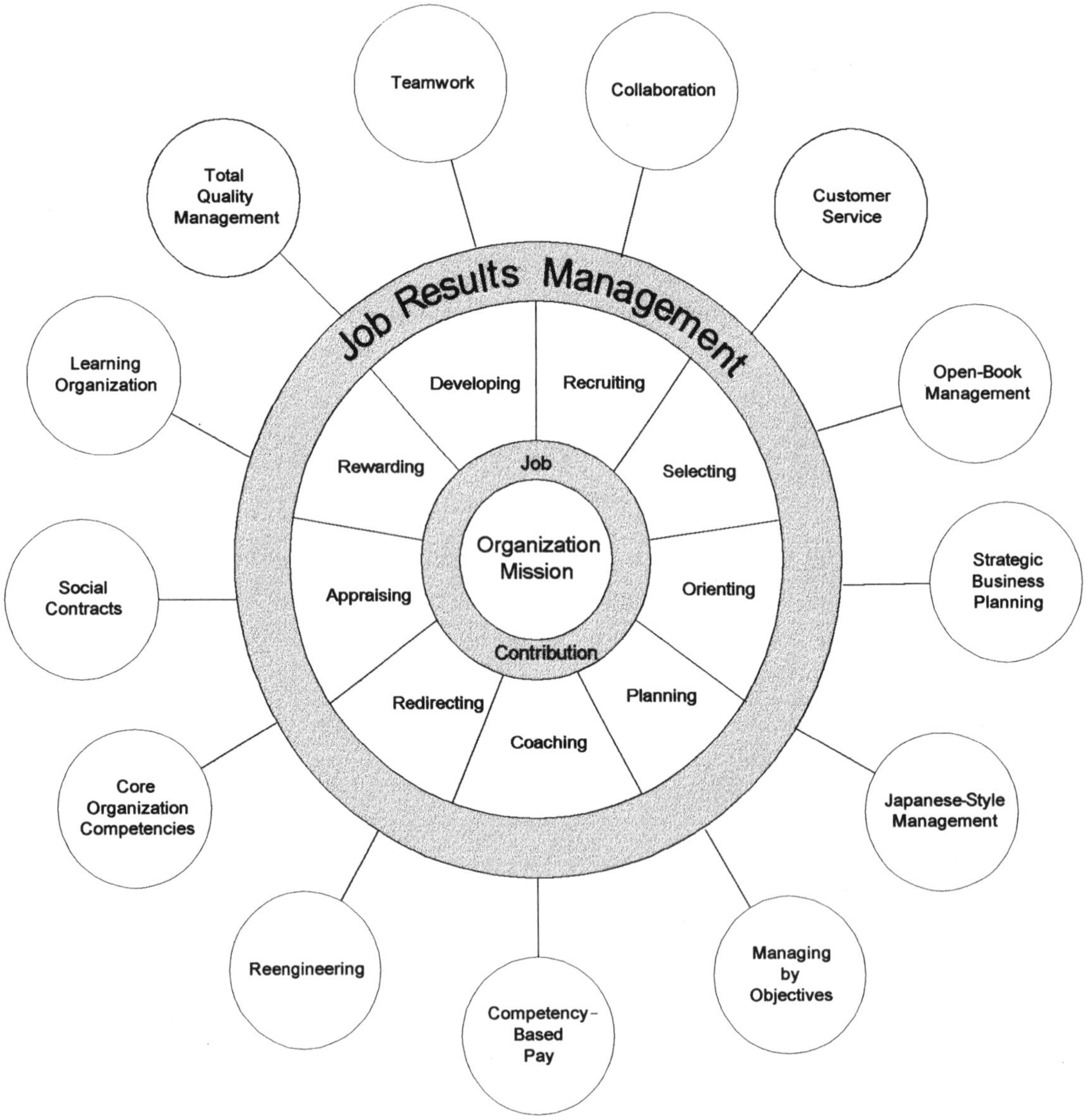

Project Analyzer 8.1

How do you manage job contributions now?

_____

_____

Does the system integrate all management initiatives?

_____

_____

Does the system support management objectives and actions?

_____

_____

What do managers think of the system?

_____

_____

What do employees think of the system?

_____

_____

What are the system's strengths?

_____

_____

What are the system's weaknesses?

_____

_____

In all fairness to managers and employees, is the structure of the system, rather than the people who use it, the cause of problems?

_____

_____

Has your system been challenged legally?

_____

_____

What was the outcome?

_____

_____
_____

8.2 Problems With Performance Appraisal

If pay is to be linked to job contributions, differentiations among job contributions must be based on a solid appraisal of job results accomplished. Traditional performance appraisal is a weak base.

Managers typically lament having to complete appraisals, and they shun the process at every turn, but it is difficult to blame them when organizations give them an appraisal system that almost certainly guarantees failure. Managers intuitively understand the reason for expanding performance appraisal into the broader concept of performance management: employees' work shouldn't be appraised if it wasn't planned with them in the first place and/or if they were not made aware of problems and given a chance to make corrections before the appraisal.

Because of inadequate appraisal systems, managers may skew appraisals in order to obtain the pay raise sought. The job results management approach is designed to build faith in the fairness of pay management by correcting the problems with traditional performance appraisal systems.

The biggest problem with traditional performance appraisal systems is that they have been perceived as the judgment of one person by another. Proper appraisal means appraising work accomplished, not appraising the person accomplishing the work.

Let's look at some other systemic problems inherent in most performance appraisal processes:

- Appraisal is only one-third of the management process. Effective management encompasses planning, monitoring, *and* appraising.

- Appraisal labels are generic (e.g., Distinguished, Outstanding, Satisfactory, Marginal, and Unacceptable). Consistency among evaluators cannot be maintained; legal challenges are difficult to support.

- Appraisal labels make managers depend on modifiers (adjectives and adverbs) to distinguish between outcome levels—for example:

Outstanding:	Performance *far exceeds* the normal requirements of the position and leaves little room for further improvement in the job.
Superior:	Performance *consistently exceeds* that of most others in this behavior area, particularly others doing similar work.
Acceptable:	*Performance is not harmful* to the organization in this behavior, but the individual could be more effective if further improvements were made.
Marginal:	Performance in this behavior area *must improve* to meet the requirements of the position.

Notice, for instance, that the modifiers *far exceeds* and *consistently exceeds* in the scale do not establish a clear and precise meaning to help the manager and employee understand the difference between the two levels.

■ Appraisal language is hurtful. You can imagine the reaction of an employee to hearing that his performance "was not harmful to the organization." Just picture yourself telling one of your employees, "Well, it was an okay performance period. You didn't hurt us."

We're reminded of an appraisal form for sale that caused us to chuckle. The criterion measured an employee's speed at accomplishing work. The scale listed Very Fast, Quick, Moderate, Slow, and one lower level. What would you guess was the lowest descriptor? Did you guess "Sluggish"? Yes, for sale in today's marketplace!

■ Appraisal labels are unclear. Numeric scales, such as 1–10, lack objective definition; one evaluator's 5 might be equal to another evaluator's 8.

■ Appraisal criteria are personality based. Words such as "aloof," "untidy," "nervous," "complains excessively," or "negative influence on others" do not lead to world-class communication experiences.

■ Appraisal criteria that attempt to label motivation frequently are demotivators or meaningless. Telling an employee she has a "low desire" for achievement makes the assumption that there are not other influences on performance other than the employee's lack of self-motivation. This commentary is a demotivator. On the other hand, telling an employee she has a "high desire" for achievement but accomplishes little is meaningless. We've all had subordinates who tried hard but just couldn't cut it.

■ Appraisal scales based on normal distribution—Superior (10 percent), Above Average (20 percent), Average (40 percent), Below Average (20 percent), and Poor (10 percent)—force organizations to skew reality. Pity the poor manager with the great department who is saddled with the same rating and pay distributions as the manager with the troublesome department. And yet it goes on all the time!

Problems Managers Create for Themselves

■ Rewarding everyone with the same pay increase clearly communicates that results don't matter.

■ Exaggerating ratings to obtain the biggest pay increase possible for an employee is a disservice to the organization, the employee, and the employee's peers.

■ Seeing only good results, seeing only bad results, always giving employees the benefit of the doubt, or feeling sorry for employees compromises the objective base on which fair pay decisions are made.

■ Using subjective criteria prevents an objective view of results.

■ Avoiding confrontation or transferring an unwanted employee merely delays dealing with the issue.

■ Not planning job objectives with employees and gaining their commitment to the plan eliminates the opportunity to hold employees to a "contract."

■ Not coaching employees along the way causes employees to ask, "Why didn't you tell me that I was in trouble earlier?"

■ Not documenting employee problems and the manager's response undermines management decisions.

Job results management is designed to eliminate or reduce the problems just cited, to make managing work a continuous process that supports natural organizational management rhythms, to give managers a structure for focusing together on work with employees, and to build an equitable base on which pay decisions can be rendered.

Project Analyzer 8.2

Is your organization still trying to resolve the "problem" of performance appraisals?

_____

_____

Is a performance management concept used?

_____

_____

Does the system promote continuous management instead of only annual appraisals?

_____

_____

Is one generic appraisal scale used for all jobs?

_____

_____

Do managers and employees agree about the interpretation of appraisal criteria?

_____

_____

Is appraisal language injudicious?

_____

_____

Have appraisal decisions been appealed because employees thought they were unfair?

_____

_____

Do managers fiddle with ratings to overcome appraisal program deficiencies?

_____

_____

Are managers guilty of filing acceptable appraisals, only to attempt disciplinary action shortly thereafter?

_____

_____

8.3 Job Results Management Profile

Job results management takes tangible shape in a profile used to communicate and manage job results. Managers and employees focus on:

- The job result from the results-oriented job description.
- Four possible job-specific outcomes defined in advance for each job result.
- Recording plans, observations, and learning requirements that augment job description and outcomes.

JOB RESULTS MANAGEMENT PROFILE

_____   **1. JOB RESULT**
        by
        duty.

☐ Result Required	☐ Problem	☐ Learning Required	☐ Performance Option

	Date	
Results Plan:		
Results Summary:		
Learning Plan:		

The *Result Required* is the outcome the organization wants. It is the initial focus of the manager's and employee's attention and the standard by which work is planned, managed, and appraised. It is the target most people choose. People are to be complimented when they hit the target. When all people accomplish the Result Required, the organization achieves all of its goals. The Result Required aims at job success.

However, as we have all found out, stating what is *not* wanted may help clarify what is wanted. The *Problem* is the outcome the organization does not want. It is the bad effect or damage produced, or potential consequences, when the Result Required is not accomplished. Examples of Problems are described. Not every possible Problem is identified; the examples demonstrate the kinds of outcomes that are considered a Problem. Any outcome that causes a similar bad effect is also a Problem.

Learning Required offers examples of what an employee may need to learn in order to accomplish the Result Required. Not every possible Learning Required is identified; the examples demonstrate the kinds of learning required to accomplish the Result Required. Specific learning plans, triggered by the examples, are developed to meet individual employee needs.

Performance Option is innovation or accomplishments that provide a role model for others. This outcome is more than what is required—a model of achievement for other people. Typically innovations are implemented that enhance the work system or the way that work is accomplished. The word "option" is used to signal the employee's decision, commitment, and motivation to pursue new goals.

One of the four outcomes is checked during appraisal to indicate the level of job contribution. When job results are accomplished, the outcome checked is either Result Required or Performance Option. When job results are not accomplished, the outcome checked is either Learning Required or Problem. In essence, then, the scale is essentially only two conditions: job results are either accomplished or not accomplished.

Here is an example Job Results Management Profile for a job result:

JOB RESULTS MANAGEMENT PROFILE

ESSENTIAL JOB RESULTS:

% of
time

_____   **1. PROVIDES CUSTOMERS WITH INFORMATION**
                by
                answering the telephone.

☐ Result Required	☐ Problem	☐ Learning Required	☐ Performance Option
The customer receives requested information, plus information we know she or he needs. The customer understands the answer. The telephone is answered by the third ring. The customer feels welcome. The supervisor is informed when the answer is not apparent. Services related to the customer's inquiry are suggested.	Customers make errors or waste their time based on incorrect information, are put on hold, complain about services, choose a competitor's services, or are able to hear negative remarks about the information retrieval system.	☐ Clarifying customer's requests. ☐ Verifying customer's understanding of answer. ☐ Studying and using information retrieval system. ☐ Verifying answer when uncertain. ☐ Studying and applying time management techniques.	Recommends improvements in information retrieval system. Develops clearer answers that become standard in the information retrieval system.

Why only four outcomes? The Job Results Management Profile is specifically designed not to have five possible outcomes, such as Outstanding, Above Average, Average, Below Average, and Poor. Ninety percent of people surveyed think they are above average. Average (acceptable) is two rungs down from the top, which most employees consider *unacceptable*. A manager is put in the position of rating acceptable work accomplishments as Above Average to avoid conflict.

The job results management four-outcome scale avoids going against the grain of most people's psychological state that they are not average. The aim of job results management is to get almost all of the people to the Results Required.

Most traditional scales are arranged from best rating to worst rating. If the Job Results Management Profile were arranged this way, Result Required would be the second category:

| ☐ Performance Option | ☐ Result Required | ☐ Learning Required | ☐ Problem |

However, an arrangement that points everyone at achieving top-rung status is demotivating instead of motivating because only 7 or 8 percent of the people actually aim for and expect to accomplish the highest rating.

Job results management takes a realistic approach. The Result Required is shown as the target because that's what most people (85 percent) choose. It communicates the basic expectation of the organization. The Job Results Management Profile arrangement focuses people on accomplishing the value-added results that the organization requires to fulfill its mission. We call that a valuable contribution and applaud employees for accomplishing the results the organization needs.

Problem is the second category because what management does not want provides a contrast to what is wanted. Learning Required is third; learning is important when accomplishments do not meet expectations. Performance Option is last because it is above and beyond expectations, and it is the employee's *option*, not a job requirement.

Three spaces are provided for documenting job results management plans before work begins, and changes or observations as work progresses, or as learning continues: the Results Plan, the Results Summary, and the Learning Plan:

JOB RESULTS MANAGEMENT PROFILE

_____   **1. RESULT**
        by
        duty.

☐ Result Required	☐ Problem		☐ Learning Required	☐ Performance Option
			☐	
	Date			
Results Plan:				
Results Summary:				
Learning Plan:				

■ *Results Plan*. The Results Plan, developed to guide future work, is used to set specific objectives, establish priorities, discuss methods, determine resources required, and set due dates. It is also used to note midcourse changes. Here is an example of a Results Plan for establishing a specific, measurable, attainable, realistic, and time-specific objective:

	Date	
Results Plan:		Identify new inventory controls to reduce expenses by 35 percent by (date).
Results Summary:		
Learning Plan:		

■ *Results Summary*. The Results Summary is used to document or explain the outcome checked, and/or offer clarifying comments. Commendations for outcomes accomplished are made here, as are warnings when outcomes are not accomplished.

If Result Required is checked, the Results Summary might note extra effort; the outcome was not Performance Option, but it was more than the Result Required. If Result Required was nearly accomplished but did not trigger Learning Required, the Results Summary could note the slight deficiency. If there were extenuating circumstances that were beyond the employee's control—for example, the new equipment was not installed on time due to extraordinary weather—the Results Summary would note the exception.

If Problem is checked, the Results Summary is used to record a warning of the consequences of noncompliance. A Learning Plan would need to be completed as well.

If Performance Option is checked, the Results Summary records exactly what the innovation was and what it accomplished.

Here are examples of using the Results Summary:

Recognize extra effort and encourage employees:

☑ Result Required			
	Date		
Results Summary:	9/21	*I appreciate the extra effort you made to fill open positions in 3.6 weeks on the average. We are far better off with maintaining an orderly flow of work and not burdening other employees. Let's talk about your suggestion of a backup log of candidates so that you can aim for the performance option.*	

Explain extenuating circumstances that temporarily set aside the Result Required (an employee should not be held accountable for events over which he or she has no control):

☑ Result Required			
	Date		
Results Summary:	9/21	*The Customer Service position was not filled until the seventh week. Even though you used excellent recruiting techniques, the scarce market of qualified candidates prevented the result required from being accomplished.*	

Warn of consequences of noncompliance:

	☑ Problem		
	Date		
Results Summary:	9/21	*We have discussed the need to have positions filled more quickly, and we have explored several methods to improve. However, filling positions does not receive your priority. You leave me no recourse but to warn you that if positions are not filled within 4.0 to 4.9 weeks on the average, you will subject yourself to disciplinary action.*	

Record the specific accomplishment of Performance Option:

			☑ Performance Option
	Date		
Results Summary:	9/21	*Your suggestion to establish a Web page tied to a telephone response system has truly given us an edge in attracting qualified candidates.*	

■ *Learning Plan.* The Learning Plan is used to establish specific learning actions and due dates for accomplishment, as well as to suggest developmental opportunities for job growth and job advancement.

If Result Required is checked, the Learning Plan can be used to record optional learning to facilitate accomplishing the Performance Option.

If Problem is checked, the Learning Plan is used to record required learning to retain the job.

If Learning Required is checked, the Learning Plan is used to record the specific learning required to accomplish the Result Required.

If Performance Option is checked, the Learning Plan is used to record optional learning to prepare for promotion, career opportunities, or job expansion.

Here are examples of using the Learning Plan:

Record optional learning to achieve Performance Option:

☑ Result Required			
	Date		
Learning Plan:	9/21	*To pursue the performance option, learn new systems to establish candidate logs and other tools to reduce recruiting time substantially.*	

Record required learning to meet Result Required:

		☑ Learning Required	
	Date		
Learning Plan:	9/21	*Attend a course on recruiting, selection, and interviewing techniques by 10/21 and successfully apply learning by 12/21.*	

Record required learning to retain job:

	☑ Problem		
	Date		
Learning Plan:	12/21	*Although you attended a course on recruiting, selection, and interviewing techniques, you have not applied the learning successfully. Review course notes and identify specific problem areas by 1/4. We will interview the next candidate, and critique the outcome together. Failure to improve may result in disciplinary action.*	

Record optional learning to prepare for promotion, career opportunities, or job expansion:

			☑ Performance Option
	Date		
Learning Plan:	9/21	*In order to prepare for possible promotion, attend a course on managing the recruiting, selection, and interviewing process.*	

Project Analyzer 8.3

Do the four outcomes appear to meet your needs?

_____

_____

Would the specific, objective language be a helpful communications tool for managers and employees?

_____

_____

Would the new arrangement of the profile, with the Result Required up front, fit your organization culture, or would people at least be willing to entertain the concept?

_____

_____

Would the concept of 85 percent of the people in your organization aiming for and being satisfied with the Results Required fit your organization culture?

_____

_____

Would the additional space provided for the Results Plan, Results Summary, and Learning Plan provide managers help for documenting job results management actions and observations?

_____

_____

8.4 Defining Job Outcomes

The four outcomes are defined in relation to each job result on the job description. Some managers groan at the thought of having to write four outcomes for each job result instead of simply using a generic scale. Yes, there is an investment of time required to fill in this architecture, but the time spent brings big advantages.

Whereas managers waste huge amounts of time trying to translate generic scales into understandable job language and explaining their point of view to employees who dispute their opinion, a Job Results Management Profile sets forth job-specific words before the work begins. Conversations are easier and less time-consuming. Once written, criteria need not be rewritten until the job changes.

Furthermore, the very nature of jobs is that they all differ from one another; therefore, they demand unique profiles. Employees are trained differently to accomplish each job. Each job is expected to accomplish different results. Logically, then, we cannot ignore this difference when job results are appraised. Separate criteria must be designed for each different job.

The true value of the Job Results Management Profile is the increased dialogue it encourages between manager and employee about important job issues. Experience with the profile demonstrates that managers and employees spend more time communicating about important job issues such as productivity, costs, quality, methods, problems, and relationships.

Following are some completed examples of Job Results Management Profiles for several jobs.

JOB RESULTS MANAGEMENT PROFILE

JOB TITLE: ACCOUNT SALES REPRESENTATIVE

JOB PURPOSE: **SELLS PRODUCT**
by
identifying prospects' needs; influencing and servicing prospects.

ESSENTIAL JOB RESULTS:

% of
time

_____   **1. INFLUENCES PROSPECTS TO BUY PRODUCT**
by
contacting them and controlling the selling process.

☐ Result Required	☐ Problem	☐ Learning Required	☐ Performance Option
Profit studies are accurately completed. Prospect file is up-to-date. Customer information file is current and complete. Sales calls are scheduled. Business deals are recommended. Prospects are willing to consider product. Sales are made.	Prospects are offended. Organization's reputation is diminished. Income is lost.	☐ Identifying prospects. ☐ Qualifying prospects. ☐ Managing time. ☐ Developing selling techniques. ☐ Understanding products. ☐ Building interpersonal skills. ☐ Developing persistence skills.	Identifies unconsidered prospects. Consistently exceeds sales quota. Finds new markets.

_____ **2. EXPANDS SALES IN EXISTING ACCOUNTS**
by
identifying customer needs; participating in the development of client plans;
introducing new products and services.

☐ Result Required	☐ Problem	☐ Learning Required	☐ Performance Option
Sales calls are scheduled. Customers are willing to consider additional product. Recommends business deals. Sales are made.	New sales are lost to competitors. Existing business is lost to competitors. Opportunities are not identified. Income is lost.	☐ Qualifying customers. ☐ Managing time. ☐ Developing selling techniques. ☐ Applying problem-solving techniques. ☐ Learning products. ☐ Strengthening financial skills. ☐ Developing persistence skills. ☐ Developing and applying research skills.	Develops new ways to help customers solve problems. Consistently exceeds sales quota.

_____ **3. ENHANCES RELATIONSHIPS IN EXISTING ACCOUNTS**
by
providing information internally and externally in conjunction with the
Client Service Manager; resolving problems.

☐ Result Required	☐ Problem	☐ Learning Required	☐ Performance Option
Customers have all the information they require. Problems are identified, communicated, and resolved. Corporate visits are coordinated. Customers become reliable references. Management reports are accurate and completed on time.	Customers complain. Customers consider competition. Customers cancel accounts.	☐ Developing analytical skills. ☐ Developing interpersonal skills.	Develops information that becomes standard response for the organization. Customers see the organization as a needed resource. Customers applaud service.

_____ **4. KEEPS MARKET AND SALES MANAGEMENT INFORMED OF INDUSTRY DEVELOPMENTS**
by
monitoring competitive products and reactions from customers.

☐ Result Required	☐ Problem	☐ Learning Required	☐ Performance Option
Market is aware of latest developments. Information on competitors is current. Customer reactions are obtained. Client Service Manager is aware of major issues.	The organization loses competitive position. Customers choose competitors.	☐ Identifying sources of information. ☐ Developing interviewing skills. ☐ Developing analytical skills. ☐ Informing corporate management.	Identifies product trends before they become obvious. Teaches and helps other Account Sales Representatives.

_____ **5. RECOMMENDS NEW PRODUCTS AND SERVICES**
by
evaluating current product results; monitoring competitive developments.

☐ Result Required	☐ Problem	☐ Learning Required	☐ Performance Option
Product results are identified and evaluated. Competitor's products are understood. Recommendations are presented and accepted.	The organization loses competitive position. Customers choose competitors.	☐ Identifying sources of information. ☐ Developing interviewing skills. ☐ Developing analytical skills. ☐ Taking risk.	Recommends product and services that become important profit producers.

_____   **6. CONTRIBUTES TO TEAM EFFORT**
                by
                accomplishing related results as needed.

☐ Result Required	☐ Problem	☐ Learning Required	☐ Performance Option
New and different work requirements are welcomed. Individual work schedule is adjusted to meet organization needs. Individual job results are completed and integrated with the requirements of other jobs.	Projects requiring joint effort are not accomplished. Work is bottlenecked or unfinished. The organization misses opportunities. Team members complain.	☐ Managing time. ☐ Adjusting schedules. ☐ Setting priorities. ☐ Understanding the job's link in the organization's value chain. ☐ Developing interpersonal skills.	Goes out of his or her way to help others apply their knowledge to organization requirements. Finds new ways to foster teamwork and resolve potential conflicts.

JOB RESULTS MANAGEMENT PROFILE

JOB TITLE: CUSTOMER SERVICE SPECIALIST

JOB PURPOSE: SERVES CUSTOMERS
by
resolving client/customer policy and coverage inquiries for financial products (direct mail and credit life); facilitating changes to billing and policy status; training and supporting clients on processing issues.

ESSENTIAL JOB RESULTS:

% of
time

_____ **1. PROVIDES FINANCIAL PRODUCT INFORMATION**
by
analyzing, researching, and resolving client/customer inquiries; maintaining product descriptions and account/client manuals; updating policies, certificates, and endorsements.

☐ Result Required	☐ Problem	☐ Learning Required	☐ Performance Option
Clients and customers receive needed information within established standards. Information is understood. Information is current and accurate.	Clients and customers are dissatisfied. Clients and customers experience service delays.	☐ Analyzing information. ☐ Identifying sources of product information. ☐ Managing time. ☐ Learning system operation. ☐ Developing relationships.	Develops new information mediums for customers. Recommends changes in processing and system procedures.

_____ **2. INTERPRETS FINANCIAL PRODUCT POLICY COVERAGE**
by
determining nature and legality of requests; responding to complex
inquiries; facilitating changes to policy status.

☐ Result Required	☐ Problem	☐ Learning Required	☐ Performance Option
Information is clear and accurate. Clients and customers have the information they need.	Clients and customers are dissatisfied. Client and customer requests are duplicated.	☐ Analyzing and interpreting information. ☐ Explaining information.	Recommends improvements in maintaining policy coverage.

_____ **3. RESOLVES CONFLICTS AND PREVENTS POTENTIAL PROBLEMS**
by
clarifying customer complaints; determining the cause of the problem;
selecting and explaining the best solution to solve the problem;
expediting correction or adjustment; following up to ensure resolution.

☐ Result Required	☐ Problem	☐ Learning Required	☐ Performance Option
Complaints are understood. Alternative solutions are explored. Correction or adjustment is made as soon as practicable.	Clients and customers complain. Time is wasted. Client and customer relationships are terminated.	☐ Analyzing information. ☐ Identifying and evaluating alternative solutions. ☐ Managing time. ☐ Evaluating results.	Receives compliments for service rendered. Identifies trends in requests and problems.

_____ **4. SUPPORTS FINANCIAL PRODUCT CLIENTS**
by
providing training on processing and underwriting issues.

☐ Result Required	☐ Problem	☐ Learning Required	☐ Performance Option
Information provided is complete, accurate, and available when needed. Clients are prepared to accomplish processing and underwriting requirements.	Clients are dissatisfied. Errors are made. Time is wasted. Complaints are received.	☐ Identifying training requirements. ☐ Developing training techniques. ☐ Developing training skills.	Develops creative training techniques.

_____ **5. DOCUMENTS FINANCIAL PRODUCT SOLICITATION DATA**
by
coordinating information flow; collecting and analyzing data in account-specific mailings; answering specific inquiries and exception issues.

☐ Result Required	☐ Problem	☐ Learning Required	☐ Performance Option
Information is clear, accurate, and ready when needed.	Decisions are based on erroneous information.	☐ Managing time. ☐ Analyzing data. ☐ Developing collection methods. ☐ Explaining information.	Recommends improved methods for collecting and analyzing information.

_____ **6. DOCUMENTS ACTIONS**
by
completing production and quality logs.

☐ Result Required	☐ Problem	☐ Learning Required	☐ Performance Option
Production and quality data are accurately documented at required times.	Production decisions are delayed or cannot be made. Time is wasted. Service reputation is diminished.	☐ Identifying information to record. ☐ Studying procedures. ☐ Managing time.	Recommends improvements in documentation procedures. Finds new ways to identify information to record.

JOB RESULTS MANAGEMENT PROFILE

JOB TITLE: DATA ENTRY OPERATOR

JOB PURPOSE: MAINTAINS DATABASE
by
entering, verifying, and balancing data.

ESSENTIAL JOB RESULTS:

% of
time

_____ **1. PREPARES DATA FOR ENTRY**
by
organizing, sorting, researching, correcting, and collecting missing data;
establishing entry priorities.

☐ Result Required	☐ Problem	☐ Learning Required	☐ Performance Option
Information is accurate and ready for efficient entry on schedule.	Sequential work is delayed. Time is wasted. Costs increase.	☐ Managing time. ☐ Organizing data. ☐ Studying procedures.	Recommends improved procedures.

_____ **2. ENTERS DATA**
by
operating data entry equipment; coding data;
resolving processing problems.

☐ Result Required	☐ Problem	☐ Learning Required	☐ Performance Option
Data entry meets production and accuracy standards. Data are coded correctly. Production schedules are met.	Sequential work is wasted. Costs increase. Work must be redone.	☐ Increasing data entry speed. ☐ Improving data entry accuracy. ☐ Studying procedures. ☐ Identifying problems and solutions.	Recommends improved processing systems and procedures. Consistently exceeds production and quality standards.

3. VERIFIES AND BALANCES DATA
by
reviewing and correcting or returning data; correcting cycle rejection errors.

☐ Result Required	☐ Problem	☐ Learning Required	☐ Performance Option
Data are accurate. Production schedules are met.	Decisions are based on incorrect data. Customers complain. Sequential work is delayed. Time is wasted. Costs increase.	☐ Checking information. ☐ Managing time.	Recommends improved procedures.

4. SERVES CUSTOMERS
by
providing information; resolving problems.

☐ Result Required	☐ Problem	☐ Learning Required	☐ Performance Option
Questions are answered and problems are resolved as soon as practicable. Information is complete and correct. Uncertain information is identified and clarified.	Customers complain. Service is interrupted.	☐ Identifying sources of information. ☐ Managing time. ☐ Studying and following procedures. ☐ Referring problems to supervisor.	Identifies trends in requests for information or in problems occurring. Recommends improved procedures.

_____   **5. CONTRIBUTES TO TEAM EFFORT**
by
accomplishing related results as needed.

☐ Result Required	☐ Problem	☐ Learning Required	☐ Performance Option
New and different work requirements are welcomed. Individual work schedule is adjusted to meet organization needs. Individual job results are completed and integrated with the requirements of other jobs.	Projects requiring joint effort are not accomplished. Work is bottle-necked or unfinished. The organization misses opportunities. Team members complain.	☐ Managing time. ☐ Adjusting schedules. ☐ Setting priorities. ☐ Understanding the job's link in the organization's value chain. ☐ Developing inter-personal skills.	Goes out of his or her way to help others apply their knowledge to organization requirements. Finds new ways to foster teamwork and resolve potential conflicts.

JOB RESULTS MANAGEMENT PROFILE

JOB TITLE: **QUALITY ASSURANCE PROCESSOR**

JOB PURPOSE: **ASSURES SYSTEM OUTPUT**
by
reconciling transactions; maintaining database.

ESSENTIAL JOB RESULTS:

% of
time

_____ **1. RECONCILES TRANSACTIONS**
by
verifying, researching, and resolving invalid entries;
following established controls.

☐ Result Required	☐ Problem	☐ Learning Required	☐ Performance Option
Transactions are accurate. Production schedules are met. Problems are identified and resolved. Controls are followed.	Work is delayed. Time is wasted. Decisions are based on incorrect information.	☐ Managing time. ☐ Identifying problems. ☐ Identifying sources of information.	Recommends improved systems and procedures.

_____ **2. MAINTAINS DATABASE**
by
entering or forwarding corrections; creating and monitoring suspense file;
updating files.

☐ Result Required	☐ Problem	☐ Learning Required	☐ Performance Option
Database is up-to-date. Production schedules are met. Outstanding problems are resolved.	Work is delayed. Time is wasted. Decisions are based on incorrect information.	☐ Managing time. ☐ Following up. ☐ Verifying information.	Recommends improved procedure.

_____ ### 3. MAINTAINS QUALITY SERVICE
by
completing audits; preparing summary information; identifying systems and procedure problems.

☐ Result Required	☐ Problem	☐ Learning Required	☐ Performance Option
Audits are completed on schedule. Summaries are accurate. Systems and procedure problems are identified.	Errors persist. Decisions are based on inaccurate information. Work is not accomplished efficiently.	☐ Following procedures. ☐ Identifying sources of problems. ☐ Managing time. ☐ Summarizing information.	Recommends improved systems and procedures. Discovers solutions to persistent problems.

_____ ### 4. MAINTAINS SYSTEM
by
analyzing and resolving operating problems, hardware requirements, and system access requests; developing procedures.

☐ Result Required	☐ Problem	☐ Learning Required	☐ Performance Option
Operating problems are resolved. Systems issues are forwarded. Work continues. Production schedules are met. Procedures are in place and current.	Work is delayed. Time is wasted. Costs increase. Customers are dissatisfied.	☐ Identifying problems. ☐ Identifying sources of information. ☐ Clarifying information. ☐ Managing time.	Recommends improved systems and requirements.

_____ **5. CONTRIBUTES TO TEAM EFFORT**
by
accomplishing related results as needed.

☐ Result Required	☐ Problem	☐ Learning Required	☐ Performance Option
New and different work requirements are welcomed. Individual work schedule is adjusted to meet organization needs. Individual job results are completed and integrated with the requirements of other jobs.	Projects requiring joint effort are not accomplished. Work is bottlenecked or unfinished. The organization misses opportunities. Team members complain.	☐ Managing time. ☐ Adjusting schedules. ☐ Setting priorities. ☐ Understanding the job's link in the organization's value chain. ☐ Developing interpersonal skills.	Goes out of his or her way to help others apply their knowledge to organization requirements. Finds new ways to foster teamwork and resolve potential conflicts.

JOB RESULTS MANAGEMENT PROFILE

JOB TITLE: **SYSTEMS ANALYST**

JOB PURPOSE: **ACCOMPLISHES BUSINESS OBJECTIVES**
by
identifying project requirements; developing and maintaining
software applications; providing support to customers.

ESSENTIAL JOB RESULTS:

% of
time

           1. IDENTIFIES PROJECT REQUIREMENTS
              by
              interviewing customers; analyzing operations; determining project scope;
              documenting results; preparing customer contracts.

☐ Result Required	☐ Problem	☐ Learning Required	☐ Performance Option
Organizational sources of information are identified and analyzed. Data are collected efficiently. Procedures are analyzed. Problem is understood and defined accurately. Customer contract reflects elements of project. The organization's methodologies are followed.	Project does not meet need. Customers complain. Resources are wasted.	☐ Identifying sources of information. ☐ Managing time. ☐ Analyzing information. ☐ Applying project management techniques. ☐ Learning and applying the organization's methodologies.	Identifies emerging issues. Develops creative solutions.

_____ **2. DEVELOPS PROBLEM SOLUTION**
by
describing requirements in a work flowchart and diagram; studying system capabilities; analyzing alternative solutions; preparing system specifications; writing programs.

☐ Result Required	☐ Problem	☐ Learning Required	☐ Performance Option
Work flowcharts and diagrams are prepared. System capabilities are understood. All alternatives are identified. Specifications accurately identify requirements. Programming is correct.	Applications will not function correctly. Resources are wasted. Customer is not satisfied.	☐ Developing writing techniques. ☐ Choosing a course of action. ☐ Studying requirements. ☐ Studying technology.	Develops creative solution.

_____ **3. DEVELOPS PROJECT ESTIMATES**
by
identifying project phases and elements, personnel requirements, and costs.

☐ Result Required	☐ Problem	☐ Learning Required	☐ Performance Option
Project estimates are accurate.	Project costs exceed expectations. Other projects are delayed.	☐ Analyzing and calculating requirements.	Consistently completes projects ahead of time and under anticipated costs.

_____   **4. VERIFIES RESULTS**
            by
            developing and completing tests.

☐ Result Required	☐ Problem	☐ Learning Required	☐ Performance Option
Comprehensive test plans are developed. Programs are checked in a test environment. Results are understood. Errors are corrected. User confirms system functionality.	Applications fail. Customers are dissatisfied. Reputation to provide helpful service is diminished. Resources are wasted. The organization is subject to legal action and/or embarrassment.	☐ Developing tests. ☐ Managing time. ☐ Analyzing problems. ☐ Studying technology.	Recommends improvements in standards and procedures.

_____   **5. PREPARES CUSTOMERS TO USE SYSTEM**
            by
            conducting training.

☐ Result Required	☐ Problem	☐ Learning Required	☐ Performance Option
Customers are prepared to accomplish job expectations. Customers obtain the consultation they need.	Customer's production is interrupted. Productivity declines. Time is wasted.	☐ Revising training content. ☐ Developing training skills. ☐ Identifying training requirements.	Develops creative training practices.

____ **6. PROVIDES REFERENCE FOR CUSTOMERS**
by
writing documentation; providing support and help.

☐ Result Required	☐ Problem	☐ Learning Required	☐ Performance Option
Documentation is current, clear, and readily available. Customers are prepared to accomplish job results. Customers obtain the consultation they need.	Customers complain. Time is wasted. Reputation to deliver complete service is diminished.	☐ Developing writing techniques. ☐ Coaching customers. ☐ Managing time.	Develops creative solutions for providing essential information to customers.

____ **7. MAINTAINS SYSTEMS**
by
researching and resolving problems.

☐ Result Required	☐ Problem	☐ Learning Required	☐ Performance Option
Systems accomplish desired results. Problems are identified correctly. Solutions correct the problem and prevent recurrences.	Customer's work is interrupted unnecessarily. Customers lose confidence in help provided.	☐ Analyzing situations. ☐ Analyzing alternatives. ☐ Choosing a course of action.	Develops creative solution to persistent problems. Detects and resolves undetected system malfunctions.

_____   **8. CONTRIBUTES TO TEAM EFFORT**
by
accomplishing related results as needed.

☐ Result Required	☐ Problem	☐ Learning Required	☐ Performance Option
New and different work requirements are welcomed. Individual work schedule is adjusted to meet organization needs. Individual job results are completed and integrated with the requirements of other jobs.	Projects requiring joint effort are not accomplished. Work is bottlenecked or unfinished. The organization misses opportunities. Team members complain.	☐ Managing time. ☐ Analyzing schedules. ☐ Setting priorities. ☐ Understanding the job's link in the organization's value chain. ☐ Developing interpersonal skills.	Goes out of his or her way to help others apply their knowledge to organization requirements. Finds new ways to foster teamwork and resolve potential conflicts.

JOB RESULTS MANAGEMENT PROFILE

JOB TITLE: **TRAINING SPECIALIST**

JOB PURPOSE: **PREPARES EMPLOYEES TO ACCOMPLISH JOB RESULTS**
by
designing, facilitating, revising, and evaluating training programs for all levels of the organization and subsidiary employees.

ESSENTIAL JOB RESULTS:

% of
time

_____   **1. ASSESSES TRAINING NEEDS**
by
consulting with managers and employees.

☐ Result Required	☐ Problem	☐ Learning Required	☐ Performance Option
Training programs are developed based on needs assessment results. Participants see relevance of program content to the job. Instructional methods are appropriate to the audience.	Participants don't understand why or how training program/need was identified. Costs increase. Participants are unclear on how to incorporate what is learned into their work.	☐ Studying needs analysis techniques. ☐ Developing working relationships' cross-functionality to assess company needs. ☐ Studying curriculum design. ☐ Managing time. ☐ Developing communications skills.	Finds new ways to assess training needs. Recommends improvements in the training assessment process.

_____ **2. PREPARES TRAINING AND DEVELOPMENT PROGRAMS**
by
designing materials; evaluating packaged training programs; working with external consultants; assessing resource materials.

☐ Result Required	☐ Problem	☐ Learning Required	☐ Performance Option
Program design matches employees' needs, interests, and learning levels. Program content incorporates appropriate learning activities and sequences. Purchased programs are cost-effective. External consultants are used efficiently. Appropriate resources are utilized.	Costs increase. Employees complain about program design and organization. Program design and materials do not support training objective. Opportunities are lost.	☐ Studying program design techniques. ☐ Studying program content and cost evaluation approaches. ☐ Reviewing consultant selection techniques. ☐ Reviewing principles of adult learning.	Discovers and applies new program design techniques. Identifies new resources of training materials.

_____ **3. PRESENTS TRAINING AND DEVELOPMENT PROGRAMS**
by
conducting classes on topics of customer service, quality improvement, and supervisory skills.

☐ Result Required	☐ Problem	☐ Learning Required	☐ Performance Option
Program presentation follows facilitator's guide. Employees understand relevance of topics to job results. Employees express satisfaction with program content and trainer presentation skills.	Grievances and lawsuits occur. Customers complain. Program content is inconsistent. Employees are confused. Employees become bored, frustrated, and angry with classroom experience. Interest in training programs diminishes.	☐ Studying principles of customer service and quality improvement. ☐ Studying state-of-the-art supervisory development techniques. ☐ Practicing platform skills. ☐ Studying trainer/facilitator techniques.	Finds new classroom techniques to inspire employees to serve the customer and focus on quality. Develops uniquely positive relationships between supervisors and employees. Identifies emerging issues and recommends changes.

4. EVALUATES TRAINING PROGRAM EFFECTIVENESS
by
grading and evaluating student quizzes, tests, and class assignments.

☐ Result Required	☐ Problem	☐ Learning Required	☐ Performance Option
Quizzes, tests, and class assignments measure employee learning.	Training program effectiveness is compromised. Employees complain about the irrelevance to job needs of quizzes, tests, and class assignments. Opportunities are lost.	☐ Studying testing methodologies. ☐ Examining class assignment structuring methods. ☐ Exploring experiential learning opportunities.	Finds creative ways to verify learning.

5. REVISES COURSE MATERIALS
by
evaluating and adjusting facilitator guides, class activities, tests, and take-home exercises.

☐ Result Required	☐ Problem	☐ Learning Required	☐ Performance Option
Revisions promote consistent learning experiences for participants. Class activities support learning objectives. Tests measure learning. Employee take-home exercises are returned completed.	Class content and structure vary among facilitators. Employees are reluctant to participant in class activities. Test scores are inconclusive.	☐ Reviewing course evaluation techniques. ☐ Studying testing techniques. ☐ Studying exercise design approaches. ☐ Studying facilitator guide design techniques.	Finds new techniques to revise course materials. Discovers new ways to achieve training course consistency among facilitators.

_____   **6. PREPARES NEW EMPLOYEES**
          by
          conducting orientation program for new employees.

☐ Result Required	☐ Problem	☐ Learning Required	☐ Performance Option
Orientation information is delivered accurately. Employees feel informed and prepared to begin their new job. Employees are eager to continue learning experiences.	Employees complain. New employees are unclear about policies and procedures; questions are raised. Retraining is required after the orientation period. Costs increase.	☐ Studying orientation training program. ☐ Applying instructional techniques. ☐ Practicing presentation motivational techniques.	Finds new ways to reduce the time requirements of orientation. Recommends creative improvements in the orientation process. Identifies emerging issues.

_____   **7. SCHEDULES TRAINING OPPORTUNITIES**
          by
          coediting the training course catalog; creating calendar of topics;
          administering the lunchtime brown bag programs; revising the
          department course catalog.

☐ Result Required	☐ Problem	☐ Learning Required	☐ Performance Option
Employees are aware of training opportunities. Employees are informed about company performance and internal operations. Employees know how to obtain business and personal information.	Employees become confused. Time is lost. Costs increase. Employees are not able to take advantage of opportunities.	☐ Applying time management principles. ☐ Utilizing communication techniques. ☐ Studying meeting coordination procedures. ☐ Coordinating activities and assignments.	Finds new ways to market training programs that create demand for services. Develops innovative ways of presenting course catalog. Develops innovative ways to communicate company, business, and personal information.

8. CONTRIBUTES TO TEAM EFFORT
by
accomplishing related results as needed.

□ Result Required	□ Problem	□ Learning Required	□ Performance Option
New and different work requirements are welcomed. Individual work schedule is adjusted to meet organization needs. Individual job results are completed and integrated with the requirements of other jobs.	Projects requiring joint effort are not accomplished. Work is bottlenecked or unfinished. The organization misses opportunities. Team members complain.	□ Managing time. □ Adjusting schedules. □ Setting priorities. □ Understanding the job's link in the organization's value chain. □ Developing interpersonal skills.	Goes out of his or her way to help others apply their knowledge to organization requirements. Finds new ways to foster teamwork and resolve potential conflicts.

Defining the Result Required

Try writing the Result Required first because it is most closely tied to the job result, which you already have defined in the results-oriented job description. The Result Required sets a reference for writing the other outcomes. Sometimes, however, you will have a better understanding of another criterion—perhaps the Problem, which describes the outcome you don't want. Start with whatever criterion is clearest to you. Remember that the four outcomes should be viewed as a single unit of four different perspectives of the same job result. If you are not certain what you are trying to describe in some criterion, look to the others for another perspective.

If the job result is not stated correctly, as when a job duty is mistaken for a job result, writing the Result Required will be difficult, if not impossible. Thus, a struggle to state the Result Required may signal that the job result should be rewritten. For example, suppose the job result and duties are incorrectly identified as, "Processes orders by categorizing and approving them." Categorizing and approving orders means the same as processing them; processing is not the end result. Off to a bad start, outcome standards will be aimed at how well orders are categorized and approved. The standards that beg to be identified center on the completion of the processing. The correct statement about job result and duties can now be written as, "Completes orders by categorizing and approving them." Now the outcomes standard can incorporate production, quality, and time standards of the completed order. When you view the job result and Result Required together, writing one helps clarify the other.

Study the job result. What is an observable event that tells you that the result has been accomplished?

Start writing the outcome with a noun, not a verb. Starting with a verb focuses on the employee's behavior, whereas a results-oriented approach focuses on the work. A behavioral focus can be particularly damaging when problems are involved, as we will see when we look at the Problem outcome.

Write in the present to create a contemporary sense as opposed to something that happened in the past. Do not use modifiers that are imprecise—for example, "usually" or "most of the time." Be as specific as possible.

Here is a job result that we will use to show how to write example job outcomes in this section:

JOB RESULTS MANAGEMENT PROFILE

RESULT   **PRODUCES INFORMATION**
              by
duty   transcribing, formatting, inputting, editing, retrieving, copying, and
              transmitting text, data, and graphics; coordinating report preparation.

The Result Required outcome written correctly:

☐ Result Required			
Information is complete, accurate, readable, attractive in appearance, and ready when needed.			

The Result Required outcome written incorrectly:

☐ Result Required			
Enters data errorlessly and returns work in a timely manner.			

The incorrect statement starts with a verb, and "in a timely manner" is vague.

The more tangible the job, the more tangibly the criterion can be stated—for example, frequency, time, number, speed, or errors allowed can be spelled out. Here is a quantitative Result Required expressing a precise range of customer satisfaction:

☐ Result Required			
Customer satisfaction survey rating of 5.7 to 6.2.			

But be careful! Numbers can also squish the humanness out of a situation. Did an employee who accomplished a 5.6 really miss? Use numbers to start the conversation, but make sure you get the assumptions and facts behind the numbers too.

Don't shy away from identifying less tangible human values, such as tact. Don't focus directly on the value; instead, focus on what the value produces. For example, to express tact, write: "Rapport is maintained" or "Disagreements are ameliorated." Don't focus directly on creativity; instead write: "New products or methods are developed." Look at what you get, not the trait or characteristic that produces the result.

Sometimes you will start to write a vague term, such as "promptly." Catch yourself, and use the opportunity to clarify the condition. For example, "promptly" might be better stated as "by the third working day of the month." Still, you may find that it simply makes more sense to describe the condition you want as "on time" or "when needed," and make it clear that the deadline must be specified to an employee when work begins and kept up-to-date as circumstances change.

Practice for Defining the Result Required Outcome   As instructions for writing each outcome are presented in this section, it will be helpful for you to practice writing the outcome. Follow the grammatical instructions (such as "Start with a noun") precisely. Sample solutions will be presented.

Here are some example phrases to use and adapt to your situation. Keep in mind quantity, quality, time, and cost:

"Customers trust the organization."
"Organization is in compliance."
"Employees are prepared to accomplish job results."
"Equipment is ready when needed."
"Inspections are completed as scheduled."
"Equipment operates as intended."
"Equipment downtime is limited to 1 percent of overall production time."
"Information is accurate."
"Work is completed on schedule."
"Reports are received within three hours of expected delivery."
"Controllable expenses are within budget."
"Budget variance is within 3 percent."
"Information and help are offered."
"Data are collected with the least use of resources."
"Adjustments are within tolerances."
"Adjustments are within 1 percent."
"Procedures and regulations are followed."
"Production is documented at required times."
"Guidelines are current, clear, and available."
"Production rates and quality standards are met."
"Production rates are within 2 percent of hourly production plan."
"Telephone is answered by the third ring."
"Customer complaints are resolved within three hours."

Here is a job result for you to use. Practice writing the Result Required before reading on.

JOB RESULTS MANAGEMENT PROFILE

RESULT   **MAINTAINS EXECUTIVES' AND SUPPORTING STAFF'S CALENDARS**
               by
duty   planning and scheduling meetings, conferences, teleconferences, and travel.

☐ Result Required			

Does the Result Required you wrote look something like this?

☐ Result Required			
Calendars are up-to-date. Calendar conflicts are resolved within one-half day. Meeting arrangements are completed as required. Itineraries are logical and efficient. Travel expenses are no more than 1 percent over plan.			

Remember that the important element here is not whether you used the precise words we did but that you described an outcome suitable for your organization following the established writing rules.

Application Project for Result Required Outcome   Now select a job result from a job in your organization that you know well. Following the writing instructions, write the Result Required outcome for this job result.

JOB RESULTS MANAGEMENT PROFILE

RESULT
by
duty

☐ Result Required			

Defining the Problem Outcome

Study the job result and the Result Required. What bad effect (the Problem) is created when the result is not accomplished and the Result Required standards are not met?

Start writing each statement with a noun, not with a verb, for the same reason as with the Result Required. Because these statements start with verbs, the implied subject of the sentence is the employee. Results statements are grammatically different; the subject of the sentence is the work, not the employee. To illustrate this point, here is an example:

Stated behaviorally: Does not meet deadlines.
Stated as results: Deadlines are not met.

The difference is subtle. You may even wonder if there is really a difference. Behavioral statements make the employee the sole reason for not meeting the deadline. Being "so accused" may trigger a defensive reaction in the employee. Obviously, a variety of other factors may influence whether deadlines are met.

More effective communication starts with the irrefutable, objective fact that the deadline was not met and works back to the reasons for the deadline's not being met. By focusing dialogue on the result, managers and employees are able to look at the circumstances to understand what happened and to find ways to prevent the problem from occurring in the future.

Do not merely state the opposite of the Result Required—for example, "Deadlines are met," "Deadlines are not met." This adds no new information. It's logically obvious that if the deadlines are supposed to be met, then not having the deadlines met is unacceptable. What's important to know is the bad effect of not having the deadlines met—for example, decisions cannot be made.

Do not use vague modifiers, such as, "Deadlines are *frequently* missed." Be specific. Write in the present tense.

Here is the Problem outcome written correctly:

JOB RESULTS MANAGEMENT PROFILE

RESULT   **PRODUCES INFORMATION**
by
duty   transcribing, formatting, inputting, editing, retrieving, copying, and transmitting text, data, and graphics; coordinating report preparation.

☐ Result Required	☐ Problem		
Information is complete, accurate, readable, attractive in appearance, and ready when needed.	Contingent work cannot proceed. Decisions cannot be made. Time is wasted. Customers complain.		

And here is the Problem outcome written incorrectly:

☐ Result Required	☐ Problem		
	Commits too many errors and doesn't give work back soon enough. Does not key documents as dictated.		

The incorrect statement starts with a verb; "too many" and "soon enough" are vague; "does not key documents as dictated" is merely the opposite of the Result Required.

It is not always possible to identify all the Problems that might occur as a consequence of failing to produce up to the Result Required. The description of the Problem is explained up front to employees as representative indicators instead of an all-inclusive statement.

Here is a quantitative Problem outcome example:

☐ Result Required	☐ Problem		
Customer satisfaction survey rating of 5.7 to 6.2.	Customer satisfaction survey rating less than 5.0.		

Here are some example phrases to use and adapt to your situation. Keep in mind quantity, quality, time, and cost:

"Time is wasted."
"Costs increase."
"Costs increase by 10 percent."
"Organization services are inconsistent."
"Customers complain."
"Organization's reputation is diminished."
"Equipment is damaged."
"Equipment repair costs are more than 5 percent over budget."
"Services cannot be provided."
"Decisions are delayed."
"Opportunities are lost."
"Resources are wasted."
"People are endangered or injured."
"Workers' compensation costs increase by 10 percent."
"Fines are imposed; citations are issued."
"Work must be scrapped or reworked."
"Telephone is not answered until the sixth ring."

Now it's your turn. Write the Problem before reading on.

JOB RESULTS MANAGEMENT PROFILE

RESULT   **MAINTAINS EXECUTIVES' AND SUPPORTING STAFF'S CALENDARS**
                by
duty   planning and scheduling meetings, conferences, teleconferences, and travel.

☐ Result Required	☐ Problem		
Calendars are up-to-date. Calendar conflicts are resolved within one-half day. Meeting arrangements are completed as required. Itineraries are logical and efficient. Travel expenses are no more than 1 percent over plan.			

How did you do?

☐ Result Required	☐ Problem		
Calendars are up-to-date. Calendar conflicts are resolved within one-half day. Meeting arrangements are completed as required. Itineraries are logical and efficient. Travel expenses are no more than 1 percent over plan.	Meetings are missed. Managerial responsibilities are interrupted. Opportunities are lost. Travel costs increase by 5 percent over plan.		

Now write the Problem outcome for the job in your organization you selected earlier. Review what you wrote for the Result Required, and think about the things that can go wrong when the Result Required is not accomplished.

JOB RESULTS MANAGEMENT PROFILE

RESULT
by
duty

☐ Result Required	☐ Problem		

Defining the Learning Required Outcome

Think about typical employees. When they are not accomplishing the Results Required, what do they need to learn in order to meet expectations and correct problems? At this point, you are only identifying general reminders; specific learning plans for specific employees will be developed in the space provided for Learning Plans when you understand specific problems and needs.

Put the language in the active (learning) context by using verbs ending in "ing." Do not describe what a person should do "more" of (such as, "Needs to be more attentive"), be "better" at (such as, "Needs to have better skills"), or "know" or "understand" (such as, "Needs to understand quality control") because these words are vague and do not provide specific learning guides.

The Learning Required articulates a key concept of the Job Results Management Profile concept: employees who do not accomplish job results do not know *how* to accomplish the Required Results; it is not that they deliberately choose not to accomplish results. Publishing typical learning requirements when outcomes fall below Results Required makes management's intent to focus on and foster learning that much more obvious. The Learning Required guides also recognize that employees are adult learners who can understand deficient work results and can find out for themselves what they need to learn by reading the guides.

Here is a Learning Required outcome written correctly:

JOB RESULTS MANAGEMENT PROFILE

RESULT   **PRODUCES INFORMATION**
                by
duty   transcribing, formatting, inputting, editing, retrieving, copying, and
                transmitting text, data, and graphics; coordinating report preparation.

☐ Result Required	☐ Problem	☐ Learning Required	
Information is complete, accurate, readable, attractive in appearance, and ready when needed.	Contingent work cannot proceed. Decisions cannot be made. Time is wasted. Customers complain.	☐ Applying technical skills. ☐ Managing time. ☐ Setting priorities. ☐ Clarifying instructions. ☐ Developing writing skills. ☐ Consulting dictionary and grammar software. ☐ Practicing word processing skills.	

Here the Learning Required outcome is written incorrectly:

☐ Result Required	☐ Problem	☐ Learning Required	
		☐ Technical skills. ☐ Be better at managing time. ☐ Writing. ☐ Get word processing skills.	

What is supposed to be done about technical skills? How does one get better at managing time? Writing? What aspects of writing? "Get word processing skills" sounds as though you might pick them up somewhere.

In the case of quantifying the Learning Required, the numbers identify the gap between the low end of the Results Required and the Problem. Specific learning will have to be identified once the reason for the Problem is clarified. Here is a quantitative Learning Required outcome example:

☐ Result Required	☐ Problem	☐ Learning Required	
Customer satisfaction survey rating of 5.7 to 6.2.	Customer satisfaction survey rating less than 5.0.	☐ Increasing customer satisfaction survey rating above range of 5.0 to 5.6.	

Here are example phrases to use and adapt:

"Studying requirements."
"Verifying information."
"Coaching employees."
"Managing time."
"Scheduling work."
"Analyzing information."
"Identifying sources of information."
"Presenting information."
"Developing relationships."
"Resolving conflicts."
"Developing techniques."
"Evaluating options."
"Choosing a course of action."
"Controlling events."
"Studying equipment operation."
"Answering the telephone on the fourth or fifth ring."

What are some possible things that might have to be learned to accomplish these Results Required or to prevent these Problems? Write the Learning Required before reading on.

JOB RESULTS MANAGEMENT PROFILE

RESULT   **MAINTAINS EXECUTIVES' AND SUPPORTING STAFF'S CALENDARS**
               by
duty   planning and scheduling meetings, conferences, teleconferences,
              and travel.

☐ Result Required	☐ Problem	☐ Learning Required	
Calendars are up-to-date. Calendar conflicts are resolved within one-half day. Meeting arrangements are completed as required. Itineraries are logical and efficient. Travel expenses are no more than 1 percent over plan.	Meetings are missed. Managerial responsibilities are interrupted. Opportunities are lost. Time is wasted. Travel costs increase by 5 percent over plan.	☐	

Are your Learning Required statements something like these?

☐ Result Required	☐ Problem	☐ Learning Required	
Calendars are up-to-date. Calendar conflicts are resolved within one-half day. Meeting arrangements are completed as required. Itineraries are logical and efficient. Travel expenses are no more than 1 percent over plan.	Meetings are missed. Managerial responsibilities are interrupted. Opportunities are lost. Travel costs increase by 5 percent over plan.	☐ Managing time. ☐ Applying scheduling techniques. ☐ Using planning models. ☐ Developing negotiation skills. ☐ Applying decision-making techniques. ☐ Controlling events. ☐ Decreasing travel costs of 2–4 percent over plan.	

Some people find the Learning Required a little tricky to write, particularly if they are coming at it from a behavioral point of view. Notice how objective and impersonal Learning Required appears. If someone needs to learn to manage time, it may well be that he or she is receiving too many personal phone calls or finds reasons to make 10 trips to the copy machine when one would do. It isn't that these behaviors will not be addressed by the manager. However, it is easier to begin a conversation addressing managing time to meet deadlines than to begin with telling a person he or she spends too much time on the telephone with personal calls.

Now write the Learning Required outcome for the job in your organization you selected earlier.

JOB RESULTS MANAGEMENT PROFILE

RESULT
by
duty

☐ Result Required	☐ Problem	☐ Learning Required	

Defining the Performance Option Outcome

The Performance Option describes a role-model employee who concentrates on innovation, new ideas, and systems development. Look at the manager's job for clues; outstanding contributors frequently do things for their manager so that the manager can get on with other responsibilities.

Start writing with a verb to make the employee the subject of attention, because the Performance Option is a compliment to the employee for extra accomplishment. Do not state superlatives, such as, "Always gives exceptional performance," because these statements are nearly impossible to attain. The Performance Option is not just more of the same as stated in the Result Required, such as, "Reports are filed when needed" or "Reports are always filed on time." The thrust of the Performance Option is value-added thinking: How can we do these better?

Here is the Performance Option written correctly:

JOB RESULTS MANAGEMENT PROFILE

RESULT   **PRODUCES INFORMATION**
                 by
duty   transcribing, formatting, inputting, editing, retrieving, copying, and
                 transmitting text, data, and graphics; coordinating report preparation.

☐ Result Required	☐ Problem	☐ Learning Required	☐ Performance Option
Information is complete, accurate, readable, attractive in appearance, and ready when needed.	Contingent work cannot proceed. Decisions cannot be made. Time is wasted. Customers complain.	☐ Applying technical skills. ☐ Managing time. ☐ Setting priorities. ☐ Clarifying instructions. ☐ Developing writing skills. ☐ Consulting dictionary and grammar software. ☐ Practicing word processing skills.	Recognizes content errors and corrects them. Develops models to simplify work. Recommends improvements in procedures. Discovers new information resources. Influences others to follow procedures. Discovers creative ways to present information. Identifies and corrects inaccurate information in documents.

Here is the Performance Option written incorrectly:

☐ Result Required	☐ Problem	☐ Learning Required	☐ Performance Option
			Documents are always typed perfectly; does her best to help out and offer suggestions. Shows initiative.

The statement starts with a noun. "Always typed perfectly" is a superlative that may realistically never be reached. "Her" is sexist language that is best eliminated to avoid discrimination charges. "Shows initiative" doesn't offer a precise guide. In what ways could the employee demonstrate initiative?

The level of outcome accomplishment has to fit your organization's culture. In some organizations, some of the Performance Options in this example might be defined as the Result Required. Whatever level of accomplishment is appropriate for Result Required, the Performance Option has to represent a higher role-model level of accomplishment.

Here is the quantitative Performance Option outcome example:

☐ Result Required	☐ Problem	☐ Learning Required	☐ Performance Option
Customer satisfaction survey rating of 5.7 to 6.2.	Customer satisfaction survey rating less than 5.0.	☐ Increasing customer satisfaction survey rating above range of 5.0 to 5.6.	Achieves customer satisfaction survey rating of 6.6 or higher.

Notice the stretch from the Result Required at 5.7 to 6.2 to the Performance Option at 6.6. Why the stretch? Because just a little bit more is not the kind of result you want to reward. The principle of the Performance Option is not working harder, but working smarter. The superstar accomplishments must be truly exceptional: a rating of 6.6 or better.

Here are some example phrases to use and adapt:

"Recommends improvements in procedures."
"Influences others to follow procedures."
"Recommends changes in requirements."
"Anticipates system errors."
"Finds new ways to keep equipment downtime to zero."
"Identifies unanticipated requirements."
"Identifies trends in requests for new information."
"Discovers new information resources."
"Increases production by 10 percent."
"Anticipates interruptions."
"Identifies emerging issues."
"Recommends creative solutions to persistent problems."
"Is sought out for help to resolve differences."
"Recommends revisions in techniques."
"Develops new methods."
"Finds ways to answer the telephone on the first ring."
"Produces desired results under budget."
"Reduces costs by 2 percent."

Before reading on, write the Performance Option now for the maintaining calendar result of the secretarial position, and you will have completed your first four-view writing experience of how the Result Required of the results-oriented job description is (or is not) accomplished.

JOB RESULTS MANAGEMENT PROFILE

RESULT **MAINTAINS EXECUTIVES' AND SUPPORTING STAFF'S CALENDARS**
by
duty planning and scheduling meetings, conferences, teleconferences,
and travel.

☐ Result Required	☐ Problem	☐ Learning Required	☐ Performance Option
Calendars are up-to-date. Calendar conflicts are resolved within one-half day. Meeting arrangements are completed as required. Itineraries are logical and efficient. Travel expenses are no more than 1 percent over plan.	Meeting are missed. Managerial responsibilities are interrupted. Opportunities are lost. Time is wasted. Travel costs increase by 5 percent over plan.	☐ Managing time. ☐ Applying scheduling techniques. ☐ Using planning models. ☐ Developing negotiation skills. ☐ Applying decision-making techniques. ☐ Controlling events. ☐ Decreasing travel costs of 2–4 percent over plan.	

Is the writing getting easier? Are you beginning to feel the connection between the outcomes? Does your Performance Option outcome resemble this example?

☐ Result Required	☐ Problem	☐ Learning Required	☐ Performance Option
Calendars are up-to-date. Calendar conflicts are resolved within one-half day. Meeting arrangements are completed as required. Itineraries are logical and efficient. Travel expenses are no more than 1 percent over plan.	Meetings are missed. Managerial responsibilities are interrupted. Opportunities are lost. Time is wasted. Travel costs increase by 5% over plan.	☐ Managing time. ☐ Applying scheduling techniques. ☐ Using planning models. ☐ Developing negotiation skills. ☐ Applying decision-making techniques. ☐ Controlling events. ☐ Decreasing travel costs of 2–4 percent over plan.	Anticipates and prevents delays. Develops models that improve efficiency. Reduces meeting and conferencing time by 7 percent. Reduces travel costs by 5 percent.

The more profiles you write, the easier it gets. When you prepare these outcomes for your organization, you will find that writing them by job groupings makes sense. You will not only see the relationships among jobs more clearly; you will see career progression planning opportunities.

Now write the Performance Option for the job you selected earlier.

JOB RESULTS MANAGEMENT PROFILE

RESULT
by
duty

☐ Result Required	☐ Problem	☐ Learning Required	☐ Performance Option

Universal Outcomes

Some job results and outcomes apply to all jobs. They can be written once and distributed for insertion in all jobs to save time.

Universal job results can be written for any job responsibility but generally fall into one of the following categories:

- Confidentiality and legal
- Education and training
- Equipment and supplies
- Information
- Management (may include standard responsibilities for different levels of management, such as supervisor, manager, director, vice president)
- Operations
- Problem solving
- Safety
- Service
- Standards and procedures

Here are some examples of universal information job results and outcomes:

MAINTAINS DATABASE
by
writing computer programs; entering and backing up data.

☐ Result Required	☐ Problem	☐ Learning Required	☐ Performance Option
Database is available to users when and as needed. Information is accurate. Programs are efficient.	Customers complain. Work cannot be processed. Schedules are not met. Services cannot be provided.	☐ Studying procedures. ☐ Managing time. ☐ Referring problems to supervisor.	Recommends improved programming. Anticipates system errors. Influences others to follow backup procedures.

MAINTAINS DATABASE
by
developing information requirements; designing an information system.

☐ Result Required	☐ Problem	☐ Learning Required	☐ Performance Option
Database is available to users when and as needed. Information is accurate. Systems are efficient.	Customers complain. Work cannot be processed. Schedules are not met. Services cannot be provided.	☐ Studying procedures. ☐ Managing time. ☐ Referring problems to supervisor.	Identifies inaccurate or unanticipated user requirement. Recommends new solutions. Improves operational efficiency.

SECURES INFORMATION
by
completing database backups.

☐ Result Required	☐ Problem	☐ Learning Required	☐ Performance Option
Information is available when and as needed. Backups are completed on schedule.	Customers complain. Work cannot be processed. Schedules are not met. Services cannot be provided.	☐ Studying procedures. ☐ Managing time. ☐ Referring problems to supervisor.	Recommends improvements in procedures. Anticipates database backup problems. Cautions others of potential backup breaches.

MAINTAINS HISTORICAL RECORDS
by
filing documents.

☐ Result Required	☐ Problem	☐ Learning Required	☐ Performance Option
Documents are available when and as needed. Filing is completed accurately, on schedule.	Work is delayed. Service is interrupted. Time is wasted.	☐ Studying procedures. ☐ Managing time. ☐ Referring problems to supervisor.	Recommends improvements in procedures. Cautions others when filing procedures may be compromised.

PROVIDES INFORMATION
by
answering questions and requests.

☐ Result Required	☐ Problem	☐ Learning Required	☐ Performance Option
Questions and requests are answered as soon as is practicable. Information provided is complete and correct. Uncertain information is identified and clarified.	Customers complain. Service is interrupted. Work is delayed.	☐ Identifying sources of information. ☐ Studying procedures. ☐ Managing time. ☐ Referring problems to supervisor.	Identifies trends in requests for new information. Recommends improvements in procedures. Discovers new sources of information.

PREPARES REPORTS
by
collecting, analyzing, and summarizing information and trends.

☐ Result Required	☐ Problem	☐ Learning Required	☐ Performance Option
Accurate sources of information are identified. Data are collected efficiently. Information is understood correctly. Reports are accurate and ready when needed.	Decisions cannot be made. Work is delayed. Service is interrupted.	☐ Identifying sources of information. ☐ Applying methods of retrieval. ☐ Managing time. ☐ Studying procedures.	Discovers new information sources. Recommends improved report formats. Finds new ways to present information.

REPRESENTS THE ORGANIZATION
by
preparing a strategy, collecting data, and presenting information at hearings.

☐ Result Required	☐ Problem	☐ Learning Required	☐ Performance Option
Information accurately reflects the organization's position. All necessary information is ready when needed.	Decisions are delayed. The organization's reputation is impaired. Time is wasted. Costs increase.	☐ Identifying sources of information. ☐ Applying methods of retrieval. ☐ Managing time. ☐ Developing presentation methods.	Develops creative approaches to understanding and presenting information.

DOCUMENTS SERVICES
by
completing forms, reports, and records.

☐ Result Required	☐ Problem	☐ Learning Required	☐ Performance Option
Services are accurately and clearly documented immediately after delivery.	History cannot be reconstructed. Services are duplicated or interrupted.	☐ Studying procedures. ☐ Observing conditions. ☐ Managing time.	Recognizes and corrects missed entries of others. Recommends improved procedures.

DOCUMENTS ACTIONS
by
completing production and quality logs.

□ Result Required	□ Problem	□ Learning Required	□ Performance Option
Production and quality data are accurately documented at required times.	Production decisions cannot be made. Incomplete shipments are made. Defective product is shipped. Time is wasted. Service reputation is diminished.	□ Identifying recordable information. □ Studying procedures. □ Managing time.	Recommends improvements in procedures. Influences others to follow log procedures.

Project Analyzer 8.4

Will the organization be willing to invest time to write outcomes?

_____

_____

What would be the best way to accomplish the writing job?

_____

_____

Should a task force be formed to consider the project and chart a course of action?

_____

_____

What training and help can be given to managers (writers) to make the job easier?

_____

_____

What job results and outcomes can be universally included in all jobs?

_____

_____

8.5 Establishing Consistent Pay Management Criteria Definitions

Each manager has a unique set of values. No amount of training will change a manager's personal values if he or she does not want to change them. However, the degree to which the personal values of managers can be blended with the organization's values demonstrates how well job results management works. Managers must interpret and apply outcomes consistently, though not identically, throughout the organization.

Organizations fail to develop consensus when they don't allow thorough discussion of the options, don't recognize that their managers have individual value systems, or don't communicate to new managers the values developed in the past by other managers.

Large organizations can use task forces throughout the organization to elicit information and opinion. Videotapes can be made of these discussions and used to initiate discussions among other managers instead of merely issuing written policy.

What may seem obvious when you state job outcomes may not be so easily applied. What may seem easy to apply may not be so easily stated. The following example illustrates how consensus among managers was developed in a small, new organization where all the managers could meet in face-to-face discussions. The managers in this organization were examining the criterion of *attendance*.

The organization stated a universal attendance criteria profile as follows:

MAINTAINS WORK FLOW
by
complying with attendance requirements.

☐ Result Required	☐ Problem	☐ Learning Required	☐ Performance Option
Required work is accomplished each day.	Absences cause a serious disruption to work flow.	☐ Managing time. ☐ Studying company attendance requirements. ☐ Setting priorities.	Takes extra precautions to be present. Works extra to alleviate the impact of others' absences.
	Date	
Results Plan:		
Results Summary:		
Learning Plan:		

In this organization, employees received pay for two weeks of vacation, five days of sick leave, two days for funeral leave, five days for jury duty, and two weeks for military-reserve duty.

Performance Option

In meeting after meeting, the managers struggled with issues such as: Should the Performance Option mean perfect attendance? Is perfect attendance an option or luck? If the employee is absent to the extent of the benefits provided, can he or she still qualify for the Performance Option, or would that encourage employees to take five days of sick leave pay, whether or not they were ill?

The managers needed to ask these questions: What does the organization really want to communicate to employees about attendance and accomplishing the organization's work? How many absences are too many? How do we deal with the employee who had perfect attendance for four years but this year had major surgery and was out three months on disability? It may seem cruel, for instance, to tell that employee that his three-month absence when he nearly died caused a serious disruption of work flow. Should we praise him instead for stockpiling his sick leave for a time when he truly needed it? Still, he wasn't at work, so we can't treat him as if he was.

Do you begin to see the complexities with a seemingly obvious criterion?

In discussion, the manager of an eighty-person department was far more laissez-faire about attendance than the manager of a three-shift, three-person department. The manager of the eighty-person department had to do a little shuffling of personnel when someone was absent, but the manager of the three-person department frequently had to work a double shift when an employee was absent. These two managers had different values because of their different environments and the different impact of absenteeism on them personally.

The manager of the three-person department suggested that Performance Option should be reserved for employees who put in extra time or spent weekends solving problems that would have caused downtime on Monday. Other managers argued that their subordinates could never reach Performance Option under such a definition, because their departments never had that kind of need to be met.

After much agonizing, the managers finally arrived at a consensus of sorts: the Performance Option demanded perfect attendance. You may be thinking, That's only attainable by a few employees. Yes it is, but this is the point of the Performance Option: to stretch employees. If anyone can achieve it with only a little extra effort, it is not Performance Option by definition.

Result Required

Some managers argued that the Result Required meant a day or two of work missed; some thought that three were okay; some said four; and some were willing to accept five. Still others thought a number couldn't be used at all. As you might expect, the manager of the three-person department felt that any missed workday was a Problem.

Because the company allowed five days of paid sick leave, the managers felt compelled to treat absences up to the five-day benefit as meeting the Result Required.

But what about employees who were away for weeks on disability? Recall the employee who had major surgery. Work was definitely disrupted. One manager could not agree that this employee should be marked less than the Result Required; he argued for a difference between planned and unplanned disruptions of work flow. Because the employee scheduled the surgery, the manager was able to plan to offset the impact of the employee's absence.

An employee who reports for work one day but may or may not report for work the next gives the manager no opportunity to plan. Yes, an employee could have emergency surgery for which there could be no planning, but at least the recuperative time is something definite to plan for. Excused absences became the key to defining the Results Required for these managers.

These managers didn't realize it at the time, but they were accepting their responsibility, as well as their right, to manage. If an employee missed work on the basis of a day here or there and those numbers started to mount up, it was the manager's responsibility to correct the situation. Although needs varied by department, generally accepted values were being developed for the organization, and consistency would be the rule.

In another organization, where consistency about attendance had not been established, an employee requested a transfer to another department. When the two department heads conferred, the receiving manager told the transferring manager, "You may allow this kind of attendance in your department, but the candidate's attendance does not meet my department's standards." What do you say to the employee who didn't get the transfer? "Your attendance is okay for Department A, but not good enough for Department B"? This is confusing not only for the employee, but for all other employees.

Learning Required

The managers in the first organization we discussed had little difficulty defining which employees would be marked as Learning Required (managing time, studying organization attendance policies, setting priorities). The employee who missed work on a sporadic basis, giving the manager no way to anticipate the absence and no time to plan for it, qualified easily for this category. Then the managers had to decide whether they would allow an employee more absences than the benefit program (five days) and still mark the employee as meeting the Result Required. They decided that more than five days' absence meant that learning was required.

How many days beyond defined benefits would be interpreted as requiring learning? Where would the cutoff be before the number of days became a Problem? The managers concluded that Learning Required meant from one to five days beyond the defined sick days benefit of five days, for a total of six to ten sick days. This would be sufficient, they reasoned, not to penalize the employee who caught an occasional cold. Some hard-nosed managers still felt that once an employee exceeded the five-day level of benefits, a Problem existed.

But what about the employee with the ten-day virus, the managers wondered, who missed fewer days of work than the medically disabled person yet couldn't meet the Result Required? If the employee with the ten-day virus had a solid record of attendance, Learning Required still should be marked, they decided, but the rating could be softened through explanation in the Results Summary space provided on the conference form—say: "Except for a ten-day virus absence in this performance period, attendance has met the Result Required."

If you wonder how you will relate the decisions these managers made to your organization, you are beginning to understand the issue of blending personal values with organization values and the hard work it takes for an organization to be consistent.

Problem

In our example, an attendance problem was defined as "over ten days missed." Why ten? Because that was the answer these managers decided on together. Your organization could decide on any number. In fact, the number itself is not important. What is important is that employees understand what the organization's values are and that managers are able to administer the organization's values without sacrificing their own. Managers can still talk to employees about the needs of the individual department and the differing impact of attendance among departments, yet apply the criteria in a way that is consistent with the ratings by fellow managers.

Intangible Standards

Establishing and maintaining organizational consistency is far more complex when the outcomes involve intangibles. How can two managers supervising different groups of receptionists in a health care facility compare intangible values for greeting patients when they arrive for their appointment? This approach is not so different from the approach used by managers who defined attendance together.

In the first organization we discussed, the managers first worked together to write the job outcomes:

RESULT   **WELCOMES PATIENTS**
                by
duty   greeting and directing them.

☐ Result Required	☐ Problem	☐ Learning Required	☐ Performance Option
Patients feel welcomed to the office as measured in patient satisfaction surveys. Patients are engaged in relaxing conversation. Required information is obtained.	Patients complain about the way they are greeted, or the way information is requested from them or given to them. Patients get lost.	☐ Identifying sources of information. ☐ Analyzing problems. ☐ Identifying alternate solutions. ☐ Referring exceptional situations to supervisor. ☐ Studying rapport-building techniques.	Verbally reaches out to patients who are distressed. Anticipates troublesome situations. Finds new ways to document patient information.

	Date	
Results Plan:		
Results Summary:		
Learning Plan:		

Next, the managers compared their interpretations of a receptionist who met the Result Required. They were encouraged by their manager to visualize successful results and to state their perceptions. (Think through this process yourself, and then compare your opinion with what the managers in this organization decided.)

These managers felt that an employee would meet their expectations by smiling, making eye contact, engaging the patient in pleasantries, and welcoming the patient to the medical facility as they would to their home.

The managers defined a Problem as complaints from the patients about rudeness, briskness, inattentiveness, or curtness by the receptionist; or patients not relaxed when they see their doctor; or patient satisfaction surveys that rate welcome by receptionist as "poor."

For Learning Required, the managers specified the learning they believed would help employees accomplish the Result Required. (From your personal experiences, think of unwelcoming styles: the receptionist who glances up as if interrupted from other duties, briefly acknowledges your presence, and perfunctorily checks you in causes you to wish that you were being checked out.)

To attain the Performance Option, the managers wanted the receptionist to go the "extra smile"; to sense patient distress, anxiety, and fear; and to alleviate these feelings by verbally and emotionally reaching out to the patient—the kind, welcoming way that frequently elicits compliments.

It's easy to agree that a receptionist should smile. How many times in a conversation should he or she smile—once, twice, continually? What one person views as friendly another may perceive as forward.

We have tried, mistakenly, to measure human behavior explicitly. We can easily measure the number of water meters an employee reads, but we cannot measure as easily the rapport a receptionist establishes. We are a technological society. We search for quantifiable measurements in every aspect of life, but we have erred. It is a worthy goal, however, to bring the extremes of human behavior into a reasonable range of understanding, to help two human beings improve the prospect of understanding each other. Nonetheless, we cannot guarantee that two people observing the same event will describe the event in identical terms.

Having managers observe each other's subordinates and talk about various perceptions of results accomplished is one of the best approaches to establish criteria and maintain consistent application. Too many managers work in a vacuum, never realizing how much help they can be to one another.

In one organization, each manager selected the job outcomes of certain of his or her employees: Results Required, Problem, and outcomes of questionable clarity. The managers then observed each other's employees accomplish their job results, without knowing which employee had accomplished which job outcome. The managers then compared notes to develop a consensus about interpreting the outcome criteria. Sometimes observing employees is awkward and inconvenient, and case study discussions will have to suffice instead. The case studies presented in Phase 8.7 can be used to develop consensus.

A great deal of effort? Definitely! This process separates the managers who want to manage from those who only want to be called managers without accomplishing the results the organization needs from its employees. Learning about each other's values is a growth opportunity for each manager. An organizational commitment to manage job contributions fairly means that managers must put a great deal of effort into establishing and administering outcome criteria, and then making sure that employees understand the job contribution appraisal criteria.

Managers may complain at first: "I haven't got the time to spend on this." The question for these managers is: Do you want to spend your time preparing for measuring job contributions consistently or chasing around picking up the pieces when employees don't accomplish what you want them to, or chasing around to support a challenged, inconsistent, management approach? A clear Job Results Management Profile puts the issues on the table early and points employees in the direction the organization wants to go. Without clear communication up front, employees are free to interpret outcome criteria as they wish, which means that managers (and customers) suffer the consequences.

Once managers accept the difference between chasing behaviors and accomplishing results, they will find the time to prepare for managing work and then build consensus among organizations about the values embedded in job outcomes. For some managers, waiting to deal with behavior until it appears seems to be easier than anticipating job contribution problems because then the behavior can be directly confronted. However, waiting locks a manager into a style of reaction instead of proaction. By being forced to discuss criteria up front with employees, managers soon realize the less-than-advantageous implications of only reacting to employee behavior when it occurs.

Exchanging Opinions

In one organization, a Result Required for managers states: "Employees are prepared to accomplish job results at the completion of the 'get-acquainted' period and throughout their employment." The senior managers who were to use this criterion to appraise the job contributions of their subordinate managers wondered together in a meeting how they would apply the standard. "How will we know that employees are prepared?" they asked. Here is some of their dialogue:

Manager 1. Obviously we can tell that employees are prepared to accomplish job results when the Result Required is accomplished.
Manager 2. But other influences besides the preparation of the employee may determine whether the Result Required is accomplished.
Manager 3. Is it fair to hold all managers equally accountable when some jobs are more difficult and more time-consuming to prepare for than other jobs?
Manager 1. The Result Required still has to get accomplished. If some job preparation is more difficult and more time-consuming, then we have to put more resources into the preparation. It's the manager's responsibility to come to us and request more resources in order to get the job done.
Manager 2. So if other influences prevent the Result Required from being accomplished and we can identify those influences, then we know that the problem was not unprepared employees, and we would not hold the manager accountable.
Manager 4. Maybe we would hold the manager accountable instead for not identifying and dealing with the outside influences.
Manager 3. Wait! We only require in the Result Required that the "employees are prepared," not that the work is accomplished. "Work is accomplished" is stated as the Result Required for a different job responsibility. Maybe we ought to think about testing employees to determine whether they are prepared.

Manager 1. You have a point there, although the proof of the pudding is in the eating. Testing is okay and maybe we can use a test at the end of the get-acquainted period, but some people can do very well on a test and yet not do well in the actual job situation.

Manager 3. You're right. We should look at both tests and actual job outcomes. The Result Required for each employee's job becomes the manager's target of accomplishment.

In this conversation, the senior managers learned about each other's point of view and came to a helpful agreement on what was important to them. Even from this brief example, the style of some of the managers begins to emerge. The first manager focused on the end result of preparation and helped some of the other managers who were not quite thinking in a results-oriented way.

As the managers talk among themselves about the meaning of job outcomes, each manager learns from the discussion. Although the wording of the four outcomes is chosen carefully, it is equally important to recognize that the *process* of discussion is the opportunity to examine different opinions. The examination is the learning. The final interpretation among the managers is the consensus.

The process is not static. The managers will meet again and again to discuss the outcome criteria. They will have their interpretations tested in the job contribution appraisals they write. Some of the interpretations will be incomplete or wrong. The managers and the organization will learn from experience. The managers will adjust their thinking when faced with new demands. Still, as they act together, they are in consensus.

In still another example organization, a group of managers looked at a Result Required for subordinate development: "Subordinates are able to accept new and more challenging assignments." Here is some of the discussion that ensued:

Manager 1. Does this mean that a subordinate must be promoted before the standard can be met?

Manager 2. I hope not, because there is no job for my employees to be promoted into in the normal job progression.

Manager 3. So "new and more challenging assignments" does not necessarily mean new and more challenging jobs. If we can document what an employee is doing more on the job, then the employee is meeting the Result Required.

Manager 1. Not just more work, but a higher level of work—for example, something that you as a manager do now but instead pass on to your employee because the employee is now capable of doing it.

Manager 4. Is the Result Required met if the employee is *able* to do the work, but someone else is already doing the work and it isn't appropriate to transfer the work to the employee who is now capable of doing it? The Result Required says, "*able* to accept new and challenging assignments."

Manager 5. I don't think that's the point of the Result Required. I think we want to pay for people who are not only *able* but actually *do* accept new and more challenging assignments. Otherwise we'd be paying for a lot of potential but not job outcomes.

Manager 6. I agree. Measuring capability instead of actual accomplishment could be very risky. We can observe an employee accomplishing a new and more challenging assignment, but we'd be in a difficult area if we tried to count potential. It's too sub-jective. Some employees think they have the capability of accomplishing other jobs because they went to a training session, but they are not really qualified, because they haven't applied those skills on the job.

Some job results, as well as the job outcomes, are written broadly because they can be satisfied in a variety of ways. The language used is not so precise as to define the various ways job contributions occur in all situations. Aiming at such precision would produce an endless list, which defeats the purpose of the Job Results Management Profile to focus attention on the essence of the issue.

Detractors may argue that the application of the statements must be consistent throughout the organization. Consistent, yes, but not absolutely identical. The application must be similar in form, follow from the same principle, and be in harmony with the intent of the statement. However, except in the case of obviously quantifiable measures, the applications cannot be absolutely alike. The conditions of job outcomes typically do not arrange themselves in such an orderly fashion.

Holes may be found in outcome statements, particularly the value-laden issues. Some people will attempt to detract from the concept by pointing out inconsequential details. The case must be made on the principle, not the detail. Of course, where the missing detail is notable, the statement must be changed.

The value of using the four-dimensional Job Results Management Profile to communicate values to employees is that *employees begin to contribute up to the organization's expectations.* Employees who need to learn more about their jobs are able to identify specifically what they need to learn in order to accomplish the Result Required. Employees who do not want to accomplish the Result Required are obviously and dramatically distanced from other employees. Employees who care to give the organization an extra effort in order to earn extra reward and recognition are given a clear direction.

Consensus Building

Getting managers to agree on organizational values to be held in common is not easy. Each manager wants to manage in his or her own way. Short of complete agreement, they may achieve a consensus. This simply means that each manager has the opportunity to argue for a point of view yet is willing to accept and respect the group's right and need to decide values for the common good.

Participants in the consensus-building process need interpersonal ability. The more experience they have at achieving consensus, the stronger will be the bond among them. Participants must talk with each other and present their point of view. Where only a few members of the group carry most of the discussion, the consensus is impaired.

In particular, participants need to listen to each other and then clarify what each does not understand. Typically people take a stand and argue to defend their position. There are precious few communication models that demonstrate respect for and a polite attitude toward an opposing point of view.

Group discussions must be managed. So-called leaderless groups have their occasional place in group dynamics, but they are inefficient in comparison with managed discussion. The group manager can help participants express their points of view, as well as help them listen to other points of view, by stopping arguments, preventing one participant from interrupting another, and separating fact from opinion.

Group managers can also ensure that all differences have been put on the table, suggest brainstorming when the conversation bogs down, help the group look at what-if scenarios, propose tests and trial runs, and suggest closure at an opportune moment.

Consensus building follows the same process, built around the same questions, as decision making: What is the problem or opportunity? What are options to solve the problem or achieve the opportunity? What are the advantages and disadvantages of each option? Which is the best option?

Someone has to decide by what standards the organization will operate. Managers—legal agents of the organization—are obligated to enforce the standards for the organization, but they must enforce them consistently and fairly. Employees understand that standards must be established; in fact, they *want* standards established so that they can feel secure in understanding how to gain rewards and recognition and to keep their jobs.

The final result is that the organization begins to pull together in stronger ways. The organization's culture becomes clearer because managers and employees have whittled away the discrepancies of varying opinions. In sum, employees and managers together now understand what's required on the job and why it is required.

Preventing Manipulation of the System

Any approach to management can be subverted, and any aspect of any system can be played with. However, the exacting language of the Job Results Management Profile helps an astute reviewer pick out the manipulations more quickly than with other systems. The toughest part for a reviewer is to pick up on the conversations that occur between the manager and the employee—conversations that the reviewer never hears, except when rebuttals occur. Let's look at the situation of an employee whose job contributions were marked by the manager as a Problem on the appraisal form: "Work is frequently bottlenecked or unfinished."

The employee argues in her written appeal that she had not only completed all assigned projects well before the agreed-on completion dates but also prepared reports, anticipating that they would be necessary. She pointed out that reports submitted to her manager had been held with no action for so long that he had to request a revised report and that her final report could not be finished on time because of this. By criticizing the employee, the manager thought he could mask his own procrastination. The more open the job contribution measurement system is, the more difficult it is for anyone to manipulate it.

Job results management is more than filling out a form; it is the essence of the relationship between a manager and an employee and their contract together to accomplish the results the organization needs to accomplish its mission. Thoughtful and consistent completion of the outcomes becomes the basis for good, meaningful conversation. Let's look at a difficult situation and how a seasoned manager might handle it.

Maintaining Consistency of Standards: A Case Study

An employee (a department manager) was faced with the serious illness of his spouse. His contributions, especially in the areas of attendance and punctuality, had slipped. The manager and the employee talked often during the job contribution period as the employee sought to find adequate care for his wife. He was frequently called away from work for an emergency and was often preoccupied with this very real tragedy in his life. This employee had been a real strength to the management team and a role model to his employees for several years; he had proved himself again and again. Then his attendance and punctuality began to become problematic.

His job contribution conference was difficult for him and his manager. The outcome criteria of attendance and punctuality were clear: the employee had not met them, though for obvious and understandable reasons. For how long, with good reason, can a manager allow the employee's lateness and absence beyond the requirements of the Family and Medical Leave Act? There is always so much more to job contributions than just outcome criteria, and it is only through effective conversations that true understanding can be attained. The conversation between the manager and the employee went like this:

Manager. Paul, because we've talked so often these past months, I feel that I understand what you are going through in your personal life. It would be easy if we could separate what's happening in your family from your job outcomes, but you and I both know that isn't possible.

Paul. I know. I'm having a great deal of difficulty balancing my personal problems and my work. You know I can't afford to leave my job even temporarily.

Manager. When we talk about your attendance and punctuality, it's impossible for me to criticize you because I have willingly excused you. However, I can't say that you meet the Result Required in these areas because you are not here, or you arrive late, or you leave early. Besides, your work is frequently interrupted during the day to answer telephone calls. I understand the compelling reasons affecting your performance in these two areas, but you are not meeting the Result Required.

Paul. You've been understanding and supportive, and generous in saying that I only need to improve. I personally would have said that my attendance and punctuality were a Problem.

Manager. Unfortunately, your personal problem seems to be affecting your department's attendance and punctuality, and some members of the administrative staff have questioned your coming and going. I have respected your wishes to keep your wife's illness private, but we have to address this issue because of its impact on the organization. You have been a role model in the past, but now your personal life makes that impossible. Do you have any ideas to help us through this difficult time so that we can maintain the organization's requirements?

Paul. I have confided in one other manager, though she promised to keep the information to herself. She agreed to cover for me when I need to leave abruptly.

Manager. Okay; that alleviates the coverage problem, but do you think it addresses the perceptions of your employees?

Paul. No. I've learned that already. One of my supervisors told me just yesterday that she resented a manager from another department stepping in when she's been managing just fine for me in my absence.

Manager. Your supervisor isn't aware, then, of why you are being called away?

Paul. No.

Manager. Have you considered telling something about your problem to your employees, your supervisors, and your fellow managers?

Paul. I can't do that.

Manager. I accept that. What can we do to minimize the impact of your problem on the organization?

Paul. I don't know.

Manager. We are at a point where we need to find some answers. Your wife's illness is not going to go away, and I believe that you have faced that reality. We have talked about community resources, and you have availed yourself of them. You know your job, and you've been one of my best managers. You have always been there when I needed you, and I've tried to return that loyalty to you now. One of my toughest jobs is balancing what the organization needs with what you need. The organization is being compromised by your personal needs, and we must find a balance soon. I want you to give plenty of serious thought to the problem. I'll be available when you want to talk. We must find a way to alleviate the problem of your attendance and punctuality.

Here are some questions to think about regarding this conversation. Do you appreciate the extent to which the human element must enter into the application of the results required by the organization? Did you notice that the manager upheld the organization's standards, yet in an understanding, compassionate manner? Had you been Paul, would you have felt okay after the conversation? Had you been the manager, would you have conducted the conversation in the same manner?

Each of us has unique values and will deal with similar situations differently. In the context of an organization, only so many style variations can be allowed. Paul faced a truly difficult situation in his life. Compassion was required, and it was given. At the same time, the organization needed to proceed with its work, and Paul had to know that.

Employees do not dispute the need for consistent application to job outcomes. On the contrary, they welcome consistency for the security that it gives them. Organizations err when consistency turns into rigidity. Employees lose faith in the system because there is no justice.

Project Analyzer 8.5

Do managers in your organization meet to define outcome criteria?

_____

_____

Are managers more likely to stick to their own opinion instead of trying to achieve a consensus?

_____

_____

Do managers in your organization have effective interpersonal skills?

_____

_____

Have managers been trained to improve their interpersonal skills?

_____

_____

Have managers been trained to improve their decision-making skills?

_____

_____

Are senior managers capable of managing discussions to achieve a consensus?

_____

_____

8.6 Job Results Management Form

Job results management forms and retrieval systems are as varied as can be, but the basic architecture remains the same. Some organizations have a stand-alone copy of the results-oriented job description and then restate the job description in the Job Results Management Profile. Others use only the profile. Among the more sophisticated applications are databases of job descriptions, job outcomes, and results plan objectives that managers can use to write and edit. Files of individual employees can be kept online and updated over the course of the job contribution period.

Sample Form

Here is a sample form that you can use or adapt:

JOB RESULTS MANAGEMENT

Guide for
Planning, Monitoring, and Appraising Job Results

Name:	I. Amgreat
Job Title:	Executive Assistant
Date of Conference:	(Date)

Our organization works best when everyone takes responsibility for and has a common understanding of—

- *What job results need to be accomplished and what duties need to be performed.*
- *Which job results have priority.*
- *How job results will be accomplished.*
- *The criteria used to plan, monitor, and appraise job results.*
- *Whether job results are achieving the agreed-on plan.*

Both supervisors and employees are expected to plan, monitor, and appraise job results together continuously, not just once a year.

JOB RESULTS ARE APPRAISED AS ONE OF THESE FOUR POSSIBLE OUTCOMES:

☐ Result Required	☐ Problem	☐ Learning Required	☐ Performance Option
Job results meet organization requirements.	Job results cause serious problems for the organization. Consequences of no improvement must be specified.	Job results must be improved. A learning plan is required to identify what must be learned to bring results up to expectations.	Job results exceed expectations. Innovation. A role model for others.

Results Plan:	(Date)	Set specific objectives; establish priorities; discuss methods; define resources required; establish due dates; make midcourse changes.
Results Summary:	(Date)	Document or explain the outcome checked and/or offer clarifying comments; document commendations or warnings.
Learning Plan:	(Date)	Establish specific learning actions; specify due dates for accomplishment; offer developmental opportunities for job growth and potential job advancement.

| **Is the Job Results Management Profile up-to-date?   Yes ___ No ___** |
| *If not, edit and attach revisions.* |

RESULTS-ORIENTED JOB DESCRIPTION

JOB TITLE: **EXECUTIVE ASSISTANT**

JOB PURPOSE: **ENHANCES EXECUTIVES' EFFECTIVENESS**
by
providing information management support; representing the
executives to others.

ESSENTIAL JOB RESULTS:

% of
time

_____   **1. PRODUCES INFORMATION**
            by
            transcribing, formatting, inputting, editing, retrieving, copying, and
            transmitting text, data, and graphics; coordinating report preparation.

_____   **2. CONSERVES EXECUTIVES' AND SUPPORTING STAFF'S TIME**
            by
            reading, researching, and routing correspondence and reports; drafting
            letters and documents; collecting and analyzing information; initiating
            telecommunications; organizing meetings; completing expense reports.

_____   **3. MAINTAINS EXECUTIVES' AND SUPPORTING STAFF'S CALENDAR**
            by
            planning and scheduling meetings, conferences, teleconferences, and
            travel.

_____   **4. REPRESENTS THE EXECUTIVES**
            by
            communicating and obtaining information; distributing and following up
            on delegated assignments.

_____   **5. COMPLETES PROJECTS**
            by
            planning, organizing, coordinating, and controlling personnel, material,
            and financial resources.

_____ **6. PREPARES REPORTS**
by
collecting and analyzing information; developing presentations.

_____ **7. MAINTAINS CUSTOMER CONFIDENCE AND PROTECTS OPERATIONS**
by
keeping information confidential.

_____ **8. WELCOMES GUESTS AND CUSTOMERS**
by
greeting them in person or on the telephone; answering or directing
inquiries.

_____ **9. PROVIDES HISTORICAL REFERENCE**
by
developing and utilizing filing and retrieval systems; recording meeting
discussions.

_____ **10. MAINTAINS OFFICE SUPPLIES**
by
checking stocks; placing and expediting orders; evaluating new products.

_____ **11. ENSURES OPERATION OF EQUIPMENT**
by
completing preventive maintenance requirements; calling for repairs.

_____ **12. CONTRIBUTES TO TEAM EFFORT**
by
accomplishing related results as needed.

JOB RESULTS MANAGEMENT PROFILE

JOB TITLE: **EXECUTIVE ASSISTANT**

JOB PURPOSE: **ENHANCES EXECUTIVES' EFFECTIVENESS**
by
providing information management support; representing the
executives to others.

ESSENTIAL JOB RESULTS:

% of
time

_____   **1. PRODUCES INFORMATION**
by
transcribing, formatting, inputting, editing, retrieving, copying, and
transmitting text, data, and graphics; coordinating report preparation.

☐ Result Required	☐ Problem	☐ Learning Required	☐ Performance Option
Information is complete, accurate, readable, attractive in appearance, and ready when needed.	Contingent work cannot proceed. Decisions cannot be made. Time is wasted. Customers complain.	☐ Applying technical skills. ☐ Managing time. ☐ Setting priorities. ☐ Clarifying instructions. ☐ Developing writing skills. ☐ Consulting dictionary and grammar software. ☐ Practicing word processing skills.	Recognizes content errors and corrects them. Develops models to simplify work. Recommends improvements in procedures. Discovers new information resources. Influences others to follow procedures. Discovers creative ways to present information. Identifies and corrects inaccurate information in documents.
	Date		
Results Plan:		
Results Summary:		
Learning Plan:		

2. CONSERVES EXECUTIVES' AND SUPPORTING STAFF'S TIME
by
reading, researching, and routing correspondence and reports; drafting letters and documents; collecting and analyzing information; initiating telecommunications; organizing meetings; completing expense reports.

☐ Result Required	☐ Problem	☐ Learning Required	☐ Performance Option
Executives and supporting staffs are free to complete managerial and staff responsibilities. Necessary information is organized, interpreted, distributed, and ready when needed.	Time is wasted. Managerial and supporting staff responsibilities are interrupted. Managerial and support staff decisions are incomplete, inexact, or delayed.	☐ Managing time. ☐ Developing writing skills. ☐ Researching time constraints. ☐ Developing reading skills. ☐ Controlling events. ☐ Organizing information. ☐ Decreasing travel costs of 2–4 percent over plan.	Discovers useful information. Develops new resources for information. Recommends improvements to procedures and processes. Resolves scheduling conflicts. Anticipates new or additional information requirements. Identifies inaccurate information in documents and makes corrections.

	Date	
Results Plan:		
Results Summary:		
Learning Plan:		

_____   **3. MAINTAINS EXECUTIVES' AND SUPPORTING STAFF'S CALENDAR**
by
planning and scheduling meetings, conferences, teleconferences, and
travel.

☐ Result Required	☐ Problem		☐ Learning Required	☐ Performance Option
Calendars are up-to-date. Calendar conflicts are resolved. Meeting arrangements are completed as required. Itineraries are logical and efficient. Travel expenses are no more than 1 percent over plan.	Meetings are missed. Managerial responsibilities are interrupted. Opportunities are lost. Time is wasted. Travel costs increase by 5 percent over plan.		☐ Managing time. ☐ Applying scheduling techniques. ☐ Using planning models. ☐ Developing negotiating skills. ☐ Applying decision-making techniques. ☐ Controlling events. ☐ Decreasing travel costs of 2–4 percent over plan.	Anticipates and prevents delays. Develops models that improve efficiency. Reduces meeting and conference time by 7 percent. Reduces travel costs by 5 percent.
	Date			
Results Plan:				
Results Summary:				
Learning Plan:				

_____ **4. REPRESENTS THE EXECUTIVES**
by
communicating and obtaining information; distributing and following up on
delegated assignments.

☐ Result Required	☐ Problem	☐ Learning Required	☐ Performance Option
Information is presented or acquired for the executives. Information and decisions are rendered accurately and in accordance with the executives' preferences.	Executives are unable to complete managerial responsibilities. Information provided causes incorrect or incomplete actions by others.	☐ Developing listening skills. ☐ Developing two-way (up and down the organization) communication skills. ☐ Explaining information. ☐ Researching information. ☐ Managing time. ☐ Developing negotiating skills. ☐ Applying decision-making techniques. ☐ Developing delegation skills.	Develops recommendations for the executives. Develops new information sources. Develops creative approaches to understanding and presenting information.

	Date	
Results Plan:		
Results Summary:		
Learning Plan:		

_____ **5. COMPLETES PROJECTS**
by
planning, organizing, coordinating, and controlling personnel, material, and financial resources.

☐ Result Required	☐ Problem	☐ Learning Required	☐ Performance Option
Projects and project phases are completed as scheduled, and within budget. Projects meet their objectives. Staff members are recruited to bring necessary talents to the group.	Group members do not cooperate. Tasks assigned do not match personal talents. Time is wasted. Decisions are delayed.	☐ Developing objectives. ☐ Developing standards. ☐ Obtaining and analyzing information. ☐ Managing time. ☐ Reporting information. ☐ Utilizing project management tools. ☐ Analyzing interpersonal styles. ☐ Resolving conflicts. ☐ Controlling events.	Anticipates and avoids work interruptions. Identifies and applies resources to projects. Anticipates interpersonal conflicts. Discovers innovative methods to present project status. Recommends improvement in project management. Discovers creative methods to present project findings.

	Date	
Results Plan:		
Results Summary:		
Learning Plan:		

_____ **6. PREPARES REPORTS**
by
collecting and analyzing information; developing presentations.

☐ Result Required	☐ Problem	☐ Learning Required	☐ Performance Option
Information is complete, analyzed correctly, understandable, and ready when needed.	Actions taken are erroneous. Managerial responsibilities are delayed. Time is wasted.	☐ Researching information. ☐ Assembling, interpreting, and presenting data. ☐ Managing time.	Discovers and includes pertinent information. Discovers creative ways to present information.

	Date	
Results Plan:		
Results Summary:		
Learning Plan:		

_____ **7. MAINTAINS CUSTOMER CONFIDENCE AND PROTECTS OPERATIONS**
by
keeping information confidential.

☐ Result Required	☐ Problem	☐ Learning Required	☐ Performance Option
Sensitive information is kept confidential.	Managerial actions are compromised. Lawsuits are filed. Advantage is lost. Feelings are hurt. Executives are embarrassed. Time is wasted. Customers complain.	☐ Following policies and procedures. ☐ Processing information. ☐ Notifying executives of potential breaches.	Develops new methods to protect information. Cautions others when security might be violated.

	Date	
Results Plan:		
Results Summary:		
Learning Plan:		

_____ **8. WELCOMES GUESTS AND CUSTOMERS**
by
greeting them in person or on the telephone; answering or directing inquiries.

☐ Result Required	☐ Problem	☐ Learning Required	☐ Performance Option
Guests and customers feel welcomed. Information provided is accurate and complete. Telephone is answered within three rings.	Guests and customers complain about lack of courtesy, or that the information they received was not helpful or was misleading.	☐ Developing listening skills. ☐ Explaining information. ☐ Researching information. ☐ Managing time. ☐ Developing empathic communication skills.	Anticipates and resolves misunderstandings or required information.

	Date	
Results Plan:		
Results Summary:		
Learning Plan:		

9. PROVIDES HISTORICAL REFERENCE
by
developing and utilizing filing and retrieval systems; recording meeting discussions.

☐ Result Required	☐ Problem	☐ Learning Required	☐ Performance Option
Information is available when needed. Filing is completed daily. Files are logical and easily used by others. Minutes of meetings are complete and accurately reflect discussions and decisions.	Information is lost. Time is wasted. Information must be reconstructed. Work is interrupted. Decisions cannot be made. Effective reasoning cannot be constructed.	☐ Retrieving information. ☐ Managing time. ☐ Organizing information.	Develops improvements to information system. Anticipates retrieval problems.

	Date	
Results Plan:		
Results Summary:		
Learning Plan:		

_____ **10. MAINTAINS OFFICE SUPPLIES**
by
checking stocks; placing and expediting orders; evaluating new products.

☐ Result Required	☐ Problem	☐ Learning Required	☐ Performance Option
Supplies are ready when needed. Inventory is not excessive. New equipment is evaluated and recommendation is submitted.	Work is interrupted. Time is wasted. Costs are excessive. Equipment does not satisfy needs.	☐ Following procedures. ☐ Applying planning models. ☐ Organizing information. ☐ Managing time. ☐ Developing negotiating skills.	Develops improved method to track and order supplies. Develops equipment specifications.
	Date		
Results Plan:			
Results Summary:			
Learning Plan:			

_____ **11. ENSURES OPERATION OF EQUIPMENT**
by
completing preventive maintenance requirements; calling for repairs.

☐ Result Required	☐ Problem	☐ Learning Required	☐ Performance Option
Equipment is operable when needed. Inspections are completed as scheduled. Repair services are capable and available. New equipment is evaluated and recommendations are submitted.	Work is interrupted. Time is wasted. Costs are excessive.	☐ Following procedures. ☐ Managing time. ☐ Researching information. ☐ Applying scheduling techniques.	Develops improvements in maintenance procedures. Anticipates equipment requirements.
	Date		
Results Plan:			
Results Summary:			
Learning Plan:			

_____ **12. CONTRIBUTES TO TEAM EFFORT**
by
accomplishing related results as needed.

☐ Result Required	☐ Problem	☐ Learning Required	☐ Performance Option
New and different work requirements are welcomed. Individual work schedule is adjusted to meet organization needs. Individual job results are completed and integrated with the requirements of other jobs.	Projects requiring joint effort are not accomplished. Work is bottle-necked or unfinished. The organization misses opportunities. Team members complain.	☐ Managing time. ☐ Adjusting schedules. ☐ Setting priorities. ☐ Understanding the job's link in the organization's value chain. ☐ Developing interpersonal skills.	Goes out of his or her way to help others apply their knowledge to organization requirements. Finds new ways to foster teamwork and resolve potential conflicts.

	Date	
Results Plan:		
Results Summary:		
Learning Plan:		

SUMMARY OF OUTCOMES			
(enter the total number of results marked on previous pages into the appropriate box)			
☐ Result Required	☐ Problem	☐ Learning Required	☐ Performance Option

MANAGER COMMENTS:

EMPLOYEE COMMENTS:

SIGNATURES		
EMPLOYEE*	SUPERVISOR	REVIEWER
Date	Date	Date

* Indicates receipt of document but not necessarily agreement with content. Employees have the right to appeal decisions with which they do not agree.

Adapting the Components and Language to Fit Your Culture

Here are some ways organizations have tailored the job results management format to their organization culture.

A medical center chose the following:

☐ High (Hospital) Standard	☐ Unacceptable Outcome	☐ Improvement Required	☐ Value-Added Results
		☐	
	Date		
Comments:			

A produce cooperative made this adjustment:

☐ Result Required	☐ Problem	☐ Learning Required	☐ Performance Option
		☐	
	Date		
Results Plan:			
Special Action Plan:	(for high-priority, one-time initiatives)		
Results Summary:			
Learning Plan:			

An insurance company named its system "Quality Results Plan" to integrate quality initiatives and modified the outcome categories as follows:

☐ Required Result	☐ Problem	☐ Required Improvement	☐ Innovative Performance Option
		☐	
	Date		
Results Plan:			
Results Summary:			
Learning Plan:			

Universal Results for All Employees

Some organizations have chosen an array of job results for which they hold all employees accountable. They include them in the job results management form. Here is an example of the universal results one organization chose:

UNIVERSAL PROFILES FOR ALL JOBS

_____   **A. MAINTAINS WORK FLOW**
               by
               reporting as scheduled.

☐ Result Required	☐ Problem	☐ Learning Required	☐ Performance Option
Work starts on time and continues without interruption.	Service is delayed. Customers complain. Other employees' schedules are disrupted.	☐ Managing time.	Takes extra precautions to be present and maintain attendance.
	Date		
Results Plan:			
Results Summary:			
Learning Plan:			

B. MAINTAINS SAFE WORK ENVIRONMENT
by
complying with procedures, rules, and regulations.

☐ Result Required	☐ Problem	☐ Learning Required	☐ Performance Option
People are safe. Safety hazards are reported. Procedures, rules, and regulations are followed. Safety meetings are attended. Work area is clean and orderly.	People are injured. Production is lost. Costs are excessive. Time is wasted. Downtime is excessive.	☐ Following safety procedures and rules. ☐ Practicing safe techniques.	Influences others to follow safety practices. Helps others clean up. Recommends improvements to safety policies.

	Date	
Results Plan:		
Results Summary:		
Learning Plan:		

C. COMPLETES TEAM PROJECTS
by
integrating individual assignment with team members' assignments.

☐ Result Required	☐ Problem	☐ Learning Required	☐ Performance Option
Team projects are completed when needed. Harmonious relationships are maintained. Individual work is adjusted to meet team requirements. Information and opinions are offered to team members.	Service is delayed. Customers and employees complain. Other employees' schedules are disrupted. Animosities develop.	☐ Managing time. ☐ Interacting with others. ☐ Solving problems.	Recommends improved work methods and ways to resolve conflict. Is a role model as a team member and for resolving conflicts.

	Date	
Results Plan:		
Results Summary:		
Learning Plan:		

_____   **D. CONSERVES RESOURCES**
by
using equipment and supplies as needed to accomplish job results.

☐ Result Required	☐ Problem	☐ Learning Required	☐ Performance Option
Equipment and supplies are used with care, and no more are used than necessary.	Downtime and costs are excessive. Work flow is interrupted.	☐ Scheduling. ☐ Following procedures and equipment manuals.	Finds new ways to economize and prevent misuse of equipment. Is a role model for others.

	Date	
	Date	
Results Plan:		
Results Summary:		
Learning Plan:		

_____   **E. MAINTAINS WORK FLOW**
by
communicating and asking for information.

☐ Result Required	☐ Problem	☐ Learning Required	☐ Performance Option
Essential information is passed on. Information is clear and concise. Rapport is maintained. Requests for information are made. Requirements for information are clarified.	Work is incomplete, interrupted, delayed, or lost. Opportunities are lost. Costs are excessive. Customers complain or seek service elsewhere.	☐ Interacting with others. ☐ Managing time. ☐ Identifying priority information. ☐ Following procedures.	Develops new ways to identify required information. Develops new ways to transmit and clarify information.

	Date	
	Date	
Results Plan:		
Results Summary:		
Learning Plan:		

F. COMPLETES WORK
by
planning, organizing, and controlling work; resolving problems.

☐ Result Required	☐ Problem	☐ Learning Required	☐ Performance Option
Work is completed as scheduled. Plans are developed. Resources are in the right place, at the right time, in the right quantity. Problems are addressed and resolved.	Customers are dissatisfied. Problems are not anticipated. Time is wasted. Costs are excessive. Resources are wasted. Solutions do not identify the essential nature of the problem and do not eliminate the problem.	☐ Gathering information. ☐ Studying and evaluating options. ☐ Scheduling. ☐ Managing time. ☐ Solving problems and making decisions.	Identifies and considers issues not presented in original requirements. Develops imaginative ways to assemble and utilize resources. Develops system improvements that prevent recurrence of problems.

	Date	
Results Plan:		
Results Summary:		
Learning Plan:		

Here are some additional universal results: attendance, confidentiality, cost-effectiveness, dress code, empowerment, punctuality, safety, and teamwork.

Job Results Management Policy

Some organizations prefer to incorporate their policy within the job results management form; others prefer to include it in their employee handbook. Figure 46 shows a policy statement you can use or adapt.

Figure 46. Example policy statement for appraising job contributions.

ORGANIZATION POLICY FOR APPRAISING JOB CONTRIBUTIONS

We believe that employees are entitled to know their manager's perception of what they are accomplishing in relation to agreed-on results and objectives, what they can do to attain accomplishment levels beyond expectations if they choose, and what they must learn if desired results are not accomplished. We believe that employees are entitled to know this, not just once a year, but throughout the year on a continuous basis.

Documented, formal job results management conferences that become part of employee personnel records are held quarterly to review organization and employee requirements and to develop strategies to meet objectives. The conference is an opportunity for managers and employees to exchange opinions about the accomplishment of results and to find opportunities for managers to facilitate, coach, and mentor results. Employees are encouraged to record their reactions to the conference on the form provided.

For new employees, conferences will be held at the end of 30, 60, 90, and 180 days following employment to ensure that employees and managers share agreement on job results expectations.

Outcomes will be examined according to outcomes published in the Job Results Management Profile as well as according to organization policy and other defined expectations required by changing organization requirements.

Additional Communication Techniques

The implementation of a job results management strategy is a major shift in thinking for most organizations. Training and orientations will be required using brochures, notebooks, posters, banners, videos, sticky notes, and perhaps even sequential multiple billboards on the drive onto the campus, saying We . . . Focus . . . on . . . Results!

Project Analyzer 8.6

What forms do you use to manage job results now?

_____

_____

What reactions to them have you had from managers?

_____

_____

What reactions to them have you had from employees?

_____

_____

What are the strong points of the forms?

_____

_____

What problems have you had with the forms?

_____

_____

How could you use the Job Results Management Profile form to improve or revise the system you now have in place?

_____

_____

Are there other labels for the four outcomes that would fit your organization's culture better?

_____

_____

_____

8.7 Case Studies for Developing Consistent Application of Job Outcomes

Here are some case studies that you can use to learn more about applying the Job Results Management Profile and to provide managers with an opportunity to develop consensus regarding the application outcome criteria. The case studies are based on the profile for the executive assistant in Phase 8.6. First, study the profile. Second, decide which of the four outcomes the employee produced. Third, write the appropriate Results Plan, Results Summary, or Learning Plan.

The solutions commonly developed by managers are presented after the case studies.

Executive Assistant Job

The Missed Meeting   You are an experienced manager. I. Amgreat has been your executive assistant for three months. During this time, you have experienced some confusion in your appointment calendar. Prior to today, you have mentioned the situation to I. Amgreat, but you are not sure that you have given him clear instructions on how your calendar is to be managed.

Your phone rings, and it's your boss demanding to know why you missed her meeting of all managers—which ended fifteen minutes ago. You review your calendar and find no notation of the meeting.

You call I. Amgreat. He rushes to your office and sees, as you do, that the meeting is not on your calendar or his. You remain puzzled and perplexed.

A week later, I. Amgreat is out sick, and the temporary worker brings you a file she discovered at the front of the filing drawer. It is marked: "Things to review before filing." You open the file and see the memorandum from your boss noting the urgency of your attendance at the meeting you missed the week before.

- Which job results are affected? (Identify all possible ones.)
- Which job result is affected the most?
- For that job result, which outcome should be checked?
- What additional documentation would you write in the spaces provided for the Results Plan, the Results Summary, and the Learning Plan?

Fill in your answers.

□ Result Required	□ Problem		□ Learning Required	□ Performance Option
	Date			
Results Plan:				
Results Summary:				
Learning Plan:				

Taking Charge of a Committee   You are a manager. Your executive assistant, I. Amgreat, was assigned to a committee of executive assistants to review the software applications in use in your organization and to make recommendations to standardize secretarial practices. For a few months, the committee met regularly and seemed to be making progress, but then interest waned and progress stalled.

I. Amgreat told you of her disappointment in the lack of progress and offered to find some ways to get the committee back on track. You encouraged her to do so.

I. Amgreat called a meeting of the committee and presented her ideas on why the committee was not making progress. She helped the committee reach consensus on defining the problems. She led a brainstorming session in problem resolution. By the end of the session, the committee members agreed to restructure the committee, get some management people involved to understand their perception of needs, and define specific objectives for committee members.

The committee has been meeting in a productive way for six months now, and tangible results of its work are positively influencing the secretarial function within the organization.

- Which job results are affected? (Identify all possible ones.)
- Which job result is affected the most?

- For that job result, which outcome should be checked?
- What additional documentation would you write in the spaces provided for the Results Plan, the Results Summary, and the Learning Plan?

Fill in your answers.

☐ Result Required	☐ Problem	☐ Learning Required	☐ Performance Option
	Date		
Results Plan:			
Results Summary:			
Learning Plan:			

Not So Pretty Documents You are the manager of public relations. You and your executive assistant, I. Amgreat, prepare media releases, letters of solicitation, and grant proposals. I. Amgreat accurately transcribes your dictation and on occasion makes good editing suggestions. He uses the spell check system, and his proofreading is impeccable. Still, the documents he produces lack visual appeal, which you consider essential for maintaining and enhancing the public image of the company.

When you have asked I. Amgreat about applying some of the desktop publishing techniques he learned in the special course you sent him to, he seemed to listen and agree, but the documents did not change. He doesn't even try such basics as bullet symbols (♦, ⇨ ☛),

borders

,

or different **type styles** or type sizes.

- Which job results are affected? (Identify all possible ones.)
- Which job result is affected the most?
- For that job result, which outcome should be checked?
- What additional documentation would you write in the spaces provided for the Results Plan, the Results Summary, and the Learning Plan?

Fill in your answers.

☐ Result Required	☐ Problem	☐ Learning Required	☐ Performance Option
	Date		
Results Plan:			
Results Summary:			
Learning Plan:			

Case Study Answers for the Executive Assistant Job

■ *The Missed Meeting.* The primary job result affected is 3, "Maintains Executives' and Supporting Staff's Calendar." The outcome to be checked is "Learning Required." The rationale is that the employee is new. The manager is not sure of the instructions given. Additional documentation might be as follows:

	Date	
Results Plan:		
Results Summary:	9/21	A memorandum noting the urgency of my attending a meeting was found in a file marked, "Things to review before filing." The meeting was not entered into my calendar, and I missed the meeting, causing me to miss out on an important discussion. During the past three months, I have been experiencing confusion concerning my appointments. My appointment calendar must be accurate.
Learning Plan:	9/21	Establish a file for all appointment-related information. Keep the file on your desk instead of in a file drawer. Post appointments at the same time each day. Indicate on the reference material the date and time posted to the calendar. We will review my calendar and the backup material every two days for the first week. We will establish subsequent reviews at that time.

■ *Taking Charge of a Committee.* The primary job result affected is 5, "Completes Projects." The outcome to be checked is "Performance Option." The rationale is that the employee took the initiative and demonstrated managerial skills. Additional documentation might be as follows:

	Date	
Results Plan:		
Results Summary:	9/21	Isabel, you certainly made a great contribution to the secretarial practices committee. Without your calling a meeting and helping the committee reach a consensus, the committee would have floundered and not made any progress. This is the kind of initiative that we really appreciate in this organization.
Learning Plan:		

■ *Not So Pretty Documents.* The primary job result affected is 1, "Produces Information." The outcome to be checked is "Problem." The rationale is that the issue has been discussed before. The employee is not using available resources. Appearance is essential in a public relations department. Additional documentation might be as follows:

	Date	
Results Plan:		
Results Summary:	9/21	While prepared documents are not unattractive, they lack the kind of visual appeal I want, especially in the use of graphics. We're not getting all of the benefits available from our software. I've checked with management information services, and they are ready to provide you with some help. Adding this knowledge to your accuracy and editing suggestions will make you even more valuable to me.
Learning Plan:	9/21	Attend a special session, intermediate-level software training program arranged by MIS for you on 10/2. Apply graphics to documents by 10/21.

Management Job

For the following case studies, use these profiles:

1. COMPLETES WORK REQUIREMENTS			
by			
assigning and monitoring employees.			
☐ Result Required	☐ Problem	☐ Learning Required	☐ Performance Option
Work is completed on schedule with an efficient staff complement.	Clients are dissatisfied with service. Time is wasted. Costs are excessive. Schedules in other departments are disrupted.	☐ Studying scheduling techniques. ☐ Assembling resources. ☐ Managing time. ☐ Observing work in process and making adjustments.	Anticipates interruptions. Devises improved work methods.
	Date		
Results Plan:			
Results Summary:			
Learning Plan:			

2. MAINTAINS STAFF			
by			
selecting, orienting, and training employees.			
☐ Result Required	☐ Problem	☐ Learning Required	☐ Performance Option
New employees are qualified to accomplish job re9sults and are prepared to accept assignments by the end of their orientation period. Employees maintain required job knowledge. Legal requirements are followed.	Clients are dissatisfied with service. Time is wasted. Opportunities are lost. Costs increase.	☐ Studying hiring criteria. ☐ Developing interviewing techniques. ☐ Revising orientation and training content. ☐ Studying legal requirements.	Recommends improvements in hiring, orientation, and training procedures. Cross-trains employees. Prepares employees for new assignments.
	Date		
Results Plan:			
Results Summary:			
Learning Plan:			

3. ACCOMPLISHES STAFF JOB RESULTS by planning, monitoring, and appraising job results; counseling and disciplining employees; providing information; providing educational opportunities.			
☐ Result Required	☐ Problem	☐ Learning Required	☐ Performance Option
Employees accomplish organization and job results according to results required. Corrective actions are taken as soon as required. Procedures are followed. Problems are resolved. Legal requirements are followed.	Clients are dissatisfied with service. Time is wasted. Employees do not understand the problems they are causing.	☐ Conducting conferences. ☐ Developing coaching and counseling techniques. ☐ Developing planning, monitoring, and appraising skills. ☐ Studying legal requirements.	Recommends improvements in counseling, appraisal, and disciplinary procedures. Reaches out to employees and helps them solve problems before problems affect job results. Models results beyond those required.
	Date		
Results Plan:			
Results Summary:			
Learning Plan:			

The New Manager Who Wants to Involve Employees   John is a new manager. Admittedly, he is not sure of himself as he approaches his employees. His usual approach is to involve employees in decision making on the best way to proceed, which has caused several problems. First, some of his employees are frustrated with all of the discussion and just want him to decide. Actually, they aren't completely convinced that a young guy with less time in the company than they have should have been promoted in the first place. Second, some deadlines came perilously close to being missed because of the time John invested in talking with his employees. Third, his boss is not the participative type.

- What job result is affected: 1, 2, or 3?
- What outcome should be marked?
- What additional documentation would you write in the spaces provided for the Results Plan, the Results Summary, and the Learning Plan?

Fill in your answers.

☐ Result Required	☐ Problem		☐ Learning Required	☐ Performance Option
	Date			
Results Plan:				
Results Summary:				
Learning Plan:				

Illness in the Family   C.J. has been a manager for several years and generally has the respect of her employees. Over the past six months, she has been under a lot of pressure because her husband has been quite ill. At least once a week, she either is late or has to leave early in order to help her husband. C.J.'s manager has worked closely with her to keep the department functioning, but work in the department is suffering because there is no continuity of management. In their attempt to be helpful, her employees take charge in her absence but argue among themselves as to whose decision should be implemented. As a result, service is falling off, and some customers have complained.

- What job result is affected: 1, 2, or 3?
- What outcome should be marked?
- What additional documentation would you write in the spaces provided for the Results Plan, the Results Summary, and the Learning Plan?

Fill in your answers.

☐ Result Required	☐ Problem		☐ Learning Required	☐ Performance Option
	Date			
Results Plan:				
Results Summary:				
Learning Plan:				

Improvement Is Her Mission   Becky is an energetic manager. She reads everything about new management techniques, attends industry conferences, and brings home new ideas to share with other managers. Her unit's production is slightly better than most others, and her employees are generally more satisfied with their jobs than other employees. Her new quality improvement initiative turned up a few interesting ideas—nothing earth-shattering, but nevertheless quite useful.

- What job result is affected: 1, 2, or 3?
- What outcome should be marked?

- What additional documentation would you write in the spaces provided for the Results Plan, the Results Summary, and the Learning Plan?

Fill in your answers.

☐ Result Required	☐ Problem		☐ Learning Required	☐ Performance Option
	Date			
Results Plan:				
Results Summary:				
Learning Plan:				

Not Prepared to Take Over   Sara has gained the respect of most other managers. She is bright and strong-willed, and usually correct in her judgments. Things happen when she takes command of a situation. But when she took an extra-long vacation, things didn't go as well as might be expected. Each of her subordinate supervisors was asked to take over for half of Sara's vacation, but neither was adequately prepared. Succession planning has never been discussed in the company, except when it hasn't worked.

- What job result is affected: 1, 2, or 3?
- What outcome should be marked?
- What additional documentation would you write in the spaces provided for the Results Plan, the Results Summary, and the Learning Plan?

Fill in your answers.

☐ Result Required	☐ Problem		☐ Learning Required	☐ Performance Option
	Date			
Results Plan:				
Results Summary:				
Learning Plan:				

My Way or No Way   Allan is a seasoned manager. Work is turned out without much fanfare. Production and quality measurements are among the best in the company. Other managers ask to study his work methods, but they never ask for his advice on getting along with employees. He's not mean or vindictive, but somehow he never got the message that a "please" or "thank you" can go a long way toward making a situation more agreeable. Allan wants his way no matter what. His employees never offer suggestions because they'll just be turned aside.

- What job result is affected: 1, 2, or 3?
- What outcome should be marked?
- What additional documentation would you write in the spaces provided for the Results Plan, the Results Summary, and the Learning Plan?

Fill in your answers.

☐ Result Required	☐ Problem		☐ Learning Required	☐ Performance Option
	Date			
Results Plan:				
Results Summary:				
Learning Plan:				

Case Study Answers for the Management Job

- *The New Manager Who Wants to Involve Employees.* The primary job result affected is 3, "Accomplishes Staff Job Results." The outcome to be checked is "Learning Required." The rationale is that the manager is new. He's not doing anything wrong, yet his employees are having a problem. Additional documentation might be as follows:

	Date	
Results Plan:		
Results Summary:	9/21	On four occasions, which we have already discussed in detail, production deadlines were nearly missed because of the time you spent discussing optional approaches with employees. Your employees seem not to be convinced that they should be involved in these discussions and seem to prefer that you simply make the decisions yourself. As you know, I'm inclined to agree with them. However, you convinced me to try your more participatory approach, and since no deadlines were actually missed, I will continue to give you my support. Besides, I know that some of the employees still think you're too young for the job, and they will get over it when you prove yourself.
Learning Plan:	9/21	In order to prevent any actual losses, we will meet each week for the next sixty days to review production, quality, and cost targets in order to anticipate situations where delays might occur, identify likely employee suggestions, and identify ways to either speed up the decison-making process or establish drop-dead times to eliminate nearly missed targets.

■ *Illness in the Family.* The primary job result affected is 1, "Completes Work Requirements." The outcome to be checked is "Problem." The rationale is that plenty of support has been given to this manager, and the situation is seriously affecting organization results. Additional documentation might be as follows:

	Date	
Results Plan:		
Results Summary:	9/21	We have discussed your very difficult personal situation many times, and you know that you have my support. As we anticipated, there may come a time when the demands of your husband's illness would be more than the organization could absorb, and that time has come. Employees are arguing among themselves, service rates are dropping, and customers are complaining.
Learning Plan:	9/21	For the immediate time, you will clarify the decision-making process in your department, assign responsibilities clearly, and have a procedure prepared and issued by 10/1. Also, by 10/1 you need to face your personal crisis and tell me your plans and proposed actions.

■ *Improvement Is Her Mission.* The primary job result affected is 1, "Completes Work Requirements." The outcome to be checked is "Result Required." The rationale is that she is making a very good effort but not an extraordinary contribution. Additional documentation might be as follows:

	Date	
Results Plan:		
Results Summary:	9/21	We continue to appreciate your quality improvement suggestions. Clearly your contributions exceed our expectations. We are pleased with the good morale that you have developed. Keep up the good work of making improvements and sharing your ideas with other managers. Keep me posted about additional conferences that you think may be helpful.
Learning Plan:	9/21	You mentioned that you may wish to make some benchmarking visits with other organizations. Identify potential organizations; review them with me; contact them for preliminary interest; develop objectives, a plan, and costs for the visits; and present your recommendations by 12/21.

■ *Not Prepared to Take Over.* The primary job result affected is 2, "Maintains Staff." The outcome to be checked is "Learning Required." The rationale is that a succession plan needs to be developed. Although the manager's absence caused a problem, succession planning was not a priority in the organization. Additional documentation might be as follows:

	Date	
Results Plan:		
Results Summary:	9/21	During your extra-long vacation, neither of your subordinate supervisors was able to manage the department successfully. Several deadlines were missed. We all learned some valuable lessons. Preparing subordinates to take over in our absence has never been a high priority in our organization, but that has to change.
Learning Plan:	9/21	All managers will participate in a session to develop guidelines that will be implemented consistently in all departments. In particular, by 10/1 you will prepare learning assessments for each of your supervisors.

■ *My Way or No Way.* The primary job result affected is 3, "Accomplishes Staff Job Results." The outcome to be checked could be either "Problem" or "Learning Required." The answer to the case depends on the organization's culture. Where production and quality are high among the organization's values, "Learning Required" would be checked. Where human relations is an equally high priority, "Problem" would be checked. Assuming that "Learning Required" is checked, additional documentation might be as follows:

	Date	
Results Plan:	9/21	Encourage employee participation in operational decision making to improve employee understanding of department operations and to improve employee job satisfaction.
Results Summary:	9/21	Clearly you have established your production and quality record. The numbers prove that you are one of our best managers in this regard. Knowing what you have been able to accomplish, I am adding a new challenge—employee involvement in operational decision making—with no hesitancy that you will be able to accomplish it.
Learning Plan:	9/21	Study operational decision making thoroughly to identify key points when employees can be invited into the process by 12/21. Visit several other organizations to review their employee involvement programs by 12/21. Attend an educational workshop to collect additional ideas to implement this new program by 1/1.

Project Analyzer 8.7

How consistently do managers apply job standards?

_____

_____

Do managers regularly exchange viewpoints regarding the consistent application of job standards?

_____

_____

How can managers be brought together to develop a consensus for applying job standards?

_____

_____

8.8 Managing Job Contributions as a Base for Pay Decisions

The job of tying pay to job contributions usually starts with the appraisal system and the calculations for pay increases based on the final rating of the appraisal system—way too late. Managing job contributions as a base for pay decisions starts when advertisements are placed to attract job candidates who are qualified to accomplish expected job results.

Focusing on the Job Results Management Profile from the start sends a continuous message throughout the recruiting, selecting, orienting, and training processes as employees join the organization. The approach is objective so that employees understand that job contributions, rather than subjective personal idiosyncrasies, are the center of attention.

A new employee cannot help but be impressed that the manager and the organization want to succeed and want the employee to succeed as well. The Job Results Management Profile gives the employee much of the information (except for operating policies and procedures) he or she needs to be successful. What could be fairer, especially when pay increases are based on job contributions?

Planning Job Results

Not planning job objectives with employees and gaining their commitment to the plan eliminates the opportunity to hold employees to a contract. Appraising their work in this situation is unjustified. Before work begins, it must be planned.

Job objectives are recorded in the space provided for the Results Plan—for example:

Result Required	Problem	Learning Required	Performance Option
		☐	
	Date		
Results Plan:	9/21	Develop a new recruiting system to reduce the average recruiting time by 2 weeks by 10/21.	
Results Summary:			
Learning Plan:			

Follow these nine steps to plan work:

1. *Review the results-oriented job descriptions and the job outcomes.* What are the basic requirements of the job? What are the employee's special talents? Has the employee expressed any desire to become involved in special projects?

2. *Review current organization objectives.* What is the current operational plan for the organization? What are key priorities? What new requirements have been assigned to your area of responsibility? Which of these would appropriately be assigned to this employee according to routine expectations in the job description? Is this employee better suited than another employee to carry out the objective? Will the employee be interested in carrying out the objective? (See Figure 47.)

3. *Write a draft Results Plan for specific issues.* Well-written job objectives have the following characteristics:

S	Specific
M	Measurable
A	Attainable
R	Realistic
T	Time bound

In addition to these characteristics, a well-written objective has four writing elements: (1) identify the action the employee will take—for example, "Identify new inventory controls"; (2) specify the reason that the action is taken—for example, "to reduce expenses"; (3) identify the measure of successful accomplishment—for example, "by 35 percent"; and (4) specify the due date—for example, "by January 2, (year)."

Although objectives are based on job results in the job description, objectives are usually not written for each job result, and in some cases, no new objectives are written, and work moves forward to accomplish basic job expectations.

4. *Put the papers away for a while.* A brief interlude gives you time to regain an objective view of the requirements and goals of the situation.

5. *Reread the Results Plan.* Is it workable? Can the employee become enthused about it? Is the information correct? Are any adjustments required?

6. *Confer with your manager.* Does your manager support your preparations? Are any adjustments required?

Figure 47. Job contribution planning format.

Our objective is: _____

_____

Our job contribution criteria are:

a. What do we want? _____

_____

b. What don't we want? _____

_____

c. What snags can be anticipated? _____

_____

d. What's better than what we want? _____

_____

What resources do we need? _____

_____

Who does what? _____

_____

When do we check progress? _____

_____

7. *Set up an appointment with the employee.* When is the best time to meet? How will you prevent interruptions? How much time should you allow? Where will you meet? Is the room setup conducive to conversation?

8. *Give the employee an opportunity to prepare.* What information does the employee need?

9. *Set a conversation strategy.* What is the result you would like to have happen? Will you need to move the conversation toward an anticipated conclusion, or should the conversation work around and explore different options? Does the employee understand the purpose of the conference?

Monitoring and Documenting Work Progress

After plans are developed or work moves forward to accomplish basic job expectations, results of work monitoring are recorded in the space provided for the Results Summary. Documentation is required to remind manager and employee about work history, support any formal disciplinary action that may be required, and substantiate pay decisions. For example, here work progress is on course:

☑ Result Required	☐ Problem	☐ Learning Required	☐ Performance Option
		☐	
	Date		
Results Plan:	9/21	Develop a new recruiting system to reduce the average recruiting time by two weeks by 10/21.	
Results Summary:	10/21	The first milestone of the new recruiting system project is on course.	
Learning Plan:			

Here, work progress is off course:

☐ Result Required	☐ Problem	☑ Learning Required	☐ Performance Option
		☐	
	Date		
Results Plan:	9/21	Develop a new recruiting system to reduce the average recruiting time by two weeks by 10/21.	
Results Summary:	10/21	The first milestone of the new recruiting system project is two months behind schedule because of project group interpersonal conflicts.	
Learning Plan:	10/21	Meet with the training department by 2/1 to identify resources to learn and apply meeting management techniques for identifying and resolving interpersonal group conflicts.	

Here work progress continues off course after the first discussion:

☐ Result Required	☑ Problem		☐ Learning Required	☐ Performance Option
		☐		
	Date			
Results Plan:	9/21	Develop a new recruiting system to reduce the average recruiting time by two weeks by 10/21.		
Results Summary:	1/21	The first milestone of the new recruiting system project is two months behind schedule because of project group interpersonal conflicts.		
	2/10	Even though we developed a learning plan for you to learn and apply meeting management techniques, the project team on the new recruiting system is in disarray and remains unproductive.		
Learning Plan:	1/21	Meet with the training department by 2/1 to identify resources to learn and apply meeting management techniques for identifying and resolving interpersonal group conflicts.		
	2/10	I will join you in the next project meeting 2/17 to demonstrate conflict resolution techniques. We will debrief the outcome afterward so that you can carry on.		

Developing Learning Plans

When work does not progress according to expectations, following the recording of the unacceptable outcomes, Learning Plans are developed and recorded to help employees accomplish expectations.

Once a manager concludes that job contributions are not meeting expectations, a conversation with the employee is in order—the sooner, the better. Some managers mistakenly assume that the employee knows that a problem exists and, furthermore, that the employee will correct the situation without any prodding. Some managers err in the opposite direction when they come down like a ton of bricks on an errant employee. Here is what should be done:

1. *State the objective.* Get agreement on what needs to happen to correct the Problem and accomplish the Result Required—what needs to be learned. Restate and paraphrase to ensure accurate understanding. Ask for commitment. Reexplain why accomplishing the objective is important.

2. *Consider the options.* Ask for the employee's ideas. Don't just state what you think. Be patient. Don't judge the suggestions. Meet again if necessary. Explore the consequences of each option. Ask: "What do you think would happen if we did that?" Avoid asking leading questions that signal the answer you want to hear.

3. *Prepare a plan.* Work together with the employee to determine what steps will be necessary to accomplish the Learning Plan. Take notes. State specifically what will

Figure 48. Learning contract format.

What Must Be Learned? (*be specific*)	Where Can Helpful Information Be Found?	How Will Information Be Acquired?	By Whom?	When?	When Will Progress Be Reviewed?	Specific Evidence That Learning Has Been Accomplished

be done, when, and by whom. Ask: "What can I do to make sure that we are successful?" Clarify job results and outcomes. Remove obstacles to contributions. Identify new sources of help, such as coworkers and experts. Improve methods, processes, systems, and procedures. Provide facilities and equipment. Write a Learning Plan.

A learning contract is a plan developed between a manager and an employee to achieve some new learning (see Figure 48 for a sample format). It begins by stating the results to be accomplished (the more specific and measurable, the better). Then a program is fashioned that allows the employee to choose the best way to learn.

4. *Make sure that both you and the employee understand and agree to the Learning Plan objectives.* Too many managers, eager to conclude these conferences, even when emotions have been minimized by focusing on job contributions first rather than behaviors first, take a "Yeah," or an "Aha!" as tacit agreement and the opportunity to move on to more "fun" conferences with employees who are accomplishing the results the organization needs. Take the time to verify the employee's buy-in to the plan.

5. *Plan to check the results.* Establish a follow-up schedule. This is critical! Employees know which managers "read the riot act" and then get bogged down in their own issues and don't bother with follow-through. Truly effective managers set specific time lines for learning required and tangible applications of the new learning to accomplish desired job contributions.

Successful managers are meticulous about follow-up. Once a Problem or Learning Plan is identified, the focus of the manager and the employee does not change from that issue until the learning is learned and the Problem no longer exists.

Redirecting Job Efforts—Disciplining Employees Whose Job Outcomes Do Not Meet the Result Required or Who Willfully Violate Rules

Usually, the process of identifying problems, setting learning objectives, preparing a Learning Plan, and following up to ensure results provides enough impetus for an employee to improve. Not always, however. Some employees do not get the message, as the saying goes, or perhaps they choose to ignore it. Under these circumstances, pay increases—if not the employee's job—are in jeopardy. Management actions must be considered carefully, and properly documented.

Organizations have a right to enforce orderly conduct and compliance with established rules. Disciplining an employee is intended to train employees to accomplish what management wants, in the way management wants it—within reason, of course. Disciplinary proceedings can turn from training into punishment for continued errant behavior. Punishment is a last resort to make the message perfectly clear.

Disciplinary proceedings should not be viewed as separate and apart from the established philosophy of managing job contributions. Thought of as only "getting tough" with employees when they do not accomplish required results, disciplinary proceedings are unlikely to motivate employees to improve and are a likely cause for a rebuke should management's actions be challenged by an employee in a judicial proceeding.

Disciplining to punish an employee cannot begin until the manager knows why a standard of conduct was violated, or why the employee continues to refuse to improve. First, the facts must be investigated.

Then the manager must ask: Is discipline necessary in this case? If yes, what kind of discipline? Is the purpose to reinforce contribution improvement measures already taken because somehow the employee did not understand, or to punish because the employee deliberately chose to disregard known standards of conduct?

Next, the manager must decide: What discipline is needed to reinforce previous discussions about lagging accomplishments, to regain order, or to punish the employee?

The basic forms of job outcome improvement discipline are *oral* and *written*. The key ingredients of both are (1) an accurate statement of the facts and (2) a clear statement of the consequences if outcomes do not improve. Disciplinary measures generally proceed from oral to written, depending on the gravity of the situation. The Job Result Management Profile serves as an excellent beginning when formal disciplinary action is required. Only the portions of the form that are used to document deficient job outcomes need to be completed.

Employees may be terminated immediately for a deliberate and severe violation of rules. Usually, however, the manager starts the job outcome improvement process with an informal conversation, to understand and correct the situation. Next come formal conversations. Notes would be made of the discussion and included in the manager's file on the employee, or possibly the employee's personnel record. Up to this point, as you can see, the process of discussing, reviewing, and recording the job outcomes is the same as that already described as managing job contributions.

If the employee fails to heed the manager's direction, however, disciplinary procedures begin with formal letters of reprimand given to the employee by the manager and signed by the employee, with copies given to the employee and placed in the official personnel file. At this point, all previous records from job outcome improvement conferences become incorporated into the disciplinary documentation. After formal letters, or sometimes simultaneously with them, employees may be put on probation, meaning that if they do not improve their job outcomes according to a specific Learning Plan, they will be subject to harsher discipline, including discharge.

An extreme form of discipline is a suspension from work without pay—used after plenty of discussion and writing have failed. The ultimate punishment is to discharge an employee for willfully failing to comply with directives.

Project Analyzer 8.8

How well do managers plan job contributions?

_____

_____

Are employees routinely involved in the process?

_____

_____

Is the job description a key document for planning individual job contributions?

_____

_____

What do managers think of the planning system?

_____

_____

What do employees think of the planning system?

_____

_____

How are organization objectives developed and approved?

_____

_____

Are managers in the habit of carefully documenting job actions?

_____

_____

Do they record actions as they are observed, or do they wait until appraisal time?

_____

_____

Does your current system make documenting easy or burdensome?

_____

_____

Are Learning Plans used?

_____

_____

Do employees participate in their development?

_____

_____

Do efforts at training and development based on Learning Plans correct unacceptable work outcomes?

_____

_____

What is the state of discipline in your organization?

_____

_____

How have disciplinary actions taken affected the general rapport between managers and employees?

_____

_____

Are managers and employees poised for discord between them?

_____

_____

Are harsh discipline and adversarial relationships common?

_____

_____

Is there a backlog of grievances and arbitration cases challenging management's disciplinary actions against employees?

_____

_____

If so, what are the causes of this breakdown in relations?

_____

_____

How well do managers conduct disciplinary actions?

_____

_____

Are managers required to have their actions reviewed before they take them?

_____

_____

What techniques are used in the training sessions?

_____

_____

Is training a continuous process?

_____

_____

Is there follow-up on training to help managers apply what they learned?

_____

_____

_____

_____

8.9 Appraising Job Contributions

After job contributions have been made, they must be appraised. Follow these fifteen steps to prepare for the appraisal conference:

1. *Review the Job Results Management Profile concentrating on specific job results, job duties, and job outcomes.* Has any new responsibility been added? Is there any new technology involved? Has the employee received any special training? Does the job still fit organizational needs? Are any changes needed? Is a new job analysis required?

2. *Review the Result Plans developed in the planning conference and any midcourse changes, if made.* Have any unexpected changes occurred? Were there any uncontrollable events? Should any Result Plans be adjusted? Were sufficient resources provided?

3. *Review progress and incident notes.* Were appropriate adjustments made along the way? How often did you request progress reports? Did you encourage discussion of differences of opinion? Did you encourage contributions? Were you available to talk

about problems and opportunities? Are you weighing information from the beginning of the planning time frame equally with information acquired recently?

4. *Use your calendar and any other records to refresh your memory.* Here is a tremendous advantage for people who keep the Job Results Management Profile online. Call up any result, review periodic notations, and memory is refreshed. Even so, you may forget to record some observations, but other recorded events may trigger recollections about the job contributions you are appraising.

5. *Get other opinions.* Who else was in a position to observe and comment on the employee's job contributions? What records offer evidence in lieu of personal observations? Use the tools available to you. If you are looking at budgeting, consult budget variance reports; if you are evaluating court cases, review documented case presentation; if you are evaluating a doctor's patient care, look at patients' vital statistics; if you are evaluating customer satisfaction, consult customer satisfaction surveys.

6. *Identify the level of job contribution.* When appraising job contributions, review recollections and documentation for the entire time frame. You know what was to have been accomplished and how well it was to have been accomplished. The possible outcomes are identified in the four dimensions of the profile. For each job responsibility, identify the condition that best describes the job contributions accomplished.

Sometimes the Result Required or Result Plan will be quite specific—say, "Thirty collections per day"—so that matching will be obvious. Other times, the outcomes will state a more general condition that should exist—for example, "Service is reviewed on a regular basis." The manager must examine the evidence of whether service was reviewed, whether the review was sufficient to identify problems, and how often and regularly the service was reviewed.

Here again, the value of planning is notable. Evidence required to support outcomes should be reviewed and decided at the time job contributions are planned so that there are no surprises or misunderstandings at the end of the job contribution period.

Job contributions below "Twenty collections per day" when the required result is thirty per day is problematic because that is what the outcome states. The service outcome states that it is a Problem when "Customers complain about the service they receive." The quantifiable measure of collections per day is obvious. "Customer complaints" need to be examined for severity and frequency. More judgments are needed to determine what is a severe complaint and how often complaints will be tolerated, but if these questions were raised and answered during planning, job contribution judgments are not difficult to make.

Furthermore, remember the internal structure of the outcomes; either a job contribution matches the Result Required, or it does not. Either "Service is reviewed" as stated in the Result Required, or "Complaints are received" as stated in the Problem. At the start of the conversation between the manager and the employee, there should be little doubt as to which condition exists.

Of course, sometimes outcomes do not quite meet the Result Required, or the Problems created are quite small. Perhaps the employee made twenty-nine calls instead of thirty, or made the service calls but not regularly, so that occasionally customers called inquiring about missed service. Outcomes are not problematic in either case, but learning is required because the Result Required is what is expected.

On the other hand, the employee may make many more collections than are expected. (Remember when we talked about "stretch"?) Or the employee may find "imaginative ways to anticipate customer service requirements" so that the manager can identify the outcome at the Performance Option level.

7. *Review previous job contribution appraisals, results accomplished, and Results Plans.* What trends have evolved? What do the trends mean? What needs to be done to reinforce positive trends? What needs to be done to stop unproductive trends?

8. *Write a draft job contribution appraisal.* Do you have sufficient information? Is the written appraisal consistent with comments you made personally during the job contribution period? Do you have a realistic balance between compliments and suggestions of required learning?

9. *Write draft Result Plans, Result Summaries, and Learning Plans based on the job contribution appraisal.* Do plans and summaries add specifics to outcomes accomplished? Do they open the door to pursue new opportunities? Will learning resolve deficiencies or prepare for job growth and possible promotion?

10. *Put the papers away for a while to let your mind clear.* It's difficult to maintain objectivity when you're working intensely, especially when you are making decisions that will have significant impact on another human being.

11. *Reread the draft job contribution appraisal.* How does the document read from the employee's point of view? How would you expect the employee to respond? Do you have your facts correct? What adjustments are required?

12. *Confer with your manager.* Does your manager support your conclusions, commentary, and plans? What adjustments are required?

13. *Set up an appointment with your employee.* When is the best time to meet? How will you prevent interruptions? How much time should you allow? Where will you meet? Is the room setup conducive to conversations?

14. *Ask the employee to prepare.* What information does the employee need? Should you give a copy of the job contribution appraisal to the employee in advance? If not, why not? Should you ask the employee to complete a self-appraisal form before the conference? Would a self-appraisal form be too threatening, or does the employee usually examine his or her own job contributions formally?

15. *Set a conversation strategy.* What is the result you would like to have happen? Will you need to move the conversation toward an anticipated conclusion, or should the conversation work around and explore different options? Does the employee understand the purpose of the conference? Is your attitude open and exploratory, or closed and in pursuit?

The Manager-Employee Relationship

To be successful, the ongoing relationship between the manager and the employee must be one of psychologically equal partners; it cannot be based on the premise that the manager is superior or that the manager's role is to judge the employee. The relationship must be structured instead on the mutual responsibility the manager and employee share to accomplish essential job contributions that help the organization accomplish its mission.

Psychologically equal people acknowledge, though not necessarily agree with, each other's view of the world. A relationship is off-center when there is no mutual respect.

Managers and employees should plan and appraise job contributions together, with respect for each other's opinion.

The tenor of the job contribution appraisal conference is determined by the quality of the relationship between the manager and employee throughout the period of time between one conference and the next. Unmistakably, the rapport of the job contribution appraisal conversation begins in the planning phase.

You should now be ready to enter the conference room and conduct a face-to-face conversation.

Project Analyzer 8.9

How well do managers appraise job contributions?

_____

_____

Do they have conversations and keep records while work continues so that appraising is a simple review of the ongoing situation?

_____

_____

Are managers confident in their observations and conclusions about work outcomes?

_____

_____

Are managers satisfied with the way the appraisal program works?

_____

_____

Are employees satisfied with the way the appraisal program works?

_____

_____

To what degree are employees required to participate responsibly in the appraisal process?

_____

_____

Is the burden all on the manager's shoulders?

_____

_____

Are employees invited or required to complete an appraisal form to bring to the appraisal conference?

_____

_____

Have there been any legal challenges to the appraisal process?

_____

_____

What was the outcome?

_____

_____

If there have not been legal challenges, have complaints been filed?

_____

_____

Are managers' ratings frequently challenged?

_____

_____
_____

8.10 Linking Pay to Job Contributions

Once job outcomes have been appraised as one of the four possible outcomes—Result Required, Problem, Learning Required, or Performance Option—pay can be tied to the level of contribution.

Valuing Job Results

The first step in distributing pay equitably is to weight each job results statement in the job description according to the value of the result as needed by the organization. For example, an accountant may be responsible for determining journal entries and for verifying assets, among other things. Arranged in order of importance to the organization, determining journal entries is more important than verifying assets.

In relation to pay tied to job contributions, what the accountant accomplishes regarding journal entries will count more than what is accomplished verifying assets. Said another way, equal accomplishments in both areas should not be counted equally. Said still another way, an outstanding accomplishment in verifying assets may not be worth as much as meeting expectations in determining journal entries.

Each job result is weighted mathematically by distributing a proportional value—a percentage of the whole job—among the job results. Some managers find it helpful to start by ranking the job results from most important to least important, and then applying the mathematics. The distribution percentage must equal 100.

Job Description Result	Weighting
Job Result 1	15
Job Result 2	20
Job Result 3	10
Job Result 4	5
Job Result 5	5
Job Result 6	10
Job Result 7	10
Job Result 8	5
Job Result 9	5
Job Result 10	5
Job Result 11	5
Job Result 12	5
Total	100

Let's look at what can happen when job results are not weighted. Here is a distribution of outcomes accomplished by two employees, each of whom has twelve job results:

Employee	Result Required	Problem	Learning Required	Performance Option	Total
Alice	9	0	1	2	12
Bill	9	0	1	2	12

Alice may have given an extraordinary job contribution in tough job responsibilities, whereas Bill, although also giving an extraordinary contribution, gave those contributions in job results that were easier to achieve. Alice needs to learn some skills that will help her accomplish desired results, whereas Bill's learning requirements occur in more important areas. Unless job results are weighted according to their significance, any pay distribution according to results accomplished would be inequitable. Similarly, unless job results are weighted, an employee with a larger number of job results would stand a mathematical certainty of winning a bigger reward.

A concern may be raised that a job result may be valued high within one job but still be valued lower to the organization than a low-weighted job result in another job. For example, a data entry clerk's input of data may be highly weighted within that job, but it is still not as valuable to the organization as verifying assets in the accountant's, which is valued low in that job.

The answer is that job results are not compared directly from job to job. Each job is a full mathematical unit—equal to 100—unto itself. Fairness is established in a job-to-job comparison. Job equity was established during the job evaluation process so that the accountant is already receiving a higher base pay to recognize the more highly valued job results, and therefore percentage increases will be calculated on a higher base. In the end, an employee who makes an extraordinary job contribution in a lower-ranked job may be able to receive a better pay reward than an employee who turns in lackluster results in a higher-ranked job.

These examples may seem obvious, yet some organizations have overlooked this consideration, only to face the problem of inequity at the moment of truth when rewards are to be distributed. Their solution is entirely subjective narrative summaries that detract more than they correct.

Unfortunately, while weighting looks as though managing job contributions is being reduced to numbers, managers and employees intuitively understand that job results are not equal and make these calculations in their mind all of the time. There is no way to avoid the reality of the differing value of job results.

Valuing Outcomes

The four outcomes also need to be valued in order to complete the mathematical calculation—for example:

Outcome	Weight
Performance Option	3
Result Required	2
Learning Required	1
Problem	0

The weighting can be varied according to each organization's culture and type of jobs, or according to a family of jobs managed with the same budget. In the following model, this organization wanted to signal the exceptional value of extraordinary job contributions:

Outcome	Weight
Performance Option	5
Result Required	2
Learning Required	1
Problem	0

Which numbers are chosen does not make any equitable difference in effect because all job contributions are calculated with the same mathematical model.

Calculating Contribution Rewards

The job results weighting is multiplied by the outcome weighting, as follows:

Job Description Result	Job Result Weight	Outcome Accomplished	Outcome Weight	Points Calculated
Job Result 1	15	Result Required	2	30
Job Result 2	20	Result Required	2	40
Job Result 3	10	Result Required	2	20
Job Result 4	5	Performance Option	3	15
Job Result 5	5	Result Required	2	10
Job Result 6	10	Result Required	2	20
Job Result 7	10	Learning Required	1	10
Job Result 8	5	Result Required	2	10
Job Result 9	5	Problem	0	0
Job Result 10	5	Result Required	2	10
Job Result 11	5	Learning Required	1	5
Job Result 12	5	Result Required	2	10
Total	100			180

Determining Rewards

The total points calculated for an employee's job contribution are used to determine the pay reward as dictated by what the organization can afford in each pay review period. For example, the 180 points calculated above would receive a 3 percent increase in the following model:

Points Calculated	Reward
275–300	6%
180–225	3%
Below 179	0%

Pay rewards can be altered to accomplish desired pay objectives by changing the point ranges and reward percentages. For example, perhaps too many awards are being given for extraordinary job contributions because employees are becoming more qualified or because managers are becoming more lenient.

The target results are between 180 points and 225 points. Notice the stretch between 225 points and the threshold 275 points to receive extraordinary rewards. From 226 points to 274 points, rewards, in addition to the 3 percent pay increase, might be nonmonetary recognition.

Below 180 points, results are not what the organization needs in order to accomplish its mission. Of course, employees who are learning their jobs are different from employees whose job accomplishments are slipping. Employees who are learning the job might receive full increases as long as they are learning and their pay rate is below the midpoint of the pay range.

Overall, flexibility and overrides need to be built into the system in order to prevent undesirable consequences. For example, special contributions that don't quite measure up might receive special rewards or recognitions, and overrides can be used to prevent employees from receiving rewards when they are under disciplinary action. Some organizations prefer not to use rigid-looking numerical scales at all and prefer instead to rely on documented managerial judgment.

When to Discuss Pay Rewards

When pay is discussed at the time that job contributions are examined in the appraisal conference, strange things happen between managers and employees. Because money is so important to most employees, they may sit in near hysterical deafness until the manager decrees the magic number. All the good value of collaborative planning and monitoring of job results, and helpful managerial coaching, may be set aside.

More crucial, if the manager walks in to the conference with a pay decision to be announced, then the conversation will hardly be that of two people sitting down to examine and understand the outcomes together, as conferences are generally proclaimed to be. Even with careful attention by the manager when monitoring job results and with plenty of conversation to ensure that both manager and employee are perceiving progress and outcomes in the same way, a manager might trip at the last moment and be embarrassed. If collaborative practices are the human relations goal, then they need to be carried through to the last step.

It is better to announce that pay will not be discussed at all in the appraisal conference and that the pay decision will be made known later, generally in two to four weeks, after all of the information has been considered. This delay also gives the manager an opportunity to confer with his or her manager to ensure fair pay decisions.

Project Analyzer 8.10

Are job results valued according to their worth within a job?

_____

_____

Do employees understand these job priorities?

_____

_____

Are outcomes weighted?

_____

_____

Are managers and employees comfortable with the way pay rewards are calculated?

_____

_____

When are pay rewards announced?

_____

_____

Are managers and employees comfortable with the way pay rewards are announced?

_____

_____

_____

Strategic Planning for Phase 8

On your *first* quick walk through the project phases, record your initial thoughts on policy issues that will have to be decided.

_____

_____

_____

_____

_____

_____

Any notes on tactical procedures?

_____

_____

_____

On your *second* time through the phases, consider the strategic influences from all the phases; decide on an integrated posture for the entire project.

Complete the section for this phase in the Master Planner (in Phase 2.8) during your *third* reading.

Phase 9

Maintaining Your Pay Program

> If your pay program is misunderstood or not up-to-date, it's worthless or, worse, damaging.

9.1 What Is Your Organization's Reputation?

People will work anywhere when they need a job; people will *want* to work for your organization when you treat them better than the "job" shops. Not just pay them better; *treat* them better.

Pay for work is a minor exchange when compared to the human relationship between employer and employee. No one wants to be paid less than he or she is worth, but people will accept lower pay in order to have a better relationship.

One company put it this way: "We know that our starting pay is lower than you can probably earn somewhere else, especially if you are starting at minimum wage with us. However, we are willing to train you—where other companies are not—and to give you opportunities to try your hand on tougher tasks if you want. We know that after you learn your skills and apply them, you will be ready for more responsibility, and more money. So though you may start for a little less with us, you will have more opportunities sooner."

Pay as a Component of Organizational Culture

The way your organization acts defines its culture. Pay is a component of organizational culture. Therefore, pay is a determinant of your organization's reputation.

Pay is important, and some people will leave an organization just as soon as they can make more money somewhere else. At the lower end of the pay scale, this is quite understandable. Even so, people will stay with you for less money—even people at the lower end of the pay scale—if you are careful about your human relations management. Now get it out of your head that if you treat people nice, you can pay them less. Be reasonable.

What about, you ask, those situations where organizations do pay less than they should, but maybe give a few crumbs in benefits, or maybe take advantage of a captive labor market? Their people stay with them, you argue. The counterargument is that those organizations will "pay" in other ways in the long term. When people perceive that they are not being treated fairly and equitably, they resent it, and they show their indignation in many ways other than leaving, such as asking unions to represent them, giving less than their all in job accomplishments, or disrupting production and service.

Project Analyzer 9.1

What is the reputation of your organization now in your industry?

_____

_____

In your community?

_____

_____

What strengths is your organization known for?

_____

_____

Weaknesses?

_____

_____

How long has the situation been like this?

_____

_____

Why do people come to work for you?

_____

_____

Why do they stay?

_____

_____

Why do they leave?

_____

_____

What is your turnover rate?

_____

_____

What is the trend of the turnover rate over the past five years?

_____

_____

What is the average age of employees?

_____

_____

Is it different among various job groups?

_____

_____

What is the average tenure of employees?

_____

_____

Is it different among various job groups?

_____

_____

What kind of a reputation would your organization like to have?

_____

_____

How does this mesh with the goals of the pay program in Phase 1.3?

_____

_____

_____

9.2 Economic Issues

Each industry has its own economy; each firm has its own economy within its industry. There is too much talk of the "average," which leads the uninitiated to follow the lead of everybody else—as in a circle. If the industry or the community is doing well but your organization is not, you will commit economic suicide if you attempt to follow that expensive lead.

Communicate the Issues

Employees understand economics when you take the time to tell them the facts—in straight talk, of course. They operate in their own personal or family economy just as your organization operates in its economy. Most organizations get a poor grade in employee communications when it comes to informing employees about financial status and outlook. Those managements that do more than the obvious "memo" always report success—unless, of course, they are trying to make a case for a poor argument. It is precisely because so few organizations really talk with their employees that you can be a hero with the suggestion that your organization make a start.

Be realistic, though: getting employees to accept that there is a financial problem neither makes the problem go away nor makes employees forgive you if you caused the problem. On the other hand, it allows employees to look at the current situation, as well as at alternative solutions to the problem, and to participate in the correction or alleviation. This can make a real difference. Witness the many cases of employees giving back pay and benefits or buying faltering companies.

When employees understand the bad times as well as the good, they accept—grudgingly, of course—reduced or frozen increases. Well-managed organizations are able to make small merit increases in bad times, because they have developed fair and equitable pay programs and have kept their employees informed. They have earned the trust of their employees.

Employees can understand that although they did not get an increase this year, at least they got to keep their jobs. It's not a nice situation, but acceptable given the alternatives. Even when employees lose their jobs, organizations that have communicated well and fully fare better because employees understand the issues of economic survival.

Don't Insulate Your Employees From Fiscal Responsibility

When an organization does not keep its employees informed, when it keeps them in a state of adolescence, it forfeits its right to challenge employees to act as adults and to expect them to participate responsibly in pay decisions.

When you do keep your employees informed, you demonstrate your confidence in and respect for them. Then you can rightfully expect them to participate with you in maintaining the well-being of the organization over the long term, through the ups and downs of economic cycles.

Project Analyzer 9.2

What is the current economic status of your organization?

What is the economic status of each location?

_____

_____

The long-term outlook?

_____

_____

Is pay management authority centralized or decentralized?

_____

_____

Which should it be?

_____

_____

How autonomous or interdependent are locations?

_____

_____

How much can you afford to pay for labor costs?

_____

_____

What is the industry outlook?

_____

_____

Do employees understand the financial status of your organization?

_____

_____

How, and how frequently, are they kept informed?

_____

_____

What more can they be told?

_____

_____

Is management willing to tell?

_____

_____

If not, why not?

_____

_____

_____

9.3 Policies and Procedures

Policies and procedures guide action. They are the lifestyle of the organization, the ways in which it operates differently from other organizations. Policies and procedures define the organization's uniqueness.

This is not a reference book on the many ways in which pay policy and procedure can be defined. Such books and software already exist. Other organizations are excellent resources; ask them how and why they deal with pay management issues. Then fashion guides to meet your organization's goals, needs, and preferences.

Here are the areas that need definition:

Job Analysis

- Purpose
- When it is required
- Who conducts it
- Who approves it
- How it is processed

Job Descriptions

- Purpose
- Who prepares them
- Preparation instructions
- Format
- Revisions
- Review
- Approval
- New jobs

Job Evaluation

- Purpose
- New jobs
- Temporary grade assignments
- Grade assignments
- Reevaluations
- Appeals
- Committee membership
- Committee chair
- Committee meetings
- Documentation
- Audits
- Employee communications

Pay Surveys

- Purpose
- When they are conducted
- Who conducts them
- Organizations surveyed
- Statistical analysis
- Benchmark jobs
- Employee communications

Pay Management

- Compensation objectives
- Personnel requisitions
- Job posting
- Hiring offers
- Probationary reviews
- Regular reviews
- Special reviews
- Merit increases
- Promotional increases
- General increases
- Special increases
- Special adjustments
- Transfers
- Demotions
- Determination of exempt and nonexempt status
- Normal work hours per week
- Overtime
- Overtime rates
- Assignment of overtime
- Shift differentials
- Geographic pay variances
- Policy consistency
- Compensation committee
- Authorizations
- Payroll
- Legal requirements
- Appeals
- Employee communications
- Confidentiality

Job Results Management

- Purpose
- When conducted
- Planning job results
- Coaching job efforts
- Learning plans
- Documentation
- Appraising job contributions
- Employee participation
- Linking pay to job contributions
- Disciplinary procedures
- Review
- Approval

Employee Benefits

- Purpose
- Vacations
- Holidays
- Other paid time off
- Religious holidays
- Life insurance
- Accidental death and dismemberment
- Travel insurance
- Short- and long-term disability insurance
- Health and major medical insurance
- Education assistance program
- Employee assistance program
- Service recognition
- Leaves of absence
- Personal leaves
- Military leaves
- Profit-sharing plan
- Pension plan
- Stock ownership plan
- Stock bonus plan
- Home purchase and sale
- Foreign relocation
- Employee communications

Project Analyzer 9.3

Are policy and procedure guides available to management?

_____

_____

Which policies and and procedures have been written?

_____

_____

Which need to be written?

_____

_____

Are managers trained to understand and use policies and procedures?

_____

_____

How are revisions considered and circulated?

_____

_____

_____

9.4 Legal Considerations for Managing Pay

The law is the law—except that it is subject to change, to interpretation, and to being ignored.

Keep abreast of new legislation and recent court decisions at the federal, state, and local levels so you always know the current requirements. Best of all, be attuned to the legislative processes, and take note as proposals for change are introduced so you can *anticipate* important changes, such as the *Income Equity Act of 1997*.

Obtain expert legal advice; do not rely on "what other organizations do" because they may not understand the legal requirements, may be subject to different requirements, or may have chosen to ignore them.

Given the transient nature of laws, interpretations, applications, and enforcements, only the major principles of significant, national legislation will be noted here. More detailed information can be found in publications dealing exclusively with these subjects; again, use the help of legal experts.

The *Fair Labor Standards Act* requires, among other things, a minimum wage and overtime pay to employees, except those employed in certain "capacities." Thus, there are nonexempt and exempt jobs. The decision depends on whether a job meets the tests of the law, not whether a manager thinks the job should be exempt or whether the employee prefers to be exempt. Be sure to check Department of Labor guidelines—for example, for methods of calculating overtime and changes in guidelines, such as new rules for using compensatory time in lieu of overtime.

The *Walsh-Healy, Davis-Bacon,* and *Service Contract* acts require competitive pay rates for specific occupations when government contracts are involved. Similarly, the *National Foundation of Arts and Humanities Act* applies where foundation funds are involved.

The *Portal-to-Portal Act* defines compensable working time.

The *Equal Pay Act of 1963* demands equal pay for men and women performing equal work under similar conditions, though some pay differentials are permitted.

The *Civil Rights Act of 1964, Title VII,* prohibits personnel decisions based on race, color, sex, national origin, or religion.

The *Age Discrimination in Employment Act of 1967* promotes the employment of older persons (at least forty years of age) by eliminating arbitrary age requirements.

Executive Orders 11141 (signed in 1964), *11246* (signed in 1965), and *11375* (signed in 1967) extend equal employment opportunities to federal employees and persons employed by contractors and subcontractors in the performance of federal contracts.

The *Rehabilitation Act of 1973* promotes employment opportunities for disabled individuals.

The *Vietnam Era Veterans Readjustment Act of 1974* requires affirmative action from federal government contractors to employ these veterans.

The *Americans with Disabilities Act of 1990* prohibits employers from discriminating against qualified persons with disabilities and requires reasonable accommodation.

The *Family and Medical Leave Act of 1993* entitles eligible employees to take up to twelve weeks of unpaid, job-protected leave for the birth of a child or placement of a child for adoption or foster care; for the care of a child, spouse, or parent who has a serious health condition; or for the employee's own serious health condition. The act requires maintenance of benefits during leave and requires reinstatement to the same or equivalent position at the end of the leave.

Also check the guidelines for distinguishing contingent workers from an actual employer-employee relationship.

Other federal legislation affects taxes and the administration of benefits. Examples are the Internal Revenue Code, the Revenue Act, the Tax Equity and Fiscal Responsibility Act, the Deficit Reduction Act, the Employee Retirement Income Security Act, and the Retirement Equity Act.

State laws vary from federal laws and from laws of other states.

Project Analyzer 9.4

Do you and your managers understand the legal requirements under which you operate?

_____

_____

Does everyone understand the implications of not adhering to these legal requirements?

_____

_____

Do you have copies of the acts and interpretive bulletins immediately available—either near your desk or with advisers?

_____

_____

9.5 Legal Considerations for Managing Job Results

Managing job results legally begins with an understanding of the rights of an employer to manage organization resources. Without a written contract, an employee serves at the will of an employer and may be discharged at any time. For what reason? For good reason, for bad reason, or for no reason at all. This is the concept of *at-will employment*.

Some states accept this notion; others do not. Some jurists believe in the concept; others do not. Many countries in the world have limited the authority of an employer to discharge an employee without good cause.

Please keep in mind that the comments in this chapter are based on a general view of the law and management practices and do not take into account the differences among the laws of different states. Check with a lawyer familiar with the laws in the states with which you are concerned.

The principal argument in favor of at-will rights for the employer is that the *employee* may end the employment relationship at any time, for any reason at all, whether or not the reason makes sense for the employer. So why shouldn't the employer have the same right? Ostensibly, legislatures attempt to protect the employee against the overwhelming economic position of the employer. The employer can continue in business without the employee, whereas the employee out of a job is out of income. Your organization's position on this matter is entirely its choice, unless your organization is within the province of a state that does not recognize the at-will concept.

Whether an employee can sue an organization for what he or she considers a wrongful discharge hinges on whether the discharge is injurious to the common welfare—that is, whether it is a matter of public policy rather than just a private dispute between the employer and the employee. The guidelines for this determination are unfortunately vague and subject to jurists' personal interpretation of what constitutes "reasonable human welfare." Obviously the interpretation may change with each examination.

Managing job results may lead to the employee's dismissal. By examining systems that the courts have decided are unreasonable, unfair, and indefensible, we can construct guidelines that will minimize challenges to a system. Furthermore, management programs designed with these guidelines in mind go a long way toward preventing the kinds of abuses by managers that give merit to employee challenges in the first place. The guidelines in this book will keep your organization as safe from challenge as any system can guarantee.

Do not be misled. No system can make managers act morally and ethically, and no system can prevent them from treating employees disgracefully if they choose to do so. However, a solid system can surely make it difficult for managers to act this way. On the positive side, a solid system points managers in the proper direction of equitable employee relations and reminds them from time to time about the proper procedures.

Most legal challenges to performance appraisal programs arise from criteria that are not job-related or from ratings that are biased. Occasionally management's inconsistent application of policy is challenged. The best defense against a challenge is a thorough, thoughtful approach, which this book is designed to give you.

One lesson has surely been learned from challenges that have been tried in a court of law: employers who do not have a formal program are hard-pressed to defend their actions against employees, and they are typically found liable. Judges have no choice, without specific policy and procedure to the contrary, but to infer what they can from established norms within the organization—not always the norms employers want paraded before them.

Essential Ingredients of an Effective and Legally Sound Job Results Management Program

Here are guidelines, distilled from court cases, that you can use to design your program. In their opinions, the courts have directly or indirectly suggested that you:

1. Identify and validate job requirements and outcome criteria through job analysis.
2. Provide employees with written job descriptions and outcome criteria.
3. Train managers to observe and appraise job contributions.
4. Require that the manager's manager review the content of the job contribution appraisal before it is discussed with the employee and approve the outcome of the conference, including results and learning plans and employee comments, after it is conducted.
5. Design a job results management form that includes:
   —Instructions on how to use the form.
   —A space for the employee to comment on the job contribution appraisal or plans.
   —A signature space for the employee to acknowledge receiving a copy of the form.
6. Tell employees how their job contributions compare with job requirements and outcome criteria.

7. Provide a procedure for employees to appeal job contribution plans and appraisals that appear unjust to them.
8. Monitor the way managers operate within the system.
9. Audit the program to assess its effectiveness, and conduct statistical checks to identify any adverse impact on minorities and other protected groups of employees.
10. Ensure the confidentiality of personal papers.

Here is some help for you with each of these legal guidelines.

Guideline 1: Identify and Validate Job Requirements and Outcome Criteria Through Job Analysis   Following the guides in Phases 4 and 8 will satisfy this guideline. Make no mistake—management has the right to decide what jobs will be performed, how, and how well. Management, however, cannot make changes in jobs without some modicum of warning to employees. Management is likely to get into trouble when changes appear to give employees little opportunity to comply with new requirements. Management is asking for trouble when it deliberately changes job requirements in order to put a particular employee in an awkward position.

In short, follow a time-honored system to identify what work you expect your employees to accomplish:

1. Clearly state the purpose of your organization.
2. Define objectives to accomplish the purpose.
3. Determine what type of organizational structure will best accomplish the objectives.
4. Define specific job expectations within the structure that will enact the objectives.
5. Define how well the objectives must be accomplished.

Guideline 2: Provide Employees With Written Job Descriptions and Outcome Criteria   Using the techniques presented in Phases 4 and 8 will help you satisfy this requirement. Surely you have had ineffective experiences with oral communications. "Is that what you meant?" "I don't remember." Some managements have not dealt honorably with employees and have claimed that information was provided to employees when it had not been.

New employees can easily be informed of job requirements and outcome criteria when they are given their orientation to the organization. Besides, telling employees what's expected of them makes all the sense in the world if management wants employees to contribute to the best of their ability. Be prepared, however, to have to *prove* someday that your employees were informed of job requirements and outcome criteria.

Include the dissemination of this information as part of your orientation package for new employees. Have employees sign to indicate their receipt of the information. Have a similar orientation package for newly promoted employees, and place a check-off reminder on job processing forms, such as on requests for job reevaluations, to ensure that job changes are always communicated to employees. A question on the form to determine that the job description and the outcome criteria are current—as shown in the model form in Phase 8.5—will serve as a periodic audit.

Should different formats for job descriptions and job results management approaches be used for exempt and nonexempt employees? No. Different systems are unnecessary. All employees, regardless of their Fair Labor Standards Act status, should have, and be informed of, their job descriptions and outcome criteria.

Guideline 3: Train Managers to Observe and Appraise Job Contributions   In most situations, managers are able to interact personally with their employees and thus observe their job contributions in order to appraise them. Some managers, however, are on different shifts or may be located in different geographical areas.

The operative word is *observe*. When outcome criteria describe how employees are to behave (that is, when they express criteria in *behavioral* terms), managers must *actually observe* the employee behaving in order to make a legitimate appraisal of performance. However, when criteria are expressed in results-oriented terms, as was demonstrated in Phase 8.4, only the *results* of behavior (outcomes) need to be examined.

This is an important shift in thinking about outcome criteria. Many guides will advise you to "express criteria in behavioral terms." Behavioral terms are certainly more appropriate than naming or describing the personal *traits* that an employee must display in order to perform effectively. However, the way an employee behaves focuses attention on what the employee *does*, not what the employee *accomplishes*. We eliminate many potential employee challenges in our job results management programs because we communicate with employees in terms of the results they must accomplish.

Nonetheless, because it's the employee's behavior that produces (or fails to produce) results, employees who do not produce the results required need to change their behavior. Thus, a manager will ultimately need to observe behavior directly in order to offer helpful guidance to the employee.

What about using team leaders to help with job contribution appraisals? Managers may designate employees as team leaders to coach other employees. Team leaders may even recommend disciplinary action for an employee. Guideline 3 means that team leaders should be trained to observe and appraise job results. However, even if team leaders offer their opinions about employees' job contributions, the managers remain ultimately accountable.

And what about using peer opinions? Should peers be asked to appraise each other's job contributions? Usually not. Employees do have opinions about each other's job contributions, but it is not their responsibility to offer these formally as appraisals in the place of management.

Legally, you could conjecture that a judge might not put much weight on a peer's appraisal, because the appraisal carries no organizational authority. The manager, on the other hand, is the legal agent of the organization. If peers were asked to render their appraisal, then they would need to be trained to participate in appraisals.

Ill feelings are easily created within a group when peers appraise each other's job contributions in a formal way. Most groups deal better with such opinions informally. Frankly, it's a good bet that any manager who asks employees to conduct appraisals on one another does not want to conduct appraisals. Exchange of opinion among peers is a reasonable tactic only when the employees relate closely with each other as a team of highly interdependent members.

Asking for peer opinions, though not appraisals, is a reasonable tactic for a manager to collect different points of view about an employee's job contributions. Similarly, opinions about job contributions should be collected from other managers and individuals with whom the employee comes in contact, and from "customers" within and outside the organization who are served by the employee. Immediately, the potentially biased judgment of one manager is reduced.

Do not place the onus of conducting job contribution appraisals only on the manager's back. The more employees are made to participate in the job results management process, the less they can sit back and complain when the process does not meet their preconceived notion of how they should be treated. Managers have put themselves in the position of making all the decisions, leaving themselves open to attack for the results of their decisions in all quarters. While the ultimate accountability may not be avoided by the manager, absolving employees from their responsibility to participate thoughtfully and responsibly is foolish. Employees should be invited to complete a self-appraisal of their job contributions and bring it with them to the job contributions planning and appraisal conference for discussion.

Project Analyzer for Legal Guideline 3

	Yes	No
Are managers able to observe their employees' job contributions?	☐	☐
Is there follow-up to training to ensure that what was taught to managers was learned and applied by them?	☐	☐
Are managers counseled when they make errors in the job contribution appraisal process?	☐	☐
Are managers appraised on their ability to appraise job contributions?	☐	☐
Are group leaders' comments made part of the process?	☐	☐
Do other employees understand the group leader's authority?	☐	☐
Are peer opinions and the opinions of others who work with an employee obtained for the employee's job contribution appraisal?	☐	☐
Are employees asked to complete a self-evaluation?	☐	☐

Guideline 4: Require That the Manager's Manager Review the Content of the Job Contribution Appraisal Before It Is Discussed With the Employee and Approve the Outcome of the Conference, Including Results and Learning Plans and Employee Comments, After It Is Conducted The manager's manager, and possibly even one manager higher, should review the appraisal documentation before the conference, but only to ensure that the opening dialogue is clear.

There is a danger here. The conference is a discussion of past, present, and future job contributions. Before the conference, the manager and the employee prepare a *draft* of an appraisal. Perceptions may change during the discussion. For example, the manager may be mistaken about some facts of the employee's past performance or personal ambition. Open dialogue will clarify the situation. If, however, the review with a higher-level manager becomes a commitment to a conclusion, the open nature of the conference will be lost. The purpose of the review is to uncover faulty thinking before it leads to emotional clashes and an appeal by the employee.

Some managers are uncomfortable with bringing problematic outcomes to their boss because the boss might be the intolerant type who wonders why problems weren't solved before they occurred. No system can stop a narrow-minded attitude. However, an objective system helps people engage in thoughtful and reasonable conversations.

After the conference, the final outcomes should also be approved by the manager's manager.

Project Analyzer for Legal Guideline 4

What is management's attitude toward reviewing documentation and plans before the job contribution conference?

_____

_____

Who is involved in the review process?

_____

_____

When does the review occur?

_____

_____

What kinds of changes typically have been made during the review process?

_____

_____

Is the review viewed as a helping or a controlling process?

_____

_____

What needs to happen to improve the review process?

_____

_____

Have reviewers been trained to counsel their subordinate managers?

_____

_____

Guideline 5: Design a Job Results Management Form That Includes Instructions on How to Use the Form, a Space for the Employee to Comment on the Job Contribution Appraisal or Plans, and a Signature Space for the Employee to Acknowledge Receiving a Copy of the Form Phase 8.5 shows a model job results management form that includes appropriate instructions on the use of the form for the job contribution conference.

Whether or not outcomes are up to par, an employee should be required to acknowledge in writing that he or she received the manager's comments about outcomes and, where appropriate, the plan for accomplishing results required. In the worst of all scenarios, an employee might deny having received proper notification of impending disciplinary action if there is no signature to the contrary. If an employee refuses to sign the form, the refusal should be witnessed.

The signature line should not require the employee to *agree* with the content of the conference, but only ask to acknowledge receipt of the words or a copy of the form. Again, Phase 8.5 illustrates a proper approach.

Employees should have space on the conference form to write a reaction to the conference if they choose to do so, but they should not be required to write anything if they do not want to. Most employees, because they are treated more fairly in a system based on job language criteria, will comment that the appraisal and the plans are fair, even though they may not agree with each of the manager's perceptions.

Employees should be encouraged to write remarks in disagreement with any of their manager's observations. This not only protects their rights but also gives the manager and the organization a chance to take another thoughtful look at the disagreement.

Most organizations file a copy of job contribution plans and appraisals in the employee's personnel record to prove that conferences were held and to make the record available when follow-up is needed. Most managers are encouraged to keep a copy to guide employee outcomes, but, unfortunately, most employees do not receive a copy for self-guidance. Oddly, management sets time aside to talk to employees about outcomes and planned improvement yet does not allow employees a copy of the plan itself as a convenient reminder. Both participants in the conference should have a record of the conversation and agreement or at least have easy access to a copy.

Project Analyzer for Legal Guideline 5

Are complete instructions included on the job results management form?

_____

_____

Are additional instructions regarding policy and procedure available for managers?

_____

_____

Do employees have access to and understand policy and procedure?

_____

_____

Is space available for employees to comment?

_____

_____

Do employees use the comments sections?

_____

_____

What kinds of reactions do employees have to the appraisals?

_____

_____

Have changes in the process been made as a result of employee comments?

_____

_____

Do employees show a reluctance to sign the form?

_____

_____

What problems have arisen in connection with required signatures?

_____

_____

Guideline 6: Tell Employees How Their Job Contributions Compare With Job Requirements and Outcome Criteria   No law requires organizations to have a job results management program. However, perhaps there *should* be a law that requires organizations to tell employees how well they are accomplishing their jobs. These guidelines, derived from court decisions, talk around the issue. The guidelines address aspects of the system, but not the fundamental issue that if an organization tells employees what to accomplish, then it ought to tell them how well they're doing. No courts have ever ordered it either.

Management may lose a legal challenge because it has made mistakes. But except for cases that employees win because of a legal technicality, management almost always wins when it designs a reasonable program and follows its own guidelines for fair treatment. Here are some thoughts regarding when job conferences should be conducted:

■ *Timing of job contribution conferences.* Job contribution conferences should be held at times that make sense in the cycle of work being performed. A reasonable guide is that outcomes ought to be reviewed at least once a year in a formal way. Informally, outcomes are reviewed each working day, as managers make routine observations. If outcomes begin to fall apart, a conversation should be held immediately, even with just a few words. Similarly, reinforcement of outstanding outcomes is most valuable at the time it is earned.

■ *Timing by employee anniversary date vs. operational cycle.* Many organizations tie job contribution conferences to the employee's anniversary date. This timing subtly emphasizes the personal cycle of the employee tenure instead of, more properly, the operational cycle of the organization. Conferences are traditionally scheduled on personal anniversary dates, instead of concentrating the conferences in a short period, in order to spread the time consumed over the whole year in consideration of the manager's schedule.

However, conferences are most effective when they are held in tandem with regular operational cycles so that they can reinforce excellent outcomes as they occur or shore up outcomes that are sagging. Cycles may be shorter than a year or longer—up to two or three years. During long cycles, outcomes can be examined at project milestones to keep outcomes on track. When outcomes are unsatisfactory, conferences are required at shorter intervals in order to clarify targets and correct the way they are being pursued.

■ *Timing of conferences for new employees.* Most organizations do not hold conferences with employees after they are hired or promoted until the third month or later, depending on the orientation cycle of the job. Most new employees should receive complete job contribution appraisals of their initial outcomes after 30, 60, and 90 days, and then again after six months, not for a legal reason so much as to establish rapport and orient the employee to the job results management philosophy.

Yes, more time is involved in managing job results when conferences are held that frequently, but the payoff comes for managers when they need not spend their time chasing problems. Instead, they can spend their time exploring opportunities. The simple question for managers is, How do you want to spend your time?

Frequent reviews pick up on problems quickly and demonstrate management's interest in helping employees succeed. Employees get used to the system and understand what job results mean to the organization. The beginning of employment is a fresh start for managers and employees alike. They are more open to discuss what is important to them before personality issues set in to detract from the relationship.

■ *Conferences after transfers or promotions.* Upon transfer or promotion of an employee, a conference with the current manager to close the books is in order. When an employee's work is the responsibility of more than one manager, such as in project work, each manager should confer with the employee to agree on what is to be accomplished and then, at the close of the project, meet again to discuss how well the work accomplished the results required. One manager would take the lead in consolidating the individual job contribution appraisals.

Project Analyzer for Legal Guideline 6

When are job contribution conferences held with new employees?

_____

_____

When are regular job contribution management conferences held? On employee anniversary dates? All at the same time? Some other cycle?

_____

_____

Have managers or employees expressed any problems with the timing of conferences?

_____

_____

What work cycles exist in your organization?

_____

_____

Can conferences be tied to work cycles instead of to employee anniversary dates?

_____

_____

Will managers tolerate conducting conferences on an as-earned basis?

_____

_____

Guideline 7: Provide a Procedure for Employees to Appeal Job Contribution Plans and Appraisals That Appear Unjust to Them   An appeal is a basic right in our legal system. Thus, employees should have the same right within their work organization.

Left unresolved, conflict festers and contaminates relationships. Appeals are a healthy process to bring misunderstanding out into the open. Though some conflict will never be resolved, it's better for the manager to know its implacability than to assume that it is a minor grievance that will eventually disappear.

The appeal process need not be complicated or fraught with hostility. When the conference takes place, the manager and the employee will learn that they disagree. If the error is of simple fact, it can be cleared up at that moment or shortly after. If the facts are not so simple, an appeal in writing will help the employee think through the situation and present an organized argument. If anger is involved in the disagreement, the act of writing serves to vent feelings.

The manager, receiving a reasoned argument, has an opportunity to consider the appeal in quiet contemplation. The process insulates the manager and reduces the possibility of an emotional backlash at the employee.

The manager and the employee who continue to disagree may need help from a third party to mediate or arbitrate the dispute. The human resources department might play a conciliatory role to help the two parties explore opposite views. A senior manager can do the same thing. In extreme situations, a person outside the organization might help. However, sooner or later, someone will have to decide which perception will prevail.

How many appeals the employee may have is at management's discretion. To allow several appeals up the management hierarchy is not too many. Look at the situation this way: If management does not give a disagreement the time and place to air within its organization, there are outside agencies that will force the time to be allotted—and management probably won't like the experience.

Project Analyzer for Legal Guideline 7

Is an appeal policy and procedure available to guide managers?

_____

_____

Do employees have access to and understand the appeal policy and procedure?

_____

_____

Do employees use the appeal process?

_____

_____

For what reasons do employees make appeals?

_____

_____

Have changes in the process been made as a result of employee appeals?

_____

_____

_____

Guideline 8: Monitor the Way Managers Operate Within the System Usually, a human resources professional participates in the development of the job results management policy and program and trains managers to manage job results accordingly. Professionals should be available to advise managers on how to proceed in ticklish situations and how to counsel employees who are not coping well with a manager's suggestions on how to improve outcomes.

Department managers should keep track of when conferences are due, properly record and document them, and be held accountable to do so. The human resources department may help ensure consistency among the managers' decisions, but the program should not be a human resources program.

The opinions that managers state when appraising employee job contributions can come back to haunt them if employees believe that their reputation has been defamed and that they have been injured in some way, such as being rejected for other jobs because of negative comments about their performance in your organization.

Employers generally have a legal privilege to appraise job contributions, and this privilege gives them a defense in such challenges. Still, fairness—and the need for a solid legal defense—dictates that managers be informed of and required to follow the specific procedures for discussing an employee's outcomes, with the employee as well as with others. In particular, managers cannot make off-the-cuff derogatory remarks. Any derogatory remarks must be based on factual evidence.

Courts of law are asking managers to be more precise in their judgments. More to the point, the courts are warning managers not to rely on their unique view of the world but instead to examine and compare their internal criteria openly in order to minimize errors of ignorance or incompleteness. The fact of life for organizations and jurists is that human beings cannot be unequivocably precise when explaining their opinions about the qualitative aspects of human accomplishments. We must learn not to try to make human beings do something beyond their capabilities. It is the open examination of our internal thought processes that is the key to more accurate and complete appraisals of job contributions.

You can use computers to process, retrieve, and analyze appraisals. With a computer, you can quickly retrieve job results management forms and analyses, including the job description and the outcome criteria; a history of all prior appraisals of the employee; a comparison of outcomes involving similar work; a summary and average of several opinions; and an index of the manager's job contribution appraisal history.

Don't be dazzled by computerized systems that move bad structures and judgments around quickly. In particular, be wary of the definitions of criteria embedded in the software, such as what a programmer might define "initiative" to be. Where computers offer a useful and natural addition to your system, use them.

Project Analyzer for Legal Guideline 8

How are human resources professionals involved in monitoring the way managers operate within the program?

_____

_____

Do managers respect the participation of human resources professionals?

_____

_____

Who else is involved in reviewing managers' outcome decisions?

_____

_____

Are any external observers used to monitor managers' effectiveness?

_____

_____

Are managers trained to be accountable to manage job results?

_____

_____

_____

Guideline 9: Audit the Program to Assess Its Effectiveness, and Conduct Statistical Checks to Identify Any Adverse Impact on Minorities and Other Protected Groups of Employees Do the policies and procedures of your program have any adverse effect on minorities and other protected groups of employees? Race, creed, national origin, sex, age, disability, and veteran status are the factors to consider as you answer that question. For example, do minority employees receive a percentage of low ratings that is disproportionate to their percentage in the total population? Do women typically receive lower ratings than men? An audit should be conducted to examine the ratings of minorities and other protected groups under the program, as well as the use of the data in personnel decisions such as pay increases and promotions.

Employers are responsible for validating employment and testing procedures, such as a job results management program. Yet one validation expert allegedly said, "I know of no studies to measure the validity of job results management procedures in an operational context." To validate means to substantiate, typically by statistical methods. However, it is difficult to validate a job results management program with quantifiable measures. Instead, because we know that judges are conditioned to think in terms of what is "reasonable," a better way to think of the validation requirement is to think of it as a requirement to be reasonable.

The job results management program should be reviewed continually as managers and employees use the system and comment on it. A formal audit of program effectiveness is best accomplished as part of the usual organizational audit of operations. In most organizations, this audit occurs annually.

Set up the job results management program in parallel with operational and financial planning and control systems. Managers who are responsible for functional and financial management in their area should also be responsible for job results management in their area.

If a task force was set up to establish or redefine the job results management program, have the task force assess the outcome of its work yearly.

If pay increases are tied to job contributions, the increases given to employees should correlate with the appraisals they received. That is, higher ratings should merit larger pay increases. The same relationship should exist if promotions, or any other forms of reward and recognition, are tied to appraisals. The warning is more obvious in the obverse. Disciplinary actions, especially termination, when based on job outcomes, should correlate with poor job contribution appraisals.

Beware. Some performance management systems we have reviewed purport to reduce "rater error," that is, the tendency of the rater to be unjustly harsh on some employees or excessively lenient on others. Other systems supposedly demonstrate a rater's decisiveness or consistency when rating employees. Most of these systems require some sort of consensus judgment and forced distribution against which individual managers' ratings can be compared. A few systems use algebraic equations to calculate an index.

The problem with these systems is that, more often than not, they only provoke the rater to concentrate on ways to beat the system. Furthermore, these systems almost universally involve a behavioral rather than a results-oriented scale.

No system can obviate a manager's prejudices, biases, or weaknesses. Feelings about race, color, creed, sex, and age—or just plain dislike—are, unfortunately, in the fabric of human relationships. Systems that allow a manager to "mark" people on personal criteria will fail when managers have a field day with their get-evens. Systems like job results management that focus on results will not prevent managers from twisting the system, but surely transgressions are more difficult when objective job results and outcomes are the focus.

Project Analyzer for Legal Guideline 9

Where are operational and financial control points in your organization?

_____

_____

Who are your principal controllers?

_____

_____

Where do you anticipate control problems?

_____

_____

How can you prevent them?

_____

_____

In what ways are human resources professionals involved in auditing program effectiveness now?

_____

_____

What is the best way for human resources professionals to audit program effectiveness?

_____

_____

Who else is involved in reviewing program effectiveness?

_____

_____

_____

Are external resources used to monitor program effectiveness?

_____

_____

_____

Guideline 10: Ensure the Confidentiality of Personal Papers   The information contained in job results management conference forms and disciplinary action documents is highly personal and, in some cases, very sensitive. Obviously employees are more concerned with keeping negative comments private than they are with having positive comments publicized. Job results management papers must be protected, and access to them limited. Careless release of information by some organizations has led to charges of libel and slander by employees.

Some employers are legally required by state law to manage information carefully and to make it available to the person whom it might affect. Where there is no legal requirement, to what degree management wishes to comply voluntarily with such a notion is up to it. However, we can expect that all employers will eventually need to comply with some sort of information management law.

Here are some information management guidelines:

1. Formal policies defining the proper collection, use, and dissemination of employee information should be written and communicated to managers and employees.

2. Employee information should be collected, used, and disseminated openly, not in secrecy, so that the process can be scrutinized.

3. Employees should be permitted to inspect information that directly affects their employment status, except for those documents that have been specifically excluded.

4. Employees should have a formal means to correct information errors in their records.

5. Releases of personal information within and outside the organization should be controlled by written procedures. Only people with a legitimate reason should have access to such classified information. Releases beyond the organization (except where required by state law) should have the employee's consent.

6. Managers should be instructed that unauthorized dissemination of personal information is a breach of policy.

7. Only relevant information should be used in decisions affecting an employee's employment status.

Project Analyzer for Legal Guideline 10

Is access to personal information limited?

_____

_____

Is release of personal information controlled?

_____

_____

Are there written policies to manage information?

_____

_____

Is only relevant information maintained on employees?

_____

_____

In Conclusion

What is reasonable and what is not differ with each observer. The decisions of some court cases beg a new interpretation, as they seem to fly in the face of reason. Still, they were so decided. There can be no absolute protection against the whims of jurists, especially when fundamental guidelines are not available to them as they make their decisions. They bring their biases and prejudices along with them to the bench. However, so does management when it manages job results.

So, organizations are best counseled to follow *traditional, tested wisdom*, as embodied in the guidelines of this chapter. Giving each employee due process invokes the very nature of the laws of our land, if not of civilized conduct. In this way, the employee learns of problems to be corrected, and managers have an opportunity to review their decisions before they are enacted. Judgments can be tested for reasonableness. Along the way, records are kept so that the process may be reviewed by a neutral party if a dispute arises. Thus, there is a good chance that reasonableness will be the final outcome.

Project Analyzer 9.5

What legal challenges have been brought against your organization regarding unfair appraisal decisions and practices?

_____

_____

What did you learn from these challenges about improvements needed in your program?

_____

_____

What challenges do you worry about that, so far, you have been lucky enough to avoid?

_____

_____

What needs to happen for you to "get legal"?

_____

_____

Does management support a legally sound program?

_____

_____

Is management willing to enforce a legally sound program?

_____

_____

Are individual managers, rather than the entire management team, the only violators?

_____

_____

What can be done to teach these managers the bad effects of continued violations?

_____

_____

_____

9.6 Explaining the Program

Employees want to know what's going on, especially when it will affect their pocket-book. We frequently wait too long before telling employees anything—generally we say something after all the decisions have been made. In most cases, that is too late. Obviously, if you intend to have employees participate with you in the development of your program, you will be communicating with them as you go along.

As you work through the phases of this book, consider what you want to tell employees and what you do not. Experience demonstrates that we say less when we are not confident about what we are saying. Adhering to the steps described in this book will give you confidence in what you do. Still, you may choose to tell this and not tell that.

Occasionally, the argument is made that some issues are too technical for employees to understand. In one report, the minimum of the next lower grade was cited as an example of a technical aspect of a pay program. There is nothing too technical about that; rather, such information is probably something we do not want employees to know.

Perhaps some design features of the pay program are difficult to explain, but none are impossible to understand. The onus is on us to find the words and devise the ways to make ourselves understood.

Plan your communication program as part of your total program. Know what you want to accomplish, and how you will accomplish it, before speaking or writing one word. Schedule communication events in tandem with each phase of the project.

Focus on Acceptance

Keep in mind that you are working toward acceptance of the program when it is announced. Do more than keep acceptance in your mind; *focus* on it. If your program is not bought by managers and employees when it is announced, you are in deep trouble. You could lose it all.

You will take much time to deliberate whether to build your program this way or that; your employees similarly will need time to accept this instead of that. If you wait to unload the entire program at once, employees will be overloaded by the quantity of information, to say nothing of the complexity of some of the concepts. Build acceptance each step of the way.

Give a Proper Explanation

Start by explaining how the program fits together and why each of the elements is necessary. (See Figure 3 in Phase 1.) Intellectual organization demands that we understand the overview of what we are trying to comprehend so that we can assemble the pieces accordingly in our mind. Otherwise, the pieces we are fed make no sense until we can discern their interrelatedness. Do not make the mistake of believing that the ultimate value of the program will unfold through its self-evident, logical design. Deal with inquisitiveness: Why are we doing this? What will we get out of it?

Communicate in the Appropriate Manner

Each organization communicates in its own manner, habitually using the same technique and form. Understand your channels of communication and use them, for they are expected, but do not be restricted by them. Be innovative. Be sharp. Be thorough. If the medium is the message, demonstrate to your managers and employees that you mean business, are thorough, and are doing state-of-the-art work.

Use announcements—written, faxed, e-mailed, intranet—from the chief executive officer; speeches by top management to large groups; department meetings; small group discussions with human resources specialists; private conversations with informal leaders; articles in the organization's newspaper; special letters to employees and families; payroll inserts; films, audiotapes, slide shows, videotapes; teleconferences; training sessions by consultants; procedural instruction sessions; impromptu hallway discussions; maybe even contests and awards. Tailor the approach to the topic at hand. Get help from trainers, public relations and advertising specialists, writers and artists, and information technologists.

Anticipate the Reception of the Program by Employees

Employees have a perception of management, which enhances or taints their perception of management's programs. Where communication has been poor in the past, the design and development of a pay program offer fruitful opportunities to open some doors. While some of the program elements are sensitive and confidential, others are straightforward and lend themselves to safe discussion.

Remind yourself that where employees have been systematically excluded from information and participation, they may be wary of sudden overtures to share intimacies. Employees may be more than guarded: they may be suspicious and feel threatened. Easy does it. A fairly reliable truism of work motivation is that employees want to know what management is doing to them, even if it is only to protect what they have.

Do You Have to Tell?

Now to the final showing of the pay program. Major strategies need to be decided up front: what are you going to tell, and when? One of the principal reasons managements shy away from projects to design or redesign pay programs is the impending divulgence of pay inequities. Little wonder, given all the sacred cows that exist in organizations. Your communication plan will derive from the strategic positions management takes.

If management is unwilling to take the heat, you may decide to tell little or nothing. If management is willing to face the music, you will need a strong theme that right will be right in the end. Although it may not be feasible in every organization, management eventually puts all the cards on the table in the best programs.

Experience has demonstrated that when management holds its cards close to its chest, employees are forced to guess what management is about; they begin to wonder whether they should continue to play the game or bluff. Management will need to think through a lot of what-ifs before embarking on any strategy.

Correct, Then Communicate

There is an escape mechanism available. You could do your design work quietly or with a minimum of fanfare. Then, having constructed a pay structure, management can administer pay, using the structure as an informal, unpublished guide. Management can buy time to correct most inequities without employees' expecting or clamoring for adjustment. When the structure is ultimately published—perhaps in six or twelve months—disgruntlements will be diminished.

Communication gives life to the project. How much to communicate, and in what style, is what management must decide.

Project Analyzer 9.6

What is the communication atmosphere in your organization now?

_____

_____

Does management communicate openly with employees?

_____

_____

What kind of a communication posture would management like to have with employees?

_____

_____

What do employees "like" to hear?

_____

_____

What do employees need to hear?

_____

_____

Will employees listen?

_____

_____

What communication techniques are used now?

_____

_____

Are people with communication arts background available to work on this project?

_____

_____

What audiovisual equipment is available?

_____

_____

How will the impact of the communications be measured?

_____

_____

9.7 Protecting the Investment

If the pay system is not maintained once it has been established, you will lose more than just the time, effort, and opportunity costs of writing job descriptions, evaluating jobs, surveying pay rates, and calculating pay structures. You can lose the goodwill of both management and employees.

A deteriorated pay program sends a message that the value of the job performed and the value of effort expended are not as important as they once were.

Control only appears to be the answer. Yes, establish procedural work flow checkpoints, such as with change-of-status requirements, and annual audits to remind people that the mechanical elements of the program must be reviewed at designated times in order to ensure that details are not forgotten and that the desired results will be produced. However, more than procedural attention to duty is required; managers must recognize the value of being current. When managers appreciate the value of an effective program, they process information properly and maintain the system without reminder. Why not? They reap the benefits.

In Phase 3.3, we noted the potential of a pay project for educating and developing managers. Now that you have proceeded this far in the project, perhaps the potential is more obvious. When managers work through the experience of considering pay goals, organization structure, jobs, management plans, and all the other dimensions of a pay project, they learn what good human resources management is all about. The educational value beats that of any theoretical training class on leadership style.

If you really want to make good management count, include the responsibility for human resources in each manager's job description, and then plan for and have his or her job results appraised on the basis of this criterion. Tie the manager's pay to the proper management of the pay program.

Planning to Meet the Predictable—and the Not So Predictable

Successful human resources management means anticipation of predictable events, preparedness to meet the unexpected, and innovation to match new realities. Human resources management is much more than the administration of the status quo; it is the development of a strategy, blended with all other strategies of the organization, for getting the results and productivity necessary to accomplish the organization's goals and objectives.

Organizations that do not plan with accurate models find themselves in an economic crunch. And people always seem to suffer first—through hiring and pay freezes or reductions, layoffs, terminations, and other cost controls. It conveys a poor message.

Organizational goals and structures are not defined or implemented apart from people. People *are* the enterprise, and their job outcomes, or lack of them, determine the success or failure of the organization. Pay is not the only relationship between the organization and its members, but it is one of the most tangible. Once you have clarified this relationship, do your best to maintain it.

Plaudits and Grievances

Listen to the participants in the system. Although no program will satisfy all of the people all of the time—not anywhere close—and there may be times when unpopular decisions have to be made, encourage people to express their likes and dislikes about compensation, in formal and informal ways.

Take the compensation program out from under the shroud of secrecy. Let the fresh air of observation and discussion invigorate the system so that it produces up to expectations. When legitimate concerns are voiced, study them. Reevaluate jobs and resurvey market values. If data are wrong, correct the error; otherwise, bask in your glory.

Don't Let Them Get You Down

Building a pay program is tough but rewarding. Try as you might, some managers and some employees just will not like it and will get a kick out of picking the thing apart or trying to outmaneuver the guidelines. Don't cave in. Hang in there, and look for new ways to educate people who seem uninterested in participating. Help them understand the benefits of a thoughtful program.

Project Analyzer 9.7

When can checkpoints be established—in planning for and processing jobs and pay—to ensure attention to procedure?

_____

_____

Can checkpoints be established during strategic planning?

_____

_____

Can checkpoints be established as part of the process of structuring the organization?

_____

_____

Can checkpoints be established when jobs are designed?

_____

_____

Can checkpoints be established while personnel requisitions are processed?

_____

_____

Can checkpoints be established while personnel changes of status are processed?

_____

_____

_____

Can checkpoints be established when jobs are restructured?

_____

_____

_____

Can checkpoints be established while planning for and appraising job results?

_____

_____

_____

Can checkpoints be established when determining and processing pay adjustments?

_____

_____

_____

Is human resources management part of the strategic planning of the organization?

_____

_____

_____

If not, how can it be included?

_____

_____

_____

What mechanisms are in place to obtain positive and negative comments about the pay program?

_____

_____

_____

What mechanisms need to be instituted?

_____

_____

_____

9.8 Program Management

To manage the pay program, you will have to depend on the managers in the organization. Managers should be made responsible for:

1. Ensuring that each employee understands the job evaluation results for his or her job.
2. Answering or obtaining answers to all questions concerning employees' pay, status, and progress.
3. Initiating action for new jobs and reevaluating jobs as required.
4. Evaluating employees' job results and recognizing excellence.

5. Recommending beneficial changes in the pay program. Changes in pay should include an interview with the employee to review:
   —The employee's job duties.
   —The employee's job results and progress.
   —The employee's current job grade and placement within the pay range.
   —The employee's job goals and interests and, where possible, appropriate opportunities for growth, transfer, or promotion.

Some sort of change-in-status authorization is a base requirement in pay management. It has many uses for communicating change:

- To initiate action for pay increases, promotions, transfers, special adjustments, and general adjustments.
- To review and coordinate recommended actions by managers and to generate pay reviews.
- To approve and control pay changes and to implement pay policy.
- To notify the payroll department of a pay change and its effective date.
- To notify an employee of any action regarding job or pay status.

Orienting Employees to the New Program

Communicate in a personal way with each employee about the new pay program and where the employee's pay and status fit into the new structure.

Make general announcements concerning the pay program in employee publications or any other appropriate communication channels. A booklet on job evaluation might be given to each employee.

Questions about out-of-line rates—pay that is too low or too high in the range—must be resolved before interviews are conducted with employees. Notations are made to record all out-of-line cases, their special treatment, and the policy decisions regarding how each is resolved.

Each employee should be personally interviewed to:

- Verify the employee's current pay.
- Verify the last increase.
- Verify the type of increase.
- Explain the pay range for the grade, giving minimum and maximum.
- Explain the employee's current pay placement in the range.
- Explain resolution of any special circumstances.
- Answer any questions about the job evaluation results or the pay program.
- Plan for employee development as suggested by the employee's placement in the pay structure.

A copy of the employee's job description can also be distributed, if this was not done already.

Any significant unresolved questions identified during the interviews should be resolved promptly.

Project Analyzer 9.9

What is the role of the manager in pay management?

_____

_____

What specifically must the manager do?

_____

_____

What is the role of the human resources department?

_____

_____

What specifically must the human resources department do?

_____

_____

How will each employee's status in the program be communicated to the employee's manager?

_____

_____

What training is necessary to help managers with their pay management responsibilities?

_____

_____

How will status in the program be communicated to each employee?

_____

_____

What topics will be discussed with each employee?

_____

_____

9.9 Planning the Pay Increase Budget

Tying pay to results begins with an assessment of anticipated pay decisions for *each* employee in the organization. Organizational pay guidelines cannot be established for the organization until a pay summary mix of all employees has been estimated. This estimate usually occurs during operational planning—generally associated with the beginning of a fiscal year. Figure 49 shows a possible format for developing pay estimates for each employee. Figure 50 shows the consolidation as a pay change calendar. A mature organization with seasoned, stable performers must establish pay management guidelines different from those of a rapidly growing organization in which results differ significantly among new employees, and also different from those of an organization intent on maximizing bonus opportunities.

The anticipated pay summary mix for employees is identified by each department manager. Financial profit and cost centers typically provide workable focal points for analyzing employee results. Specifically, each manager must study the contributions of each employee and estimate what each employee's contribution will be at the conclusion of individual job contribution periods.

Estimates of the first-level operating units are collected and combined upward into estimates for major operating units. The control point of management within an organization is an operating unit of approximately 200 to 300 employees—about as many employees as one manager can reasonably track. These managers are the "consistency controllers" of the organization.

Pay mix estimates are gathered according to divisions, groups, regions, and so on, paralleling the organizational structure, until information for the entire organization is assembled. Consistency controllers must meet with other controllers in order to compare their values and achieve a consensus on the interpretation of outcome criteria. Group controllers meet with division controllers, who meet with department controllers, until all controllers understand one another. There is no shortcut if fairness is to be achieved.

Only when planning is concluded and a consensus achieved can pay guidelines be structured. Most important, the guidelines must match the unique economic limits of the organization.

Some managements, in an attempt to remain consistent with their competitors, construct guidelines that they cannot afford. They are then forced to take drastic protective actions by freezing pay rates or, worse, laying off employees. In difficult economic times, the spotlight has to shine even more brightly on results so that small increases are made to mean a lot (and no increase means that you get to keep your job). Additionally, other forms of recognition in lieu of pay rewards must be identified.

Managers can use several techniques to help them assess their situations and plan pay increase budgets. First, they need to identify the range of result contributions that exist in their unit.

A *forced ranking* of employees places each employee in relation to every other employee in the unit, in order of contribution. If there are ten employees in the unit, the manager ranks the employee who is first, the employee who is second, and so on until the tenth-place performer is identified. There is no inference that the tenth employee is not accomplishing acceptable results. The ranking merely means that in comparison with nine other employees, this employee is tenth. Once the ranking is determined, the contribution of the first and the last is estimated in order to understand the range of contributions.

Figure 49. Format for estimating pay increase budget.

EMPLOYEE NAME	CURRENT BASE PAY STATUS	Grade Percentile Amount ($)
Job contribution conference due date Pay change due date	Date Date	
Last base pay increase Last bonus	Date Percentage Amount ($) Date Percentage Amount ($)	
Anticipated base pay increase	Date Annual percentage Annual amount ($)	
Actual base pay increase	Date Annual percentage Annual amount ($)	Variance (budget to actual)
Anticipated bonus	Date Annual percentage Annual amount ($)	
Actual bonus	Date Annual percentage Annual amount ($)	Variance (budget to actual)

When the number of employees becomes too large to comprehend in a simple ranking, the *paired comparison technique* can be used. Each employee is compared to every other employee, one at a time. The employee's contribution is estimated as better or worse than the other employee's. The employee who most often is estimated as contributing better is the top employee in the group; the employee receiving the next fewer marks is second; and so on.

Figure 50. Sample master pay change calendar.

Name	\multicolumn{12}{c}{Specific Due Date}
	J	F	M	A	M	J	J	A	S	O	N	D
Arlene	13											
Bob	18											
Cindy		2										
Don				14								
Evelyn				23								
Fred					19							
Gerry							1					
Howard									14			
Inez											29	

An overlay of mathematical distribution can then be placed on the ranking and the range of contributions identified. In large populations, our concept of job contribution and pay management produces the following distribution:

Result Required	Problem	Learning Required	Performance Option
85 percent of employees	0–1 percent of employees	7–8 percent of employees	7–8 percent of employees

Be careful! The normal distribution should *never* be applied directly to employee populations to determine pay. People just don't fall into such neatly arranged piles. Use the statistical techniques to gain a reasonable estimate, not as a decision crutch.

Time-of-Year Implications When Planning the Pay Budget

Most organizations prepare base pay and bonus increase budgets expressed in annual dollars. What some managers fail to take into account is that the time of year of each pay action affects the annual percentage differently. If the pay increase budget is 4 percent, only 4 percent increases awarded at the start of the fiscal year will have a 4 percent impact on the employee's salary and the pay budget in that year.

For example, here are two employees who earn the same base pay percentage increase but whose increases will occur at two different times during the year:

Employee	Percentage Increase	Due Date	Percentage Impact on Calendar Year Budget
Randy	4	January 2	4
Rodney	4	July 1	2

Randy's increase is in effect for 12 months; Rodney's increase is in effect for six months, or 50 percent of the year. Fifty percent of 4 percent equals 2 percent.

When awarding job contribution bonuses, there are several payment options, among them lump sum, quarterly, monthly, and weekly. Payment methods have different impacts on the financial condition of the company. Let's look at two examples using the same calendar fiscal year as in the previous example:

1. If job contribution bonuses were paid in a lump sum:

Employee	Job Contribution Percentage Bonus	Due Date	Percentage Impact on Calendar Year Budget
Randy	5	January 2	5
Rodney	5	July 1	5

2. If job contribution bonuses were paid over the following twelve-month period:

Employee	Job Contribution Percentage Bonus	Due Date	Percentage Impact on Calendar Year Budget
Randy	5	January 2	5.0
Rodney	5	July 1	2.5

Whether bonus amounts are paid weekly, monthly, or quarterly will have an impact on that financial reporting period. Payment considerations also must weigh the impact on cash flow. Particularly in seasonal businesses, where huge influxes of cash appear in a given month or two, the awarding of lump sum bonuses will warrant close examination.

We particularly like the concept of larger lump sum bonuses rather than an integration in the weekly or monthly paycheck. The message is that this money is for job contributions over a specified period of time and not to be considered as a given within a paycheck.

The pros and cons of payment methods must be weighed alongside the financial ability of the company, of course, and tested against Internal Revenue Service regulations.

Compiling the Organization's Total Pay Budget

When all managers have estimated pay statuses for all their employees on the basis of historical and current indicators, the manager at the next higher organizational level collects the data and determines the total contribution dollars to be expended at that level. Data are summarized until one budget is determined for the organization.

Budgets are typically returned to managers in order to shift allocations from one area to another. One manager may request more contribution dollars for a large group of high achievers, whereas another manager may forgo contribution dollars because they are not needed for low contributions.

If job results management conferences are held at one time during the year for all employees, and pay increases are distributed shortly after, then management has an opportunity to review the actual distribution and adjust pay requirements to money available.

Let's look at two departments in an organization: a computer department of three people and an accounting department of seven people.

The computer department consists of a manager, a programmer, and a night operator. The manager is a model manager. The programmer has learned the manager's job in order to keep the department operating smoothly in the manager's absence. The night operator has learned programming so tasks can be completed while nightly reports are run. All three perform at the performance option level. With good conscience, their pay increases cannot be distributed on a normal distribution, because two of them would be unfairly penalized, since they could not receive increases at the performance option level.

The accounting department is another story. Employees perform only what they must. There are no shining stars; two of the employees have received problem reviews. The normal distribution doesn't work in this department because some employees would be overrated.

The pay increase budget is reviewed each time a pay conference is planned; managers must justify to their managers proposed changes to their plans. For example, during the budgeting process, the manager may anticipate that employee Angela will meet results required. Eight months later, Angela may begin to exercise performance options. The manager cannot be influenced only by the last four months of contributions and must be reminded that the contribution period is one year. As we warned before, make sure that the process does not become predictable so that employees do not feel that their raises were determined a year earlier and that there is nothing they can do to outperform the budget.

Senior managers in control of organizational results can use the contribution ratings produced by each manager to review how each manager interprets and applies outcome management. "Hard" and "soft" raters can be counseled to manage more consistently with the rest of the organization. Control can also be exercised when one department's contribution is out of line with other departments.

Project Analyzer 9.9

Are pay increases tied to the financial condition of the organization or to the going rate of increases in other organizations?

_____

_____

Are senior managers the only managers who determine who shall receive how much?

_____

_____

Are managers included in the budget planning process?

_____

_____

Do managers anticipate pay decisions for their employees?

_____

_____

Is the process formal and attentive or haphazard?

_____

_____

Do senior managers examine pay recommendations as closely as they examine other operational recommendations?

_____

_____

_____

Are senior managers held accountable for pay decisions in their area?

_____

_____

_____

9.10 Ongoing Adjustments

Installing the pay program is not the end of the story. Periodically, you will need to make both adjustments to the structure and changes to accommodate individual employees.

Structural Adjustments

Pay is dynamic; it is influenced by market conditions and the organization's plans. Although adjustments to the pay structure are not made daily, be aware daily of influences that may impinge on the guide that your organization uses to pay people.

What are such influences? Several job candidates for one job ask for salaries a bit higher than you had anticipated; employment ads in the newspaper for another job have quoted the same pay for quite some time; at the local gathering of human resources professionals, you hear talk of tough economic times coming next year; a group of employees complain that more and more responsibilities are being added to their jobs with no increase in pay; the CEO would like to see some special incentives introduced to spur productivity; the benefits manager is worried about the cost of dental insurance; trade talk in your industry centers on foreign competition; the sales manager is looking into new geographic markets; and so on, and so on.

Periodically, survey market conditions to ascertain exactly what is happening. How often you do this depends on the dynamics of your organization's situation. When changes start occurring quickly, you cannot afford to wait another three months for the next scheduled survey. Almost everyone looks at particular issues as the occasion arises.

One has to conjecture that the annual program review, while in part a response to a need for stability in planning and operations, also owes its existence to the time and effort involved in conducting a survey. In the pencil-and-paper, type-it-over-again era, a year was soon enough. The information revolution has changed all that. Modern pay managers use online networks that enable them to make fast and accurate decisions, just as in the stock market.

Plans for adjustments to pay structure are made in consort with the organization's economic cycles and planning routines, and adjustments to the structure are made at economically appropriate moments in the operational cycle. Organizational needs and desires dictate what you do. Pay management is not a distribution of what is left over after planning for other operating expenses.

Individual Adjustments

Balancing organizational consistency and individual attention is the challenge. The pay structure, including policies and procedures, guides management as it determines the pay for each employee. The guides must be clear and certain so that employees witness equitable treatment throughout the organization, yet not so defined and restrictive that individual needs and preferences cannot be considered, even if not accommodated.

The specific guidelines in your organization are decided by management. Here are some of the major issues, including frequently found formulas:

■ *Hiring rate*—as close to the minimum as possible, assuming little or no previous experience; up to the first quartile or the midpoint at the manager's discretion; approval required to hire above the midpoint.

■ *Promotion*—increase to the minimum of the new pay grade, and give some sort of tangible recognition, such as a bonus.

■ *Transfer*—can be lateral (no adjustment); to lower pay grade at organization's request (no reduction); or to lower pay grade at employee's request (reduction if current pay is higher than the new maximum).

■ *Demotion*—reduction to appropriate level of new grade.

One common thread runs through the policy: who is responsible or whose convenience is being served? If it is the organization, it suffers the burden; if it is the employee, he or she assumes the burden.

Keeping a Long-Term Perspective

During harsh economic times, some organizations, scratching for cost-cutting measures, look long and hard at the large numbers of senior employees sitting at high pay rates. In total disregard for the basic principles of pay management, but under the guise that cost reductions are necessary for the organization's survival, some fanciful notions have been developed—for instance, freezing the more expensive employees and hiring new employees at new and lower minimums. (At the same time, the management group may be taking off for a strategic planning meeting at some distant retreat location, or the top executives may be awarded huge bonuses.)

Organizations have no choice but to respond to the economic demands placed on them. In some cases, survival is the issue; but cost-cutting measures that involve pay are viewed as making the employees suffer for the problem. Unions get particularly feisty at these times, and not without cause when more rational means could have been adopted.

Part of the problem is that not all the economic woes of an organization can be alleviated by cutting one aspect of the costs. Another part of the problem is that surgical means are an action of last resort. Compensation management—involving not just pay but benefits costs as well—cannot be brought up on the agenda Monday and solved on the spot; as with any other aspect of good management, the organization must position itself.

Management must also own up to its share of the predicament. Yes, trade unionism has bargained wages upward, but management has agreed. The short-run view typically wins out, whereas pay issues should be placed in long-term perspective.

Management's Changing Perspectives on the Distribution of Resources

Economic conditions in the organization determine the amount of money available for structural and individual pay changes. An anticipated poor year may mean that no change is made in the structure, and that whereas "exceptional" outcomes meant a certain level of increase last year, it means less of an increase this year. Pay must be planned alongside all the requirements of the organization if scarce resources are to be divided fairly. Employees must be taught to expect change.

All pay is pay for results when considered from the perspective of the organization's ability to pay and the employee's ability to earn. Management must then design strategies to accomplish two goals: maximize the organization's ability to pay and distribute the amount it can afford to pay in the most effective way.

Some managements prefer to distribute the resource as evenly as possible, using group incentives, profit sharing, pension plans, and general increases. Increasingly, however, managements are putting their money on their top performers by extending individual executive-style incentive programs throughout the organization and granting spot or deferred cash awards, performance shares, stock grants and options, and, simply, more and larger pay increases.

Project Analyzer 9.10

In what ways do you keep abreast of changes in your labor markets?

_____

_____

What can you do to obtain more information?

_____

_____

What is your organization's financial planning cycle?

_____

_____

How often should compensation programs be reviewed?

_____

_____

What is the best way to integrate compensation planning into organizational and financial planning?

_____

_____

What are the economic realities of your organization now?

_____

_____

How are employees moved through the pay range now?

_____

_____

How well do these approaches work?

_____

_____

What changes are in order?

_____

_____

Have any hypocrisies developed?

_____

_____

In what ways do you keep in touch with employee sentiments?

_____

_____

_____

9.11 Maintenance, Audits, and Appeals

Analyzing jobs, writing job descriptions, and evaluating jobs are projects that most folks prefer to enjoy only once in life. The work is demanding, tedious, and time-consuming, and it frequently only confirms what we suspected anyhow.

Keep the system up-to-date. Keep managers involved. Hold them accountable to keep the program up-to-date. On a daily basis, as changes in job descriptions occur, maintain records. When a job is vacated and is to be advertised or posted, verify the job content with the manager and record the audit or the change on the job description master file.

When managers propose job changes, examine them for significant changes. If you find some, take the job to the job evaluation committee and have it reevaluated. The committee should meet as required to consider job changes, depending on the frequency of job change.

New jobs are evaluated as they are proposed, to determine the range of pay offers. Descriptions and evaluations for new jobs are usually treated as tentative to accommodate changes necessary to fit the job into the organizational scheme.

Once a year, review all job descriptions that have not surfaced for audit to determine whether changes have been made but not recorded. A simple checkpoint is a question on the job results management form: Is the job description current, and are all revisions recorded?

Also once a year, the job evaluation task force ought to meet and assess whether the pay plan still meets the organization's needs. Perhaps a word here or there has taken on a new meaning. More substantial changes in job evaluation plans should not be necessary for five or more years, and even then, changes should be minimal.

However, as the organization evolves to a new purpose, structure, and operating philosophy, fundamental changes in the job evaluation plan may be required.

Examine the impact of job evaluations on career progression, turnover, affirmative action, pay equality, and the other major indicators of human resources management. Look for negative trends and make appropriate adjustments.

Maintenance During the Pay Project

Months will pass between job analysis, job evaluation, and the presentation of pay ranges—enough time for jobs to have changed. Inform managers that these changes should be incorporated into the project as they occur, not saved until the conclusion of the project, when job changes may look like a deluge.

Generally changes during the project are not numerous, since managers assemble proposed changes during job analysis and have them incorporated into the project at that time. Good planning on your part, with plenty of advance notice to managers and encouragement to make proposals at the appropriate time, will reduce midproject adjustments. However troublesome midproject adjustments may be for you, demonstrating the flexibility to deal with change is an excellent message to send to managers and employees about your program.

Appeals

Job incumbents and managers ought to have an official opportunity to complain when they believe that the system is not treating them fairly.

To begin with, of course, employees and managers should receive an explanation of the task force's decision and the validation process. After all, a number of people examined the results for fairness and equity—a point that should be made to sell the results.

When the explanation fails to convince, provide a mechanism for a case in opposition. Require a written rebuttal and a presentation to the task force. Make the mechanism formal enough to discourage random grumbling yet open enough to encourage fair processing.

The task force can be made the final arbiter, the ultimate authority may be placed with a senior executive, or a more formal alternative dispute resolution system might be established.

Project Analyzer 9.11

How much job change do you experience in your organization?

_____

_____

Can managers be relied upon to incorporate job changes into the official record?

_____

_____

What mechanisms are in place to capture job changes?

_____

_____

What mechanisms need to be introduced?

_____

_____

How often should the job evaluation task force meet to consider job changes?

_____

_____

How often should major audits be conducted?

_____

_____

Can the maintenance and audit procedures be incorporated into other planning and review processes?

_____

_____

Strategic Planning for Phase 9

On your *first* quick walk through the project phases, record your initial thoughts on policy issues that will have to be decided.

_____

_____

_____

Any notes on tactical procedures?

_____

_____

    On your *second* time through the phases, consider the strategic influences from all the phases; decide on an integrated posture for the entire project.

    Complete the section for this phase in the Master Planner (in Phase 2.8) during your *third* reading.

For Further Reading About Pay Management

Books

Belcher, J. *How to Design and Implement a Results-Oriented Variable Pay System*. New York: AMACOM, 1996.

Boyett, J., and Conn, H. *Maximum Performance Management: How to Manage and Compensate People to Meet World Competition*. Lakewood, CO: Glenbridge, 1994.

Chingos, P. *Paying for Performance: Models for What Works in Compensation*. New York: Wiley, 1997.

DeLuca, M. *Handbook of Compensation Management*. Englewood Cliffs, NJ: Prentice-Hall, 1993.

Evans, E. *Compensation Basics for HR Generalists: Understanding the Role of Pay in Human Resources Strategy*. Scottsdale, AZ: American Compensation Association, 1997.

Fay, C., and Risher, H. *New Strategies for Public Pay: Rethinking Government Compensation Programs*. San Francisco: Jossey-Bass, 1997.

Flannery, T., Hofrichter, D., and Platten, P. *People, Performance and Pay: Dynamic Compensation for Changing Organizations*. New York: Free Press, 1995.

Frost, K. *Fundamentals of Flexible Compensation*. New York: Wiley, 1995.

Gross, S. *How to Design and Implement Team-Based Reward Programs*. New York: AMACOM, 1995.

Harvard Business Review Staff. *Compensation: Fair Pay for Executives and Employees*. Cambridge, MA: Harvard Business Review, 1991.

Henderson, R. *Compensation Management: Rewarding Performance*. New York: Prentice-Hall General Reference and Travel, 1993.

Heneman, R. *Merit Pay*. Reading, MA: Addison-Wesley, 1992.

Hewitt Associates Staff. *Fundamentals of Flexible Compensation*. New York: Wiley, 1992.

Jorgenson, K. *Pay for Results: A Practical Guide to Effective Employee Compensation*. Santa Monica, CA: Merritt, 1996.

Kohn, A. *Punished by Rewards*. Boston: Houghton Mifflin, 1993.

Lawler, E. *Strategic Pay*. San Francisco: Jossey-Bass, 1990.

Martocchio, J. *Strategic Compensation: Human Resources Management Approach.*
Englewood Cliffs, NJ: Prentice-Hall, 1997.

McCoy, T. *Creating an "Open Book" Organization: Where Employees Think and Act Like
Business Partners.* New York: AMACOM, 1996.

Milkovich, G. *Pay for Performance: Evaluating Performance Appraisal and Merit Pay.*
Washington, DC: National Academy Press, 1991.

Milkovich, G., and Newman, J. *Compensation.* Burr Ridge, IL: Richard D. Irwin, 1995.

Rock, M., and Berger, L. *The Compensation Handbook: A State-of-the-Art Guide to
Compensation Strategy and Design.* New York: McGraw-Hill, 1991.

Schuster, J., and Zingheim, P. *The New Pay: Linking Employee and Organizational
Performance.* San Francisco: Jossey-Bass, 1992.

Watson Wyatt Data Services, Inc. *The ECS Decision Maker's Guide to Salary
Management.* Rochelle Park, MD: 1995.

Wilson, T., and Moss-Kanter, R. *Innovative Reward Systems for the Changing Workplace.*
New York: McGraw-Hill, 1995.

Periodicals

ACA Journal (American Compensation Association), Scottsdale, AZ.

ACA News (American Compensation Association), Scottsdale, AZ.

Compensation and Benefit Management, Panel Publishers, Frederick, MD.

Compensation and Benefit Review, American Management Association, New York.

HR Focus, American Management Association, New York.

HRMagazine, Society for Human Resource Management, Alexandria, VA.

Training, Lakewood Publications, Minneapolis, MN.

Index

About the Authors

Roger Plachy and Sandra Plachy are principals of the Job Results Management Institute consulting firm located in Winston-Salem, NC. The culmination of their consultations and best-management-practices research, presented in this book, is an integrated and coherent results-oriented strategy for managing and rewarding employee job contributions aimed at fulfilling an organization's mission. They have applied their results-oriented thinking to a concept of rewards based on results, to restyling job descriptions, to defining objective job-evaluation criteria, to identifying four specific outcomes tied to each job result, and to refocusing the manager-employee relationship to a collaborative exploration of opportunities and problem-solving. They are the authors of *Results-Oriented Job Descriptions*, 1993, and *More Results-Oriented Job Descriptions*, 1997, both by AMACOM.